BADASS
RETIREMENT

Shatter the Retirement Myth

LIVE WITH MORE MEANING, MONEY, AND ADVENTURE

ROBERT PAGLIARINI, PH.D., CFP

ALSO BY ROBERT PAGLIARINI

THE SIX-DAY FINANCIAL MAKEOVER (St. Martin's Press)

THE OTHER 8 HOURS (St. Martin's Press)

THE SUDDEN WEALTH SOLUTION (Harbinger Press)

GET MONEY SMART (Harbinger Press)

BADASS
RETIREMENT

Shatter the Retirement Myth

LIVE WITH MORE MEANING, MONEY, AND ADVENTURE

To my loving and supportive family.
You have encouraged me to live an adventurous and bold life.
To my dear clients who have trusted me to be their guide.
You have inspired and expanded my view of what's possible in retirement.
We are on this journey together...

JOIN THE FAMILY

The online **Badass Retirement Community** is where you will connect with other people just like you who want to experience more meaning and purpose, joy and adventure, energy and confidence, and growth and impact than you ever thought possible.

Members get these exclusive benefits:

- ✔ Investment Updates & Strategies
- ✔ Asset Allocation Analysis
- ✔ RetirementGrader Assessment
- ✔ Community Challenges
- ✔ Portfolio Reviews
- ✔ Exclusive Discounts
- ✔ Video Library
- ✔ Health Checkups
- ✔ Interviews, Meetups
- ✔ Live Workshops
- ✔ and so much more...

Surround yourself with other ambitious retirees.

BADASSRETIREMENT.COM

TABLE OF CONTENTS

INTRODUCTION

We've been conned.

The traditional approach to retirement is failing us. It's based on the belief that retirees and aging are synonymous with becoming weaker and less capable. That retirement is about winding down and playing it safe, because, you know, retirees are frail. This outdated and patronizing view assumes that when you retire from your job, you also retire from life.

Like hell you do.

In retirement, you have more time, money, resources, and wisdom than you've ever had. You can be more adventurous, pursue your dreams, and have a greater impact. But that's not the message we tell retirees.

If you think taking it easy, avoiding challenges, and creating a life of comfort leads to happiness and fulfillment after you stop working, you've fallen for the Retirement Myth.

The Retirement Myth is the widely held belief that a successful retirement is about pulling back and doing less. That you'll be happy and content just puttering around the house, golfing a couple days a week, and simply spending your time relaxing.

If you buy into the false idea that retirees need to be bubble-wrapped and that fulfillment comes from doing, achieving, and becoming less after you stop working, you are guaranteed an Average Retirement.

Average Retirement is the pursuit to disengage, remove challenges, and create a life exclusively of relaxation. This describes the ideal retirement for many. It's easy and comfortable. But this is also what makes it unfulfilling and unexciting for *some* (maybe you?).

The biggest mistakes I've seen retirees make is that they aim far too low, experience far too little, and never come close to reaching their human potential. You've got one shot at this. There are no do-overs. No second chances. There is no next. Retirement is it.

You need to stop playing the long game as if next year or even tomorrow is guaranteed. Instead, you need to start playing the short game. You've been conditioned to focus on some distant future. Guess what? In retirement, the future is right damn now. Don't hesitate.

Don't delay. Don't postpone. Whatever it is you want to do, achieve, or experience, get on it.

The life philosophy of too many retirees is "I came. I saw. I retired." You didn't come this far, work this hard, and accomplish so much just so you could kick back and disengage, did you? Don't let an outdated and BS view of retirement define the rest of your life and what you can achieve. Let's flip retirement on its head. You came. You saw . . . and you kicked some Average Retirement ass.

The aim is not to simply *improve* retirement; it's to *replace* retirement with something far better.

If you want your best days to be ahead of you. If you want to take on big challenges that give you purpose. If you want to feel stronger and have more energy with each passing day. If you want to make an impact and feel valued. If you want total financial security. If you want to live a bold life that's rich with excitement and adventure, welcome to Badass Retirement!

Why "badass"? I have a client to thank for that. After I told him my view of retirement – that we need to do more, achieve more, and live with more passion and adventure – he said, "Sign me up! That sounds like one badass retirement!" And so, it's been Badass Retirement ever since.

Average Retirement is safe and conservative. Badass Retirement is rebellious and bold. Average Retirement is passive and restrained. Badass Retirement is uncompromising and adventurous.

Instead of stripping away the things that give your life purpose and meaning, Badass Retirement is about pursuing passions you never had time for, challenges you thought were too big, and adventures you always dreamed about. Average Retirement is subtraction. Badass Retirement is addition.

After nearly 30 years working with retirees, here's what I know to be true:

Average Retirement is a death sentence – somewhere you go to die.

Badass Retirement is a life sentence – somewhere you go to live.

Of course, not everyone thinks about and approaches retirement the way I do. Badass Retirement is just one version of life after work, but it's not for everyone and that's okay. It's like when someone tells me I should like sushi or jazz – I don't and I shouldn't.

But for those who are looking for something more, I don't want you to just live a Badass Retirement; I want you to become a Badass in retirement.

That means you figure out what drives you, do not compromise on what's important, go after your biggest goals, seek challenges, push yourself, routinely live beyond your comfort zone, take risks, get stronger, and surprise yourself by doing stuff you didn't think you could do.

I know this may seem a little intimidating. I get it. I call it "Badass Retirement" and there is a tough-looking surfer on the cover of the book! But don't dismiss Badass Retirement as being out of reach or too challenging. If the story you are telling yourself is that you can't do this or it's not who you are, give yourself a chance.

A Badass Retirement doesn't have to be extreme. You don't need to be in shape or jump out of planes. You don't need to ride waves or hike trails. But you do need a challenge – something that lights a fire within you and propels you forward. You need a mountain – real or metaphorical – that you can climb throughout retirement.

Badass Retirement is about *psychology*; not *chronology*.

There are no prerequisites to living a Badass Retirement. No application. No permission. It doesn't matter how you've lived up to this point. If you've neglected your health, ignored your finances, or haven't connected with friends in a while, that's okay. Shifting your mindset doesn't require years of planning, deep discussions with a therapist, or even a profound event. Change can happen in an instant. Age doesn't matter. All you need is desire.

Whether you are approaching retirement or already in retirement, this book is going to help you build the best life possible. I've worked with countless clients over the past several decades to create and live their best lives after they stopped working.

Intrigued? Good. A little skeptical? Good. Retirement is your life. I want you to get it right.

But why listen to me?

If my early childhood was any indication, I would be the last person from whom you would want to take financial and retirement advice. Why? Growing up, we never had any money! Every day was a struggle for my single mom of five kids. She used to sell pieces of our furniture when things got tight. One day, I came home from school and my mom made me a snack. I noticed our coffee table was missing. I asked her where it was, and she answered, "You're eating it."

At a very early age, I knew I didn't want to be poor and struggle for everything. I knew I wanted to enjoy life and experience it to the fullest. I'd watch adventure movies such as *Raiders of the Lost Ark* and dream of going to exotic countries and on adventures like Indiana Jones.

From those early years, I've been committed to creating and living the best life possible. I overcame my background and created a life my younger self would not have believed.

Over the past almost three decades, I have dedicated my professional life to helping clients grow their wealth and enhance their lives in retirement and during significant financial transitions through my investment and wealth management firm. I earned a Ph.D. in financial and retirement planning, studying and conducting research on retirement income distribution planning, behavioral finance, and investment strategy. Additionally, because of my fascination with the intersection of finance and psychology, I went back to school and earned a master's degree in psychology. I've also written five personal finance books and have had the privilege of appearing on *Dr. Phil*, *20/20*, *Good Morning America*, *The Today Show* and many others. I've even gone on adventures that would make Indiana proud.

But why listen to me?

This book and message are personal for me. I remember what it felt like to have little and to struggle for everything. I remember dreaming of escaping what I saw as an average existence. I've seen family members and clients sacrifice and work their entire lives only to pass away shortly into retirement. Life is precious. There are no guarantees. All we can do is make the most of every moment.

That's my promise to you.

I'm on this journey with you. I didn't write this book for you as much as I wrote it for us. I want to create and live a Badass Retirement as much as I want you to.

If you want extra guidance and more hands-on tools, I suggest you download the *Badass Retirement Workbook*. It's so much more than a workbook – it's a blueprint for helping you create and live a Badass Retirement. This step-by-step guide includes quizzes, reflection questions, assessments, and additional content that will help you get the most from this book.

To get the full experience, also be sure to join the Badass Retirement Community, an online membership platform that provides financial guidance and lifestyle design for retirees who want to thrive. It's for people like us – people who want more from their lives in retirement.

The community needs you. I need you.

If you're ready, let's *Escape Average Retirement* together.

Robert Pagliarini, Ph.D., CFP®

SECTIONS

MAGNIFY

MINDSET

MEANING

MONEY

MOMENTUM

1

CHALLENGE

Shatter the Retirement Myth

What you've been told will lead to happiness and fulfillment in retirement may lead to disappointment and discontentment.

CHALLENGE 1

There is a battle for your happiness, your life, and dare I say, a battle for your soul.

This battle starts years before you retire but will affect every day of your retirement.

This battle is how you *think* about retirement. You have a choice. A choice of two very different retirements and of two very different lives. You can choose to see the truth or continue to believe the myth.

Will you expand your perception of what retirement can be and live your life to the fullest, or will you buy into what you've been told retirement should be and succumb to a shriveled version of your potential?

This Challenge is your red pill moment. Will you look away and hope you are comfortable living an average life, or will you open your eyes and reject the most pervasive and damaging myth we all face?

THE RETIREMENT MYTH

There is a widespread belief about retirement that all but guarantees you will live an Average Retirement and struggle to create a truly remarkable life. That belief is the Retirement Myth. If you buy into the Retirement Myth and the ensuing Average Retirement, you will achieve exactly what you think you want – a retirement where you relax, withdraw, and avoid challenges.

I've helped hundreds of clients plan for retirement and talked to thousands more *in* retirement about their hopes and fears. These conversations have taught me what most people <u>think</u> they want in retirement...

They want to relax.

They want to step back, unwind, and withdraw from the responsibility of work life.

They want to have more time for hobbies. They want to travel more.

They want a carefree life with little stress and challenge.

Unfortunately, this is all many retirees want in retirement. It's because they bought into the Retirement Myth. The Retirement Myth is a series of commonly held beliefs that contribute to frustration, disappointment, and malaise for some retirees. It can be easily summarized as:

RETIREMENT MYTH = LESS > MORE

Nobody should be surprised that "less" is the goal of Average Retirement – it's right there in the word "retire." Retirement is all about stopping – from work and your career.

What image comes to mind when you think of retirement? Two beach chairs facing the ocean? If so, you're not alone. The beach scene is often used to depict the ideal retirement. For the fun of it, Google "retirement" and then click on *Images* and you'll see exactly what I'm talking about. Over 60% of the photo results feature a beach. The beach theme shows up in articles, commercials, advertisements, book covers, podcast art, and in many other areas related to the topic of retirement. Why is that? When did sitting on your ass, staring at the ocean become the rallying cry for life in retirement? A vacation sure, but your entire life?

SHATTER THE RETIREMENT MYTH

Do you want to sit on the beach or live your best life in retirement?

THE SCOURGE OF AVERAGE RETIREMENT

I've been working with retirees for close to 30 years, and I've seen the Retirement Myth play out over and over again. I've met people who are ambitious workers pre-retirement, working hard to achieve big goals. They have purpose in their days and their lives. They have a mission. Each day they go into the world to learn, grow, and accomplish. They feel a palpable energy, and those around them feel it, too. They have strong social networks and a sense of community. They are doing important things and making something of themselves in the process. And then they retire...

It's like a light gets switched off. They lose all that energy that once illuminated the world and are now just vacant vessels. They lose their spark and their spirit. They forget what day of the week it is – what I call "calendar coma." They complain of having no energy or drive. They'll claim that retirement is great because they don't have to set the alarm clock and have all the free time in the world to do whatever they want. But a few might share what so many others think but do not say:

I'm so grateful I've been able to give up a lot of the things from work I didn't enjoy now that I'm retired. But if I'm being honest, there are also things I miss. I miss the feeling of accomplishment and purpose. I miss the feeling of teamwork and contribution. I miss how good relaxing felt after working hard. I miss the person I was. I don't want to go back to my job, but I thought retirement would be something more.

These disgruntled retirees were infected by the Retirement Myth and now suffer from Average Retirement. Since every good story needs a villain, ours is Average Retirement. The enemy is real. With 10,000 Americans retiring each day, millions of workers fall for the Retirement Myth every year.[1]

The Retirement Myth says that you can (and should) give up your alarm clock but also your goals. Give up your morning drive but also give up what drives you. Give up deadlines but also give up making a difference.

The Retirement Myth perpetuates the idea that less responsibility is better than more responsibility. Less activity is better than more activity. Less effort is better than more effort. Less achievement is better than more achievement. It is a myth that, once you retire, you have arrived – that retirement is the final stop along life's journey. But does this lead to happiness?

There is no doubt that these words describe the perfect retirement for some people. In fact, many soon-to-be retirees slogging through long commutes and working 60+ hours a week cling to this view of retirement because it represents a break from their current daily grind. What I've learned while helping clients financially plan for retirement is that those who have been able to look beyond this traditional perspective seem more fulfilled, enjoying this next stage in their life more than those who get stuck in the Average Retirement mindset.

There is no problem with relaxing and taking it easy in retirement. You've worked hard for several decades and sacrificed to reach a position where you can retire. You need some well-deserved rest and recuperation.

Don't get stuck there, however, thinking that relaxation and slowing down are the only ingredients for a fulfilling long-term retirement. For a select group of retirees, that's a recipe for disappointment. If you think you just want an Average Retirement, be warned that you may wake up one day and discover you crave more joy, happiness, adventure, connection, and purpose.

"THAT'S THE DUMBEST THING I'VE EVER HEARD"

Based on my conversations about retirement over the past few decades, I've discovered that my views on the topic are not mainstream. I've been laughed at and ridiculed. Heads have shaken and eyes have rolled.

It turns out that the beach chair retirement theme is so popular because, well, it represents what many retirees want. In a very unscientific survey I conducted of 100 adults age 55 and older, only about 10% preferred a Badass Retirement.

The truth is most people are content with an Average Retirement. Are you?

I've found there are three types of retirees:

1. **Comfortable.** They want an average and traditional retirement and find that they are quite happy with it.

2. **Confused.** They want an average and traditional retirement but find they are not as satisfied and happy as they thought they would be.

3. **Concerned.** They want something different than an average and traditional retirement but aren't sure how to get it.

Most retirees are thrilled with their new life – they enjoy stepping back, unwinding, and having more time to relax. Godspeed to the Comfortable.

But my message is not for the masses.

My message is for the few – the Confused and the Concerned. If you're a few years into retirement and feel underwhelmed, or if you are close to retiring but are already worried that you might be bored or listless in retirement, you may not be in the majority, but you are not alone.

Once I started questioning Average Retirement, I discovered I wasn't the only one who had doubts. Before I published my *Forbes* article, "Rage Against Retirement," I was worried it would rub readers the wrong way or maybe come across as preachy or too ambitious. It did in fact rub readers the wrong way, but more importantly, it didn't rub <u>all</u> the readers the wrong way. Instead, it got an incredible response from those that shared my concerns and frustrations.

There are a few of us out there looking for something more – more adventure, more meaning, and more fulfillment – than what we see happening in Average Retirement. My clients are a special breed. They think differently and want something different. Exactly zero times has a client asked me to help them achieve an Average Retirement. Every client – and I'm guessing you as well – has the same wish. You want the best retired life possible. It's that simple. Maybe your version of a best life includes jet skis and yoga retreats, but someone else may be focused on grandkids and volunteering at the local animal shelter. You want your version of the best, not average.

If that message resonates with you, welcome to the club. We aren't large in number, but we are passionate. It's a shame that more retirees don't share our vision because not all retirees are happy with average.

AFTER THE HONEYMOON

Retirement is the promised land where you can ditch your morning drive, employment responsibilities, and pressure, and instead, enjoy plenty of time for relaxation, travel, and hobbies. Retirement represents the finish line and the prize for a lifetime of work, saving, and sacrifice. Retirement should be one of the happiest periods in your life, and for many, it is. For some, however, the transition from work to retirement is not smooth.

In fact, research shows that many retirees experience a honeymoon phase – a period lasting between a few months and a couple of years where retirees' moods are elevated. The novelty of their new freedom and the possibilities of retirement lead to increased feelings of well-being and life satisfaction.[2] After this brief phase, some retirees experience a big drop in well-being and life satisfaction – sinking to levels even lower than when they initially retired.[3]

Some retirees lament that they know they should be loving their new retired life, but after the brief honeymoon period, they feel lost or unprepared. Most eventually find a good rhythm and settle in, but the transition can be long and uncomfortable. Researchers found that approximately 25% of retirees experienced negative changes in psychological well-being during the initial transition stage, with only 5% experiencing positive changes.[4] In another study, nearly 70% of retirees said that their retirement transition was not smooth.[5]

In a separate survey, participants were asked, "All in all, would you say that your retirement has turned out to be – very satisfying, moderately satisfying, or not at all satisfying?" Over 40% of respondents reported that they were not at all satisfied or only moderately satisfied with retirement.[6]

In a follow-up question in the same survey, participants were asked, "Thinking about your retirement years compared to the years just before you retired, would you say the retirement years have been better, about the same, or not as good?" Nearly 50% said that their lives in retirement were either not as good or about the same.

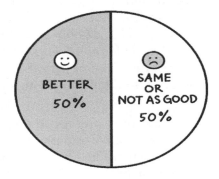

ARE YOUR RETIREMENT YEARS
BETTER THAN WORKING YEARS?

BETTER 50%

SAME OR NOT AS GOOD 50%

Only half of retirees think their retirement is better than their working years. What's going on?

Think about that for a minute. For many, the dream of retirement is less jubilant and more... meh.

THE DANGER OF THE RETIREMENT MYTH

The Retirement Myth leads to passivity, especially since far too many equate retirement with relaxation. *I'm retired; therefore, I relax.* The belief is that relaxation will lead to happiness. If stress is bad, then no stress must be good. Imagine a life with no challenges, effort, or hard work – just day after day of carefree, stress-free living. I know there are some who just read that last sentence and thought *That is the ideal retirement.* It is what they fantasized about for years when they were stuck in traffic, working late nights, and inundated with never-ending deadlines. I get that. Trust me. I've worked hard for decades. I've been stuck in the country's worst traffic (I-405 in Southern California). I've sacrificed just like you. The natural response is to want the opposite.

I cannot emphasize this more strongly: If you think retirement is all about relaxing and living a life with few challenges, responsibilities, and stress, you may wake up one day in the future and feel like something is missing. And you'd be right. The Retirement Myth would have you believe that the opposite of work is doing a lot less. The opposite of a stressful work life is a life with no stress. The opposite of a demanding and achievement-oriented career is a life with few goals and responsibilities. These are all myths.

The less-is-better Retirement Myth will lead you to set your sights far too low. When doing, achieving, and working less is the goal of retirement, your retirement and life will fall far short of their full potential. Nevertheless, the myth permeates our culture, affecting millions of new retirees every year. It's not just pervasive; the Retirement Myth is cruel.

What makes it so cruel? It leads to deep dissatisfaction. Retirement is the part of your life when you have the most time, money, and ability to embark on important, fulfilling, and life-changing pursuits, yet it's when most retirees do the least. We believe we need to do less, but when we do, we are left with a feeling of emptiness. The Retirement Myth is like taking a caged tiger into the wild and, just as it is about to step outside of captivity and begin a life of adventure and meaning, slamming the cage door in its face.

The Retirement Myth tells people that doing less and pulling back is the way to achieve joy. But is this true? Think of the times in your life when you felt the best and the most fulfilled. Were you sitting on a beach or were you actively pursuing a big goal?

Notice I didn't ask when you felt the most relaxed. It's easy to feel relaxed sitting on a warm beach, listening to the waves lapping against the shore. I love hanging out and reading a good book on the beach as much as the next guy. It's also easy to feel relaxed watching TV, meditating, or curled up in a chair with a blanket, watching it rain outside. Relaxation is a state of being – a healthy and pleasurable state of being that should be a daily part of retirement life – but it shouldn't be your *only* goal in retirement. The Retirement Myth has equated retirement with relaxation – retirement causes relaxation. You are retired and no longer work. Therefore, you are relaxed.

But is this how relaxation works? Think about your own experience with relaxation. Often, you feel the greatest relaxation after hard effort. You run the race, then you get to take a break. You put in a long day at work, then you get to unwind. Relaxation requires polarity – push/pull, on/off, move/stop. It is more beneficial to think of relaxation as a form of recovery. Relaxing isn't simply the state of being at ease. Relaxing is the recovery that occurs after effort. In the absence of effort, relaxation just leads to malaise.

A two-week vacation where you lounge by the pool and sip drinks works because it is a temporary reprieve from the physical and mental demands of your career. Checking out makes sense during your working years because you know that, after the vacation, you must check back in. A vacation is a short-term break, not a way of life.

What if every day was Christmas morning? Would that lead to happiness and fulfillment? I don't think so. I remember Christmas mornings as a kid like they were yesterday. They were magical because they happened just once a year.

The Retirement Myth can lead not only to dissatisfaction but also depression. What advice does a psychologist give someone who is depressed? Step back? Do less? Relax? Achieve less? No, just the opposite. The recommendation would be to exercise, get outside, spend time with family and friends, start a new hobby, do something scary, set goals, and quite simply, do more.

The Retirement Myth tells a whole group of people who have spent their entire lives striving and accomplishing, who have accumulated 40 years of wisdom and experience, and who have more time and money than ever before, that the best thing they can do in retirement is… less.

THE RETIREMENT MYTH IS OFFENSIVE

Frankly, the Retirement Myth is patronizing. Successful people who have more time, connections, experience, wisdom, and ability than those in any other age group are told that they should pack it in and do less. The collective message to retirees seems to be "Thank you for your time, but we've got this now." *Like hell you do.* Just because you've stepped away from your day-to-day job doesn't mean you don't still have a lot left to do and contribute.

Our value, meaning, and purpose don't have to retire when we do. Just because we may not "work" in retirement doesn't mean we still can't contribute, produce things, and have a meaningful impact on the world around us. In fact, I'll suggest throughout this book that we can do all these things even more in retirement.

The Retirement Myth is not just condescending – it's dangerous. It's dangerous for you and for the rest of us. You don't sideline your best player at the height of their career during the most important game of their life. Nevertheless, that's exactly the message of the Retirement Myth. Millions of people retire every year at the height of their careers. One day, they are working and contributing, and then – *poof!* – they are done. Goodbye responsibility. Goodbye mentoring. Goodbye creating. Goodbye learning. Goodbye growing. Goodbye camaraderie. Goodbye goals. Goodbye achievement.

Reject the Retirement Myth. An Average Retirement is mediocre. Don't settle for less; demand more. More adventure. More money. More joy. More challenge. More relaxation.

Yes, even more relaxation. This surprises some people. I love to relax and watch TV, read a good book, or have a lazy day just as much as most people. Being in *go go go* mode all the time is not healthy and is certainly not the reason you worked hard and sacrificed for years. Pull back, recuperate, and rest so you can then move forward again. This was true in your working years – clocking out at night, enjoying weekends and vacations – and it should be true in retirement.

But a break where you temporarily step back and recharge is not the same as a lifestyle of inactivity and ease. The Retirement Myth perpetuates the idealization of a lifestyle of endless relaxation and happiness. At least, that's the promise. The truth is something entirely different.

RETIREMENT DOESN'T ELIMINATE PROBLEMS – IT REPLACES THEM

One of the best gifts you can give yourself is the space to wrap your head around the idea that retirement doesn't remove anxiety, discomfort, or problems; it merely changes them. The belief that retirement is a state of nirvana made up of carefree days and frolicking on the beach – or maybe lounging in one of those omnipresent beach chairs we discussed earlier – is a recipe for surprise and disappointment.

Retirement is not a panacea that will automatically eliminate your problems. Remember – retirement doesn't remove problems; retirement replaces them.

Here are some of the recurring comments I've heard over the years from people in their working years and in retirement. You might not experience all of these, but you will likely identify with a few of the sentiments.

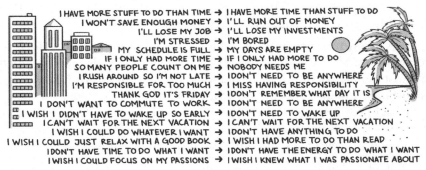

Our fears and concerns may change in retirement, but they don't go away. Which of these statements do you identify with?

Retirement could be the best time of your life, and if this book and the Badass Retirement Community have anything to say about it, it *will* be the best time of your life! I want you to look back and appreciate your working years, but not pine for the glory days that have passed. Instead, I want your Badass Retirement to be so fulfilling, meaningful, and fun that you kick yourself for not having retired sooner.

But few anticipate retirement is one of the most significant and stressful transitions in life...

ANIMALS DON'T RETIRE

If you're at all unsure about how to create a retirement of meaning and fulfillment and worry that you might feel like a caged animal, you may not be wrong. What do animals in captivity have to do with retirement? More than you may think.

Animals have natural instincts to hunt, forage, and mate, but when they are kept in prolonged captivity and are provided everything they need, they can exhibit zoochosis – a term for the signs of extreme depression, boredom, and frustration some animals experience in captivity. Animals will work to obtain food even when abundant food is readily available. Their inner drive to hunt and achieve – at least in some animals – may be stronger than their need to eat and survive. According to a 2005 report in the *Foundation for Wildlife*, the "psychological problems encountered in captive animals are frustration and boredom due to their being prevented from fulfilling inherited biological needs."[7]

The takeaway is that animals aren't the only creatures that can lose their oomph when provided an environment that prioritizes comfort and security over challenge and achievement. You're no different from a tiger. You have an inner drive to achieve and a need for challenge. This is true throughout your life, regardless of your work status. If all your needs are placated, stripping away all challenge, you run the risk of experiencing your own version of zoochosis – Average Retirement.

It's time you get out of the cage and enter a beautiful, bold, and adventurous retirement filled with meaning, fulfillment, and wonder. But how?

RETIREMENT ROULETTE?

What I've learned over the years is that you should rage against the Retirement Myth and do everything you can to avoid Average Retirement. It's telling us to rage right there in the name . . . Ave_rage_ Retirement.

Rage against the myth that you need to pull back, step down, and withdraw just because you are retired.

Rage against the culture who tells you that, once you are retired, you need to "act retired."

Rage against the belief that, in retirement, you need to take fewer risks instead of more.

Rage against the Retirement Myth.

Really? Rage? Isn't that too dramatic or intense? I don't think it's extreme enough. Retirement isn't a two-week vacation. We are talking about your life for the next 20 years. Or 30 years. Or 40 years. Or more. You don't want to wake up near the end of your retirement wondering if you could have done it better.

But your perfect dream retirement isn't going to happen by itself. This is the great retirement fallacy. There is little chance you'll stumble upon retirement happiness. You need to put the same effort and zest into designing your retirement as you did into your work. The difference is that designing your retirement should be fun! This is your life! If you are fortunate enough to have the financial security to retire, you get to think about and plan what you want your life to look like post-work. This can surely be a fun and rewarding exercise, but it can also be frustrating and challenging. Why?

Not everyone knows how to design their perfect retirement or knows what makes them feel fulfilled or happy. If you're in that group, that's okay. This book, workbook, videos, exercises, and supportive online membership community will help. When it comes to trying to determine how best to spend your retirement, work as hard as you did in your career because your retirement may last longer than your career!

Some retirees sit back and expect a great retirement to materialize out of thin air, putting very little thought into what would be an ideal retirement or how to create one. They figure that Rome wasn't built in a day, so their retirement just needs some time to develop. *I'll sit back and relax and wait to see what happens,* they tell themselves. *Besides, I've worked hard for years, and this is my time to kick back and check out.*

Even though they can see retirement on the horizon, this group looks the other way instead of preparing to design a new life. Hope and luck may work in Vegas, but they are not the foundations of a great retirement.

Rome wasn't built in a *day*. Rome was built *daily*.

It's time to start building a Badass Retirement.

JOIN THE FAMILY

If you are intrigued by the idea of experiencing something more and something better in retirement, join the online Badass Retirement Community to get access to additional resources, meet others, and make an impact.

GO TO BADASSRETIREMENT.COM

2

CHALLENGE

Discover Badass Retirement

If you are hoping for something more meaningful and exciting in retirement, welcome to Badass Retirement.

CHALLENGE 2

"You're telling me there's something different?"

Those six words have been the launching pad for creating a whole new life in retirement for many retirees skeptical of Average Retirement.

I remember one conversation with a client that changed his life and mine. He was a successful business owner who was in the middle of selling his company. He had worked long days and sacrificed for decades. He said he was ready to stop working, but confessed he wasn't sure if he wanted to retire. "I don't know what to do. I know I don't want the grind anymore, but retirement scares the hell out of me," he admitted. He had seen family members and friends retire and witnessed a gradual but steady decline in their health, sense of purpose, and zest for life. He also saw several become obsessed with every up and down in the stock market and endlessly worry about their finances. He continued, "The thought of retiring and just sitting around sounds depressing. I don't want to keep working, but I just don't think I can retire either. I know this is what I've been working for, but I'm telling you I wouldn't last five years."

I think he was exaggerating about the five years. He would have survived Average Retirement, but he wouldn't have enjoyed it. He wouldn't have felt engaged and connected. He wouldn't have felt meaning and purpose. And he certainly wouldn't have felt alive and inspired.

But that's when I told him there was an alternative. I shared my vision for what retirement could be. I told him he could stop working, recharge, and have time to do all the hobbies he had put off, but also continue to grow, create, achieve, contribute, and experience life to the fullest. I didn't have a name for it at the time, but I knew it felt right. He did too.

That conversation changed his life. For the first time he saw an alternative and he seized it. He created a life that inspired him. That conversation also changed my life. I think it was the first time I realized that there is real fear and angst among *some* soon-to-be retirees (and even retirees). I always knew I felt a pang of doubt when I thought about normal retirement, but I figured I was just weird. That conversation helped me see that while I may be different, I wasn't alone.

2 IN THE BUSH > 1 IN THE HAND

Think back to the times in your life when you felt the most alive and inspired. Can you find a common theme? Do they share any characteristics? Perhaps a certain geography? Maybe a relationship or social connection? Most likely, they're not tied to a particular place or person. The common thread for those times when you feel the best and most aligned with your purpose is often a particular state of thinking, being, and doing.

Happiness, it turns out, is a verb.

What are the elements to happiness? This can vary from person to person, but I've worked with enough people over the years to identify some main themes that certainly help. I think the two big contributors to overall happiness are the pursuit of a meaningful goal and a sense of contribution. There are others, obviously, but each of these (and both together) can provide a great deal of fulfillment and happiness.

This reminds me of a surprising conversation I had several years ago with a client. "We are thinking about making a change," they said. I could hear the sense of excitement and apprehension in their voice. I wondered what kind of change they were contemplating. Both had worked hard for years, but they still had another 10 years before typical retirement age. What kind of change were they thinking about making? Getting a vacation home? No, they already had one on the beach. Traveling more? No, they didn't enjoy flying or traveling. New job or career? No, the husband was a banker at a large credit union and enjoyed the work and people. What could make them so giddy that they couldn't wait to share it with me to get my thoughts? Then they said something I didn't expect and haven't forgotten: "We are thinking about retiring, moving to Texas, buying some land, and raising cows."

Come again?

They had lived in Los Angeles their entire lives. They belonged to a nearby country club and played golf several days a week. Their friends and family all lived within 20 minutes of them. They had a great income and were diligent savers. "Can we afford it?" they asked.

Having worked with them for many years, I knew their dream was to have more land where they could ride horses. We had talked about their goals for retirement and the kind of life they wanted to live. It was clear neither wanted an Average Retirement. "The things most people do in retirement just don't interest us," they told me. "We want something different – more challenging." I always knew that their retirement would be anything but average, but raising cows in Texas? Now, that was a surprise!

After many discussions, dozens of financial simulations, and a few trips to Texas, they had their ranch within three years – complete with horses and cows. As I write this, I'm on a plane flying home from visiting them in Dallas. They are living their dream retirement, and it looks and feels nothing like retirement. They make less money now than when they worked, but they both joke they have never worked harder or longer. They are pursuing a meaningful goal and taking care of their animals provides them with a sense of contribution. Their retirement consumes them, and they've never been happier (and they even named a cow after me – Roberta!).

RETIREMENT POTENTIAL GAP

The greatest punishment is not to be stripped of everything you have, but to be given everything you want. – Robert Pagliarini (I know it's pompous to quote yourself, but I couldn't help it.)

Retirement is full of gaps between what we have and what we want. We want to take a trip to Italy, but we don't have anyone to go with. We'd love to write a children's book, but we don't feel like we have the skill. We want a 1969 Mustang, but we can't afford it. We want to hike the Inca Trail, but we are out of shape.

When we desire something, we direct our frustration at the gap. It can take months or even years of struggle to finally close the gap and achieve our goal – saving the money, learning the skills, getting into shape. Life would be so much better if only we could snap our fingers and get whatever we wanted, right? Easier? Definitely. But better? Maybe not.

RETIREMENT GAP

The gap between where you are and where you want to be provides meaning, passion, and fuel.

The gap between "want" and "have" is what fuels our effort. The gap is what provides the angst to keep pushing. Pre-retirement, we'd get up early to go to the office and stay late. We'd sacrifice today to achieve a better tomorrow. The gap can provide purpose and meaning. Psychologist Mihaly Csikszentmihalyi coined the term "flow" to describe the sense of being fully immersed and engrossed in a challenging and mentally stimulating activity. Contrary to expectations, his research indicates that the "great majority of flow experiences are reported when working, not when in leisure."[8] Relaxation is important, but we experience the most fulfillment when we are sufficiently challenged. The gap is what creates the hunger and the challenge of the hunt – the focus to pursue something that we don't have.

But what happens when there is no gap? When there is no distance between what you want and where you are? When there is no struggle? When hunger is replaced by satiation?

This is what happens for those in an Average Retirement. The initial thrill of finally closing the gap transforms into weariness and discontent. They grow increasingly bored and despondent because there is no longer a gap to close. At this point, some retirees experience a feeling of emptiness – a void. Ironically, even though they have what they thought was their dream retirement, they feel like they are missing something.

Meaning is the degree to which we feel our lives have value, purpose, and impact. If someone no longer feels they are making a difference, contributing, or having any impact, they will experience a deep dissatisfaction in retirement. No one wants to feel like they just exist. They want to feel they are here for a reason and that they are making a difference in the world – or at least in their world.

The Retirement Myth perpetuates the belief that retirement itself transforms not just our lives, but us in the process. But that's not what happens...

MEET THE NEW BOSS; SAME AS THE OLD BOSS

Everything changes in retirement... except us.

Retirement changes our lives – not us – overnight. It transforms everything from our daily routine to our finances to our social environment. Although retirement turns our lives upside down, it doesn't change who we are and what makes us tick. None of our deeply held needs go away just because our careers do. We're the same exact person we were before, but now without a job.

We still want to feel needed. We still want to contribute. We still want to be part of a group that understands and appreciates us. We still want to overcome challenges. We still want to feel pride and accomplishment after reaching our goals. We still want to feel that our lives have purpose – that *we* have purpose.

But the Retirement Myth would have us believe that all the things that drove us throughout our 40-plus years of working can instantly be discarded just like our commute. But we are the same person on the last day we work as we are on the first day of retirement. None of our deeply held needs vanish just because we retired.

This is why I always find it so surprising when soon-to-be retirees tell me they have no big goals or dreams for retirement and that they're looking forward to doing as little as possible. When I press them, asking if they enjoyed contributing through their work, the answer is always *yes*. Making a difference? *Yes*. Being part of a team or group? *Yes*. Setting and pursuing challenging goals? *Yes*. Working hard? *Yes*. And now they want to do as little as possible? This is the toxic myth that informs how we view retirement – we'll be happy doing less, achieving less, and being less just because we're retired?!

Ask a retiree about themselves and they will either tell you what they used to do for a living or will simply say, "I am retired." Retiring is just something you've done. It's not who you are. We need to detach ourselves from this idea that retiring and retirement define who we are. It does not explain who we are or what we hope to accomplish. Retiring merely represents a decision we made in the past to not continue working.

Who you are isn't determined simply by the absence of something you used to do. While it's interesting to learn about what someone has accomplished, I find it even more fascinating to learn what they still want to achieve. What someone has done tells you who they were; what someone does now tells you who they are; what someone wants to do tells you who they hope to become.

We do not suddenly change once we retire. We don't morph overnight into somebody else with different aspirations and desires. Retiring is what we did. It's not who we are.

It pains me to think we spend 40-plus years working and answering to others only to reach retirement – the point in our lives where we have the most time, money, and ability to become and pursue anything we want – only to let the opportunity slip by. The future is always unknown. I've had clients who diligently worked hard and saved their entire lives only to pass away shortly after retirement. Nothing is guaranteed. None of us know how much time we have.

FINDING YOUR "AND"

You should relax, take that cruise, see the world, and spend as much time as you can with the grandkids. And, yes, get out there on the golf course and try to perfect your game! But to live your best life in retirement, you need an "and."

The "and" is what separates Average Retirement from Badass Retirement. At some point, you must stop coasting and shift into gear. This is the promise and power of "and." You are retired *and* what else? Retiring is what you did – it's your past – but that's not who you are. Your "and" is what you are doing now – it's your present *and* your future.

To achieve a successful retirement filled with purpose, meaning, joy, adventure, and contribution you need something more – an "and." That is the purpose of the rest of this book, the workbook, and the online community. It is about filling in the "and" to create the very best retirement and life possible.

In our working years, we had a lot of needs. We needed to work. We needed to commute. We needed to get that report done. We needed to hit our numbers. We needed to keep our job. In retirement, this burden of needs reduces overnight. We retire from needs, but that's one of the selling points of retirement, right?

What does a retiree *need* to do? Sure, retirees have all kinds of *wants* – we want to take that cruise, we want to play golf, we want to join a book club, etc. – but needs? Not so many. While there is freedom in reducing the number of needs we must satisfy, there is real danger in eliminating them.

An Average Retirement has few, if any, needs. This is consciously done by intentionally eliminating responsibilities. Badass Retirement, on the other hand, recognizes the value of needs. Needs create a gap and provide drive to close it. But not just any need is valuable. No retiree longs for the meaningless responsibilities and busywork they did while working. The goal isn't to create stuff to do. It's to create needs that move you.

THE BADASS RETIREMENT SYSTEM

What does it really mean to live a Badass Retirement? It doesn't mean you need to be Type A – always pursuing and grinding to get better without ever resting. The more zealous will want to push themselves to create a retirement where they have their feet firmly pressed on the gas pedal. Others may look at that level of effort as being too much like work and opt for something a little less ambitious.

You may laugh at my definition of "badass" as being too extreme (or maybe too timid!), and that's okay. Retirement is not a scorecard where one tries to compete with others to live the most badass life. Nobody wants to be judged for trying to improve their life just because someone else is insecure.

Your vision and implementation of Badass Retirement will likely look very different than mine, but the **Badass 5** are the essential drivers that comprise a Badass Retirement:

Badass Driver #1: **Greater Meaning**

Badass Driver #2: **Total Financial Security**

Badass Driver #3: **Upgraded Health**

Badass Driver #4: **Deeper Relationships**

Badass Driver #5: **Real Adventure**

If you truly want to live a Badass Retirement, you must nail these five core drivers. Not just once in a while. Not just occasionally when you feel motivated. You need to nail them *consistently*. I like to think of making daily deposits into each of these five areas. If you let any one of the **Badass 5** slip for too long, you'll get off track and you may not even notice it until you wake up one day and wonder what the hell went wrong. It doesn't happen overnight, but believe me, it will happen. Gradually your enthusiasm and energy may start to fade. You might worry more and feel less fulfilled. Imagine a life where you are missing just one of the **Badass 5**...

Without **Greater Meaning**, you might have the money and ability, but you'd likely feel like your life had no purpose. You'd bounce from one activity to the next – ever chasing the next dopamine hit but never really feeling grounded or fulfilled. You don't need to solve the world's problems, but you do need to feel you are growing and contributing.

Without **Total Financial Security**, you might be plagued by worry and insecurity – never fulling feeling comfortable and not being able to afford the things or experiences you'd really like. You don't need to be rich, but you do need to feel secure that you aren't going to run out of money or have your finances turned upside down.

Without **Upgraded Health**, you might have all the desire to live a bold life, but it would be a constant struggle. Compromised health would put you at a distinct disadvantage. You might not have the energy or the ability to do the things you really want. You don't need to have six pack abs or train like an Olympian, but you do need to have ample energy to undertake the activities you want.

Without **Deeper Relationships**, you might have the money, energy, and resources in retirement, but you likely would feel disconnected and lonely. Your days would be full, but you may feel unfulfilled. Our relationships provide connection, the feeling of camaraderie, and love. You don't need to have a romantic partner or have dozens of friends, but you do need to feel valued and appreciated and a sense of belonging.

Without **Real Adventure**, you might have the foundation of a normal retirement, but you'd be missing the spark and the excitement. You'd have no *joie de vie* as the French say. Your life would be stable and secure, but perhaps a bit mundane and boring. You don't need to rock climb or jump out of planes, but you do need to push your comfort zone and feel a sense of excitement.

All five elements are crucial to living life at the fullest. The mission of this book is dedicated to uncovering and exploring how to create a retirement with Greater Meaning, Total Financial Security, Upgraded Health, Deeper Relationships, and Real Adventure.

You're going to read and learn, but by the end of the book, you're going to have a plan for what you need to do to create and sustain a Badass Retirement. Remember, you don't have to work *in* retirement, but you have to work *on* retirement.

The first step? Expand what you think is possible.

JOIN THE FAMILY

Does the idea of creating and living a Badass Retirement excite you? If so, you're part of a small group that wants something better in retirement. Plug into the Badass Retirement Community and continue your journey.

GO TO **BADASSRETIREMENT.COM**

3

CHALLENGE

Expand Potential

Don't settle. You and your retirement can be so much more than you think.

CHALLENGE 3

I was in the middle of giving a live presentation to a large group of people when I started to tear up. As I kept talking, I became more and more emotional. I remember hearing the words come out of my mouth and becoming more consumed with each passing sentence. I also remember thinking, *What the hell is going on?*

Many grown men cry and express their emotions freely and unabashedly. I'm not one of those people (my wife still gives me a hard time because I didn't cry at our wedding). Surely the presentation I was giving must have been about a loss I experienced, a tragedy involving a client, or something – anything – that might lend itself to strong emotions. But it wasn't. The presentation was about . . . retirement. Yup. Just plain old, boring retirement.

Somehow, I was able to continue the presentation while conducting an internal dialogue with myself at the same time. *What's your problem? People are going to think you've lost it. You're just talking about retirement. Get it together!* Eventually, I was able to compose myself and continue the speech, but that moment has stayed with me since, and it's the reason you're holding this book.

I've always been passionate about doing, achieving, and being more. I've always thought about my own potential in life and trying to reach it. I love to coach and inspire others to set big goals. I feel at home with others who push themselves in the pursuit of their dreams.

I've also always thought there wasn't something quite right about how most people approach retirement. I saw how content some people were with retirement, but I also knew I'd struggle with this version of retirement when the time came for me to retire. I have had the opportunity to observe hundreds of clients over the years as they approached and entered retirement. It has been fascinating to see how different clients respond. Some ease into their new lives of rest and leisure and seem satisfied, while others become increasingly agitated as they try to pull back and relax.

How could I sit stone-faced through classic tearjerkers like *Titanic, The Notebook,* and *A Star Is Born* but become emotional over a presentation on retirement? It struck a nerve – a nerve I didn't even realize was so tender. I was talking about how people work so hard all their lives. Many of us are fortunate to do things we love and to make a difference, but it's still hard. We get up early, battle traffic, sometimes answer to not-so-great bosses, work when we don't feel well, suffer injustices and toxic work environments, sacrifice our mental and physical health at times, and lose time with our kids and loved ones that we can never get back. We do all this for years, for *decades*, and then, one day, we get the opportunity to retire.

That's when it hit me. We devote our mind and our body to our career for 40 or more years. We reach that critical point in our lives where retirement gives us the gift of doing anything we want, but most of us don't live up to our potential. Some experience health issues and don't have the ability to do everything they want. Others get illnesses that cut their lives short. These thoughts crush me.

Most retirees, however, are healthy and able to set big goals, chase lifelong dreams, and live the best 30 years of their lives but don't. We're constantly told that retirement is the "final chapter" in our lives, and what do too many retirees do? We drift, pull back, and let go. At the point in our lives when we have the most time, money, and ability, we do less. It kills me to think that people are giving up on achieving and doing important things in their lives. We push our big dreams and plans off to the future, thinking we have the time. Until we don't. We wake up one day and realize we don't have the time or energy anymore. We missed our opportunity. We missed the one last chance to experience everything we wanted, to achieve our deepest ambitions, and to live our best lives. And what really gets to me is that there are no do-overs. We have one shot at retirement. In the best-case scenario, we will wake up one day in the future and realize our game is coming to an end. The question that haunts me is *Will I make the most of my life?*

Maybe I was projecting my own insecurities or doubts about retirement or maybe I was facing an existential crisis, but that is why I started to cry during my retirement presentation.

If you believe in God, would your God want you to waste the life you have been given? You were not put on Earth to casually sit back on life's couch and binge-watch your retirement. You are here for a reason. Even if you're not religious and don't believe in a higher power, your time here is just as important. If there is no afterlife, it means this life is the only one you have.

One day, you're going to discover that the game is over. You'd better make the most of it while you can still play.

RETIREMENT GREATNESS

This is personal for me. My core belief is that each of us has the highest potential for our life. Of course, everyone's highest potential is different, and our potential in our working years often looks different than our potential in our retirement years. Some call it "living my best life," and others refer to it as being the best version of themselves, but however you label it, we all have vast amounts of potential.

The problem with an Average Retirement is we get further from our potential day after day and year after year.

The goal of Badass Retirement is to shrink the retirement potential gap – the gap between Average Retirement and what your ideal retirement could be. There is a large chasm between what is (or what will be) and what *could* be. Your new "job" in retirement is to work on closing that gap and getting a little closer to your ideal. This continuous pursuit is your opportunity for meaning, purpose, and deep satisfaction – this is the Retirement Opportunity.

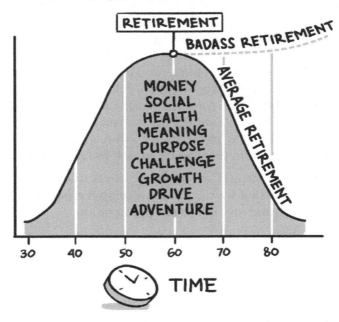

Most people experience their peak at retirement and then see a rapid decline.
Those living a Badass Retirement avoid the drop and continue to experience
growth.

The goal is to do more of the things that make you feel happiest and most fulfilled. In retirement – even an Average Retirement – we all find things that give us meaning and that we enjoy. It could be spending time with the grandkids, reading, painting, or volunteering. I've never met a retiree who hadn't found something that gave them joy or hadn't experienced times of deep satisfaction. But an Average Retirement is just that – average – certainly not terrible but not fantastic, either. Again, there is a decent percentage of the population (a majority?) that is content with average. Not surprisingly, most retirees live Average Retirements, but "average" means there is opportunity for improvement.

DON'T DIE WITH A SONG STILL INSIDE YOU

You don't need to cure pediatric cancer or solve homelessness in retirement (unless you'd like to try!). This is a judgment-free zone. If your highest potential is improving your golf score or knitting sweaters, congratulations! Go forth and slay. Live your retirement and be happy!

If you feel even a twinge of anxiety about retirement, however, keep reading. If you feel you were meant to do something more than live an Average Retirement, keep expanding your vision of what's possible in retirement. You may not have all the answers now, but the goal of this book is to help you find your purpose and drive – to help you find that thing that makes you excited each morning.

Some clients intuitively chart their own paths that look different than the Average Retirement. Maybe for some (you?), the choices you make in retirement will provide even more meaning and purpose than you experienced during your working years. Maybe you'll create and contribute more while you are "retired" than you ever have before. Maybe you'll find more joy, adventure, and excitement as a retiree than you did in your career. That's my goal for you. Badass Retirement shatters the Retirement Myth that less is better. A Badass Retirement is one where you jump out of bed in the morning with purpose. You have the health and energy to propel you forward. You have the financial security and confidence that you will have a lifetime of income and never have to worry about running out of money.

The yellow brick road to retirement is long and hard, but the hope is that, once you reach it, you will be rewarded and not disappointed by an angry and pudgy figure staring back at you in the mirror, making you feel like you've been tricked and that the entire journey was a waste. Dorothy realized the wizard wasn't going to save her. She was and always had been the hero of her story…

HOLDING OUT FOR A HERO

You may be aware of the term "hero's journey." The phrase was coined by Joseph Campbell and is used to describe the common three-act literary structure found in many novels and movies. The idea of the hero's journey has been expanded over the years, but the original premise remains. The story starts with the main character living an ordinary life, only to be suddenly thrust into unknown territory where they face challenges and trials that they must overcome. At the end of the third act, the hero gets to comfortably look back on all the struggles they faced and the battles they won. The hero's journey has been fulfilled. No more challenges. No more adventure. No more dragons to slay.

Although this story sequence shows up over and over in fictional work, we all want to be the hero of our own story. Unfortunately, the Retirement Myth leads to us conquering our working years only to close the story with our retirement – the seeming resolution of our journey. We triumphed over our career and have achieved success by reaching retirement.

If you buy into the Retirement Myth and aspire to live an Average Retirement, you are at the end of a three-act play. Story over.

But is the story over? Or is it just the beginning of a new adventure with different missions, challenges, and dragons to slay? Be proud of what you've accomplished in your working years and having the luxury of being able to retire, but don't reminisce too long. An Average Retirement says, "Look at what I've done and the life I have led," but a Badass Retirement says, "Look at what I'm going to do and the life I will lead."

You have more time, energy, and money than you've ever had to create and live the best life possible in retirement.

If you ask an ambitious 20-year-old what their goals in life are, you'd better get comfortable, because it might be a long list. On the other hand, if you ask someone living an Average Retirement about their future goals, you might get a blank stare or hear about a few items on their bucket list.

If you just scoffed at that last sentence, it is because you still view the world through the lens of the Retirement Myth. That lens has clouded your judgment and your ability to live a much greater-than-Average Retirement. Why do you think it is so normal for a 20-year-old to have much greater aspirations and goals for their future than a 65-year-old retiree? Why do you think a younger person who has little free time, no money, almost zero experience, few resources, and decades of work ahead of them should have more goals (professional or personal) than a retiree with decades of experience and skills, vast connections and resources, more money than they've ever had, and unlimited free time?

Something is not adding up. It's insulting to retirees that those around them think so little of their potential. It should be insulting to you that you think so little of yourself. Demand more. Be the hero of your own story.

CAPABLE > COMFORTABLE

The paradox is that the easier and more comfortable you try to make your life, the more you need things to be comfortable and easy. The more capable you become; the easier things get.

The Retirement Myth wants to hold your hand as you cross the street. It wants to cut your food for you. It wants to shield you from effort and challenge. But that's a mistake.

Don't fall into the trap of thinking that making your retirement life as easy as possible will lead to happiness and fulfillment. Does this mean you need to live a stoic life or fly economy when you can afford first class? Of course not! Enjoy the finer things. Travel well. Hire help for around the house. But don't eliminate challenge.

We spend so much time and energy making things easy and comfortable, but we should spend that time and energy making ourselves capable. Don't hope things are easy enough; hope that you are strong enough.

This is what I've found to be true:

The easier you try to make your life, the harder it becomes.

The harder you make your life, the easier it becomes.

Isn't this true? The more things we do to make our lives easy and comfortable, the more we become irritated over the little things. It's a great paradox.

But expanding your view of what's possible in retirement isn't easy. You don't have to work *in* your retirement, but you do need to work *on* your retirement. That takes effort, and frankly, not everyone wants to put in the work.

BORN TO BE... LAZY?

Sorry, Steppenwolf, but you got it wrong. We were born to be lazy. Or maybe a kinder description would be that we are judicious about how we exert physical and mental energy. Scientists suggest that we are "efficient" with our energy expenditure, but however you look at it, we have evolved to exert as little energy as possible.

It makes sense that we will exert energy if it leads to increasing our chance of survival. Although lions lounge for 20 hours a day, when they get hungry, you can bet they have no problem exerting a lot of energy to chase down a meal. Our survival doesn't necessitate chasing down food, but it does require us to chase down a paycheck. There is no doubt you have exerted tremendous energy during your working years – staying at the office late, putting in more hours than your colleagues, and out-hustling others to get new clients. We will work hard if we predict it will lead to a greater outcome.

In retirement, however, the impetus for financial survival and success has been eliminated. There is no shiny pot of gold driving our actions. It's the same reason you'll see a lion run 50 mph after dinner, but you won't see one on a StairMaster or doing crunches (okay, there are many reasons you don't see this, but you get the point!).

If we are predisposed to conserve energy and take the easy route, where does this leave us when we stop working for money? Are we destined to live a life of leisure and idleness in retirement since there is no survival benefit or financial reward for exerting effort?

It's not just culture tempting us to aim low, it is evolution. In terms of the survival of species, the advantage goes to those who are energy frugal. But you aren't reading this book just to survive, right? If you wanted an Average Retirement, you certainly don't need to read a book

– average is the default. Average Retirement is your consolation prize just for showing up.

But that's not you. You want something more. You want to escape Average Retirement. Just know that you will need to confront a culture that tempts you to take it easy and years of evolutionary biology encouraging you to do less.

You weren't born to retire. You were born to create, to achieve, to make a difference, to contribute, to have an impact, to better your life and the lives of those around you, to experience, to grow, and to become more.

I hope that, after reading this Challenge, you have a new appreciation for what retirement can be. The goal is not just to help you elevate your view of retirement, but to elevate what you can do in retirement. That's next...

JOIN THE FAMILY

Your retirement can be so much more than average. Join the Badass Retirement Community, and you'll have access to exclusive tools, live webinars, and content to help you continue to expand your vision for what's possible in retirement.

GO TO BADASSRETIREMENT.COM

44

SECTIONS

MAGNIFY

MINDSET

MEANING

MONEY

MOMENTUM

CHALLENGE

Take
Control

A successful retirement isn't based on
hope or luck; it's the result of intention
and effort.

CHALLENGE 4

According to Sioux legend, there was a time long ago when it did not rain for many months. The land became dry, plants withered, and animals perished. The people of the land struggled to survive without life-giving water. They became fearful that they too would become victims of the drought. Fear spread from village to village across the prairie, eventually reaching a small village with children and elders.

The children asked the elders, "What is this thing that has come to visit us?" "Fear," the wise elders replied. The children asked, "Does Fear want to play?" to which the elders answered, "Fear has forgotten how to play."

The children decided they would try to help Fear remember how to play. They jumped and danced and sang songs. The sounds of their joy echoed across the prairie. From far and wide, other villagers came to this little village where everyone was singing and dancing. They became overwhelmed with emotion and began to cry. The wind carried their tears across the land, filling the rivers and lakes and providing water for the plants and animals.

Many indigenous people from all over the world still practice rain dances and rituals to this day – those people are known as Rainmakers. They make it rain.

Then, there are meteorologists, scientists who attempt to forecast the weather. They analyze charts and mathematical models to predict what the weather will be in the future.

The Rainmaker controls the weather; the meteorologist predicts the weather.

The Rainmaker makes the future; the meteorologist observes the future.

Don't sit back and observe. Your retirement is a blank slate. You get to design it however you want.

Be the Rainmaker in your retirement.

There is only one requirement for embarking on a journey toward Badass Retirement: desire.

Your prior career, financial success, or achievements are irrelevant. As the saying goes, past performance is no indication of future performance. I've seen just as many people who had ordinary careers, lives, and ambitions during their working years go on to create amazing retirements – fully embracing and benefiting from the Badass Retirement lifestyle – as I have those who you would expect to seek out a Badass Retirement.

If you feel like you didn't fully live up to your potential during your working years, now is your opportunity. Retirement is the great reset. You can change the course of your life in an instant by deciding to reject the Retirement Myth and an Average Retirement and to do, experience, and become more with a Badass Retirement.

Nobody is going to look at your previous jobs, call your professional references, or dissect past decisions. No prior experience or success is required. You don't need to have made a fortune or started your own business. You don't need anyone's permission or approval. You get to decide what kind of retirement you want and how you will live the rest of your life.

You have no boss making demands. There is no looming deadline. You don't have clients expecting something from you. Retirement can be lonely. You'd think things would be easier because you have so much free time, but it can be difficult when there are no external forces asking anything of you.

It's all on you.

MOBILITY > NOBILITY

Who are you? What are you capable of achieving? For thousands of years and across different parts of the world, the answers to these questions were clear and unalterable. Your social status, the jobs you could perform, who you could marry, and your life were not determined by your talents or efforts. Instead, they were based on heredity – the family into which you were born. Imagine having the desire and drive to achieve but never having the chance to pursue greatness simply because society didn't deem you worthy. There is nothing noble about nobility.

I prefer a system that allows for movement or mobility. A system where you have the opportunity to grow, expand, and become successful. A system where what you do and what you achieve are not based on arbitrary rules or the approval of a gatekeeper. In retirement, you get to determine how you want to live your life. You don't need permission. You don't need approval. You are free to shred any preconceived ideas about what you can or can't do. Even today, this is a luxury not everyone has.

But retirement's great reset gives you this luxury. You are not tied to your past. In retirement, you have the ability and the freedom to pursue anything you want and to create the life you want. You do not live in a society with a caste system that determines what you can achieve, though too many people create internal caste systems, deferring their agency to others.

Don't look to your past and don't seek approval.

RETIREMENT HAPPENS BECAUSE OF YOU

Retirement can feel like it is something happening to you – like you are just along for the ride. The healthier interpretation of retirement is not that it's happening *to* you or even that it is happening *with* you, but that it is happening *because* of you. That's the goal for this Challenge – to help you appreciate the influence you have over your life in retirement and to put you in a mindset where you don't surrender, gladly taking control instead.

For most of us, the mindset of having control isn't something that comes naturally. We've worked our entire lives in careers where we had varying levels of control. We had bosses and clients. Whether we were at the bottom of the corporate ladder or the top, we all reported to someone. Even if we were the boss, clients and changing market conditions could make it hard to feel like we ever had full control over our fate.

There is a perception that retirement is this force that exists independently from ourselves, a separate entity living and operating on its own. You might interact with it and have some influence over it, but it has its own life and, ultimately, controls itself.

If you listen to how people describe retirement, you may hear this hands-off view reflected in comments such as "I hope I have a good retirement," "I wonder what my retirement will be like," and "I hope retirement makes me happy."

It's easy to view retirement as this thing with a mind of its own. Except it's not. Retirement does not exist outside of yourself. You are your retirement. Yes, there will be things that happen to you in retirement that are beyond your control – some positive, some negative – but ultimately your retirement is the result of the decisions you make and the actions you take.

Retirees who adopt a passive role tend to be less satisfied. They view themselves not as active participants in their retirements, but as observers. They sit back and let retirement happen to them. They "go with the flow," hoping things work out. Retirees who accept control and take ownership over their retirements feel more empowered, satisfied, and do much better than the ones who sit back and hope things go well. Hope shouldn't be the basis of your retirement plan.

It's the difference between roulette and poker. You either let the ball bounce around and hope it lands on your number or you make decisions and do your best to improve the hand you are given. You might win or you might lose. But with poker at least you're in the game instead of just watching it all happen.

If you are merely a participant, you relinquish control. If you do not feel like you have agency over your situation, you are less likely to become involved in the process. The difference between experiencing retirement and effecting retirement may be subtle, but it's significant. If you believe that your decisions and actions do not meaningfully influence the outcome, you are a lot less likely to do things to improve your retirement and your life.

So, how can you regain your footing – especially in the first few weeks or months of retirement – despite the apprehension you may feel? Here's how you can become the master instead of the puppet...

RISE TO THE OCCASION

In order to "take control," you need to believe that you have the ability to influence the future. Psychologists call this "self-efficacy" – the belief in your ability to perform actions, accomplish goals, and have an effect on your life.

Self-efficacy is a big deal. It's not some pop psychology fluff. I conducted research on financial self-efficacy for my doctoral dissertation.[9] It has real-world implications. In short, those who believe they have greater control over their behaviors and influence over their future don't just have better outcomes – they have better lives. How can you hope to live your greatest retirement if you believe you have little control over your actions or your future? Badass Retirement doesn't rely on hope or luck. To live the best life possible, you need to strengthen your self-efficacy.

Oh, I don't think I could do that. How many times have you encouraged a child, partner, or even a parent to do something they didn't believe they could do but you knew they could? We've all had that experience. It's painfully obvious to us that they can do it, but they lack the confidence.

I just don't think I'm ready yet. This is another all-too-common utterance from perpetual planners. Getting "ready" is a disease of confidence. The advice to "take control" does not mean "get ready." Taking control means you jump in and figure it out, even if you are unsure. If not now, when? What are you waiting for? To be *more* ready? Sometimes, you must take the plunge, even if you don't feel 100% ready. The truth is that you can never feel totally ready when you are doing hard things and being bold. The point is to push yourself beyond your comfort zone. If you felt confident and ready, it wouldn't be a stretch.

This might sound counterintuitive, but the goal isn't to reduce discomfort or anxiety. You aren't trying to minimize your apprehension by getting "ready." You don't want to move away from the tension; you should seek it and move toward it. Waiting until you feel ready is counter to what you need.

You don't have to be ready. You just have to be willing.

In our working years, our lives and livelihood were contingent upon how confident, capable, and ready we were. The more experienced and rehearsed we were, the better we did. Competence plus confidence is a winning formula. There's a reason we spent our entire career sharpening and growing our capabilities. It feels good, and we are rewarded for it. "Winging it" was clearly not a successful strategy during our professional lives.

We spent our entire professional lives building competence and confidence. We went to school, got advanced designations or degrees, worked for years and decades in our field, gained experience and greater responsibility, and maybe even managed or mentored others along the way. When we retire, we are at the top of our careers. We have more knowledge, experience, competence, and confidence than at any other point. We haven't just gotten used to knowing the answers and feeling assured, we've also become masters at learning how to become ready.

It feels better to be confident than to be insecure. It feels better to be in control than to be helpless. This mentality, however, is also going to work against you in retirement. Don't run from insecurity; embrace it. Be warned – this may feel uncomfortable.

In my experience working with retirees, I've found that the more competent and confident someone was in their career, the less likely they were to put themselves in a position where they felt unsure or insecure. This isn't always the case, but it seems to be true more often than not. It's something for you to consider for yourself. How open are you to feeling incompetent? How willing are you to feeling like an amateur? How likely are you to do something where you feel insecure in your ability and/or knowledge?

When was the last time you felt nervous or like you were stretching your abilities? Last week? Last month? Or has it been years? If you can't remember how long it's been since you felt the wonder of having learned something or felt a tug of insecurity, you are not alone. We get to a certain point in our careers and our lives when we pull back. Instead of growing and pushing ourselves by taking risks and stretching our abilities – getting in a little over our head – we become stagnant, content in our competence.

It's time to make the call.

MAKING THE CALL > WAITING FOR THE CALL

In an earlier Challenge, I discussed the hero's journey – the character arc found in many movies and novels. One of the most significant steps of the hero's journey occurs early and is the start of the adventure – the call to action. The call to action is the critical point that introduces an event or challenge that pulls the main character from their ordinary life into an extraordinary mission, thrusting a normal person into something special.

DON'T WAIT FOR THE CALL

Passivity isn't going to cut it. You need to take control.

Isn't this what we all want? None of us wants an average and ordinary life. We want to feel as if we are living an extraordinary life and that our experience is special and meaningful. We want to answer the call. We want to rise up. We want to help. To contribute. To excel. To challenge ourselves. To push. To sacrifice. To be part of something. To feel needed.

It's one of the main reasons we enjoy movies. We get to vicariously answer the call and go on an adventure – even if only for a couple of hours. Our mirror neurons – special neurons that fire when we perform or observe an action – light up when we watch movies and sports. But then the movie ends or the clock runs out on the game.

Some want to answer a call that will shake them loose from their normal lives; they are looking for a major transformation. Others want a call to provide them with a nudge or a little more purpose – something that gently shifts the arc of their story.

We binge watch the next digital adventure as we wait for our call. But most of us never get a call – especially in retirement. In our working years, there was more opportunity to rise to the occasion because there were more occasions – we had our careers, new projects, raising kids, etc. We also had people above us – bosses, boards of directors, clients – who could push us out of our comfort zones. Our work increased the chance we would need to step up. Although we have now more time in retirement, we often have fewer opportunities to be called to action.

We must be more purposeful than the characters we watch in movies. We can't sit back and wait for the call to come. We must make it ourselves.

The strategy for creating a Badass Retirement is not to just retire and hope for the best. It's really hard to fall into a great life. I suppose it's possible, but I've never seen it. Instead, what I've seen time and time again is that living a remarkable life, whatever that may mean for you, doesn't just happen by accident. Creating a good life requires thinking, planning, and effort. This is true for everything – a career, marriage, health, relationships, and even (maybe especially!) retirement.

TIPS TO GAIN MORE CONTROL OF YOUR RETIREMENT

The following are a few ideas on how to feel more in control of your retirement and life:

Ask yourself these questions. In therapy, psychologists will often say that awareness is half the treatment. Why? Because our attention matters. If we don't notice or recognize we have an issue, it becomes nearly impossible to resolve. It's like having a defective operating system running in the background. If we view the world through this flawed lens, we can't address it. When we focus our attention, we start to see things we wouldn't have noticed.

If you struggle with the belief that you don't have as much control over your life as you'd like, ask yourself: Do I have any control over my life in retirement? If yes, what should I do? If no, what would I do if I had some control?

Get a coach. If you live 30 years in retirement, that's 262,800 hours! Would it make sense to invest a few of these hours into seeing a coach or therapist that can help us feel like we have control over the remaining 262,790 hours? I think so. Work with someone who can help you see the world through a lens where you have control. Consider using a cognitive-behavioral therapist, as their approach is a good fit for this task. Be sure to join the Badass Retirement Community, where you'll have access to webinars and interactive videos with therapists and coaches who specialize in this area.

Dial up your insecurity index. It may sound counterintuitive, but one way to feel more confident is to put yourself in situations where you feel anything but confident. One way psychologists help patients overcome anxiety and phobias is through systematic desensitization therapy. Part of this treatment involves exposing the patient to increasing levels of the fear stimuli. Patients who have a phobia of spiders might first be asked to talk about spiders, then draw one, then see a photo of a small spider, then a more intimidating photo, then a video, then being in the same room with a caged spider, and maybe even holding one. Each step along the way is scary and a step beyond the comfort zone, but not quite terrifying enough to prevent patients from participating. As they work their way to the end goal, they become increasingly desensitized. The photo of the spider that caused them to shriek a week ago is blasé today.

You can use this same approach to gain more confidence. You just need to do more things that create feelings of insecurity. The more often you do scary things to test your limits, the more you become desensitized to feeling insecure.

Change is possible. If you have little to no belief that you have control over your future, you won't take any steps to make it better. You must first open your mind to the possibility that your retirement can improve. If you are still having a hard time accepting this, ask if it is possible for your retirement to get worse because of the steps you take. If your retirement can get worse because of your actions, there's no reason it can't also get better.

Set goals. Just the act of setting goals will help you overcome the feeling that you have no control over your future. The energy and thought process required to set goals will get your mind thinking in a whole new way. In the section on meaning, you will learn what drives you and what goals you should pursue.

Review the past. Have there been times in your life when you've felt confidently in control? Where you felt your success hinged on your ability? What is the biggest challenge you have overcome? What has been your greatest accomplishment? What are your top three most significant strengths? What are three compliments you've received of which you are most proud? Review these moments as proof that your actions matter.

Consider a different viewpoint. Martin Seligman's research on learned helplessness inspired him to look at optimists and pessimists and examine how both types of people explain good and bad events. He writes in *Authentic Happiness*, "Optimistic people tend to interpret troubles as transient, controllable, and specific to one situation. Pessimistic people, in contrast, believe that their troubles last forever, undermine everything they do, and are uncontrollable." If you can change the way you explain the events that occur in your life, you will be more likely to feel in control and less likely to suffer from learned helplessness.

Keep a journal. We don't usually have strong memories. Even when we do, we might not be able to trust them. There is what happened, and then there is what you *think* happened. The only truth is what you believe. Think about an important event from your past where you felt you didn't have control over the outcome. Objectively, you may have had a lot more control than it seemed, but you may be viewing the world through a lens that blocks your ability to see clearly, which is why keeping a journal can be helpful. Keeping a journal forces you to document your feelings in real time, preventing your perception from getting clouded as time passes. Your task in journaling is to notice and document the things in your life over which you feel you have control as well as those things over which you feel you don't have control. Write what you've done and what happened. Find instances in your records where your actions had a big influence on the outcome. These are the action-consequence moments that can be helpful to identify so you are reminded that you often have more control than you think.

To summarize, I want you to appreciate the importance of exerting control over your retirement. Unfortunately, many retirees take a passive approach without even realizing it. We can blame the Retirement Myth for this. When the focus of your retirement is relaxation and comfort, "control" and actively working toward creating a better life can feel foreign. You might be thinking, *I thought I was done working!* As I like to remind clients, you no longer need to work *in* retirement, but you still need to work *on* retirement.

To give yourself every opportunity to live the best life possible in retirement, it requires focusing on the **Badass 5** and doing the small things every day. It's going to take effort though. That's the "work" I am talking about when I say you need to work *on* retirement. You can't phone it in and expect an amazing life. Think about any of the success you've already had in life whether it's financial, family, friendships, happiness, contribution, or health. It didn't fall into your lap, did it? You had to work at it – even the fun stuff. Think about the vacations and the adventures you've had. Those had to be planned and organized.

Badass Retirement requires your participation. You can't do it if you are passive or watching from the stands. It requires you to have the mindset that it's all up to you.

I also want you to appreciate that you can't control everything (nor do we want to!), but that doesn't mean you still don't control *some* things. Is retirement full of uncertainty and challenges? It is. Do you have control over some of it? You do. As wonderful as it would be to have security and predictability throughout the entirety of our retirement, there will be times and things that throw us off guard. The trick is to distinguish between what we can and cannot control, and just as importantly, to not let the things we can't control cause us to lose sight of what we can control or influence. Control is not something that is either on or off, black or white – there are a lot of shades in between.

If you operate under the old paradigm of having to know all the answers and require feeling like you are "ready" before you can engage in a new hobby, travel to a unique place, or join a group, you're going to spend a lot of time preparing for retirement instead of enjoying retirement.

Your goals are patient, but you shouldn't be.

JOIN THE FAMILY

Shifting your mindset in retirement from passive to active is not easy. We are conditioned to "go with the flow" and "unwind" in retirement, but if you want to create a unique retirement that provides you with more joy, adventure, and fulfillment, you need to take control. The first step you can take to create an active mindset is to join the Badass Retirement Community.

GO TO BADASSRETIREMENT.COM

5

CHALLENGE

Re-Think Time

In retirement, you have more time and less time than you've ever had in your life. Use it wisely.

CHALLENGE 5

My mom has always wanted to visit Paris. She's talked about it for years – decades, even. It has been a dream of hers for as long as she can remember. Every Thanksgiving, Paris would inevitably come up in conversation. For years, I would encourage her to go. "Take the trip," I'd plead, "Paris is amazing, and you'd love it." Her response was always the same: "Maybe next year."

I would show her photos of my trips to Paris, recount the beauty of the Eiffel Tower at night, and tell her stories of visiting shops and cafés. "I want to go, but I'm not ready to go this summer," she'd say.

After I achieved some professional and financial success, I told her I'd plan and pay for the whole trip – all she would have to do is pack, and I'd take care of everything else. "That sounds great, but let's wait a few months," she'd counter. This went on for many years. As she aged, she had more health issues and less energy. One day, she looked at me and said, "I don't think I'm ever going to see Paris."

At that moment, she realized she would never witness the City of Light, smell the scent of freshly baked croissants, or sip on a latte in a streetside café. "I wish I would have gone," she confessed. I know this is one of her only regrets in life.

We don't talk about Paris anymore.

What big dream have you been putting off?

If you buy into the Retirement Myth and settle for an Average Retirement, you will undervalue the most precious, limited, and valuable asset you have . . . time.

Time is life. How you spend, invest, and enjoy your time defines your life.

If you discount the hours, days will have little value. A lifetime of empty days leads to an empty life.

But if you cherish the hours, your days will be full of value. A lifetime of meaningful days leads to a lifetime of meaning.

If you want a Badass Retirement, you need to change your mindset concerning time. This shift in thinking requires a reassessment of your relationship with time and starts with appreciating this paradox:

In retirement, you have more time than you've ever had… and the least amount of time you've ever had.

In retirement, you get back the 50+ hours a week you had always dedicated to your career. All the time you spent getting ready, commuting, working, and traveling for business is once again yours. There has never been a period in your life when you had more free time than right now. But all this free time isn't actually free – it comes with a price.

You've never had *less* time in your life than you do in retirement. Your life – however many more decades it may span – is shorter today than it has ever been. This can be a depressing realization that keeps you stuck in place, or it can be a great awakening that liberates you.

You may be familiar with the law of scarcity. This is a principle in social psychology and economics that explains our tendency to place a higher value on things we perceive to be rare. Conversely, the more abundant something is, the less we value it. If you've ever gone camping, you may be intimately familiar with this theory. I refer to it as the toilet paper effect. In the early days of camping, when the roll is large, you don't think twice about how much you use. But as the days go by and the roll shrinks, every square becomes more valuable.

The godfather of persuasion, Robert Cialdini, writes that scarcity is a "weapon of influence."[10] The law of scarcity permeates marketing and commerce. For example, if you've ever felt compelled to buy something because time or supply was limited, you've experienced the law of scarcity firsthand.

The same thing happened to me a few days ago. I came across an offer for membership to an online community, but to get the accompanying video course, I had to become a member that day. If that wasn't enough, there were also a limited number of memberships available. Once they filled those, the community and course would be closed. I have a master's degree in psychology, I've read every one of Cialdini's books, and I'm a student of marketing, so I knew exactly what they were doing . . . and I still pulled out my credit card. That's the power of scarcity.

But that's only half of the law. The opposite is also true. If something is available in abundance, we value it less. In retirement, you will be awash with time. You go from having slivers of free time – hours or even just moments during your working years – to having more than you may know what to do with. It can feel unlimited. Some retirees joke that they "have nothing but time."

You hear a lot about "time affluence" in retirement – the idea that retirees are rich with time. But time is agnostic. It doesn't care if you take the trip, go to the gym, volunteer, climb the mountain, enroll in a class, or start a non-profit. Time is like a train that just keeps rolling along. It doesn't care if you are happy or depressed. It keeps rolling. It doesn't care if you feel fulfilled or restless. It keeps rolling. There's no slowing down or reversing. Time will pass. Tomorrow will come. Having more time doesn't necessarily mean a better life, just like having less doesn't mean a worse life. It's not about *how much*, but *how*. How will you use your time?

If you squander it, you will look back and wonder where it all went. But if you acknowledge and respect the retirement time paradox, you can cherish the sanctity of each hour, using them to create a life of meaning, purpose, and fulfillment. Badass Retirement doesn't require more free time; it requires more fulfilling time.

THE GIFT OF GREED

What's the opposite of being selfish? According to the dictionary, an antonym of "selfish" is "caring." Really? Selfishness isn't the opposite of caring. Selfishness *is* caring. It's simply caring about yourself and what's most important to you more than competing interests that are less compelling. It's okay to be self-focused and to do things that give you meaning and pleasure. It's okay to spend money on activities and stuff that only serves your needs. The retirees who do the best are the ones who know exactly what drives them and are happy to use their money to enhance their lives, in addition to making an impact by being generous with their money, giving to people and projects they care about.

One of the most common regrets is the feeling that you haven't truly lived *your* life. Maybe it's the pressures of work or family life or a sense of fear, but for many there is a gnawing feeling that they haven't been true to themselves. You may have focused your time and energy on everyone but yourself, but retirement is your time to live life to your fullest. That's not selfish; that's brave. It takes courage to become something different. If you feel there is something you've hidden or just neglected, right now is the time to rise up and become the person you want to be, do the things you want, and create the life you desire. Retirement is your (last) opportunity to squeeze out every bit of courage you have to do the things and become the person you've always wanted.

GIFT OF GREED

Use "greed" to improve your life and those around you.

If you're like most people, I imagine that you've played by the rules, done what you could to fit in, and tried to be a reasonable person. You've lived the last 50+ years dutifully compromising – maybe at work with your boss or clients, maybe at home with your family or spouse. Aren't you a little sick and tired of being reasonable?

Listen, I get it. There is a time and place for being reasonable and compromising. That time, however, is not all the time, and that place is not everywhere. What got you here may not get you where you want to be. It's okay to take a stand on the things that are most important to you. Go ahead. Compromise on the little stuff, but don't ever compromise when you know what you want. Do you want to live a measured and reasonable life that is steady but stagnant? Stable but unfulfilling? If you know what would make you happy and give your life meaning, be very unreasonable about going after it. This is not meant to create friction or tension in your most important relationships. Instead, the goal is to live a life that is true to you and your passions and desires. Don't forgot, you've got one shot at retirement. Now is the time to chase down what drives you.

SLOW TIME > FAST TIME

Aristotle observed that time does not exist without change. Why? Because what we call time is simply our measurement of the difference between "before" and "after." The paradox is that the faster things change, the slower time can often feel. Conversely, the slower things change, the faster time seems to pass. The pace of activity and change can alter our perception of time.

In Average Retirement, the days can bleed into months, into years, into decades. When you are standing still, your life can quickly pass by without you noticing. Your days blend together forming an amorphous collection that comes to define your life. You can look back and wonder what happened. This is fast time and it's the enemy of a Badass Retirement. Fast time is what happens when you fall for the Retirement Myth and believe that doing, becoming, and achieving less will somehow make you more. You can't expect a full life if your days are empty.

If you want a lifetime of fulfillment, you need years, months, weeks, days, and moments that are fulfilling. Slowing time is about enjoying time – investing in activities that provide meaning and fulfillment instead of distraction and monotony. Slow time isn't about time management; it's about attention management – identifying and prioritizing those things that will bring you closer to your ideal retired life.

Doing this well requires you to take a close look at what moves you and gives you meaning. It also requires you to get a little greedy. Since it feels like you have unlimited time in retirement, you may not assign it the value it deserves. Badass Retirement demands that you learn how to say no. If you freely give your time away to people, activities, or commitments you don't love or that don't provide you with meaning, you are wasting the most important asset you have.

I love to spend money because it means I'm using it to buy something I value, but I hate to squander it because that means I'm wasting it on something insignificant. When you fill your days in retirement with activities that don't fulfill you, you are not spending your time, you are blowing it. When you recognize the value of your time and start to say no more often, it will allow you to say yes to things that are important to you.

Every day, for the rest of your retirement and your life, you will have a decision to make. What will you do with your time? Will you waste it or invest it? Slow time is about being intentional with this decision.

Your mission in retirement is to create firsts. Lots and lots of firsts. First experiences. First activities. First visits. First hobbies. First everything. Novelty is the key to slowing time. When things are familiar and each day is a copy of the last, time becomes an amorphous blur. That's fast time, and it's the enemy. This is your retirement and your life. You don't want it to be an indistinguishable blur. You want your days to be exciting, poignant, inspiring, and remarkable. The trick is to do things for the first time. That creates slow time. We need novelty and variety throughout our weeks – those first experiences create markers in the sand for our memories.

INVESTING TIME

Time isn't just life, it's capital.

Elon Musk wrote, "Time is the ultimate currency."[11] He isn't wrong. Like all currencies, time (and more specifically, your *attention*) can be spent or invested. If you can view it through the lens of an investor, you will make better short and long-term decisions.

What does every investor want? A return. As an investor, you can invest in assets or liabilities. Assets have value, producing a positive return and growing over time. In contrast, liabilities decrease in value over time. Assets give; liabilities take.

The Attention Investment Quadrant helps us evaluate our focus as an investor might analyze an investment.

ATTENTION INVESTMENT QUADRANT

FEELS GOOD NOW

		NO	YES
GOOD FOR YOU LATER	YES	DISCIPLINE	DELIGHT
	NO	DESTRUCTIVE	DANGEROUS

Use the Attention Investment Quadrant to make the most of your time.

The Quadrant can help you identify if you are investing your time in assets or liabilities based on two factors: does it feel good, and is it good for you?

Assets are the activities you invest your attention on that are good for you, although they may not always be fun, relaxing, or pleasurable.

1. **Delight.** These kinds of activities are ones that you enjoy doing while also providing long-term benefits. They should be the cornerstone of retirement. Examples of these investments include volunteering, physical activities you enjoy (e.g., golf, walking, or yoga), and time spent cultivating relationships. The more you can fill this quadrant in retirement, the better your life will be and feel, because these investments provide the best of both worlds – they feel good and are good for you.

2. **Discipline.** The investment of attention in these activities requires the most effort and willpower since they don't feel good, but they are good for you. The problem with activities in this quadrant is that it feels better NOT to do them, plus the ramifications of avoiding them are not immediate – they might sneak up on you months or years later. What makes them even more challenging is that, if you invest in these activities, you experience the displeasure immediately, but you may not experience the benefits for months or years. That is what makes this quadrant so hard. We are bad at delaying gratification. Even worse, investing our time in this quadrant's activities requires us to endure discomfort now *and* wait for the rewards.

That's a tough sell. Examples include strenuous exercise, eating well, reducing your expenses, investing in new relationships, having difficult (but necessary) conversations, and marriage counseling.

Fortunately, if you had success in your working years, you likely became adept at making these tough investments. You may have earned advanced degrees, worked on the weekends, attended networking events, written a weekly blog, or spoken at industry events, trading your short-term enjoyment for long-term success by investing in this quadrant. This quadrant is anathema, however, to those who believe in the Retirement Myth and view retirement as something exclusively relaxing, carefree, and enjoyable. As someone who aspires to live a Badass Retirement, you need to concentrate on this quadrant because it will be the easiest to neglect.

Liabilities are the activities you spend your attention on that are not good for you, even if they feel good.

3. **Destructive.** These are activities that aren't good for you and don't feel good either. Examples include staying in a bad marriage, supporting toxic friendships, addiction to drugs or alcohol, or compulsively following the news. Why would we engage in things that aren't good for us and don't feel good? Usually, it's because we aren't making decisions based on logic; we are making them based on our guts or our hearts. Other times, it's because they become habits – things we do without thinking. Over time, we get hooked. As much as we want to stop, we can't. That's what makes this quadrant so destructive. The time you spend here can rob you of your retirement and your life if you let it. If you struggle with negative activities, addictions, or compulsions, invest more time in the asset quadrants. The more that your day and attention is focused on healthy alternatives, the less time and opportunity you will have for harmful activities.

4. **Dangerous.** This is the most dangerous quadrant because, at first, you get all the pleasure and no pain. In the financial realm, the best example is credit cards. You get to buy fun stuff you can't afford right now, but you don't have to pay for it until months or years later. Activities in this quadrant include excessive drinking, eating poorly, or watching too much TV.

When done in moderation, there is nothing wrong with any of these activities – a few drinks, a cheat day, or some TV time can all make your retirement and life more enjoyable. The danger is when we do these in excess or invest most of our time in this quadrant. Average Retirement is full of activities that would fit in this quadrant –enjoyable while providing few long-term benefits. We don't pay the price for these activities immediately. Rather, their effects grow over time until we have a drinking problem, a health problem, or a meaning problem.

Even if you concentrate on investing your attention in assets that produce positive benefits, there are often countless options from which you can choose. Investors are always looking for the best possible returns for the least amount of risk – the proverbial biggest bang for their literal buck. The same principle holds when it comes to choosing how to invest your attention. It's about getting the most from the least. What are the areas in your life where a small investment of focus will produce the biggest return – the most satisfaction, happiness, and well-being?

When it comes to creating the best retirement, every Challenge in this book represents an investment in an asset that produces an asymmetric return –the biggest bang (value) for your buck (time). When you focus on positive pursuits, such as expanding your vision for what is possible in retirement, upgrading your health, growing relationships, creating lifetime income, and building resilience, you are maximizing the return on your time by creating a better retirement and life.

Don't make the mistake in thinking your time isn't worth anything just because you are retired. Your time is worth *everything*. I won't mention names, but there are several people close to me that will spend three hours on the phone or online just to save a few dollars or get a refund. This is ludicrous. Just because you have more free time doesn't mean your time is free. Wasting your precious time and mental health arguing with customer service reps is literally killing you. If the amount you are haggling over is meaningless to your finances, spend that time doing something that will provide you a better return on your investment instead – take a nap, take a hike, or take food to a shelter. Anything but devaluing your time and sanity.

Your time is as much capital as the money in your bank. In retirement, how you allocate your time becomes more consequential because it is limited, shrinking each day. You can choose to squander it on insignificant things, or you can invest it in assets that will continue to pay you benefits for years to come.

SHORT GAME > LONG GAME

One of the rewarding things about my work as a retirement financial advisor is that I get to help clients plan the future – sometimes, over decades. But then something fascinating happens . . . one day, the future arrives.

The transition from work to retirement – from planning for the future to living in the moment – is momentous. It's an incredible transition that requires a different mindset. It's challenging to change how we look at time in retirement because, over the past 50+ years, we've been trained to think about, focus on, and plan for the future. From the time we enter school, our focus is always forward – the next test, grade, school, and degree. Then, we enter the workforce and continue this fixation on the future – the next project, promotion, employer, and title. Our financial lives are no different, as we save and invest for – you guessed it – the future.

In mastering the art of delaying gratification, we have become experts at playing the long game, emphasizing tomorrow over today and often sacrificing the present for the future. Saving instead of spending. Working longer now so you can enjoy the fruits of your labor later. Putting off travel, expenses, and enjoyment so you can reap the rewards in retirement. If you had success in your career and your finances, it's likely because you played the long game. This is the formula we've been taught for achievement. Tomorrow's success is built on today's sacrifice. What can you do today to improve your tomorrow?

But what happens when you retire and, suddenly, later is now and tomorrow is today? We've become so conditioned to discount today for tomorrow that most retirees undermine their happiness by failing to shift their mindsets. If you want to live the best life in retirement, don't play the long game; play the short game.

Playing the short game means abandoning the belief that we need to delay gratification. You're retired! What are you delaying it for? Stop thinking you have enough time. You don't. Don't put the important things off. Make a plan to do them while you still can.

I tell clients to frontload their retirement, doing as much as they can in their early years. Your time is limited. You don't know how much you have or if you'll feel healthy or have the energy later. This might sound pessimistic or even morbid, but I don't see it that way. For the first time in your life, it's all about right now. I think that's inspiring and liberating.

One of the most painful and damaging emotions you can feel is regret. Unlike pain, sadness, or even grief, which all tend to get better over time, regret often grows with time. Studies confirm that regret can be increasingly distressing as we age.[12] The ramifications are not limited to painful memories – although that is certainly a factor. Regret can also manifest in both our bodies and our lives. The research shows that regret in older adults can compromise our well-being and our health.[13] What do we regret more, the things we didn't do or the things we did? We can regret both, for sure, but the research finds that our greatest regrets are the things we wish we would have done but didn't.[14]

Regret extends beyond the domain of things we do or don't do. It's also a factor in who we become or don't become. In a study examining regret and how we view ourselves, the single biggest life regret of the participants was not acting when it would have helped them get closer to realizing their ideal selves.[15] Co-author Tom Gilovich concludes, "When we evaluate our lives, we think about whether we're heading toward our ideal selves, becoming the person we'd like to be.

Those are the regrets that are going to stick with you, because they are what you look at through the windshield of life."

The lesson? In retirement, you have a whole lifetime of future decisions about doing things you really want to do. It will be easy to say no. Maybe the timing won't be ideal. Maybe the circumstances won't be quite right. There are always reasons not to do something. But if not now, when? Retirement is your time to live a regret-free life.

While my mom was thinking about tomorrow, Paris was waiting.

Tomorrow is the enemy of action because tomorrow fosters paralysis. While you're preparing today and getting ready for tomorrow, your dreams, goals, and life are waiting. They won't wait forever.

Sometimes you have to take the plunge even if you are afraid. Learn how in the next Challenge…

JOIN THE FAMILY

Your time is precious and more valuable today than it ever has been in your life. Invest your time in activities that support your dreams and vision for your future and help you become the best version of yourself. One of the best time investments you can make is to become part of the Badass Retirement Community. Join us!

GO TO **BADASSRETIREMENT.COM**

6

CHALLENGE

Increase Boldness

Overcome fear and experience meaningful adventures throughout retirement.

CHALLENGE 6

Increasing boldness is about pushing your boundaries and living outside your safe and secure comfort zone (at least, some of the time). Why would you do something that makes you a little uneasy or nervous – maybe something riskier, bolder, or more adventurous than what you're comfortable with? Isn't retirement supposed to be relaxing and safe? Well, you know how I feel about that. The Retirement Myth makes retirees especially vulnerable to centering their lives around being easy and relaxed, ensuring that they never come close to the edge of their comfort zone. When you are perpetually content and comfortable, it means you are not expanding, experiencing, and living. It often means you are coasting and merely existing.

The retirees who live Badass Retirements do not shy away from taking risks and experiencing adventures. They intentionally do things they know will test their boundaries and make them uncomfortable. They don't avoid challenges; they create them.

And you can, too. Whether you're a Type A personality who is highly ambitious and has led a life full of taking risks and creating challenges, or you're someone who has taken a more careful and less audacious approach, you can still increase your own boldness. It's not a competition with anyone else.

The goal is to incorporate activities and challenges that help you sustain a high degree of boldness throughout your entire retirement. Although this is an objective for everyone wanting to live a Badass Retirement, *how* we reach and maintain that level will vary for each of us.

Think of boldness as a scale from 0-100. With everything you know about the Retirement Myth, what boldness level would you give someone living an Average Retirement? Would it be anywhere near 100? Not likely. When I've asked retirees what level of boldness they typically experience, it's normally below 20. What's striking about this self-assessment is that the boldness scale does not measure your perceived boldness compared to someone else – an active neighbor, a younger sibling, etc. – but against your perception of how bold and adventurous you think you *could be*. It's measuring how close you get to exceeding your comfort zone.

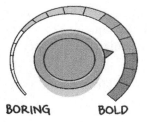

The Boldness Scale. How far can you turn the dial?

The more adventurous among us may indeed need to hike mountains, SCUBA dive, or rock climb to keep their boldness dial near 100. In contrast, others may reach 100 by joining Toastmasters, taking improv classes, or writing a novel. This is one of the reasons I love working with retirees so much. I get to understand what moves them and scares them, and it's different for everyone. It's not about pushing arbitrary boundaries; it's about pushing *your* boundaries. It's like going to the gym and seeing a fit person curling 50-pound dumbbells with relative ease versus an out- of-shape person sweating and struggling to lift 10 pounds. Which is growing and pushing their boundaries more?

Increasing boldness is not about outcomes or extreme feats; it's about getting out of your comfort zone – both physically and mentally. Happiness is raising your boldness level from 20 to 40, not about doing more than your spouse or friend.

Let's start with overcoming our fear of failure.

THE "F" WORD THAT WILL F-UP YOUR RETIREMENT

You need to shift your view of failure in retirement.

In our working years, a healthy fear of failure may have benefited us, since taking too many risks and failing at work could have a real impact on our lives. A failure could jeopardize a promotion, cause us to lose a client, or even get us fired. Our reputation, career, and livelihood depended on succeeding, but also, to a large extent, on not failing. Being bold and taking big risks early in our careers was smart – we had little to lose and much to gain. I always tell younger people to take huge risks since they have no mortgage to pay or family to feed. It's like playing roulette with someone else's money; there is nothing but upside. But then we get older, and the risk-reward dynamics change.

The consequences of failure become more meaningful – our health insurance and our 401(k) balance are in the crosshairs. Playing it safe and only taking highly calculated risks serves us well during the bulk of our working years.

But you are retired now. How should that change your perception of failing and risk?

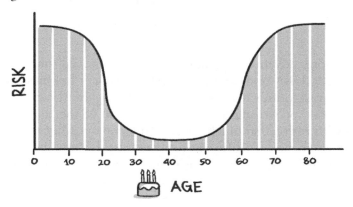

Don't believe the myth. You should increase your level of risk in retirement.

I think this is a healthy perspective on risk. As you enter retirement, you can shed the fear of failure because, for so many of the risks you'll encounter, it just won't matter if you fail. You're not going to lose your job, employee benefits, or company 401(k) match. In economic terms, you have an asymmetric risk/reward. That is, there is a massive imbalance between the small amount of risk you are taking for the huge possible reward you could achieve. The lottery is an example of asymmetric risk – bet $1 for the chance to win $200 million.

You've lived for 40 years consciously or unconsciously doing this risk-reward analysis, and you've given too much weight to risk avoidance. Now, however, you get to be 20 years old again. Sadly, you don't get the body, metabolism, or energy of a 20-year-old, but you can handle as much risk as they can. Actually, you can take even more risk and be a lot less worried about failure. You just need to re-program how you view risk.

Contrary to popular belief, it's smarter to take more risk when you are older.

Why do you fear failing? Because you don't want to feel like a failure. If you are asked to play a game of billiards, darts, or miniature golf, but you don't regularly do any of these activities, there is little chance you will be afraid of failing at them because you don't care how well you do. That is, your identity is not associated with your skill at these games. On the other hand, you may fear failing at things that are much more closely tied to your ego – what I call "identity proximity." You can only feel like a failure if your identity is wrapped up in the activity at which you have failed. Failing is a very different experience than feeling like a failure. The former is a momentary loss, while the latter is a state of being.

Obviously, not succeeding at something shouldn't brand our psyche as a failure, but too often it does. We're not good at separating an unsuccessful effort from our self-worth. Much has been said and written about failure: *You can only fail if you don't try. Failing is just one step closer to succeeding. Failure is part of learning.* These cliches are true but ineffective.

I used to have a metal paperweight on my desk with the inscription, "What would you do if you could not fail?" It's another nice platitude, but I realized it's the wrong message. Anybody can fail at anything. We know this. It's not helpful to try to deceive ourselves into thinking we are invincible. A much better and more useful message is, "What would you do if it didn't matter if you failed?" To me, that's much more realistic and powerful.

To transform this message from a nice-sounding bumper sticker into something useful, you need to shine a light on your fear of failure.

The natural reaction is to avert your attention from it, but that only makes it worse. A healthy approach is to make the unknown into something known – to take the mystery out of it by exploring it. The only way to settle your heart rate and fall back asleep when you hear a creak in the night is to turn on the lights and explore the noise. The alternative is to pull the covers over your head and try not to have a panic attack until the sun comes up.

If your goal is to live a Badass Retirement, you need to expand beyond your comfort zone, take risks, and do hard things. The good news is that it's really hard to fail in retirement.

Many of the things you will attempt in retirement don't have a time limit or a score. Most things are works in progress, which means you can be continually failing but never fail. In your working years, it was black and white – land the new client or not, get the promotion or not, make payroll or not, succeed with the startup or not. Fortunately for us, the rules change in retirement. There is no scorecard and nobody to judge us. This means we can take bigger risks without suffering the same consequences.

Failing is when your team is losing at half-time. They may be behind, but they have not lost. Instead of failing, we just haven't succeeded yet. This isn't glib advice meant to make you feel better. Retirement rewrites the rules of risk-taking and what it means to fail. The idea that you can be failing but not fail is powerful. The retirees who recognize and appreciate this new dynamic become empowered to try things they would never have in their working years. That's my hope for you, too.

OVERCOMING THE FEAR OF FAILURE/BOLDNESS

What are you fearful of doing even though it would give you great joy? This question attempts to identify if there is a fear holding you back from doing what you really want to do. What is a big thing you dream about but can't imagine doing because you are afraid? Maybe you don't currently have a "big thing." That's okay. Just keep reading – you will think of something. Once you have identified your big thing, some level of apprehension, anxiety, and even fear is bound to come to the surface. When it does, use these strategies to reduce some of those negative feelings.

Ask the genie. Sometimes, we are fearful but aren't even sure why. When you make a wish to a genie, you are forced to get specific in your wording. If you could instantly eliminate any three fears you have, what would they be? Which of these impacts the quality of your retirement?

For example, I have an aversion to spiders. Would I like to get rid of this fear? Sure. Is it impacting my life? No. Our big fears, however, can often prevent us from doing the things we want to do. Focus on the consequential fears that get in the way of your dreams, not on the trivial fears with little impact. These big fears can be physical, such as flying on a plane or traveling alone, or mental, such as speaking in public or being rejected.

Is there a way to cheat your fear? In some cases, you can still do the thing that scares you by removing the fear. For example, if you've dreamed of embarking on an African safari, but you are afraid to fly, could you take medication that reduces your anxiety or helps you sleep on the plane? Or, if you want to write a book, but the fear of rejection or embarrassment prevents you from writing, could you write it under a pseudonym? Or, if you've dreamed of running a marathon but don't want to look like a failure if you can't finish, could you do it without letting anyone know?

What is the worst thing that could happen? This is one of my favorite questions to ask retirees contemplating a big decision or challenging goal. Again, we aim to make the unknown known. The worst feeling is being anxious without being able to pinpoint exactly why you feel that way. The only way to understand the fear is to explore it. Simply writing out all the bad things that could happen can be productive. Listing your fears and concerns is much better than them constantly swirling around in your head, unable to be resolved, festering. On paper, you can look at them. They become separate from you – your fears are there, on paper, rather than within you. Think about and document everything that could go wrong – everything you are worried about, no matter how big or small– until there is nothing left undocumented. You can do this on a sheet of paper, on your phone, or my preferred method: index cards where each concern is a separate card.

This exercise's purpose is twofold. First, it's empowering to point to a worry and say, "That is the very worst thing that could happen." Sometimes, the worst-case outcome is awful – the loss of a relationship, death, or financial ruin. But surprisingly, it's often not that bad. When the fear is in our heads, our worry leads us to think the worst scenario is this horrible and life-altering event. Once we get it out of our heads, however, we may find that it is a lot more manageable and innocuous than we thought.

Second, by writing down all your fears, you can start to develop ways to mitigate them. My fear of "I'm going to drown in the ocean" turned into "I need to learn a better swimming technique that requires very little energy." The fear inspired a solution. You'll never act with a cloud of worry hanging over you. This exercise can help you identify the next steps to mitigating the negative outcomes. The process of taking small steps in the direction of our fears helps to minimize them, giving us more confidence to take even larger steps. It's a virtuous spiral that can only happen if we get out of our heads and become unparalyzed by our fears.

Does the benefit outweigh the risk? Before you attempt something with the potential for serious negative consequences, ask yourself if it's worth it. You may discover that, for some goals, what you will gain far outweighs the risks, while they do not for others. In cases where there is too much risk and too little reward, place your bets elsewhere.

Is there a way you can partially move forward? It's all about baby steps. What is the smallest and least scary action you can take that will move you in the direction of your goal? Don't get caught up worrying about the end, which can be frightening – just focus on the next action. For example, when I thought about doing an Ironman triathlon, my mind would start racing about how hard it would be, how I can't swim well and might drown, how I had never run anything close to a marathon in my life, and on and on. So, I tried not to think about the morning when I would actually participate in the race. Instead, I focused only on the next immediate action, such as registering for the event, watching swimming videos on YouTube, going to the pool, putting in miles on my bike, etc.

Be comfortable not having all the answers. I get it. Big goals are daunting. Thinking about doing something that seems impossible to you is bound to create worry and anxiety – maybe so much that you decide not to pursue it. Ironically, it may also be the mission's boldness that propels you forward, giving you energy and purpose. It would be a shame to lose that spark just because you are worried. Part of the reason we get anxious when trying to accomplish big goals is that we don't know how to do it. If we knew how, then it wouldn't seem impossible for us. The trick is to get comfortable with not having all the answers when you start but having confidence that you will with time.

Make a date with scary. If you had an important meeting that was crucial to your job during your working years, wouldn't you schedule it on your calendar? Just because you've retired doesn't mean you shouldn't still schedule important events and activities. Included on the list of things crucial to creating and living a Badass Retirement is ample amounts of boldness. You can't sit back and hope boldness falls in your lap. Make a point to include it in your schedule. How often you do this is up to you, but I'd aim for at least one bold activity a week. Get it on the calendar and stick to it just like you would an important business meeting.

Shuffle the deck. I've often thought it would be fun to create a deck of cards for unique and different activities to do in retirement – simple and quick things that take, at most, a couple of hours. You could then randomly choose three cards and decide on one of the three activities to do. I haven't created the "Retirement Deck" game yet (I'll add this project to my list in retirement!), but I have sent a list of ideas to retirees and encouraged them to add to the list. This ever-growing list serves as a constant supply of new and bold things to be tried.

Say yes. When we had full-time jobs, we had so little time to say yes to anything. It might take some practice but try saying yes more often. If a friend invites you somewhere you wouldn't normally go or asks you to do an activity you wouldn't normally do, say yes and yes. Being bold and overcoming fear often means doing things you haven't done – even things you think you might not enjoy.

Join a group. Find a friend or join a group of people who do fun things and stretch their limits. Boldness is contagious! It's hard not to get excited when others around you are growing and experiencing life. Meetup groups are an easy way to connect with others. You can also join the Badass Retirement Community to get some virtual (but very real!) inspiration and connection.

Experiment. Being curious and open is the name of the game. Try everything at least once. Find what works and what doesn't. Retirement is your time to have fun, explore, and play.

Find a mentor. Friends or partners are great because they are usually at a similar level of boldness and adventure as you. If you want even more inspiration, immerse yourself in boldness by finding a mentor who is at the level you want to reach. Read adventure magazines or blogs. Listen to podcasts. Watch YouTube videos of people doing things that excite you (and scare you a little).

Create an alter ego. If you are still struggling to think of yourself as someone who can do something bold or risky, try creating an alter ego. An alter ego is a way to take a step back from the engrained and perpetual thoughts and fears that hold you back and create a new identity that is more empowering. Alter egos are not just for superheroes. They have been used by performers such as Beyonce (Sasha Fierce), athletes such as Kobe Bryant (Black Mamba), celebrities such as Dwayne Johnson (The Rock), as well as by countless others wanting to tap into a different identity, and they can be a powerful tool for you. During my master's program in psychology, I had the opportunity to lead several hundred hours of individual and couples counseling sessions. Some of the greatest breakthroughs were when we tapped into alter egos. They can be powerful tools to explore new, and maybe stronger, bolder, or more confident versions of yourself. Your identity is everything. It shapes your thoughts, decisions, and actions. If creating an alter ego has piqued your interest, check out the *Retirement Myth Workbook* for additional exercises and join our online community to participate in the discussion.

SEEK MEANINGFUL ADVENTURE

I've observed that most people – especially retirees – do not consider themselves to be adventurous. I get it. Not everyone reading this is an adrenaline junkie who craves pushing boundaries. I've found that some people do not value adventure or are intimated by it.

Increasing boldness is an important component of living a Badass Retirement. It creates an environment of uncommon emotions such as fear, excitement, and thrill. Few things ramp up these feelings like pushing beyond your comfort zone and having an adventure.

Like so many other things, "Real Adventure" is entirely subjective. Your version of adventure may look a lot different than mine. A road trip across state lines is an adventure for some, while, for others, it's hiking 491 miles on the Camino de Santiago.

It is meaningless to compare your level of adventure against someone else's. In fact, it's worse than meaningless. It can be harmful if the comparisons have a demotivational effect. We are social creatures, and we can't help but make comparisons, but these comparisons can sometimes undermine how we view our plans for ourselves. How? If you're doing X, but your best friend or someone on Instagram is doing X+100, you might think what you are doing is not "good enough" and decide to give it up. It's been said comparison is the thief of joy, and anyone who has spent any time on social media can attest to the power of social comparison. The research[16] shows that, if we compare ourselves to an idealized reference, it can negatively impact how we feel about ourselves (although, in some cases, "upward" comparisons can create hope and inspiration[17]).

The goal is to elevate *your* adventure. But why?

BENEFITS OF ADVENTURE

In addition to being a lot of fun, adventure provides us with many other benefits. While I would argue that a dose of adventure is important regardless of your age or work status, adding some more to your life in retirement is especially beneficial. Adventure is so crucial to a Badass Retirement, it is one of the **Badass 5** drivers. But for too many living Average Retirement, confronting fears, taking on bold challenges, and adventure can get overlooked.

In our hectic working lives, as we focused on raising families and building careers, we were plenty busy. There was always something for us to do – we had responsibilities and lots of boxes to check. Those who navigated this lifestyle the best were the ones who could manage the stress by mastering the work/recovery formula. When it came time to unplug from work, the go-to solution was to relax and recover. Setting out to climb a mountain was less attractive when it already felt like your entire life was one big mountain to climb.

But in retirement, our lives and our relationships with stress change. Rather than needing and seeking recovery – a respite from the grind of our daily working lives – we now benefit from adding challenge and risk.

The following are a few benefits of adventure.

Transcend normal life experience. This is not to suggest that our lives are mundane, but it's easy to fall into a routine. And sometimes that routine can feel a little like a rut. The research suggests that adding adventure can help us break away – even just for a short period – from our daily routines.[18] Most of us are creatures of habit because it feels comfortable and gives our lives structure. As you read earlier, humans are naturally ~~lazy~~ energy conscious. Maintaining our daily routines and habits conserves energy and takes a lower toll in operating our lives. These routines provide security and certainty, but if we rely on them too heavily and for too long, the once loose routines can become rigid and confining. We can lose a sense of wonder and excitement in our normal life experience. Adventure forces us off autopilot and away from the feeling of going through the motions.

Feel alive. If our normal lives in retirement can feel a little routine, adventure provides the antidote by giving us novelty and challenge – boredom killers. When I've taken clients on "adventures" – whether around the world or in our backyard – the result is always the same: we all feel alive. There is a difference between living and feeling alive. Retirement can make living easy, but one of the casualties is a lack of enthusiasm. Psychologists have a term for this feeling of stagnation and emptiness – "languishing."[19] Individuals with this problem often feel a bit aimless and joyless. Languishing exists on a spectrum somewhere between depression and thriving. You may be functioning, but you are not flourishing. We can experience languishing at any time in life – not just in retirement. Considering the reasons highlighted, however, I think retirees are particularly prone to experiencing this mental purgatory. Fortunately, there is a vaccine. It's called adventure and it won't give you a sore arm.

Researchers studying the benefits of adventure suggest that it can help us experience a "sense of thrill" as we confront fears, perceived risks, and uncertainty.[20] A sense of thrill repels those who buy into the Retirement Myth. But for those of us who want to live Badass Retirements, a sense of thrill is crucial. Researchers looking at adventure as a remedy for our fast lives conclude that adventure "can partly aid the treatment of 'affluenza' and move people away from languishing toward flourishing."[21]

Pre-adventure spike. If all the benefits highlighted above (and the many others not listed) are not encouraging enough, adding adventure into retirement can even provide you with a boost of happiness just in the planning stage! There is ample research[22] that shows we experience an anticipatory bump in well-being and positive emotions weeks before an exciting adventure – long before we board the plane, strap on our boots, or dive into the ocean.

Good for the body and soul. Novel adventure is good for you. Researchers have discovered that it provides many positive benefits,[23] including improved well-being, resilience, physical health, self-esteem, and enjoyment. Abigail Marsh, a professor of neuroscience and psychology at Georgetown University, has identified another important benefit: "Over time, adventurous activities may actually improve your brain health."[24] Researchers posit that adventure promotes increased feelings of well-being by providing autonomy, competence, and feelings of social connection and having a positive impact on the lives of others.[25] Although the why behind this phenomenon is complex, we just *know* that adventure makes us feel good.

Get into the flow. My favorite class in high school was psychology. When the book *Flow: The Psychology of Optimal Experience* by Mihaly Csikszentmihalyi was published in 1990, I immediately got a copy from Powell's Books in Portland, Oregon. I fervently dug into the pages. Csikszentmihalyi describes optimal experiences as those times when we feel in control of our actions, a sense of exhilaration, and a deep sense of enjoyment. He is quick to dispel the optimal experience myth, writing on page three, "Contrary to what we usually believe, moments like these, the best moments in our lives, are not the passive, receptive, relaxing times. The best moments usually occur when a person's body or mind is stretched to its limits in a voluntary effort to accomplish something difficult and worthwhile. Optimal experience is thus something we *make* happen."[26] I've been fascinated with and written about flow for years.[27] The takeaway is that adventure creates a wonderful environment for flow to flourish if the skill and challenge of the adventure are in balance.[28]

You don't even have to believe the research. Just think back to the adventures you've had in your own life. How did they make you feel? Were they unpleasant or did you feel alive? Did they make you feel insecure or powerful?

Adventure is a potent elixir that helps remedy the doldrums of Average Retirement.

Before we continue, we should try to wrap our heads around what adventure really is.

WHAT IS MEANINGFUL ADVENTURE?

Let's start with what adventure is not: a death wish. I call this tendency to confuse adventure with danger the X-Games Fallacy. Adding more adventure into your retirement doesn't mean you need to be an extreme athlete and rock climber, jump from planes, or complete triathlons. Of course, some of you will gravitate toward those activities. Still, most people who want to improve their retirement will never summit a mountain or navigate Class V whitewater rapids.

Injecting your Badass Retirement with adventure has nothing to do with extreme physical feats or stunts.

The traditional view of adventure focuses on selfish adrenaline-seekers trying to conquer nature.[29] That's not my idea of adventure, nor is it the prevailing view in the literature. There's no doubt the right kind of adventure can provide a thrill, but recent research on the subject suggests a more nuanced view. Adventure participants (at least, many of them) do it more for a sense of goal achievement and social connection and less for sheer thrill and selfish, hedonistic motives.[30] This is why I like to think about these activities as "meaningful adventures."

How should we think about meaningful adventure in retirement? For some, it could mean hiking in the woods and, for others, taking up free diving. A vacation to an exotic location might feel adventurous, too. Getting out and doing something that you consider exciting or bold will always be beneficial. The goal isn't to judge or prioritize one activity over another. A walk in a park may not seem like an "adventure," but it may provide a great deal of health and psychological benefits. Again, any activities that get you moving and thinking are positive and have a place in retirement. The goal is to not get hung up on semantics.

If you want to experience the unique benefits of meaningful adventure, it's also important to clarify what adventurous activities have in common so you can dial in the right kind of experience for yourself. Relying on academic research,[31] my work with clients, and my personal experience is how I've come to understand meaningful adventure.

Out of the ordinary. Novelty is key. Adventures should not be part of your everyday life. Adventures are infrequent and unique. If your mountain bike ride is something you've done for six years, certainly keep it up but consider doing something new. The activity needs to be distinct from your normal, familiar routine.

Physical. Your adventure needs to require physical activity. Ideally, it would require a decent amount of effort – something that pushes you and couldn't be done easily. Again, your version of strenuous physical activity may look very different from your spouse's, and that's okay. The goal is to push your physical limits so that it is a worthwhile challenge for you to accomplish.

Challenging. The adventure must present you with some challenges and difficulties that you voluntarily accept. Involuntary, unwanted challenges do not lead to adventure – they're just a pain.

Your adventure should have mental and/or physical challenges that you welcome. If you are not challenged, it's not an adventure.

Bravery. When you think about your adventure, do you feel butterflies in your stomach? Does your breath quicken? Most adventures require you to overcome fear. Think back to the discussion of the hero's journey. In novels and films the hero must conquer their fear to complete their journey. There should at least be an aspect of your adventure that worries you to some degree. You know you're onto something exciting when you feel compelled to engage in it even though it scares you. Retirees will often share with me that they haven't felt nervous in a long time and that adventure stirs emotions in them that they haven't experienced for years.

Uncertainty/risk. An unknown outcome is one of the keys to an adventure. Will I succeed, or will I fail? Will this be a victory or a disaster? The research is clear; there needs to be uncertainty and risk involved. There is a sweet spot, however, that you are trying to achieve. Too low and it will feel too pre-ordained. Too high and it will be overwhelming. The uncertainty needs to be "bearable," which is entirely subjective and different for everyone.

Heightened arousal. This means your adventure must dial up your level of thrill. You are looking for activities outside of your everyday life. You need something that heightens your senses. Adventure participants will often talk about their "Spidey senses" – the feeling that they could see, hear, feel, and smell better. Researchers say your "senses are enlivened."[32] If your activity doesn't heighten or change your arousal level at all, it may not be challenging enough or provide as much fear/uncertainty as you need.

Outside your comfort zone. This goes without saying: completing your adventure must stretch your physical and mental limits. If the activity fits cozily within your comfort zone, it most certainly is not an adventure. Researchers have called this sweet spot the "stretch zone" – in between the home-based comfort zone on one end and the panic zone on the other.[33]

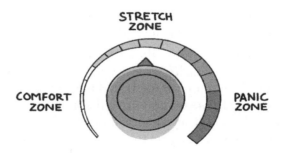

Escape your comfort zone in retirement.

Nature-based. I'm sure some adventures do not take place outdoors, but most will. Nature provides unique challenges and risks thanks to its varying terrain, uncertain weather, and variety of wildlife. These elements require heightened senses and bravery and can often push people outside of their comfort zones. We've discussed the positive benefits of physical activity, but when you combine exercise with nature you have a recipe for adventure.

Requires/develops personal skills. For an activity to be a meaningful adventure, it should both require and develop your skills. This gets at the uniqueness of the experience – not just anyone can do it – as well as the challenge – you must work for it. At my age, you would think I would know how to walk and breathe, but I had to relearn both skills when I hiked Mt. Kilimanjaro in Africa. Yes, really. To successfully summit, I had to learn how to walk differently and breathe differently. These were real skills that required training and practice. Think about any adventure you are considering. Does it require you to learn new skills or improve on those you already have? If so, you are on the right track.

Transformational. The best adventures are the ones that change you. Maybe you face a challenge that scares you, but you do it anyway, realizing that you are braver than you thought. Maybe you overcome a fear by letting go of the worry and realize that you can be composed. . . or even that you appreciate the comforts of your everyday life more because of the struggle. Maybe you witness something that gives you a renewed sense of the goodness in others, or you might help someone else overcome a challenge and start to see more value in yourself as a result. Adventures can be transformational. You won't often see this in the marketing material. Still, anyone who has experienced a real adventure will tell you that the greatest benefit they received was becoming someone different. We come to see ourselves, others, or the world differently. These transformations usually occur in brief moments – flashes – and are often the things that get remembered years in the future when everything else about the trip has become a blur. This is why we adventure.

These are just a few factors that make up a meaningful adventure – I'm sure there are others. As you start to think about what adventures you might tackle in retirement, consider what factors are important to you and add them to this list. When you return from your adventures, you can evaluate which factors were the most significant and provided you with the most enjoyment and meaning. You may find a perfect combination that resonates with you best.

I love talking to people about adding adventure into their retirement because the excitement and energy are infectious. Almost everyone lights up and becomes animated when they start thinking and talking about what these adventures might be. Some have detailed ideas of what they want to do, but others aren't even sure where to start.

Here are a few things to consider as you think about embarking on your next adventure.

HOW MUCH ADVENTURE DO YOU NEED?

How do you find the sweet spot of adventure – the activity that provides just the right amount of challenge, fear, skill, uncertainty, and transformation? If too few of these elements are present, the "adventure" becomes mundane. Many vacations and trips provide elements of adventure but fall short of achieving a meaningful adventure's full scope and benefits. On the other hand, activities that are too challenging – requiring skills you don't have – or too extreme with too much risk and uncertainty – just aren't fun. You want to explore the area between dull and overwhelming. When you are just getting started, it can be hard to find the ideal sweet spot, which can make you think you shouldn't even try.

In the early 1990s, two researchers developed a novel way to think about and classify adventures, which they called the Adventure Experience Paradigm.[34]

ADVENTURE EXPERIENCE PARADIGM

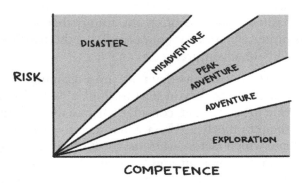

*Find your sweet spot of risk and competence between
Peak Adventure and Adventure.*

Rather than finding some perfect middle ground, their classification system contains five categories of adventure based on risk level and competence.

Disaster is achieved when you combine high-risk environments with very low-level skills. This is a recipe for disaster and should be avoided at all costs. There's no problem with getting into a situation where you are well over your head (this is encouraged!), but you don't want to combine this with high risk. Think rock climbing a formation well above your skill level or night diving when you just got SCUBA certified. In taking on high-risk activities, make sure you have a commensurate level of competence first.

Misadventure occurs when the level of risk is higher than your level of competence. Unlike the dangerous *Disaster* category, the *Misadventure* category is highly unpleasant. You're able to survive, but it's not fun. If you're looking to feel burned out and generally frustrated, this is your category. Otherwise, you'll need to either decrease the risk and/or increase your skill.

Peak Adventure is an ideal level of risk and competence, albeit a bit of a stretch for your skills. For the truly adventurous who want to push their limits, this is the category to target.

Adventure is a balanced level of risk and competence that results in you feeling challenged yet comfortable. This is an excellent combination of skills and uncertainty/fear and should be your desired balance for your adventures in retirement.

Exploration is a great place to start. This category is high on competence and low on risk. This is the ideal mixture when testing new activities because it is low risk, but since the activity is different, there is still some novelty to it. Start here if you are at all unsure.

Here are a few more things to consider as you start planning meaningful adventures in retirement.

Start slow. You have the rest of your life to enjoy all kinds of adventures. If you are new to these types of activities, start slowly and start small. I'd rather you spend more time in the *Exploration* category above than jump in too quickly and either get hurt or become discouraged. This is the biggest mistake I see people make is that they try to do too much too soon. That never ends well. Work your way up to longer and bigger adventures. Purposefully do less than you think you can in the beginning. This way, you can determine your actual boundaries and adjust accordingly.

Schedule adventure. Adventure doesn't just happen. It must be planned and scheduled. Yes, I know. This feels counterintuitive. It's because we've watched too many movies where adventure just seems to fall into the character's lap. That doesn't often happen in the real world, though, and when it does, it's not called adventure; it's called calamity. Meaningful adventure requires thinking, researching, and planning . . . and, yes, scheduling. You must schedule adventure. Do not wait to feel motivated or tell yourself you'll get to it later. Ideally, you should always have several meaningful adventures on the horizon – as far out as a couple of years if needed. Big or small, long or short, just make sure you have them earmarked on your calendar.

Find a partner. In case you haven't noticed, so many of the suggestions in this book involve finding a partner. This is not by accident. It may be the best advice I share with you. Adventures, retirement, and life are better shared with a partner. But this doesn't mean a spouse or romantic partner must join you on these adventures. I've gone on many adventures with friends. One benefit of having a partner is accountability – someone is counting on you to do it with them. You also get the benefit of someone else's ideas – someone who can help research and plan the adventure. Lastly, it's just more fun when you have someone by your side, pushing both themselves and you.

Go solo. If you can't find someone to join you, go alone. I've traveled to India, the Middle East, Australia, Brazil, and many other places by myself.

Me hang-gliding in Rio on a solo adventure.

But if you are feeling a little nervous about taking on adventure by yourself, you don't need to go so far. A single female client of mine had always shied away from adventure. She had talked for years about wanting to travel to Europe but couldn't drum up the courage to book a trip. Part of the problem was that she didn't have anyone to go with, which increased her anxiety. Her solution? Forget the trip across the globe and do a road trip across her state instead! She visited small towns – all about four hours from her home – and she loved it. She found it exhilarating and still talks about her adventure to this day. She's since done even more road trips and has even taken some short flights. Increasing boldness is entirely subjective. Figure out your comfort level and then push the boundaries just a little. She said she never felt more alive than when she was driving and exploring new areas. You'll never feel more alive than when you are exploring the outer boundaries of your comfort zone.

Experiment. Unless you're an adventure junkie, a lot of this might be new to you. You may not know where to start, what you think you'd enjoy, or what you should attempt. If that sounds like you, start by trying a lot of different activities. Instead of scheduling a two-week river rafting trip when you have no idea if you'd enjoy it, schedule a day trip instead. Keep testing and experimenting, making sure to keep an open mind. I can assure you that, if you try enough activities, you'll find several to which you gravitate, and you'll also find several that you can't stand. Don't let those deter you. Keep testing and trying.

Do what works. Think about the most adventurous things you've ever done. How did they make you feel? What did you do? The answers to these questions are a great place to start if you are unsure. If you've enjoyed an activity in the past, test it to see if you still enjoy it. You can always expand into uncharted territory, but as you are getting started, it can be helpful to gain momentum by doing something you know you will enjoy and have some competence in.

Make boldness, nature, activity, and adventure a part of your retirement and a part of your life.

BOLD > BABY

In my household, we have a saying: "Don't be a little B." When my daughter was younger, she asked what the "B" stood for, and I told her it meant "baby." Now that she's older, she knows better.

We say this to each other when we know the other family member is underestimating their ability, doubting themselves, or just taking the easy way out. I'm on the receiving end of that phrase more often than I'd care to admit. My immediate reaction is to reject the label and justify my position. Soon enough, though, I let down my defenses and admit that I really was being a little B.

I can honestly tell you that my favorite thing to hear from my daughter – right below her saying "I love you" or "You're the best daddy" – is when she tells me, "Don't be a little B." It's because I know she recognizes that I'm setting my sights too low and could do better. If she can see that in me, there's a better chance she can see it in herself.

Be bold in retirement. Don't be a little B.

JOIN THE FAMILY

Boldness often doesn't come easily or naturally. Sometimes, we need a little help as we Increase Boldness in retirement. If you want a shot in the arm of motivation and inspiration, join us in the Badass Retirement Community.

GO TO BADASSRETIREMENT.COM

SECTIONS

MAGNIFY

MINDSET

MEANING

MONEY

MOMENTUM

7

CHALLENGE

Strengthen Purpose

Discover what will get you to jump out of bed in the morning and provide you meaning throughout retirement.

CHALLENGE 7

There is a question that has gone through every retiree's mind. I bet it's gone through yours as well. This question may be a fleeting thought that is quickly disregarded, or it may haunt you in the middle of the night.

Will I be bored in retirement, or will I have meaning and purpose that gets me out of bed every morning?

Sergey Young is the founder of the $100 million Longevity Vision Fund, which invests in longevity breakthroughs that extend human lifespans and overcome the negative effects of aging. In his book, *Growing Young*, he poignantly writes, "We have created technologies to extend our life, but we haven't created a life we want to extend." Why is that?

There are two simple words at the heart of achieving a Badass Retirement and a life worth living: meaning and purpose. When we were young, learning and obtaining a degree provided meaning and purpose. In our working years, we certainly had responsibilities. We had a reason to get out of bed – even if that reason didn't provide deep meaning. We had places to go, things to do, people to see. Our purpose was to provide value in our work and earn an income. Maybe we weren't saving lives every day, but our work provided purpose.

Raising a family certainly provides meaning and purpose. Although it's a job that never ends, a significant number of parents go through empty nest syndrome once their kids move out of the house.[35] This "syndrome" isn't a medical or psychological diagnosis, but it is associated with depression and decreased overall well-being.

Now that you have the degree, raised the family, and left work, it's normal to feel unsure of your purpose or what is now going to provide you with meaning. It's common to confuse activities and hobbies for meaning and purpose. It's easy to fill our days with things to do, but having a full calendar is not the same as being fulfilled.

We're all going to have 168 hours a week every week in retirement, but some of us invest that time in things that produce returns for us. This Challenge and its exercises are all about discovering what gives you meaning and provides fulfillment – filling your heart, brain, body, and soul. My goal is for you to have a clearer sense of your values, your vision for your life, and what will fuel your days and nights throughout retirement.

Pre-retirement, we had so many demands on our time (work, responsibilities, etc.) that it was challenging to think deeply about the life we wanted because we were too busy actually living it. In talking to many new retirees, I've noticed a belief that they will figure things out or that their ideal lives will come to them. The thinking is that when they retire, they will automatically create this "best life" filled with joy and meaning. The reality is that this doesn't happen automatically. Just because you have a lot more free time in retirement doesn't guarantee you'll figure it all out.

Creating a life with meaning and purpose doesn't happen by accident. Achieving Greater Meaning requires consistent attention and effort to the **Badass 5**. As I've said before, you don't have to work *in* retirement, but you do have to work *on* retirement.

The big shift in retirement is that compensation is no longer a deciding factor in our choices. Even if we didn't like what we were doing in our working years, at least we were getting paid. In retirement, our "compensation" is entirely personal and not economic. The result of this shift is that we need to get better at evaluating opportunities. Most of us are not used to making work choices entirely based on non-financial metrics. This is one of the benefits of going through this Challenge. Even if you think you already know yourself and what makes you tick, these exercises will undoubtedly help you gain a better understanding of what really drives you and provides meaning.

BORED > BUSY

Pre-retirement, your time wasn't necessarily your own. You had commitments and responsibilities. There were things you had to do, places you needed to be, and people to whom you had to answer. The promise of retirement is that you get to own more of your time and your decisions. It is the time in your life when you have real freedom – no constraints and few responsibilities. You can go wherever you want and do whatever you want. Retirement is independence. But when you wake up that first morning in retirement and don't *need* to do anything, what will you do?

This is the "retirement void," and it is real. It is experienced by nearly everyone entering retirement. What you do in the face of that void determines whether you live an Average Retirement or a Badass Retirement. It seems like an easy choice, but when you come face to face with the void, your natural response is to fill it.

Although nearly one in four retirees worry that they won't find purposeful ways to pass the time, most quickly try to fill their time with stuff – activities, hobbies, appointments, get-togethers, etc.[36] This makes sense. The void is uncomfortable, leading them to feel like the busier they are, the better. The solution? Schedule more trips, do more activities, and start new hobbies. It's not just possible to stay busy doing stuff, it's incredibly easy. There are so many things you can choose from to keep busy and occupy every waking minute. It turns out, however, that being busy doesn't lead to fulfillment.

Need help finding your purpose?

GET THE WORKBOOK AT BADASSRETIREMENT.COM

If you are stuck in this cycle of taking on more and more to feel fulfilled, it's better to step back from being busy and to be bored instead. Live in the boredom. Avoid the instinct to "do something" or schedule yet another activity. Being busy is a distraction and a deception – jumping from one thing to the next supports the pretense that what you're doing is important. A full calendar doesn't mean you are fulfilled, though. Having a lot to do isn't the same as having a lot of meaning. Don't confuse being busy with improving your well-being.

Average Retirement can create emptiness – a feeling that there must be something more. You've worked for so long and looked forward to this stage in your life when you have the freedom to do whatever you want. The "more" you are looking for is not more appointments or activities; it is more meaning and fulfillment.

You won't have the time or energy to determine what truly moves you if you are perpetually busy. It's better to be bored than busy because, when you are bored, you will seek answers. When you are busy, you will seek the next distraction. Do the work in this Challenge.

Discover what gives you meaning and what leads you to feel fulfilled. Maybe that *will* include a full calendar, but you need to do the work first, and you can't do that if you are always busy.

Before you jump in, I think it's important to see the big picture. The following is a brief roadmap of this Challenge and the themes we will explore to help you find a little more meaning and fulfillment throughout your retirement – and to help you strengthen your purpose.

Part I: What is important to you?

- Needs
- Values

Part II: Where do you go to give/get energy?

- Interests
- Passions

Part III: What do you want your future to look like?

- Vision
- Purpose

This Challenge has a lot of exercises for you to complete. If you want more detailed step-by-step instructions throughout this process, I recommend you download the *Retirement Myth Workbook* at BadassRetirement.com. It has additional insights and exercises that will help you identify and amplify your purpose throughout retirement.

Get ready to work and have some fun while you learn something about yourself!

PART I: WHAT IS IMPORTANT TO YOU?
Discover Your Needs

NEEDS –▸ VALUES –▸ INTERESTS –▸ PASSIONS –▸ VISION –▸ PURPOSE = MEANING + FULFILLMENT

The first step is discovering what is truly important to you – your top needs and values. Why do we do what we do? This question has fascinated me since I took an introductory psychology course in high school as a 15-year-old. Psychologists and researchers have plenty of theories on the subject – I've studied many of them – but there is one theory that has risen to the top and has helped me understand my behavior and that of others. This theory, called human needs psychology, provides a lens through which you can decipher behavior and not only understand why we do what we do but also predict what we might do in the future. If our goal is to create more meaning and fulfillment in retirement, understanding our needs is an important part of that process.

Unlike other needs-based theories, such as Maslow's hierarchy of needs that attempt to organize and prioritize psychological and physiological needs, human needs psychology takes a different approach. Human needs psychology is a theory of human behavior developed by Cloé Madanes and Anthony Robbins with a simple premise: there are six psychological needs every human being on this planet shares (excluding physiological needs). So, even though we may be differentiated by wealth, race, religion, or geography, we all have the same six fundamental needs. They are universal.

Like any theory, especially one trying to identify universal needs for the 7+ billion people on the planet, it is not perfect. Whenever I've introduced this theory to clients, however, I've found they almost immediately gain insight into themselves and their motivations. For retirees, it can be helpful not just to understand their needs but also how they can fulfill them.

Although we all share the same six needs, we tend to emphasize two of them that influence our decisions and behavior more than the others. Again, these are *needs*, not hopes, wants, or desires. We are compelled to fulfill all our needs, but two stand out. They constantly pull at us, and we'll make decisions to satisfy them – sometimes at the expense of our other needs, relationships, and even our finances.

The better you understand the six needs (and especially the top two), the more conscious you will become of why you've made some of your decisions. This understanding of what drives you can also help you better evaluate future decisions.

The six needs, according to human needs psychology, are:

1. **Certainty.** The need for stability, security, and comfort, as well as the confidence to avoid pain and gain pleasure. Avoiding pain and uncertainty is key. High-certainty people will avoid risks and plan carefully for the future. They are predictable, seek control, and prefer stable work over challenging work. Because they focus on stability, they may seem unenthusiastic and even

boring. Their strengths are their organization, reliability, and dependability. Can you recognize the need for certainty in your life?

2. **Uncertainty/Variety.** The need for change, new stimuli, the unknown, and the ability to exercise your physical and emotional range. Many need the excitement that comes from variety and many interests. As a result, others see them as dynamic, entertaining, and fun to be around. People who have a strong need for uncertainty can get involved in too many things at once, bouncing from one experience to the next. They may even put themselves at risk physically, emotionally, and financially. They dislike habits and routines. Boredom is anathema and will be avoided at all costs.

3. **Significance.** The need to feel important, special, unique, and wanted. Individuals with a high need for significance believe that happiness comes from feeling respected and people looking up to them. They may work hard at being different or taking on leadership roles. Pre-retirement, they often worked long hours and focused on rising in their professional careers. They have high standards for themselves and are relentless in accomplishing their goals, but because they constantly need to feel important in the eyes of others, they can seem arrogant and full of themselves. They are often disciplined and competitive and can be perfectionists.

4. **Love/Connection.** The need to belong and to feel closeness to someone or something. High love/connection people are generous to those they love and can be very protective of them. They are often nurturing, responsible, supportive, and helpful, but this can come at a cost. Some will repress their own needs, unable to say no to others. Their desire to feel love and meet others' needs can become intrusive without them realizing it. They will do whatever it takes to avoid disappointing others and feeling dispensable or unappreciated, making rejection difficult to deal with.

5. **Growth.** The need to expand, learn, and grow. People who value growth feel the need to develop themselves intellectually, emotionally, physically, and/or spiritually. They love to learn and to challenge themselves. They can become detached and unwilling to share, and they may undervalue some relationships while, at the same time, being respectful of others. They are

typically thoughtful, calm, and dependable. Others may look up to them as a model of self-improvement, although high-growth people don't do it for the respect of others, they do it for the respect of themselves.

6. **Contribution.** The need to give beyond oneself and to support others. Individuals who highly value contribution believe that their lives are incomplete unless they contribute to others or a cause. Even though they care for others, they may neglect to take care of themselves or even those closest to them. Others may resent the time and energy they put into the cause. Their strengths are their compassion for helping others, bravery, persistence, and generosity. They are often outgoing and enthusiastic but can become confrontational and angry in the face of unfairness or injustice.

Can you see how the decisions of a retiree who values love/connection and contribution may be quite different from someone else who values uncertainty/variety and significance? It's important to point out that one need is not necessarily better than another – each need has value, and we all must fulfill all six – but you can begin to see how we might make vastly different decisions based on the primary needs that drive us.

What are your top two needs? There are a few different ways to determine this. First, it can be as simple as reading the list above and choosing the two that seem to resonate with you the most. For some, two of the six needs will fly off the page and just feel right. If you're not sure which two are most important, then you can take a brief online assessment at BadassRetirement.com, which will provide you with an analysis of all six needs and will identify which two are most important to you.

Understanding your top needs is not just entertaining, it also provides actionable information you can use as you identify and strengthen your purpose and create your life in retirement. Although everyone looks to fill all six, we get more satisfaction and reward by focusing on our main needs. In terms of getting the biggest bang for the buck, our top two needs provide it. If you spend significant time and energy focused on your least desirable needs, you won't experience the same level of fulfillment.

Needs are part of the story but not the whole story. Our primary needs determine what we move toward – our drive. The need is the place you want to arrive at and experience – the destination. We can, however, move toward and satisfy our needs in different ways. The actions, beliefs, and behaviors we use to reach our needs are vehicles. Your top two needs create the pull, but the vehicles we choose and the rules we create determine the decisions we make and what we do in retirement.

Here's an example of how the vehicles we choose shape our actions. Let's imagine your primary need is to feel important, wanted, and special – significance. How might you satisfy this need in retirement?

To quench your desire to feel important, you might join a country club or buy a new car you can't really afford. Alternatively, you could meet your need for significance with an entirely different vehicle. You might donate a considerable sum to a charity and relish in the attention and feeling of importance and significance your big check provides. Same need, different vehicle, different life.

It's important to differentiate between needs and vehicles. Having money is not a need. Being a member of a fancy country club, taking your family on a European cruise, or paying for your grandchildren's college tuition are not needs. Finishing your degree or sitting on the board of a non-profit are not needs. Remember, there are only six actual needs (i.e., certainty, uncertainty/variety, significance, love/connection, growth, and contribution). All those achievements are simply vehicles – things we think will fulfill one or more of our needs.

In retirement, when you have more time than you've ever had before, you have more opportunities to meet your needs in different ways. For example, someone who places growth and uncertainty above all others may choose to meet their need for learning and personal development by traveling to exotic places around the world. Someone who requires growth and certainty may choose to meet their need for learning and personal development by taking classes at a local community college – same primary need but a different vehicle to satisfy it.

Needs and vehicles provide powerful insights into what gives us meaning and satisfaction, but our values provide another layer to explore.

Finding Your Values

NEEDS —▸ **VALUES** —▸ INTERESTS —▸ PASSIONS —▸ VISION —▸ PURPOSE = MEANING + FULFILLMENT

Needs and values both help us understand what is important to us. They influence our decisions and play important roles in our satisfaction, happiness, and pursuits. The difference between them is that needs are universal and more of an unconscious drive or longing, whereas values are more of a conscious choice and unique to the individual.

Try this exercise to uncover your values.

What are your greatest accomplishments – the things of which you are most proud? Why did you pursue those goals? What about those things makes you proud? Why do they hold a place in your heart and mind even now?

Think about a couple of times in your life when you felt the most fulfilled or satisfied. What were you doing? Why do you think that experience gave you meaning?

Think about a time when you got angry, deeply sad, or upset. What happened? Looking back, why do you think this experience caused such a strong reaction? Sometimes, we can best identify our values by examining those times when they are absent.

Who are your role models or people you admire (living or not)?

What is it about them that you admire or inspires you?

How do you spend your time and money when given a choice? Time and money are limited and valuable resources, so if you would purposefully exchange both for something, that could be a clue for you. Why do you buy what you buy? What are you getting in return? How are you spending your time? What are you doing and what are you getting back?

Next up, you will discover where you go to give and get energy.

PART II: WHERE DO YOU GO TO GIVE/GET ENERGY?

In Part II, the goal is to determine what gives us energy and where we are happy to exert it. Why focus on energy? Because energy is everything. If we can track down those activities, interests, and causes that give us energy, they can function as signs of what gives us meaning and purpose. Likewise, discovering where we freely give our energy offers us clues about what we find important and meaningful.

Uncovering Your Interests

NEEDS —▸ VALUES —▸ **INTERESTS** —▸ PASSIONS —▸ VISION —▸ PURPOSE = MEANING + FULFILLMENT

This Challenge aims to help you understand what moves you and gives you a sense of meaning and purpose. One way you can think of your retirement is as a series of bets or investments of time, energy, and even money that you hope to turn into happiness and fulfillment. The more you know, the better your investments are going to pay off.

What are your interests? What activities, hobbies, or pursuits do you enjoy? Unlike our needs or values, which are often below the surface, our interests are usually more obvious. These are the things we spend time doing because we enjoy them.

If you're having trouble, look to the past. What books do you enjoy reading? Historical fiction or mysteries? What podcasts do you listen to? Self-help or business? What YouTube videos or documentaries do you watch? *How Stuff Is Made* or WWII? These can provide clues to your interests.

The gift of retirement is that we have more time to explore and try things we didn't have time to pursue when we were working. You may have identified several things in which you are interested, but this list is not complete. There are countless other activities and interests that you've never tried, so you don't know if you like them or not.

I encourage you to experiment. Get curious and try as many diverse activities and hobbies as you can. Is paragliding one of your interests? If you've never done it, the answer is not "no." It's "I don't know." Maybe jumping off the side of a mountain with only a fabric wing keeping you from plunging a thousand feet to the ground is something you'd enjoy. Or maybe it's not. The truth is, we are poor predictors of what will make us happy – what psychologists refer to as affective forecasting.[37] It seems strange that we wouldn't necessarily know what would give us pleasure in the future, but if you think about your past, you can likely recall situations where the thing you thought would be amazing and make you happy didn't.

The best way to predict what's going to make you happy is to get out and try as many things as you can. Writing and performing your own poetry at open mic night? Worth a try. Improv classes? Worth a try. Off-roading? Worth a try. Learning about the history of famous art? Worth a try. Cooking Filipino dishes? Worth a try.

Sometimes we need to get out of our heads and just go for it. Engagement is key, and it's really the only way we can truly know if we enjoy something or not. So, your homework for the rest of your retirement is to be curious and keep trying new things, even if you think you might not enjoy them.

Interests alone are not enough. We can have superficial interests in dozens of activities, hobbies, or causes. Still, to dig deeper into what really provides us with meaning and fulfillment, we need to continue to climb the ladder. The next rung concerns our passions.

Unlocking Your Passions

NEEDS → VALUES → INTERESTS → PASSIONS → VISION → PURPOSE = MEANING + FULFILLMENT

The difference between an interest and a passion is the level of enthusiasm and energy you get from it and/or give it. Interests are things you enjoy – they are fun and rewarding. Passions, on the other hand, require more. Attention is like flirting, interests are like dating, and passions are more akin to much deeper relationships. You can have dozens of interests, but you probably only have a handful of true passions.

Passions aren't just strong interests, though. Passions also have strong emotions connected to them but are less likely to meet one or both of your top needs and/or connect with one or more of your values.

The goal is to have several things about which you are passionate in retirement because passions aren't simply enjoyable and entertaining. Passions can also provide meaning and fulfillment, which we all want to experience more throughout retirement.

Interests are great, and you should have many of them – the more, the better. Passions tend to require more time and energy, but you also get more from them.

How can you begin to discover and define your passions? I have a few ideas to get you started.

Find overlap. Examine your interests and try to find the ones that intersect with your top needs and values. This ensures you are connected to them and that they are serving you. If it's helpful, write the need and value each interest provides (or could provide) next to each interest.

Get into the flow. Csikszentmihalyi pioneered work on the mental state of flow, which you read about earlier. In an interview for *Wired* magazine after nearly a decade of this research, Csikszentmihalyi described the state of flow further: "The ego falls away. Time flies. Every action, movement, and thought follows inevitably from the previous one, like playing jazz. Your whole being is involved, and you're using your skills to the utmost."[38]

Can you think of times over your life, the past year, or even the past month when you felt a shift of time and strong concentration or focus? When you felt mentally and/or physically engaged, connected to an activity, and challenged? What activities were you doing when you experienced this state of flow? This is a tell-tale sign that the activity is of extreme interest to you.

Go with your heart. If creating lists and rankings doesn't resonate with you, try using your heart instead. Is there something you already love doing? What are a few things that come to mind? Do they provide you with a sense of meaning? Do they give you energy when you think about them or engage with them? Can you do them with others? Do they positively impact others? Are these activities good for you and sustainable? If so, chances are you already have a strong passion. It's common for a retiree to already have a passion. It can be beneficial to dig a little deeper or search a little wider. If you *had* to develop a few more passions, what might they look like for you? Using what you've learned about your top needs and values, explore your list of interests further to see what resonates with you. And, of course, continue to explore and experiment!

PART III: WHAT DO YOU WANT YOUR FUTURE TO LOOK LIKE?

Part III is focused on the future. Now that you have a greater sense of your needs, values, and those interests that provide you with the most energy, you can use that information to shape your future and create sustainable meaning and fulfillment throughout your retirement. This section focuses on vision and purpose.

Creating Your Vision

NEEDS → VALUES → INTERESTS → PASSIONS → **VISION** → PURPOSE = MEANING + FULFILLMENT

It's common to work toward achieving goals in our working years. As you read earlier in the Retirement Achievement section from Challenge 2, however, a precipitous drop-off in goals usually occurs in retirement. Many activities, trips, and events are planned, but not many people have goals to pursue in retirement.

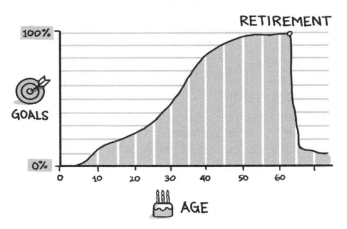

% PEOPLE WITH GOALS

You've had goals all your life. Don't eliminate them just because you've retired.

This is one of the key differences between Average Retirement and Badass Retirement. I want you to look to the future and close the Retirement Gap. This is where your vision about the future becomes important. You can think about a goal as just a sliver of your future that you want to look different than it does today. If your goal is to become healthier and lose 30 pounds, your vision of your future self looks thinner. If your goal is to take the grandkids on a Disney Cruise to Alaska, your vision of your future includes a cruise with your grandkids. Goals are essential because they provide a bridge across the Retirement Gap, helping us get closer to reaching our potential. If you closed the Retirement Gap across all areas of your life and reached your potential – whatever that may be for you – that is the realization of your vision.

This exercise should be fun because I want you to think about your future – but not just any future. I want you to think about your *ideal* future. Focus on your needs, what you value, and your passions. And please, don't be too hard on yourself. If you're not thrilled with where you are today or are worried about what your future might look like, this is your opportunity to think a little bigger and paint the future you'd like to see. If your compelling vision isn't so compelling, it's not going to draw you in, give you energy, or provide the fulfillment you are hoping to achieve in retirement.

- What is possible for you in retirement?
- What does your retirement look like if it is successful?
- What will the world around you look like in retirement if it is successful?
- When you imagine your ideal retirement, what do you see? What are you doing? How do you feel? Who are you with? Who are you in that vision?
- What words come up when you think about living this ideal retirement?
- What visuals come up when you think about living this ideal retirement?
- What emotions come up when you think about living this ideal retirement?
- What are you doing in this vision of the future to create and live this ideal retirement?
- Who do you have to become to live this ideal retirement?
- What would the experience of working toward that vision in retirement be like for you? What words would you use to describe the process?

What was it like to answer these questions? About half the people who answer these prompts love the process. They find it motivating because it creates positive energy for them. The other half, however, struggle with the process. If that's you, it's okay. We are trying to think into the future and answer tough questions. If you found this process of dreaming up a compelling vision for your future frustrating, let's go in the opposite direction. It can be challenging to identify what we want but easier to pinpoint what we *don't* want. Try these questions:

- What would your retirement look like if it was not successful?

- What will the world around you look like in retirement if it is not successful?

- When you imagine a retirement where you are unhappy and unfulfilled, what do you see? What are you doing? How do you feel? Who are you with? Who are you in that vision?

- What words come up when you think about living an inferior retirement?

- What visuals come up when you think about living an inferior retirement?

- What emotions come up when you think about living an inferior retirement?

- What are you doing in this vision of the future to create and live an inferior retirement?

If you can clearly identify what you don't want, it may help clarify what you do want. Investigate your responses to the questions above and look for clues that help you determine what an ideal retirement would look like. For example, if an inferior retirement is one where you have no energy and are in physical pain, what would an ideal retirement look like instead?

Living with Purpose

NEEDS —▸ VALUES —▸ INTERESTS —▸ PASSIONS —▸ VISION —▸ **PURPOSE** = MEANING + FULFILLMENT

You've been laying the foundation for your purpose as you complete each exercise. You likely have a clearer sense of your needs and values. You have insight into your interests and passions. You've explored and created a vision you want to make. But your work is not quite over.

Understanding your purpose provides you with the insight that answers the question of why you are here. What is the meaning of your life? There is ample scientific evidence that having a sense of purpose is associated with mental and physical health benefits as well as improved quality of life.[39] Having a purpose may even help you live longer.[40] In one study of nearly 7,000 adults over 50 years old in the United States, they found that a "stronger purpose in life was associated with decreased mortality."[41] Specifically, those who did not have a strong sense of purpose were more than twice as likely to die during the five-year study.

Purpose is important in any language. Studies conducted in Japan asked participants if they had *ikigai* – something to live for, the joy and goal of living. Results showed that those who felt they had *ikigai* also had greater longevity.[42]

But purpose isn't just about living a *longer* life; it's about living a *better* life. A study looking at the factors associated with older people leading a meaningful life reported that "feeling life is worthwhile contributes to subsequent well-being and human flourishing at older ages."[43] Purpose is a gift in the present, and it can continue to provide beneficial outcomes throughout your retirement.

The goal for all retirees who want to live Badass Retirements should be to increase their feelings of purpose – to feel like life has meaning and goals. Your purpose answers the questions: *Why am I here? What is it that I am meant to accomplish? What big problems am I hoping to help solve? What impact do I want to have on the world and my family?*

You can certainly live a wonderful life and retirement without ever uncovering the great meaning of your life. If you can get close to it or find a few things that inspire you, however, life will certainly be more fulfilling. That is what makes this process so rewarding. It's not all or nothing. Your happiness and fulfillment aren't contingent on having 100% clarity about your values or purpose. That said, the greater your proximity to what really moves you, the more you will feel contentment and fulfillment in the days of your retirement.

Another common misconception is that your purpose needs to be grandiose or change the world. If the thought of making a huge impact on the world keeps you up at night and gets you out of bed in the morning, go for it! But even if changing the world doesn't inspire you and your motivations are less zealous, they are still every bit as important. The goal isn't to see who can develop the best-sounding mission statement or purpose. The goal is to help you uncover what is most meaningful for you. End child trafficking in SE Asia? Great. Be the best grandparent you can be? Great. We all get inspiration and meaning from different things. Don't for a second minimize what really moves you just because you don't think it is significant enough.

So, yes, this is hard work, and there are no easy answers, but I guarantee you that it is worth it. Having even a little more insight into what moves you and gives you joy will pay dividends throughout your retirement.

Based on what you know about yourself, play around with different purpose statements. Think back to your vision statements and think about *why* you want to create this vision. It's okay to have multiple purpose statements if they all resonate with you and feel right. Remember, your purpose statements don't have to have a global impact or solve the world's problems. It's okay to be self-focused but strive to have at least one purpose that creates an impact outside of yourself, since these often provide the greatest meaning for retirees.

This is all a work in progress, and you can change the wording at any time. Don't get stuck trying to craft the perfect purpose. Instead, use your purpose statements to move you forward and give meaning to your life and your days throughout retirement.

When you think about your purpose in life and retirement, it should feel right. It doesn't matter if it sounds good; it needs to feel good. The ultimate test is whether you're still thinking about your purpose statements when you set this book down or move on to the next Challenge. Do you get excited about them? Are you anxious to share them with others? Re-read them in a couple of days. Do you still feel connected to them? Do they still inspire you? That's when you know you have something meaningful.

For your entire adult life, you worked for somebody. You worked for your teachers in school. You worked for your boss at your job. You worked for the approval of your colleagues. Even if you ran your own company, you still worked for your clients. But not anymore...

Now that you're retired, it's all about you.

Think about all those early mornings you pulled yourself out of bed when it was still dark out, or the countless times you arrived home well after the sun had gone down. The years of your life you spent in traffic. The unforgiving boss and the relentless deadlines. Your job and the world were always demanding more and more from you. But not anymore...

Now that you're retired, it's all about *you*. But what if it isn't *all* about you?

JOIN THE FAMILY

Finding and strengthening your purpose is one of the most important things you can do to create a retirement of meaning and fulfillment. While I hope this Challenge was helpful, I also know it's a process, and it's often not easy. Join the Badass Retirement Community and participate in one of our purpose-building workshops to go even deeper.

GO TO BADASSRETIREMENT.COM

8

CHALLENGE

Make an Impact

We need you. Discover the mission
that moves you and the mark you want
to make in the world.

CHALLENGE 8

In the last Challenge, you put a lot of work into uncovering your purpose. This clarity around what drives and inspires you will help create a more meaningful and fulfilling retirement. Frankly, if you don't have this level of understanding about yourself, it will be difficult to create the very best life possible in retirement. Instead, you may bounce around from one activity or trip to the next, always hoping to create more meaning but feeling like something is missing. That's not living a Badass Retirement. That's living far below your potential. If you haven't done the work yet, please do it now, because this Challenge will have you digging even deeper.

Your needs, values, interests, vision, and purpose are deeply personal and self-centered, but that doesn't mean they have to be selfish. You can create and live your ideal retirement but still not feel a sense of meaning or fulfillment. You may achieve the vision you painted, but that doesn't guarantee you'll be satisfied with it.

Fun? Check. Adventure? Check. Passions? Check. But something is missing. The most common reason I've observed for retirees who work on their retirements but still feel unfulfilled is that they didn't think about the impact they wanted to make.

I think selfishness has a bad reputation. I don't think there is anything wrong with being selfish. This is your retirement and your life, after all. Shouldn't you pursue the things you want? I don't just think it's okay to be selfish; I think it is essential.

Being self-focused helps you figure out what you like and want to do, achieve, and become in retirement. It lets you answer the questions about your needs, values, and interests and gives you the ability to determine your passions and vision for the future. My advice is to be as introspective and self-focused as possible in determining what drives you and makes you the most fulfilled. Don't shy away from it because you think it's not appropriate. It's not only appropriate, it's crucial.

IMPACT > IMPOTENT

There is no doubt you can fill your days in retirement by pursuing enjoyable interests and activities. This is the playbook, however, for achieving an Average Retirement – replacing work with a few entertaining hobbies. Maybe a couple of trips a year, an extra round or two of golf a week, or a bit more reading.

Perhaps you've decided you want something more than an Average Retirement, so you've dialed up the challenge and adventure and gone all-in on a handful of deeply rewarding activities or hobbies. Is that enough? For some, I think it can be. I've seen retirees who are so passionate about something that it becomes an obsession to which they dedicate their entire retirement, going on to live amazing and full lives. If something can occupy your time and fill your soul throughout retirement, take advantage of that.

Being entirely self-focused, however, is not the only (or best) path for most people trying to live Badass Retirements. Sure, there are endless hobbies and adventures you can pursue that would be fun and challenging, but they rarely become obsessions that can sustain someone throughout retirement. To experience the deepest levels of meaning and fulfillment, we also need to look beyond ourselves. We should embrace the power of "and" by ensuring we are both self-focused *and* selfless. We need to look inward *and* outward. We need to make a difference in our own lives *and* the lives around us. These things are not mutually exclusive – we can and should seek both.

One of the fears of retirement is that the retiree may become irrelevant, overcome by a feeling of insignificance. This is a common concern felt by many entering retirement and those already retired, but it is especially pressing for those with a strong need for Significance. Regardless of your top needs or values, nobody wants to feel unimportant. We all value feeling valued, but in retirement the fear (and sometimes the reality) is that you are no longer needed. Still, there is hope. The cure for feeling irrelevant is to provide value. The cure for feeling unimportant is to do important things. The cure for feeling impotent is to have an impact. The cure for feeling hollow is to do what you can to make a difference.

The surefire way to feel that your days and life in retirement have meaning is to be a hero – to mean something to someone else. During the years we worked and raised our families, we had opportunities to feel needed and valued. Every day, we were affecting the world – or at least our small parts of it. The big projects to which we contributed at work and the small things we did at home provided us with a sense of meaning. In an Average Retirement, there are fewer opportunities to experience meaning. As a result, some retirees crave the feeling of making a difference and having an impact. When you tap into your needs and values to create a vision that impacts others, you will experience meaning and fulfillment. Many retirees report that they feel more satisfaction and fulfillment than they ever did in their careers.

PROXIMITY OF IMPACT > MAGNITUDE OF IMPACT

If you're concerned that you need to try to solve the world's biggest challenges to have an impact, don't be. After working with hundreds of retirees, I learned a secret that seems counterintuitive. The benefits you will experience from making a difference seem to have little relationship to the scope and scale of the impact you are making. In other words, you may get as much meaning and fulfillment from being a hero to just one person as you would from helping many.

I've seen clients find purpose and meaning in volunteering at the local library or in a hospital gift shop, providing financial advice to those with little money, picking up groceries for the elderly, helping kids read, coaching out-of-work single moms on how to interview better, and teaching personal development courses to disadvantaged girls. Why does the magnitude of the impact have a minor effect on the amount of meaning you feel?

It's all about the proximity of impact. That is, how close are you to the difference you are making? You must feel like your efforts and actions are resulting in a tangible difference. The further you are from the change, the more abstract the connection. Giving money to causes you care about is critical in supporting these organizations' efforts. Writing a check and thinking about how your money will help the cause can certainly make you feel good. That feeling is often temporary, though. Our goal in a Badass Retirement is to create elevated and sustainable meaning all throughout retirement – not just in brief spikes.

The magnitude of impact is much less important than its proximity.

This is good news. It means you don't have to be wealthy and write big checks to feel significant. It also means you don't need to feel obligated to solve the world's most important challenges. Making any difference – even a small and seemingly insignificant one – can provide fulfillment if you are near the change and feel your actions were responsible for the improvement.

You don't have to help everyone – just one person. You don't need to improve everything – just one thing. If you are motivated to tackle the biggest and hardest challenges, we need you! If your ambitions are less lofty, however, you can still find meaning and fulfillment in the smallest of tasks, whether it's holding the hand of a grieving parent, playing with a puppy at a shelter, or delivering a meal to a hungry family.

If you want to feel like your days have a purpose, get as close to the change as you can.

MAKE IT MEANINGFUL

I remember having a poignant conversation with a retiree about her volunteer work. She told me about all the work she was doing for an organization and how it felt like a chore. She said she felt stressed while she was volunteering and couldn't wait to leave. After giving her time and energy to this charity for a couple of years, she still never felt excited about it. When I asked her what the organization did, she told me all about her duties. When I clarified and asked her what the organization's mission was, she started to explain that they did something with the homeless and the less fortunate, but then just stopped and stared at the floor. She looked up, gave me a half-smile, and said, "I honestly don't really know." It was at that point the problem became clear to her.

If you are going to work for an organization – spending your precious time and energy – and not be financially compensated, you'd better find the work deeply meaningful. If you don't, it's just work without a paycheck! Find organizations that inspire you and make you want to jump out of bed in the morning. Here's how...

Charities are businesses, but they are not in the business of making money. Instead, it's about the *change*, not the dollars. Your task is to think about the changes you want to see in the world. What issues do you see that pull you in, that make you want to get involved, that beckon you to make a difference, and that you can't turn your back on?

To help you get started, answer these questions:

- What big problems do you notice?
- What causes are you the most interested in?
- What problems cause you to want to cry, scream, or both?
- If you had a magic button you could press that would instantly eliminate one problem in the world, what would that problem be?
- What hardship have you or a loved one overcome that gives you meaning?

- What are you willing to fight for? Is there a cause for which you'd be willing to risk your life?

- What is something in the world that you feel needs to change?

- If you were to start a non-profit organization, what would be its focus?

- What topics do you lose yourself in when you talk about them with friends?

- If you had to watch a documentary about an issue, what would you choose?

- If you had to donate your entire estate to charity, which one(s) would get your money?

Given all of your thoughts and answers to those questions, think about the problems you'd like to see solved in the world. Do any of these stand out to you? Knowing what you know about your values and interests, can you narrow the list from ten to five? How about two or three?

Are you having trouble coming up with causes you care about? It can help to ask family and friends what issues they think you are passionate about. If they've noticed your passion, chances are these are topics that mean a lot to you. You may even be reminded of events that highlight these meaningful issues. Maybe there have been experiences in your life that you've forgotten and that a conversation with a friend or family member could help uncover.

Now that you have narrowed the list to a couple of big problems that are most meaningful to you, what's the next step? Choose one. Yup, just one for now. That can be hard. There are so many challenges and so many worthwhile causes that it's easy to want to solve them all. But I encourage you to identify a cause and focus your efforts (at least initially) on just that one. Turn it from *a* cause into *your* cause. Your mission.

Now that you have discovered the big cause you want to dedicate time to solving, here are a few ideas to move it forward:

Find like-minded organizations. Now comes the fun part. After working on all the exercises and digging deep, you've identified a couple of issues that resonate with you. Out of the millions of problems and causes you could have chosen, you've found your few. Now you get to research people and organizations dedicated to solving the very same problems that are most important to you. Just think about that for a moment. You can find your tribe of people who feel just as passionately about your causes as you do. When you find them it will feel like home.

Start a charity. I've had many clients start their own non-profit organizations around causes they believe in. It's a much bigger commitment than simply volunteering or joining an existing organization, but if you have the passion and the desire, it's a way to go "all in" on a cause. I've found this works well if you have a spouse/partner or friend who feels just as strongly as you do. Starting and administering a non-profit takes time and know-how, so it's a good idea to get professional help along the way. In the mid-2000s, several friends and I started a non-profit organization to support disadvantaged kids worldwide. We've had projects across SE Asia, including Vietnam, Cambodia, Thailand, Burma, the Philippines, Indonesia, and other countries in the region. We didn't know what we were doing when we started it, but we learned and it's still operating and impacting kids to this day. If you want to be moved, create a movement.

Start a personal foundation. If you have the financial resources, a foundation can be a way to use your wealth to support causes and organizations that are meaningful to you. A foundation is a corporate entity that you set up and contribute money into, donating a certain percentage to charitable causes at least once a year. The best application I've seen of a foundation is when a 50-year-old client of mine sold his company to Microsoft. After the sale, he retired but still wanted to be active and do something with his three kids and wife. The solution? A personal foundation. He donated a large sum to the foundation, got a significant tax deduction (which helped offset the gain on the sale of the business), and got his family excited about supporting causes they care about. In addition to some bookkeeping requirements, he also had to donate at least 5% of the value of the foundation each year. To make the personal foundation even more personal, I suggested that each family member research and donate 1% of the money. My client was into sustainable farming and the environment, so he found like-minded organizations. The youngest daughter was all about animals – specifically horses. She found several organizations that shared her love and passion. The foundation provided a family "business" of sorts and it got them working together to make an impact.

Be a hero to just one person. If your dream is to go big and start a foundation or non-profit organization, that's amazing. The world needs your talents and enthusiasm! But don't think for a second you have to impact thousands or even hundreds of people. You. Just. Need.

To. Help. One. Person. Full stop. In the process of helping them, you will feel valued, wanted, and a deep sense of purpose.

Regardless which route you choose, if you invest your time and energy into causes you care deeply about, the experience will be meaningful for you.

MISSION

Your purpose and vision can provide you with a boost of energy and meaning, but it can also feel a bit abstract. It's one thing to know your purpose in life and what drives you, but it's another thing to know what to do. That's where having a mission can help. Your mission provides the *what* for the *why* you've been uncovering. Your mission describes what you will do to fulfill your purpose, make an impact, and create your ideal vision.

For example, if your purpose is to eliminate animal cruelty, that cause might give you energy and meaning, but what specifically are you going to do to eliminate animal cruelty? You could start a non-profit that rescues abandoned animals. You could write a book that highlights the advantages of a plant-based diet. You could start a company that creates lab-manufactured meat. You could organize events around the world that protest animal testing. One purpose can have many possible directions. Your mission is what you want *to do* to realize the vision you dream of creating.

One purpose I have is to help people make the most of their lives. There are countless ways I could seek to accomplish this, but my mission – my *what* – is to create and support an online membership platform of passionate people who want more meaning and purpose, joy and adventure, energy and confidence, and growth and impact in retirement than they ever thought possible.

My mission is the continuous process of building and supporting the community. Such a mission is never-ending. That's what makes it different from a goal, something which you strive to complete. Unlike a to-do list or bucket list with activities you scramble to accomplish and check off, a mission provides endless motivation and meaning. You can think of a mission as a combination of *what* you are going to do to create your vision and fulfill your purpose and *how* you are going to do it. You may have dozens of goals and projects to help you accomplish your mission, but these are shorter-term and may change over time.

At this point, don't get too caught up in thinking about individual goals. They can be distracting and frankly, overwhelming. Instead, focus on the bigger mission. What and how will you seek to fulfill your purpose and vision? Without a specific mission related to each purpose, you will likely lose motivation. Remember, the reason you are doing any of these exercises is for the payoff – a lifetime in retirement of feeling energized and inspired each morning by the impact you will have. Each night, you'll go to bed feeling like you've done something special that provides you with meaning and fulfillment. It's a good investment.

On every client's birthday, I like to remind them of their uniqueness and purpose. I send them this quote by Scottish theologian William Barclay: "There are two great days in a person's life – the day we are born and the day we discover why." I hope today you got a little closer to answering that question.

JOIN THE FAMILY

What impact will you make in retirement? Join the Badass Retirement Community to share what you are doing or learn what others are doing and get ideas and inspiration.

GO TO BADASSRETIREMENT.COM

9

CHALLENGE

Grow Relationships

Take a fresh look at the people in your life, deepen the connections with those most important to you, and continue to build new relationships that provide joy and meaning.

CHALLENGE 9

A foundation of Badass Retirement is relationships. There's a reason Deeper Relationships is one of the **Badass 5** drivers. Our friends, family, and spouse/partner provide meaning and fulfillment unlike anything else . . . but don't just take my word for it!

Imagine studying hundreds of individuals for 75 years to see what factors were associated with success or hardship. Imagine if these participants completed questionnaires providing insights into areas like career happiness, retirement, and marital quality every couple of years. What if, every few years, physicians provided mental and physical health information on every volunteer? Can you imagine the insights you could glean from such a comprehensive data source?

Well, you don't have to imagine. Harvard Medical School psychiatrist and researcher George Vaillant conducted that exact study. It's called the Grant Study, and it has been in operation since 1942.[44] Multiple books have been written about the study and its takeaways. But in a 2008 interview, Vaillant was asked what he had learned from the participants. After decades of painstaking research and hundreds of thousands of data points, what do you think Vaillant's conclusion was? Find a job you love? Follow your passion? Get a good education? Exercise and eat well? Nope. Vaillant remarked, "The only thing that really matters in life are your relationships to other people."[45]

Cultivate deeper relationships. It's an investment that will likely do more to improve your physical and mental health, well-being, and happiness in retirement than anything else you do.

Will I be lonely, or will I have meaningful relationships?

The answer to this question has profound consequences for your well-being and satisfaction in retirement, as well as your mental and physical health. It may even impact how long you live.

Many retirees have robust social networks they can rely on for support, connection, and camaraderie. If that describes your situation, consider yourself fortunate. Strong relationships are an asset that you will benefit from greatly throughout retirement.

If you don't have a strong social network or are hoping to deepen the relationships you already have, you are not alone. Not all of us are extroverts who require constant social interaction, but we all require some. We crave connection, so the thought of being lonely (which is different from being alone, as you will see) is both frightening and common. When pre-retirees are asked about their fears for retirement, one in four admit they are afraid of being alone and isolated.[46] That fear was just below concerns about health and money. It's staggering that 25% of people worry about not having relationships in retirement. But then, once they enter retirement, something interesting and concerning happens. Of people who are already retired, nearly half worry about becoming more isolated and alone as they age.[47] The number of people who worry about not having social relationships in retirement doubles once they enter it.

Unfortunately, this worry is not unfounded. The research shows that over 40% of individuals over 60 years old report feeling lonely and that nearly one in four adults over the age of 65 are "socially isolated."[48] This is tragic. In their prime retirement years, such a large percentage of retirees shouldn't feel lonely. Worse yet, we are getting lonelier. According to research from the Stanford Center on Longevity, those in the Baby Boom generation are even less socially engaged compared to just 20 years ago, though the researchers aren't sure why.[49] What causes so many retirees to be lonely in retirement?

One good reason is that our work provides the largest contribution to friends and social interaction.[50] It's the number one source of friends and we are almost guaranteed to have some form of social interaction every day we work. Like so many other things, this changes in retirement. The day after retiring, we face a large social void that wasn't there just 24 hours ago. This social void is real, and it doesn't go unnoticed. The number one thing retirees miss most about work? It's not the paycheck. It's not the structure. It's not even the sense of accomplishment. It's the people and the social stimulation.[51]

WE > ME

Over 200 people participated in a survey on happiness. About half of the respondents reported feeling happy. What was more interesting is that the largest contributor to feeling unhappy was found to be loneliness. Loneliness was a larger contributor to unhappiness than religious beliefs, disability status, or even perceived health![52]

There is no doubt about the power of relationships. They have a profound effect on our psychology and physiology. If your goal is to create more meaning and fulfillment throughout retirement, cultivating relationships is your best bet. Let this Challenge be your guide to growing and deepening the relationships in your life.

One more note about the study mentioned above: all the respondents were homeless. Loneliness – not their housing situation – was still the most significant contributor to unhappiness!

Of course, you probably don't need research to confirm what you already know – relationships play an important role in your happiness and life satisfaction. What you may not fully realize is the extent to which your relationships affect all aspects of your life, including your health.

It makes sense to attribute poor health in retirement to simply getting older. Unsurprisingly, research finds many negative biomedical factors that increase with age.

The story, however, is more nuanced.

Disease, disability, and death are also influenced by psychosocial distress.[53] Exercise and eating well will go a long way in helping you live a long and healthy life. Still, less obvious contributors, such as your relationships, also play important roles in your short and long-term physical health,[54] as well as in improving psychological health outcomes (e.g., higher levels of life satisfaction and well-being) in retirees.[55] Having close relationships doesn't just feel good, it's good for you. And the research shows that the benefits only increase as we get older.[56] According to the author of a research project that included almost 280,000 participants and spanned nearly 100 countries, "Friendships become even more important as we age. Keeping a few really good friends around can make a world of difference for our health and well-being."

The benefits of meaningful relationships are important at any age, but they may be even more important for retirees. One of the most common fears in retirement is cognitive decline. A lack of social connections is linked to a myriad of negative physical outcomes, including cardiovascular disease, high blood pressure, stroke, dementia, and cancer.[57] These diseases don't need extra help from us, as they are all conditions that already increase with age. Still not convinced of the power of relationships? A lack of meaningful relationships is associated with a much greater risk of death – nearly twice as high in some studies.[58]

Neuroscience and psychology professor Julianne Holt-Lunstad has conducted considerable research in the field of loneliness. Her initial study, which combined the data of 148 other studies of 300,000 individuals worldwide (and was later replicated and expanded to include over 3.4 million people around the world), provided a wealth of new information on the association between perceived loneliness and our health.[59] Most notably, her research suggests that a lack of social relationships increases health risks as much as smoking 15 cigarettes a day and that loneliness is twice as harmful to mental and physical health as obesity! She concluded that there "is robust evidence that social isolation and loneliness significantly increase the risk for premature mortality, and the magnitude of the risk exceeds that of many leading health indicators."[60]

Why are social connections so important to mental and physical health? Dr. Steve Cole, a genomics researcher and Director of the Social Genomics Core Laboratory at UCLA, hopes to understand how loneliness affects the functioning of both body and mind.[61] After years of studying the link between relationships and health, he artfully summed up his observations: "Loneliness acts as a fertilizer for other diseases. The biology of loneliness can accelerate the buildup of plaque in arteries, help cancer cells grow and spread, and promote inflammation in the brain leading to Alzheimer's disease. Loneliness promotes several different types of wear and tear on the body."

We are wired for social connection.[62] But is our need for relationships as strong as our need for food, water, and shelter? Matthew Lieberman, a professor of psychiatry and biobehavioral science at UCLA, thinks so: "Being socially connected is our brain's lifelong passion. It's been baked into our operating system for tens of millions of years."[63] He's not alone. Stephen Porges, founding director of the Traumatic Stress Research Consortium and professor of psychiatry at the University of North Carolina, concluded that "Our biological imperative is to be connected with others. Through the process of evolution, social connectedness evolved as the primary biological imperative for mammals in their quest for survival."[64]

Social connection has served us well over the millennia, and it will serve you well throughout retirement. Growing relationships is one of the key contributors to creating a Badass Retirement. Even if you dedicate your time and energy to strengthening your purpose and making an impact, your retirement experience can still be lacking if you neglect to grow and deepen your relationships. To create the most meaning and fulfillment in retirement, it is essential to focus on your relationships.

LEVERS OF GROWING RELATIONSHIPS

We all seek connection. We want to feel like we are part of something. We want to feel a bond with others. More important than having friends or family, more important than having people to do things with, we want to feel togetherness. We want to feel connected.

Except it's not easy.

As we age, our bandwidth for adding new friends and cultivating new relationships tends to narrow. So does opportunity. Although there is more time for relationships in retirement, there are fewer opportunities for *new* connections. Work once provided ample chance to meet new people and develop ties. Retirement (especially Average Retirement)? Not so much. Why? Remember the Retirement Myth – *less is more*. In an Average Retirement, the world contracts. The friends and relationships we already have going into retirement are often the ones we keep throughout it.

If you have a strong social network and deep friendships that provide you with a sense of connection and fulfillment, this may not be a concern for you. With nearly half of retirees feeling lonely,[65] however, you are certainly not alone if you feel a desire for greater connection.

One of the most significant benefits of living a Badass Retirement is the relationships you will forge. When you are clear on your mission and purpose, pushing to reach your potential, going on adventures, and making an impact, you will surely have more opportunities to meet people.

But Badass Retirement's most significant advantage isn't that you will meet new people (although you will). The most significant benefit is the *type* of people you will meet. Remember, we don't crave people; we crave connection.

Who are these people you will meet while living a Badass Retirement? Imagine finding someone or even a whole group of people who share your ambition to create the best life they can in retirement. What do you think that would be like? Imagine they share your enthusiasm for the activities you do. How would that feel? Now imagine they also share your passion for the same cause and that they jump out of bed each morning with the purpose of solving those challenges that mean the most to you. Does that feel good? Does it inspire you?

I've taken dozens of multi-day hiking trips with clients in all corners of the world. Many things could go wrong on these trips – sickness, injury, language issues, crime, etc. – but there's one thing I never have to worry about: the other people on the trail. No matter what country I'm in or how supposedly dangerous it might be, once I'm on the trail, I never worry. I know everyone I meet out there or at camp is pursuing the same adventure I am. Regardless from where they come, their culture, religion, political beliefs, race, or sexual orientation, we are on the same physical and spiritual path. No matter how different we may be, there is literal and metaphorical common ground.

When you live a Badass Retirement, you attract others who share your spirit for seeking more, doing more, achieving more, and becoming more. We may be very different, but our sameness connects us. The best people you will ever meet may not look like you or believe the same things you do, but a shared path and enthusiasm for living will connect you.

PASSION > PROXIMITY

It's common to have a handful of closer friends. These are people you've probably known for years – you have history and shared experiences. They have seen you at your best and worst. They will celebrate your successes and be there in the tough times. These are important relationships to nurture throughout retirement.

Many retirees, however, may not have relationships like this. Still others may acknowledge that, while they have plenty of people and even friends in their lives, they seek relationships that can offer more. One retiree lamented, "I don't need more friends. I need more connection." Maybe you feel something like this as well – but why?

One of the challenges during both our working years and retirement is that many of our friendships are relationships of convenience. Our friends are our neighbors or co-workers, people from church or the club, our spouses' friends, or classmates from school. Proximity is the strongest predictor of friendship, at least according to some research in the field.[66] In fact, just sitting next to someone greatly increases the chance of making a best friend.[67] Remember, we are inherently lazy. We seek the path of least resistance. We became friends with people because they were near us, which was comparatively easy. It's no wonder why so many retirees feel lonely and crave connection – even among those with pre-existing social networks.

If you want to make deeper connections and create more meaningful relationships, the path of least resistance and proximity will not get you there, but the path of shared interests and passions might.

FIND YOUR TRIBE

You have the opportunity to create deeply meaningful connections with others who share your passions and vision. Rather than let chance and ease of effort determine your relationships, you need to be more intentional. Your goal is to find your tribe – or, more accurately, your tribes.

A tribe is a group that shares a collective objective and interests. Your tribe will feel like home. It will be a place where everyone knows not just your name but also what drives you. A tribe is deeply meaningful because there is a common cause – a reason for membership. It creates connections because of the underlying shared interests and shared purpose.

Your goal should be to have at least one place where you have a tribe and where you feel you fit in. It could be a regular meetup group, an organization in which you volunteer, or even something as seemingly insignificant as a Peloton class. Yes, you can be alone in your basement at 1 a.m. but feel totally connected for the duration of your 30-minute bike ride because it's a shared interest and a shared struggle – you're all in it together.

Your tribe is waiting for you. You just need to find (or create) it. Here are a few places to start:

Focus on your passions. What interests are you most passionate about? Find groups focused on these passions to connect with others who are just as enthusiastic as you are. Do an online search. Are there any Meetups near you? Reach out to the leadership and introduce yourself. Get involved.

Advance your knowledge. A great way to connect with others who share your love for a topic is to learn more about it. Find classes or courses related to your passions. Search for clubs related to your interests. The teachers, students, and participants are your tribe.

Connect with organizations. Look for organizations dedicated to solving the problems that you've identified as being most meaningful to you. These are your people. They share your vision for tomorrow and are working today to make it a reality.

Go virtual. If you have a hard time finding local groups, go online. Even if you connect with others near you, I'd still recommend connecting online, too. The wonderful thing about the Internet is you can find a tribe dedicated to the most obscure interests imaginable.

Self-improvement. Over the years, I've noticed that the retirees who work at creating Badass Retirements are the same ones who value and work on improving themselves. If you are attracted to pushing your limits, having adventures, and making an impact, you are likely interested in becoming the best version of yourself you can be. Some of the most inspirational people I know are the ones who are focused on getting better each day. Find groups, courses, or communities with others who share this same passion for improvement.

Become a fan. There is a surprising amount of research that shows there are real benefits to being a sports fan. Fans have lower levels of loneliness, higher life satisfaction, and higher self-esteem levels than those who aren't interested in sports.[68] According to Daniel Wann, a psychology professor and expert on fan behavior, the "simple fact is that people are looking for ways to identify with something, to feel a sense of belongingness with a group of like-minded individuals."[69] Isn't this what we are all looking for? A sense of connection and the feeling of belonging? Dust off that jersey from your closet and attend a game or visit a bar to watch the action. I remember being alone in Chicago on business in the 1990s during the NBA finals. The Chicago Bulls were playing for the championship and Michael Jordan was a god. I was not a fan of the Bulls, basketball, or any sport at the time, but I went to a bar (full disclosure: I may have gone to a few bars), and I remember the experience like it was yesterday. I've never felt more instantly connected to a group of strangers than I have watching that game. The power of fandom and community is real.

Join a retirement community. If you've made it this far in the book, that tells me something about you. Connect with others who share your desire to make the most of retirement by joining an online retirement community of other like-minded people. Our Badass Retirement members may be very different from you in all the ways that don't matter – how they look, where they live, how much money they have, or what they did for work – but they are the same in the one area that does matter – their desire to experience more meaning and purpose, joy and adventure, energy and confidence, and growth and impact in retirement. You don't have to join the Badass Retirement Community. There are other retirement communities that you can explore. Find the one that resonates with you and jump in. It could be one of the best investments in your retirement you will make.

Start your own tribe. If you can't find your tribe, create one. I guarantee that there are (many) people out there who share your passion and would love to connect. Create an online community. Arrange a monthly in-person meetup. Start a podcast around your topic. Your people are out there. You just need to find and organize them.

YOUR ENVIRONMENT IS *EVERYTHING*

One of the most important lessons I have learned in life is also one of the simplest. Your environment shapes you. And not just in a minor or casual way, but in significant and meaningful ways. Our physical environment can play a big role. Think about the energy you feel when you are listening to your favorite song or your emotions when you gaze at the ocean or a stream. We like to think we are independent and autonomous masters of our universe single-handedly charting our own destiny, but that's not entirely true. Your environment shapes your thoughts, feelings, decisions, and even your genes. And that's okay. Don't fight it; embrace it.

The *What* in your environment has a significant impact on your life, but the *Who* is even more consequential. If you forget everything else in this book, please remember this:

The people you choose to spend time with in your life will either be a positive force or a negative force.

I know. That can sting. It might not feel fair. But it is as true as anything I know. And if you think about your experience in life, you're likely to agree. Just think back to the times in your life when you were surrounded by greatness – people who were reaching higher and working harder to do something meaningful. The people who were supportive and encouraging. The people who inspired you and gave you energy. The people who made you think you might be able to achieve and become more. Think back to how that made you feel. Amazing, right?

Now conjure a time when the Who in your life were negative or maybe just uninspiring. Did you feel the same level of passion and purpose? The same level of inspiration or potential?

You have a choice. Unlike in your working years when you likely didn't have much control over the Who in your life, in retirement you have more say about who you want in your inner circle. Be intentional. Quality matters.

QUALITY > QUANTITY

In our working years, our social networks tend to be more fluid. For example, we would change companies, move houses, or join new groups on a nearly regular basis. In retirement – especially an Average Retirement – our social networks become more rigid and fixed, with fewer opportunities for change or expansion.

It can take time to enter new social networks and build new relationships, which is why I coach clients to start the process before they enter retirement. Regardless of your age or how long you've been retired, the work you do to cultivate relationships will be worth it.

The question isn't if you *can* grow your relationships, it's what kind of relationships do you *want* to grow? The quality of your friendships matters at any stage in life, but even more so in retirement. Finding and deepening high-quality relationships takes effort and intention. It also requires an understanding of what you want in and from your social circle. Relationships are investments in others and yourself. We all have a limited amount of time and energy for maintaining relationships, but if you're living a Badass Retirement, you will manage.

You need to be discerning about who you want in your life and deliberate about finding and cultivating those relationships. My goal for you is to think deeply about the qualities and attributes you want in your most meaningful friendships – what standards do you require? And, just as importantly, what qualities don't you want? This filtering isn't to limit the number of deep relationships with quality friends, it's to limit the number of substandard relationships in your life.

I know this philosophy on friendships is not shared by everyone. Some may scoff, finding this approach too calculating. Indeed. It is calculated by design. If you think this is too extreme, you need to remind yourself of what's at stake. There is a reason you are reading this book, after all. You have just one life and one retirement. What is it about living your best life in retirement that draws you in? Think about your purpose and your mission. What are the important things you still want to accomplish? What are the adventures you haven't taken? What is the impact you have yet to make?

What's at stake? Your vision, your fulfillment, your retirement – your life.

Your relationships *may* be significant contributors to your happiness and may provide meaning in retirement. They may also be a drag. Simply having relationships – even deep relationships – isn't sufficient. The goal isn't to find and deepen just any relationship, it's about cultivating the right relationships.

Years ago, when my daughter was young, I talked to her about the importance of forming the right friendships. After a string of toxic friendships, we wanted an easy way to communicate to her how to think about forming friends. I came up with a red, yellow, and green method. It worked for her, and it's helped me think about my own relationships. When I use this same taxonomy with clients to describe relationships in retirement, it clicks for them, too. Granted, it's a bit hokey, but it's also easier to understand and actionable. The latter quality is key. You want a framework that will allow you to evaluate existing and future relationships.

Red relationships. We've all experienced the deleterious effects of negative relationships. It should go without saying that there is no room for these in retirement. If you are carrying the baggage of caustic relationships, sever ties immediately. Nobody deserves to be subject to the negative consequences of harmful relationships. I've seen the devastation created by bad ones. It's heartbreaking. Red relationships are damaging at best and dangerous at worst. Do whatever it takes to extract yourself from them – whether they are friends or family. It's not easy. In fact, it could be one of the hardest things you do. It could also be one of the most important things you do. Get help if needed.

Yellow relationships. The consequences of destructive "red relationships" are often obvious – maybe not initially, but eventually. There is another type of relationship, however, that is far more common and is also pernicious: the yellow relationship. What makes these relationships harmful is their concealed corrosiveness – you don't even realize the damage is being done. Yellow relationships undermine your potential and the vision you have in retirement without you even realizing it. How? Social contagion.

The adage that we are the average of our five closest friends has merit – and a lot of research to back it up. It is well documented that our social networks have a powerful influence over us. Research shows that they strongly influence our moods, affecting our happiness, loneliness, and depression, as well as our behaviors, such as sleep, speeding, and criminality, and our health in the form of smoking, substance abuse, alcohol consumption, and obesity. They can even contribute to divorce.[70]

Yellow relationships are comfortable, but they provide little value and can deplete your energy. You aren't inspired to become a better person when you are with these people. They may have bad habits that rub off on you, or they may simply have an uninspired vision for the future that gradually and surreptitiously undermines yours.

Environment matters. We are social creatures. We are not only wired for connection, but we are wired to learn from those connections. The quickest way to become unhealthy, unmotivated, and unhappy is to be around others who are unhealthy, unmotivated, and unhappy. The quickest way to fall back into an Average Retirement is to fill your social network with those living Average Retirements.

As independent and sovereign as we might think we are, our relationships change us. The question isn't *if* they influence us; it's *how* we want them to influence us.

Green relationships. The influential power of social connections is agnostic, as they can exert negative or positive influences. Red and yellow relationships promote less desirable outcomes. Green relationships promote positive ones.

These are the relationships you want to find and cultivate throughout retirement. Green relationships are those that give you meaning. They bring out your best qualities and the best version of yourself. You like who you are when you are in them. There is a natural give and take. You give as much inspiration, energy, and value as you get. Green relationships are the ones that support and encourage you to reach your potential. These people may join you on adventures or share your vision to make an impact.

Take an inventory of your relationships, and immediately do whatever you need to eliminate the most caustic red ones. These are harmful to your retirement success and your health. Reduce (or at least contain) your yellow relationships. I know they seem innocuous, but if your entire network is yellow, it's going to be a struggle to create and sustain a Badass Retirement. Instead, focus on increasing or expanding your green relationships. These are the most enjoyable and healthy, but they can take time to find and develop.[71]

HIGHER-RISK GROUPS

After working with hundreds of retirees from diverse backgrounds, I've identified a few groups at a higher risk for neglecting relationships in retirement. As you've learned throughout this Challenge, cultivating the right relationships is one of the most important things you can do to create more meaning and fulfillment in your retirement. But even if you agree with this, there can be challenges.

If you fall into one or more of these groups, you might need to focus more attention or work a little harder on growing and deepening your relationships. Let me assure you that you are not alone. Many retirees struggle with building relationships – especially the right kinds.

Men. The research is clear. Men have a harder time cultivating relationships. One of the reasons is that men may enter retirement with fewer and/or more superficial friendships. Part of this is because men are much more likely to sacrifice friendship to focus on career and family.[72] The number of men who report having at least six close friends has been cut in half over the last 30 years.[73] As a result, men are less satisfied with their social relationships compared to women. Surveys also show that, compared to men, women tend to be more satisfied with the number of friends they have.[74] There are plenty of theories for why men are not quite as adept at friendships – everything from being too competitive, not asking enough questions, not opening up emotionally, or simply not talking enough. As a man, I understand and experience these challenges. If you do as well, just know that you are in good company. While some men seem to effortlessly make close and meaningful connections, others struggle. If this is an area you want to improve in retirement and would like additional resources, go to BadassRetirement.com for webinars, interviews, and other tools that can help.

Singles. The strongest social connection for most married couples is the spouse – your built-in social network right at home. The unmarried or unpartnered, however, must rely on external social networks for connection. Of course, this is not insurmountable, as there are plenty of single and social folks doing just fine in retirement. Nevertheless, research shows that single people living alone are at a higher risk of having a low quality and/or low quantity of social relationships.[75] Single retirees can benefit from having both more and deeper friendships.[76] Some retirees like to have separate circles of friendships based around shared interests. For example, I have several single retiree clients who have "travel buddies" they can count on to explore the world with them. These buddies are different from their book club friends and different from their volunteering friends. This is not to say there isn't any overlap between the social circles, but this segmented approach works well for some retirees. If you are single and entering retirement, invest more time and energy into expanding and deepening your social network. As you know, it can take time to build strong relationships, so it's helpful to say yes to more groups and opportunities before retirement begins. If you are already retired, this just means you have more time to dedicate to finding the right relationships.

Concentrated work social network. If most of your social interaction and friendships have been related to your work, you are at a higher risk of feeling a void as you enter retirement. I've seen this countless times with retirees, and if they are not prepared, the sudden loss of their social network can feel dramatic. Many surveys have proven that the fear of losing connections at work is one of the top concerns. In one survey, half of the respondents feared losing their social and friendship network at work.[77] This is understandable given that you spend more time at work than anywhere else, and that work is the most cited place where friendships are made. It can be challenging when your strong social network – with its daily interactions and camaraderie – suddenly disappears overnight. This isn't to say you will necessarily lose your work friends, but you'll certainly lose the daily interactions, the after-work drinks on Friday afternoons, and the company potlucks and holiday parties. You retire, but their lives at work go on. If your social network is concentrated around work friendships, continue to invest in those relationships, but also start to diversify. Ideally, you would start this process a year or more before retiring, but it's okay to start now if you are already retired and are feeling the void. Not only do you have plenty of time to expand your social network, but you can also focus on hobbies and new activities where you can find connections.

Strong family ties. This high-risk group is counterintuitive. Strong family connections – close ties to your children, siblings, and even spouse – can provide needed social support and meaning throughout retirement. The research does show, however, that friendships have a more significant link to health and happiness than family relationships for older adults.[78] Explanations for this unexpected finding are that we choose our friends but not our families and that family relationships can involve "serious, negative, and monotonous interactions," according to a lead researcher.[79] Additionally, it's likely that, if your social network is primarily made up of your family, you may not take the time to develop other friendships. In contrast, a diverse set of friends may expose you to new activities and interests – potentially providing you with a greater set of experiences and increased fulfillment.

Few friends. Quality matters. You're better off having one deep friendship than several superficial ones. Nevertheless, the research shows that quantity also matters. The size of your social network makes a difference, as increasing your number of friends is associated with better mental and physical health, greater well-being, improved health behaviors, decreased loneliness, and decreased mortality risk.[80] In the same study, researchers found that doubling one's number of friends produces the same effect on well-being as a 50% increase in income. Your quantity of friends seems to be even more important for adults over 50.[81] How many friends do you need? There is no hard and fast rule but be aware that significantly more negative consequences come from having too few friends than too many. If you feel like you could benefit from increasing your social relationships, consider the suggestions throughout this Challenge – especially finding like-minded people with whom you share an interest. This seems the most efficient and least threatening way to connect with others, since you are connecting over a hobby or shared activity.

Social anxiety. Social anxiety symptoms can range from mild to extreme and include fear of interacting with strangers, avoidance of doing things or speaking to people, and intense fear of social situations. While approximately 7% of the adult population is affected by a social anxiety disorder,[82] many more have lower forms of social anxiety that don't meet the clinical criteria to earn the disorder diagnosis. This means many retirees have some degree of fear and nervousness related to social situations, being around new people, or interacting with others. If you are one of the millions with some form of social anxiety, the good news is that there are proven therapeutic methods and medications that can help. You don't need a hundred close friends or to be the center of the party to live a Badass Retirement. You really just need one or two good friends you know and trust to enjoy a meaningful retirement. Find a therapist and/or psychiatrist who specializes in helping clients overcome social fears.

Social apathy. This is not to be confused with social anxiety, where you fear interacting with others. If you have social apathy, you just don't care or have the desire. If you are introverted or have many solo interests, you may not find any need or think there is a benefit to having a social network. There are real rewards to being alone, including mental, emotional, and even social benefits.[83] As highlighted earlier, being alone is not the same as being lonely. There are plenty of people (myself included) who are perfectly content being alone. But even the most diehard introverts need some social interaction and a strong social network. For introverts and others who experience social apathy, creating new friendships can feel like work. And that's okay. Just like how we exercise even though it feels like work, we do it because we know it's good for us. Approach cultivating relationships as work. It's going to take effort, and it will likely drain you of energy – at least initially – but do it because it's an investment in your future happiness. To make the task less like a chore and more enjoyable, take a cue from researchers who explored how to accelerate intimacy between strangers. They devised a list of 36 questions that can jump-start any new interaction, such as, "Given the choice of anyone in the world, whom would you want as a dinner guest?" and "What is the greatest accomplishment in your life?" among others.[84] For the full list, go to BadassRetirement.com.

SPOUSE/PARTNER-SPECIFIC ISSUES IN RETIREMENT

Disclaimer: I'm not a marriage therapist. I am not giving marital advice. I think it's important to know what you know and defer to the experts. In fact, if my wife knew I was even indirectly discussing relationships, she'd be the first to scoff. This section merely introduces common relationship issues I've seen arise in retirement over my career. It's not meant to provide answers but rather to help you start thinking about the issues and asking your own questions. There is no shortage of excellent resources available to you, including books, workshops, online seminars, and, of course, marital counselors and coaches. It's hard to live a Badass Retirement if you are having issues in your marriage. This is why we provide resources and programs at BadassRetirement.com to guide you and your partner in creating a strong relationship throughout retirement.

I was recently on a conference call with husband-and-wife clients. The husband had just retired, and I told him I was writing a book about the advantages of living a Badass Retirement. Basically, I gave them this book's high-level overview – how it's about finding meaning, purpose, and fulfillment through making an impact and being bold.

"Yes, fine, sure, good, all makes sense," they said, but then immediately asked, "Are you going to have anything in the book about spouse issues in retirement?"

I heard them loud and clear. They were at the beginning of the retirement transition and in the throes of negotiating their new lives together. It was obvious that the dream of perpetual retirement bliss was experiencing a hiccup or two. And they are not alone. What's more uncommon is to slide gracefully into retirement without encountering any spousal issues!

If you are worried about experiencing marital friction or are already in the thick of it, rest assured that this is normal and that you'll navigate your way through it. But could we make the transition a little smoother? I think so. You must recognize that the road may not be as clear as you thought, and you may have to work at it – especially in the first couple of years in retirement.

In the literature covering retirement research, you will often read about retirement's honeymoon phase – the first few months after retiring, when excitement and euphoria run high. During this phase, retirees revel in the novelty of not working and the freedom this provides. Staying up late, waking up later, maybe a few extra rounds of golf or more time for hobbies, and an overall sense of contentment are all common. But sometimes, just below the surface and masked by the thrill of the new stage in life, there are growing relationship challenges. I call this the "un-honeymoon" phase, and these spousal issues can last a couple of years in retirement.[85] Phyllis Moen, professor at Cornell and sociology researcher, observed that "It's not being retired, but becoming retired that seems most stressful for marriages."[86] The challenge is the transition. The friction isn't caused by what you are leaving behind or even where you are going necessarily. It comes from crossing the bridge between them.

Here is how to make the transition smoother:

Negotiate expectations. In our working years, we juggled careers, kids, and life. There may have been little time left over to devote to your spouse. When there is too much to do and not enough time, our relationships are typically the first victims, followed closely by sleep. In retirement, however, we don't have the same demands on our time or schedule, which means we have a lot more available time with our partners.

This extra time can be a welcome change from your working years' hectic and chaotic schedules. A more relaxed and stress-free environment can allow you to connect or reconnect. The busyness of pre-retired life can also create a distraction from marital issues, masking relationship problems. Like so many other things in retirement, this all changes overnight. A client once remarked, "I went from this go-go schedule to a no-go schedule, instantly." Unless you fill your calendar with trips, hobbies, and activities, you will suddenly have a lot more time – and time together.

Being together is not the same as togetherness. Spending more time together can feel lonely if you are not on the same page, which requires an understanding of your needs and negotiating expectations with your partner. The work you did earlier on your needs, vision, and purpose should go a long way in understanding what moves you. Have your partner do the same exercises to gain more insight into what gives them energy and meaning. You can then look for overlap of interests and passions.

Unsurprisingly, research has found that we can smooth the retirement transition by participating in shared activities.[87] What activities can you do together? Which hobbies do you both enjoy? This is an easy and natural place to start. For some it's playing golf, and for others, it's overlanding. I had one client who was an avid tennis player. He played several times a week before he retired and even more afterward. His wife didn't enjoy tennis, though. They talked and discovered they both had an interest in learning how to golf. Since he had a lot more time in retirement, he could learn to golf without sacrificing time playing tennis. After a year of doing both, he discovered that, while he still loved tennis, he also loved spending time on the course, bonding with his wife over bad shots and not having the sore knees that accompanied an afternoon of tennis. They now travel to golf courses all over the world together.

What fun, exciting, and adventurous activities can you and your partner do together?

What aspects of your vision for the future are similar? Even if you both do the vision exercise and find that you each have very different views of the future, look past the differences and try to find some areas of similarity, however small they may be.

I once worked with a married couple who seemingly had very different ideas of their retirement future. She wanted to stay near their children and grandchildren, while he wanted to move to Florida and get a place on the beach. They seemed like two very different plans, but similarities were lurking below the surface. Both spouses valued time spent with their grandchildren. They both enjoyed sailing. They were both deeply concerned about the environment and wanted to make a difference. These similarities were more than enough for them to negotiate and construct a life in retirement that met their needs, which included buying a small beach cottage, volunteering together, and spending ample time with the grandkids at their house and their cottage.

Do you share the same impossible dreams? What adventures can you go on together? One of my clients likes to take big adventure trips through countries around the world – things like snowshoeing up mountain pikes, ice climbing, and whitewater rafting. His wife? Not as much. Did this create a problem in retirement? Not at all. They negotiated. Sometimes, she participates in the adventures – the ones that stretch her comfort zone without breaking it – and other times she travels with him but doesn't do the adventure part. Instead, they'll stay another week or two in the country and turn it into a shared vacation that often includes several visits to wineries – one of her passions.

Do you have a similar vision for the impact you want to have on the future? Is there a cause about which you both feel passionate? After my wife and I lost our son eight months into the pregnancy, we found a shared cause. We became board members of a nascent non-profit organization helping couples deal with pregnancy and infant loss. Can you and your spouse volunteer together? Can you join an organization? Can you host an annual fundraiser? Do you both feel so passionately about something that you want to start your own organization?

If you discover that you can't get enough of each other and find great fulfillment in spending all of your time together, more power to you. Keep in mind, however, that you don't *have* to do everything together. In fact, believing you must be glued together may be doing you more harm than good. Marriage therapists suggest that it is normal and healthy to have a mix of things you do together and things you each do separately. The trick is to get on the same page, though. Failure to do so can lead to unmet expectations.

Imagine you've worked for the last 40 years, and in retirement, you have dreams of fishing, taking adventure trips with your buddies, and playing golf a few times a week. Seems reasonable. Now, let's imagine that your stay-at-home spouse has been waiting for your retirement so you could spend more time in the garden, read together, and go on walks. Seems reasonable, as well. But it doesn't take much of an imagination to see that these conflicting expectations might lead to hurt feelings, resentment, or likely both.

Imagine a different scenario. This time, you are retiring, but you don't have any obvious interests or hobbies. You putter around the house and watch a lot of TV. Your spouse, however, isn't used to having someone at home all the time and must adjust to your constant presence. Again, different expectations can lead to disagreements and issues.

These are just a couple of scenarios that are all too common in retirement, but there are limitless variations that can contribute to a less-than-ideal relationship. Again, this section isn't meant to resolve issues – just to raise them so you can be prepared.

Reconnect. Some clients benefit from entering retirement with an open and curious mindset regarding their partner. Even though they may have been together for years, even decades, and have maybe even raised a family together, they may not be the same people as when they first met. Rarely are the changes radical, but nevertheless, they can be significant. A husband once remarked, "I thought I knew my wife, but I had an outdated view. I needed to see her as she is today and not what she was." Okay, I lied. No husband has ever said that, but you get the idea.

Priorities, needs, and interests naturally change over time. Get to know your spouse. Get curious about what they want and need to experience a fulfilling relationship and an amazing retirement. You may think you know – and maybe you do – but in my experience and research, it helps to have an open and curious mindset.

You can explore together, or you may benefit from doing group workshops or even marital coaching. What's marital coaching? The term "marriage counseling" feels pejorative – like there is something wrong that needs to be fixed. "Coaching" communicates quite the opposite. Instead of fixing what's wrong, coaching is about improving what's right. I've found that it is a much better way to think of the process, and it's easier to get buy-in from couples if they view the process as making the good better instead of changing the bad.

Marital checkup. Love is in the air – or is it? How strong is your marriage or relationship with your significant other? You may think you know, but are you sure? What would your spouse say? Your marital relationship's strength is more important than any investment you'll ever make. It can influence not only your well-being but your health. Marital strain can erode physical health, compromise immunity, and be linked to depression.[88] The "good" news – at least for retirees – is that the divorce rate for those younger than 50 is about twice as high as it is for older adults. The bad news, though, is that the divorce rate for those over 50 has roughly doubled since the 1990s. One of my married clients joked, "Even though I stopped working, I can still get fired. It's called divorce!"

Marriage therapists will be the first to say that divorce doesn't happen overnight – it's usually a slow and gradual process. One strategy they recommend is having frequent marital check-ins, just as you might with your health or even your money. You can go to a doctor to get a physical that will determine your current level of health with great accuracy – everything from your BMI to your cholesterol level, blood pressure, bone density, and more. The same holds true with your finances. It's just as easy to get a snapshot of your current financial health by calculating your net worth and cash flow.

But when it comes to our relationships, we often don't have a clue. Wouldn't it be nice to have a checkup? Here's where we can learn a few things from the business world. Every quarter, public companies disclose the previous three months' sales and income. As an investor, this gives you a clear snapshot of how the company did, what went well, and what went wrong. There is no guessing. The numbers don't lie. A couple of bad years for a stock, and the board may fire the CEO. A couple of bad years in a relationship and you-know-who might get replaced!

There's an old saying: "What you measure, you can improve." I recommend that you schedule a quarterly date with your spouse to measure what is and isn't working in your relationship – call it a quarterly marriage report. Why not just go with your gut? Because your gut is wrong. Has your spouse ever been upset with you for something, and you had no idea? Or have you ever been upset with your spouse, unbeknownst to them? It's not enough to "feel good" about the relationship. You need to test it. But how?

Asking your partner "We good?" in the few seconds before Netflix auto-plays the next episode just isn't sufficient. There are many useful assessments can help you gauge your relationship's health, including the Couples Satisfaction Index, Marital Adjustment Test, and the Relationship Assessment Scale.[89] Assessments like these can be helpful because they can bring minor issues to the surface before they become major problems.

Take the relationship partner assessment a few times a year to stay on track.

I'd also recommend scheduling an hour-long session with a marriage counselor every three months. This can be done in person or using an online service. Visit BadassRetirement.com for a list of online counseling apps/services. A small amount of time and money could prove to be a valuable investment in your relationship. It can also be helpful to have an expert review your assessment results and help resolve any issues that arise.

Retire together. If you and your spouse/partner haven't retired yet and are considering a staggered retirement where one spouse retires months or even years after the first, you may want to reconsider. The research suggests that spouses tend to do better when they retire together.[90] There can be a host of financial benefits to staggering spousal retirements, but if you have the financial resources, the relational benefits of retiring together may outweigh the monetary benefits of doing it separately. In fact, a long gap can easily lead to decreased retirement satisfaction. If you think about it, it makes sense. If one spouse is retired and the other isn't, it can be hard to travel together or do shared activities. Some people navigate this effectively and find no problem with this arrangement, but others struggle with it. For financial reasons, it may be better for you to work a little longer and for your spouse to retire a little sooner. If you have a choice about who retires first, the research suggests that the man should be the one who works longer (sorry, gentlemen!).[91] If you are considering retiring a year or more before your spouse, think this through.

Your relationships are the cornerstone of living a Badass Retirement. Your friends and loved ones will raise your hand to help you celebrate the good days and hold your hand to comfort you on the bad days. They will make your life richer and provide you with meaning throughout your retirement.

Even if you manage to maintain strong relationships, there is still another fear that can crush your retirement happiness: worrying that you're going to run out of money.

It is impossible to truly enjoy your retirement if you are worried about money. Money insecurity will impact every area of your life – your happiness, health, and relationships. Retirement success is made possible by total financial security and confidence.

The next section is focused on creating Total Financial Security, which is one of the **Badass 5** drivers to living a retirement free of financial worry. You'll learn how to create a lifetime of income, maximize your investment portfolio's longevity, and de-risk your finances.

JOIN THE FAMILY

One of the most important things you can do to create a meaningful and fulfilling retirement is finding your tribes — those who get you and to whom you feel connected. If you are dedicated to improving your life in retirement, we want you to become part of our tribe by joining the Badass Retirement Community.

GO TO **BADASSRETIREMENT.COM**

SECTIONS

MAGNIFY

MINDSET

MEANING

MONEY

MOMENTUM

10

CHALLENGE

Create
Lifetime Income

Effective strategies to generate steady
income you can count on throughout
retirement.

CHALLENGE 10

Congratulations. You just left the only steady source of income you've ever known.

When you retire, you don't just leave work. You leave behind a stable source of income. You don't just let go of a paycheck. You let go of financial security. It's common to hear that retirement is a transition, but it's also a disruption for many. For decades, you benefited from and relied on a steady supply of income, and every couple weeks like clockwork, the deposit of new funds arrived in your account. Over your working years, the income you earned paid for your house and utilities, cars and insurance premiums, food and fun. The income funded not just your lifestyle but your life. And then you retired.

Overnight, the income stops and the fear starts.

What's your biggest concern about retirement? Money, right? Specifically, you do not want to run out of money. This is the number one fear reflected in the results of every retirement survey I've ever seen, with upwards of 90% or more retirees admitting that running out of money worries them.[92] And it's not just an occasional worry. It's pervasive for a huge swath of retirees.

How would you answer the question, "Which do you fear the most, outliving your money in retirement or death?" According to one survey, 61% of respondents said they were more afraid of running out of money than dying![93] It makes sense. The thought of running out of money is absolutely frightening. Your entire world would be turned upside down if you no longer had the income to pay your bills and support yourself.

Without enough income, it's difficult to experience a rewarding retirement. Money may not solve all your problems, but it sure can help by providing options and freedom. Money can give you the power to shape your life on your terms. It can purchase food, stability, security, shelter, education, and medicine. This is why the path to Total Financial Security begins with creating lifetime income.

USING MONEY > SPENDING MONEY

You get to use money to improve your life. Let that sink in. You can use your savings and assets to experience more, achieve more, and become more. This sounds obvious, but you'd be surprised how many retirees do not enjoy the fruits of their labor. Some spend it lavishly on things that neither improve their life nor provide much joy. Others become too worried about using their money. Paradoxically, hoarding money and keeping a tight grip around it doesn't provide more financial security. It often does just the opposite. Of course, you want to be smart about your money – knowing what you can afford and not afford – but as long as you are not jeopardizing your finances you should freely use it to improve your life.

Invest it in your health – eat better food, hire a trainer, get preventive medical tests, use a health coach, hire a masseuse to come to the house once a week, work with a nutritionist, sign-up for a healthy meal service, buy supplements, invest in smart health devices, get a better bed, etc.

Invest in your personal growth – take courses, hire a private language tutor, work with a golf pro, start a new hobby, take martial arts lessons, etc.

Invest in experiences – take your family on a cruise, hike to Machu Picchu, visit the outer edge of the atmosphere in a space balloon, learn how to ice climb, drive Alaska's Dalton Highway to the Arctic Circle, etc.

Invest in people and projects that make an impact – start a non-profit, donate to causes you care about, help your kid start a business, etc.

This is money well used.

This Challenge will help you create a lifetime of income, allowing you to worry less about running out of money and enjoy your Badass Retirement more.

INCOME > ASSETS

Everything changes. That seems to be the theme of entering retirement. To live a Badass Retirement, you need to think differently. You need to elevate your retirement view, reimagine what you're capable of accomplishing, and adopt a more proactive mindset. One of the other ways in which you need to recalibrate your thinking concerns money. How you thought about money in your working years allowed you to create the retirement portfolio you have today. What worked so well pre- retirement, however, may not serve you as well when you are living it.

For your entire adult life, you had one financial goal: convert income into assets. That was the winning financial formula. Success was a function of how well you could exchange the income you earned from work for investment assets. And for those who are still working, that really is the formula for financial success.

WORKING YEARS

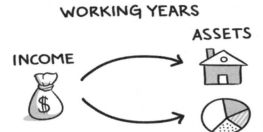

In your working years the focus was on converting your earned income into financial assets.

In retirement the financial formula doesn't just change, it gets reversed. Financial success in retirement is contingent on your ability to successfully convert assets into income.

RETIREMENT

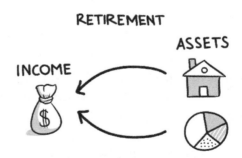

In retirement, the focus needs to be on converting financial assets back into an income stream.

There's only one problem: it's not easy to do.

We lack experience and knowledge. Workers have become experts at converting income into assets, but retirees have little idea how to convert assets into income. For every 1,000 books or resources on building *assets*, you may find one focused on creating *income*. In fact, the entire financial industry is built around helping you save excess income. The message they promote is that they will help you save for your future, but what they're really teaching is how to convert your income into assets. Your 401(k) is the perfect example of this in action. It makes converting part of your income into assets so easy, you don't even have to do anything – it happens automatically every paycheck. When you're working, progress is easy to establish – just look at your growing account balance each month. The size of your retirement portfolio defines success.

What's success in retirement? *Lifetime* income. Not 10 good years of income. Not 20 years. Lifetime. Why income? Because income is how you pay the mortgage and insurance premiums, buy groceries and prescriptions, and afford your hobbies, trips, and adventures. Retirement runs on income – not assets.

This focus on income requires a mental shift in retirement. Although you may have become adept at converting income into assets, if you are like most retirees, you have no experience and likely no clue how to properly convert those assets into lifetime income. That's okay. I've been helping clients do this for nearly 30 years, and I can help you.

Let's tackle this challenge together!

INCOME PRIORITIES

I like to tell clients that income in retirement needs to have "ESP." No, I don't mean mind reading or the ability to see into the future. Retirement runs on income, but not just any income. Your retirement income needs to be *Escalating*, *Sustainable*, and *Predictable*.

Escalating

When I was a kid, I had to walk to school in three feet of snow in June, uphill both ways. Okay, that might be a bit of an exaggeration. But when your grandpa complained about paying $15 for a movie or

$10 for a hamburger because "movies were a nickel and hamburgers were a dime" when he was younger, it may not have been such an exaggeration.

It's called inflation, and it results in the erosion of buying power. It's like carbon monoxide – silent, traceless, and invisible. Slowly and gradually, your savings are worth less and less. If you can comfortably live on $10,000 a month today, there is a very low chance you will be able to live on the same amount 20 or even 10 years from now. Things like healthcare, groceries, travel, prescriptions, and utilities get more expensive with time. If your $10,000 a month income stays static while everything around you becomes more expensive, the $10,000 will buy less and less with each passing year.

Nobody wants to reduce their expenses and lifestyle as they age in retirement. The goal for your retirement income should be to retain its buying power. In short, you need it to escalate at least as much as inflation does each year. It might be $10,000 a month the first year, but by year 10 your income should have increased to an amount closer to $13,500 a month. This is what I mean by escalating.

Sustainable

A financial advisor tells a couple, "I've run the numbers and the good news is you can afford to cover all of your living expenses in retirement." The clients reply, "That's great! What's the bad news?" The advisor replies, "You'll run out of money in three years."

Your retirement income needs to last a lifetime. How long is a lifetime? I don't know. If we knew, it would make financial retirement planning a lot easier. But because we don't, we must assume your income will need to last a long time. While the worst outcome is running out of money early in retirement, the second-worst outcome is running out of money later in retirement.

I may not know anything about you, but I guarantee you do not want to run out of money. After all, that's the most important objective in retirement financial planning!

Your retirement income needs to be sustainable. It needs to last your lifetime – however long that may be.

Predictable

One of pre-retirement's advantages was income stability. Unless you worked solely on commissions, your income was predictable. You knew how much you were going to get each month, and you could plan around it. The predictability gave you control. You knew what you could save and spend with a great deal of certainty.

Imagine if, in retirement, you got $12,534 one month, $3,985 the next, $7,320 the following, and a different amount every month thereafter? How would you know what you could spend if you never knew how much money you were getting? Should you live it up in the good months and then cut back for the leaner months? It would be financial chaos and you'd never be able to have any financial confidence. It would be a terrible way to live.

Your retirement income needs to be predictable. You need to know how much you are getting, not just this month, but next month and next year. Your retirement income needs the same stability from which you benefited during your working years.

In summary, the best retirement income is escalating, sustainable, and predictable. That certainly sounds good, but how do you achieve it?

There are three broad sources of retirement income – each with its advantages and disadvantages. The best retirement income plans are composed of a mixture of these three sources:

1. Investment Portfolio
2. Stable Sources
3. Alternative Sources

#1 - INCOME FROM INVESTMENT PORTFOLIO

The foundation and the largest source of income for most high-net-worth retirees is their investment portfolio, while the less affluent will rely more on Social Security as their primary source of income (more on how to maximize Social Security later in this Challenge). Still, for many retirees, the money they receive from their portfolio dwarfs all other sources of retirement income.

At first glance, earning income from your investments is easy to understand – you simply withdraw money from your portfolio. But it's important not to let the simplicity deceive you. As simple as it is to understand, it is equally difficult to execute successfully. It may be one of the most challenging things to do in finance. But don't take my word for it.

William Sharpe, a Ph.D.-holding economist at Stanford University and winner of the Nobel Prize in Economics, described spending down assets in retirement as "the nastiest, hardest problem in finance." Why should we care what Dr. Sharpe has to say about retirement planning?

For one thing, he is one of the originators of the Capital Asset Pricing Model – basically, the model investors use to measure risk and reward.

His comment surprised the investment and retirement planning community because there are countless challenging issues related to finance. Nobody expected him to say that the most significant, most challenging problem is figuring out how best to draw income from an investment portfolio in retirement.

Why is creating a sustainable retirement income distribution plan so difficult? The answer, in a word, is *uncertainty*.

To create a perfect retirement income plan, you would need to accurately predict several important variables in the future. But of course, we don't know what the future holds. We can only make informed decisions based on educated assumptions based on the data we have today. Due to the future's uncertainty, we can't know if our decisions were optimal until we witness their results.

There are several significant questions we can't definitively answer when someone is ready to retire, such as:

- How many years will you be retired?
- What average annual investment return will your portfolio produce?
- What is the sequence of investment returns that will produce the average annual return?
- What will income and capital gains tax rates be in the future?
- Will there be large and unexpected expenses, and if so, what will they cost?
- What will the rate of inflation be each year in retirement?
- How much will your living expenses be each year in retirement?

These are just a few issues that make creating a sustainable stream of retirement income difficult. Challenging? Yes. Impossible? No. There is a solution. It's called the Lifetime Retirement Income Solution and it includes three steps:

(1) Lifetime Retirement Income Percentage

(2) Lifetime Retirement Income Portfolio

(3) Lifetime Retirement Income Paycheck

The Lifetime Retirement Income Solution attempts to eradicate fears and uncertainty while providing a stable and predictable lifetime stream of income in retirement.

Step 1: Lifetime Retirement Income *Percentage*

If you are nearing retirement or are already retired, chances are you've heard of the 4% rule for determining how much money you can withdraw from your portfolio in retirement. But what does the 4% rule really mean? A few years ago, I conducted an informal survey for a podcast episode and *Forbes* column, asking retirees and retirement advisors what they knew about the rule. Almost everyone had heard of the 4% rule, but there was a lot of misunderstanding and uncertainty about what it meant. Most people said it was the percentage of money you could withdraw from your retirement portfolio and never run out of money. That is definitely not what the 4% rule means.

I shared 17 surprising facts about the 4% rule in a *Forbes* column, but here are the top four things you need to know.[94]

1. **Limited time frame.** The 4% rule was initially calculated using a 30-year retirement time frame. Many mistakenly think the portfolio will never run out of money, but the study only accounted for 30 years of retirement.

2. **Calculating 4%.** One of the most frequent misconceptions about this rule is how to calculate the 4%. Nearly everyone (yes, even other financial advisors) thinks the 4% rule means that you could withdraw 4% of the balance of your investments each year in retirement. For example, if you had

$1 million, you could pull $40,000 from the account. If the portfolio had grown to $1.1 million the next year, the belief was that you could then take $44,000 in that second year (4% of $1.1 million). In essence, you do the same calculation each year to determine how much you can withdraw.

This is not, however, how the 4% rule is calculated. Instead, you only calculate 4% of the investment balance *once*, in the first year of retirement. Whatever amount you derive becomes your annual income throughout retirement (plus inflation – see #3 below). Using the example above, you could withdraw $40,000 the first year of retirement. At the start of the second year, your investment balance doesn't matter. You still withdraw $40,000 – even if your account is worth $1.1 million or $900,000.

3. **Inflation protection.** The money you withdraw from your retirement investments will lose purchasing power because of inflation, which makes the cost of most products and services go up over time. The 4% rule takes this into consideration by allowing retirees to increase their initial 4% in accordance with the inflation rate each year. Continuing the $40,000 example above, if we assume that the inflation rate was 2.7% during the first year, you could actually withdraw $41,080 ($40,000 initial withdrawal amount + 2.7% inflation rate) in the second year.

4. **Asset allocation.** The original 4% rule used a retirement asset allocation of 50% stocks and 50% bonds. The S&P 500 index was used for the stock allocation, and intermediate-term government bonds were used for the bond allocation. Any other asset allocation would have returned different results.

Based on the research used to develop the 4% rule, it was found that an initial withdrawal of 4% from a portfolio was the highest withdrawal rate over the period analyzed that didn't leave the retiree broke after 30 years of withdrawals. However, in 2006, the author of the original research raised the withdrawal rate from 4% to 4.7% after including other assets classes such as international stocks and small cap stocks to the allocation. Does this mean you are guaranteed to never run out of money in retirement if you rely on the 4% (or 4.7%) rule? Unfortunately, no. It's a good place to start when thinking about how much money you can safely withdraw from your retirement portfolio, but you shouldn't rely on it exclusively.

The 4% rule should really be called the 4% *consideration* because it is not a hard and fast rule. The global economy and markets are quite different from when the 4% rule was first publicized back in 1994, before Amazon, the iPhone, and the wide adoption of the internet. As such, there is some research that suggests withdrawing 4% is too aggressive and that a safer withdrawal rate is less than 4%.[95] Even the author of the rule recently lowered the safe withdrawal rate from 4.7% down to 4.4%.[96]

Confused yet? I don't blame you! We have experts suggesting a 5% or even higher withdrawal rate will likely be safe and leave a lot of money for beneficiaries, and other experts warning that a withdrawal rate closer to 3% is as high as you should go. So, which is it? Should you stick with 4.7%, 4.4%, 4%, 3.3% or something else? It's as clear as mud as they say.

What's a retiree to do with all this conflicting (and seemingly ever-changing) guidance? First, realize that there is no one-size-fits-all approach to ensuring you have lifetime retirement income. If your retirement time horizon is 20, 30, or more years, don't blindly follow any "rule of thumb". You need to be flexible. Second, if you have sufficient assets and can live the lifestyle you desire in retirement by only withdrawing 3%, then this will provide you with greater portfolio longevity. On the other hand, if you run the numbers and can't or are unwilling to "get by" with a lower withdrawal rate, you need to create some flexibility in your finances.

One simple option is to not increase your annual withdrawal amount for inflation in any year during which your portfolio return is *negative*. Let's go through an example. If inflation went up 3.5% for the year and your portfolio return is positive, you'd adjust for this by increasing the amount you withdraw each month by 3.5%. If your monthly withdrawal amount was $10,000, then, for the next 12 months, you would increase this to $10,350. If the market and your portfolio were negative for the year, however, you would stick with the $10,000 a month withdrawal, even though inflation increased by 3.5%. If your portfolio generated a positive return the following year, you could resume the inflation adjustment and increase your monthly distribution. This easy strategy can meaningfully increase your portfolio longevity.

Another strategy is to ensure your expenses in retirement are manageable and flexible. Why? You want to be able to reduce your monthly withdrawal amount if necessary. I know having to cut back on spending in retirement isn't anyone's dream, and it is rare, but it can be necessary if the market and your portfolio experience extended declines. While the second-worst outcome is having to reduce your monthly income, the worst outcome is not being able to. This happens when a retiree's fixed expenses are so high that they cannot reduce them and must continue pulling money at a rate that puts their portfolio in jeopardy. If 90% of your expenses are fixed, you have very little opportunity to reduce the amount you must withdraw from your portfolio. If your fixed expenses are only 50%, however, you can cut your monthly income by half and still cover your fixed expenses. This financial flexibility provides a huge advantage in ensuring that you are creating income for life and that you'll never run out of money.

The 4% rule uses specific assumptions that may or may not apply to you. There are many factors to consider when determining how much you can pull from retirement accounts. A slight shift in any of these factors – which include expected investment returns, retirement length, desire for leaving an inheritance, inflation rates, and sequence of returns, among others – can make a big difference in your overall retirement income plan.

So, what's better than the 4% rule? The chicken rule.

Chicken Rule > 4% Rule

I'll never forget a conversation I had with a client many years ago. I'm 15 minutes into explaining the 4% rule and retirement income planning when my client stops me mid-sentence and says, "So, basically, don't kill the chicken." I pause. I pause some more. She looks at me like I'm an idiot, and I look at her like she's crazy. Guess who was right?

My client explains, "Your chicken lays eggs. Those eggs are like income. If you try to get in there and get more eggs, you'll kill the chicken, and then she can't produce any more eggs for you."

What a great metaphor – your portfolio will produce for you, but if you spend it down, it can't keep up.

So, in the end, my client was right, and I was the one that looked like a fool. It was definitely worth it, though, to hear her chicken and egg metaphor. It is a great explanation of portfolio withdrawal theory, and I've used it with clients ever since.

The income you withdraw from your portfolio to live on in retirement is only as secure as the portfolio's health and longevity. What determines the health of an investment portfolio? It's asset allocation.

Step 2: Lifetime Retirement Income *Portfolio*

Step two of the Lifetime Retirement Income Solution is to invest your assets using a "bucket" asset allocation. It sounds weird but stick with me on this. It's a game changer for retirees. The most challenging financial aspect for people entering retirement is the uncertainty around income and the volatility of the stock market. We've had 40 years of steady and stable paychecks every couple weeks and then – *poof* – it stops. If you've relied on the certainty and predictability of a regular income for your whole life, losing that can be difficult.

Additionally, many retirees are worried about the ups and downs (actually, the downs more than the ups) in the stock market. They worry that if there is a big drop, they may have to cut back or even run out of money. Badass Retirement shouldn't be filled with financial worries.

Here's how you and/or your financial advisor can implement the Lifetime Retirement Income Portfolio strategy to create lifetime income in retirement and a steady monthly paycheck despite any turmoil in the stock market.

Divide your investment portfolio into three "buckets." These buckets can be separate investment accounts, or they can be mental accounts. These three account buckets will be invested differently. You will have an Investment Bucket, a Low Volatility Bucket, and a Cash Bucket.

Investment Bucket

This is your general investment account, where you will have the bulk of your investments including stocks, REITs, mid to long-term bonds, precious metals, etc. Investing can be confusing, but in the next Challenge you will learn strategies on how to allocate your Investment Bucket.

Low Volatility Bucket

This account should consist of CDs, low duration bonds, and other lower risk and low volatility investments equal to about three years' worth of living expenses.

Cash Bucket

At the start of each year, your Cash Bucket should have approximately two years of living expenses in cash (e.g., money market accounts, higher yielding savings accounts).

The goal is to start each year with three years of living expenses in your Low Volatility Bucket and two years of living expenses in your Cash Bucket. As you withdraw money from your Cash Bucket each month to live, it will gradually deplete. So where do you get the cash to replenish your Cash Bucket? You take it from the Low Volatility Bucket. And where do you get the assets to replenish the Low Volatility Bucket? From the Investment Bucket.

Each year you need to shift assets down through the buckets – from Investment to Low Volatility to Cash – to ensure you have plenty of liquid and lower-risk investments to continue funding your monthly retirement paycheck.

LIFETIME RETIREMENT INCOME
PORTFOLIO

STOCKS, BONDS,
REAL ESTATE

INVESTMENT
BUCKET

REPLENISH THE
LOW VOLATILITY
BUCKET
EACH YEAR

SHORT TERM
BONDS, CDS
(3 YEARS OF
LIVING EXPENSES)

LOW
VOLATILITY
BUCKET

REPLENISH THE
CASH
BUCKET
EACH YEAR

MONEY MARKET,
CASH
(2 YEARS OF
LIVING EXPENSES)

CASH
BUCKET

Shift investment assets into low-volatility investments and cash to ensure you have plenty of income to cover your living expenses.

This seems like a lot of work to do each year. What's the advantage? There are two. One, it provides you with a steady source of cash to pay your bills and enjoy retirement. Two, it helps you stay invested. Imagine turning on your TV and seeing that the market dropped 40%. You'd immediately start to worry about how that would affect you. Would you need to cancel your upcoming trip? Would you be able to afford rent?

One of the biggest financial risks you'll face in retirement isn't the stock market dropping, it's the stock market dropping *and you selling*. Getting spooked by market volatility and getting out of the market can create short-term relief, but it also can create long-term financial consequences that can be difficult to recover from.

But when you utilize the Lifetime Retirement Income Portfolio strategy or something similar, you can catch your breath and remind yourself that you have planned for this. I can't tell you how many times I've had conversations with clients during a volatile stock market where I've reminded them they have five years' worth of living expenses in safe assets not tied to the stock market (three years in the Low Volatility Bucket plus two years in the Cash Bucket). You might have 99 problems in retirement, but a market drop shouldn't be one.

You can live the same lifestyle for five years without ever having to sell a single share of stock. That's five years for the market to recover. That's five years of comfort and security. Are there other portfolio investment strategies that *may* provide a higher return? Possibly. But what the bucket approach does is provides peace of mind and financial security. For most retirees, that's better than trying to get the highest possible investment return.

Step 3: Lifetime Retirement Income *Paycheck*

As soon as I explain the Lifetime Retirement Income Paycheck, clients immediately breathe more easily. Seriously. I've had clients audibly breathe a sigh of relief. It's amazing. They sit back in their chairs. They nod their heads. They smile. It's simple to understand and set up, but it is powerful.

There are numerous benefits to having a steady paycheck deposited into your checking account each month. For one, you can plan around it. If you know you are getting the same amount each month, you know what you can spend. Also, knowing that you get another deposit to live on and enjoy each month provides consistency and security.

The Lifetime Retirement Income Paycheck is where you have your investment custodian such as Charles Schwab or Fidelity automatically withdraw and deposit the monthly amount you calculated in Step 1 into your checking account at the start of each month. This monthly deposit mimics the salary you received while employed. Although the amount may be different, the monthly transfer's consistency will make it feel just like the paycheck you have been so used to receiving. For those larger but occasional expenses (e.g., new car) or unexpected expenses (e.g., medical bills), you can pull more from your Cash Bucket and/or your Low Volatility Bucket.

As soon as your salary stops, your Lifetime Retirement Income Paycheck can start. In fact, I often recommend starting the money transfers a month or two early so that clients can see it work and get comfortable with it even while they are still earning paychecks from their jobs.

#2 - INCOME FROM STABLE SOURCES

In the previous section, you learned about how to create income from an investment portfolio. As someone who has likely invested for decades, you don't need me to tell you that the stock market can be volatile. If the goal is to create lifetime income, relying exclusively on a capricious investment portfolio can create anxiety for some.

Fortunately, there are other, more stable sources of income that you can use to supplement your portfolio income. The three most common sources of stable income are:

1. Social Security
2. Pensions
3. Annuities

Social Security

Social Security is the most common source of stable income for retirees. The Social Security Administration estimates that 97% of retirees receive retirement benefits. On the surface, Social Security seems straightforward – in your working years, you and your employer contribute, and when you reach a certain age, you get a monthly benefit for the rest of your life. While that is accurate, it's not the full story. Social Security is actually quite complicated and knowing when to start benefits is even more challenging.

Entire books have been written to help retirees navigate Social Security benefits. A slew of software programs exist just to determine the ideal timing of Social Security for those entering retirement. This section is not meant to be a comprehensive tome on all things Social Security. If you want customized advice for when you should start Social Security benefits, consider working with a financial advisor who specializes in retirement planning, using one of the many popular online software programs, or making an appointment with a Social Security benefits specialist at your local Social Security Administration office.

There are a few important areas I've found that many retirees do not consider when thinking about their Social Security benefits. Use the following as an introduction and starting point on your journey.

Social Security Benefits Timing

When should you start receiving Social Security Retirement Benefits? This is one of the more consequential financial decisions you can make in retirement, but it doesn't get enough attention much of the time. There are generally three popular times retirees will start benefits:

Age 62. This is the earliest you can start receiving benefits. Since you are getting the benefits early, the monthly amount you receive will be the lowest amount possible. I almost always advise against starting benefits at age 62, with one exception: poor health. Social Security benefits are meant to last for the rest of your life. If you are in poor health and have a shorter life expectancy, you should consider taking benefits at the very earliest opportunity.

Full retirement age. For most retirees, Social Security defines "full retirement age" as 66 to 67 years of age. This is the age at which you can receive your full stated monthly benefits. Most retirees who don't take early benefits will wait until they reach full retirement age. Although this is a popular option, this doesn't mean it's the best one.

Age 70. This is the maximum age to which you can delay Social Security benefits. But why would you want to delay getting a monthly check until age 70? Because if you do, you'll get a larger amount. Your benefits will be considerably higher for each year you delay taking them. Your monthly check will be approximately 75% higher if you wait until you are 70 years old than it would if you started benefits at 62. If you are getting close to full retirement age and are in good health, your monthly benefit increases by about 8% for each year you wait until reaching 70. For wealthier clients who are in good health and have access to sufficient income from other sources, I strongly recommend waiting until they are 70 before starting benefits.

Spousal Considerations

If you are married and both have Social Security benefits available, you have several options. I've found that spouses tend to start their benefits when they each reach full retirement age. This may not be ideal, though, and may result in you forgoing tens or hundreds of thousands of dollars over your lifetimes without even knowing it. To avoid this fate, you'll want to determine if it makes sense for you or your spouse to file for benefits early and for the other spouse to file later.

The calculations can get complicated quickly, so it's best to plug in your data (e.g., birth dates, projected benefits, etc.) and let software crunch the numbers for you. I've run these scenarios thousands of times over the years, and I'm always surprised by the differences in the total benefits by choosing one timing strategy versus another. I can only imagine how much money most retirees leave on the table because they aren't aware of their options.

To review your options, go to BadassRetirement.com and plug in your information and/or work with a retirement financial advisor who can help you optimize your Social Security benefits.

Signing up for Medicare

You do not want to be without health insurance in retirement, but that is an all-too-common outcome. Fortunately, the solution is easy and simple. Sign up for Medicare when you turn 65. Medicare becomes your primary insurance payer, so, if you do not sign up for it at age 65, it's possible you will have a gap in your insurance coverage. The rules seem to be ever-changing. To get the most up-to-date guidelines, visit Medicare.gov or work with your financial advisor.

Badass Retirement is about enjoying retirement and not having to fret about health insurance. Mark it on your calendar to register for Medicare as you approach age 65.

Pensions

These days, pensions are rare. Fewer and fewer private companies and governmental organizations offer them to employees. Although the economics of pension plans are challenging for companies, they are an incredible vehicle of financial security for workers in retirement.

If you and/or your spouse have a pension available in retirement, you will need to select a payout option. These options are typically listed on a single page and include lump sum, single life annuity, 50% joint and survivor option, and life with 10 years certain, among others. The form often looks innocuous and is mixed with several other forms you need to complete before you start receiving your pension benefits. Some HR departments are excellent about explaining the various options and helping the employee figure out what is best for them, but

I wouldn't count on it. You need to know what you're looking at, since your payout decision has significant long-term financial consequences, and you cannot change your mind after your benefits start.

Properly evaluating which of the dozen or so options is best for you will depend on your and your spouse's health, your ages, and your overall financial situations. There are circumstances where a lump sum payout is the best choice and other times when the 50% joint and survivor option or 100% lifetime annuity are better.

If you have a pension, do not make a fast or uninformed decision regarding the payout option. Take your time. Work with a financial advisor – even for a couple of hours – so they can analyze each of the options and help you decide what makes the most sense for you.

Annuities

Annuities are (almost) universally despised. They are notorious for their excessive fees and mind-numbing complexity. I'm confident writing that *most* annuities are absolute trash for retirees, though certain ones can be valuable tools for creating lifetime income. So, which is it? Are annuities a curse or a blessing? The short answer is . . . yes.

I could write an entire book about annuities. There are so many different options that it would make your head spin, but let's touch on a couple of the main ideas. An annuity is an investment where you contribute money and hope for a return. An annuity is different from other investments in that some annuities provide certain guarantees. For example, the annuity company (an insurance company) will guarantee a certain minimum rate of return. They might say, "Invest your money in our annuity, and we'll give you a 5% return each year," kind of like a CD investment. They might also guarantee a certain amount of income for as long as you live, similar to Social Security, so no matter how long you live, you keep getting a check in the mail. Again, there are many different flavors of annuities, but the guarantees set annuities apart from most other investments.

The most common types of annuities are:

Fixed. Fixed annuities offer the least risk and the most predictable income. The insurance company providing the annuity guarantees a certain fixed interest rate. For example, if the fixed rate on your annuity is 5%, it doesn't matter what happens in the stock market or if interest rates go lower. The annuity will continue to pay 5% each year. Their consistency and non-correlation to economic recessions or declines in the stock market set this type of annuity apart from other annuities and other investments. You pay for that stability, however, in the form of lower and fixed returns over time.

Variable. A variable annuity doesn't have a fixed rate of interest that it will pay out. Instead, the rate will vary based on an investment portfolio's performance. Variable annuities have more risk because the interest they pay can decrease, but there is also more opportunity for growth.

Indexed. Indexed annuities – also called equity-indexed annuities – share characteristics of both fixed and variable annuities. They provide a minimum guaranteed interest rate and an interest rate linked to an investment index, such as the S&P 500. If the index does well, it's possible that the annuity's value can increase. If the index declines, the annuity typically has a floor under which its value cannot fall. The marketing of indexed annuities suggests that investors get the benefits of stock market gains with the protection of not losing money if the market drops. All gains and no losses surely seems too good to be true. And it is. Insurance companies are in the business of making money, so you can bet that there are all kinds of rules and caveats in these policies. For example, I had a client who had previously purchased an indexed annuity. Each year, the client received an annual statement that showed how the annuity performed. When I reviewed the statement, I thought there was a mistake. The annuity was supposed to participate in the growth of the S&P 500, and because the S&P 500 was up nearly 20% the previous year, I expected to see a nice return for the client. Instead, I saw that the annuity produced a return of just 0.24% for the year.

No, not 24% – just 0.24%. That was less than a quarter of 1% return for the entire year. To make matters worse, the annuity assessed a rider fee that wiped out their return completely. Even though the index this annuity was tied to returned nearly 20% for the year, the annuity returned -0.78%. I had to call the insurance company to get them to explain how that was possible. It's all in how they calculate the index returns, which is obviously very favorable for the insurance company. Not all indexed annuity contracts are written so poorly, but they are often complicated. The marketing is very enticing, but you must be very careful if you are considering this type of annuity.

While I'm not a fan of most annuities, they can still make sense as part of an overall lifetime income strategy. Although they offer the least growth, fixed annuities provide guarantees that can be an excellent supplement to an investment portfolio income plan.

If you are interested in exploring whether an annuity may make sense for you, don't talk to an insurance annuity advisor. Work with a fee-only financial advisor who can evaluate different annuities and who isn't compensated based on whether you buy one or not. Remember the adage *If you're a hammer, everything looks like a nail.* For insurance and annuity salespeople, everything can be solved with an annuity or life insurance policy – even when it can't.

#3 - INCOME FROM ALTERNATIVE SOURCES

We've covered the most common sources of income in retirement – portfolio income, Social Security, pensions, and annuities. But that doesn't mean there aren't other notable sources available, including real estate and reverse mortgages.

Real Estate

The most popular alternative source of income is real estate – and for good reason. Real estate can provide everything we want for retirement income. Remember ESP? Income from real estate covers all three requirements: it's escalating, sustainable, and predictable. In fact, it's hard to consider real estate as an "alternative" source of income, but few retirees think about it when building their lifetime income plans.

There are dozens of different real estate types, but you should appreciate the difference between developed and undeveloped land if your goal is income.

Undeveloped land – also called "raw" land – means land with no manmade structures on it. Drive out to the middle of the desert or forest, and you'll find raw, undeveloped land. Drive down the block, and if you see an empty plot of land with nothing on it, that is also undeveloped land.

On the other hand, developed land has some manmade structure on it – maybe a house, an apartment building, a strip mall, a Starbucks, or a parking lot. All these things were constructed and put on the formerly raw land.

For retirees, the biggest difference between developed and undeveloped land is that you don't earn income on undeveloped land. You aren't going to earn rent by just owning it. In fact, it will cost you to own raw land because of property taxes and other expenses. There is also much greater risk with raw land because you won't earn rent until you first build something there and rent it out.

If you invest in developed land, on the other hand, the building or structure is already there. There may even already be a business present, with renters who can pay you money. You could start earning income immediately. For example, if you buy an apartment building today, you could start earning rent checks from tenants as early as next month.

How else can you think about real estate? There are three main types: residential, commercial, and industrial.

RESIDENTIAL
- SINGLE FAMILY
- MULTI-FAMILY

COMMERCIAL
- OFFICES
- RETAIL

INDUSTRIAL
- WAREHOUSING
- MANUFACTURING

The many different types of investment real estate.

These are the three main categories, but there are certainly others, which are often hybrids of these. For example, think about a hotel. It's residential in that people sleep there, but it's also commercial. Or think about self-storage. It has similarities to commercial real estate, but also a bit industrial.

Each type of real estate has unique characteristics, and they are going to perform differently. If you own a single-family house and rent it, you'll get a monthly check in the mail, but you may also get a call at 3 a.m. about a plumbing issue. Compare that to a large office building. You're unlikely to get the proverbial 3 a.m. plumbing call, but you'll have different challenges.

I have many clients who receive income in retirement from their real estate holdings – everything from office buildings to apartment complexes, public storage units, industrial buildings, warehouses, trailer park land, and even single-family homes they rent on long- or short-term bases (i.e., through Airbnb). Some manage the properties themselves, and others hire property managers to help offset some of the work. The clients love the predictable rent checks and the fact that the rents increase to keep up with inflation over time. In many locations, the clients have earned nice investment returns from the monthly income they receive, and the value of their property has also increased. Remember, however, that no investment is perfect.

There have been times when clients didn't receive tenant checks or their property was vacant while they tried to find a new tenant. Delayed rent payments and even no payments are possible – think about the rent moratorium enacted during 2020 and 2021 in some areas because of Covid-19. Retirees counting on rental income for their living expenses had to scramble if their tenants stopped paying rent.

Some retirees make the case that they want to enjoy retirement and not worry about broken pipes or dealing with unhappy tenants. If you want a hands-off real estate income investment, a triple net lease may be a good fit.

Triple Net Lease (NNN) Real Estate

Consider a triple net lease if you are looking for a real estate investment with virtually no management needed. A triple net lease – often abbreviated NNN – is a term for an investment where the tenant is responsible for all expenses, such as property taxes, building insurance, maintenance, etc. The owner (you) is freed from paying any expenses related to the building. Under a true triple net lease, if there is a storm and your building's roof is damaged, the tenant would pay to get it fixed. If the AC unit breaks, the tenant is responsible.

I've had many clients invest in triple net lease real estate projects over the past several decades. Their experience has ranged from good to excellent. It's an ideal investment for retirees because of the hands-off nature and because of the escalating, sustainable, and predictable income it generates.

Triple net lease investments can make a lot of sense, but they are neither perfect nor right for everyone. As with any real estate investment, your money is tied up until you sell the property, which can take time – especially if real estate is in a slump. You will also pay a commission of 5% or more when you sell. The tenant can go bankrupt and/or stop paying rent. Additionally, as with other forms of income-producing real estate, the property's value can be closely tied to and fluctuate with broader interest rates. This means your property's value could decrease simply because interest rates rise over time. Knowing and considering these risks (and others) is important if you consider NNN investing.

As with any investment, it makes sense to understand and evaluate all the risks. This is where you can lean on professional tax, legal, and financial teams to help you analyze the investment. Although there are unique risks with real estate investing and specifically with NNN investments, they can provide stable and recurring income throughout retirement.

I've analyzed hundreds of NNN real estate offers for and with clients. Some have been for commercial office spaces, such as medical buildings and office buildings, but most have been in the retail and fast-food areas. For example, I have a client who owns a couple of nationally branded convenience stores on the East Coast. The tenant is a large international company with strong financials and an excellent credit rating. On the first of every month, my client gets a large deposit into his checking account, and the deposit keeps growing over time because of rent escalators built into the lease agreement. This income covers nearly all his living expenses, and it requires no management from my client.

Another client owns a couple of fast-food properties. Remember, these are NNN investments, so she doesn't operate the fast-food stores and is not a franchisee. Instead, she simply owns the building and the land. The fast-food operator pays her rent. Her properties are diversified geographically – in different states – and diversified financially, with each tenant being part of a different company. Every month, she receives three deposits into her checking account that cover almost half of her retirement living expenses. Before the NNN investments, she owned a mid-sized apartment complex. Although she had an on-site manager, managing the property still required considerable time. She wanted something that produced ESP income but didn't want the headaches of management.

If you are interested in exploring NNN properties, find a good commercial agent specializing in this area. Learn the language of these deals so you can analyze and compare different properties. After reviewing so many deals and helping clients negotiate and purchase properties, I've learned a few things that seem to separate the great NNN investments from the good ones.

Cap rates. Cap rates – or capitalization rates – are interest rates you earn on your investment. You can think of them like the interest rate you might earn on a money market account or CD. The higher the cap rate, the higher the amount of rent you will earn from your investment. For example, if you buy a $1 million NNN property and the cap rate is 6%, you will earn $5,000 a month or $60,000 per year in rent. Cap rates can differ dramatically across properties depending on various factors, such as location, tenant quality, length of the lease term, and others. Higher cap rates typically suggest there is more risk.

Increasing rents. One of our goals for retirement income is that it escalates at least at the pace of inflation. One of the advantages of most NNN investments is that rents increase over time – either every year or, more commonly, every several years. Look for properties where rents increase at least as much as inflation, which will ensure that the rent dollars you receive from your tenant in 15 years have the same purchasing power as they do today.

Valuation. An NNN property's value is a combination of two factors: (1) the rental income and (2) the physical land and building. Sometimes, the investment's value is skewed more toward one or the other. For example, one client purchased an NNN investment in a remote part of Arkansas. The investment was nothing more than a concrete building – a big box. The tenant was a national company with strong financials and 12 years remaining on their rental agreement. The investment was valued at over $1 million. During the due diligence, I calculated that the land was worth less than $100,000 and the building itself was worth no more than $300,000. So, why was the property selling for three times the actual intrinsic value? The price was based on the future stream of rental income over the next 12 years. In comparison, I reviewed a fast-food NNN investment located in the heart of Nashville, Tennessee. The location was busy and growing. The tenant was also large and stable. The cap rate was considerably lower because more value was placed on the land and building versus the income stream. The advantage of the higher cap rate investment – such as the big box in the middle of nowhere – is that you get a larger monthly deposit, but as the lease term comes to an end, the property may not be worth very much. The advantage of the fast-food restaurant in the middle of a thriving city is that, even when the rental term comes to an end, the owner will likely be able to sell the property for a good price. Of course, the disadvantage is that the monthly rent payment will be lower.

Location. Not surprisingly, location is an important factor with NNN investments. I've reviewed deals in the most obscure places in the United States – towns I'd never heard of in counties I didn't know existed in states I've never been to. Most NNN marketing brochures will have several pages on town demographics, population, income, etc., providing an important glimpse into the location. I've had clients invest in remote locations, but I'm always much more comfortable when they choose more popular and populated sites. A NNN is still real estate, and we all know that location matters in real estate. Don't let higher monthly rental income tempt you into going to lesser-known places. Stick with larger areas that are growing.

Tenant creditworthiness. Most new NNN properties have rental agreements spanning between 10 and 20 years. This means that your tenant agrees to pay you rent for a decade or two into the future. The last thing you want is for a tenant go bankrupt a few years into the lease and leave you scrambling to find another tenant. One way to mitigate this risk is to ensure that your tenant is financially stable, will be in business, and can make monthly payments for the entire term of the agreement. If you start looking at NNN investments in the retail or fast-food space, you are bound to come across three types of tenant guarantees: individual, franchisee, and corporate.

An *individual* tenant guarantee is the weakest. The "guarantee" is often nothing more than a single tenant's signature promising to continue paying rent. If they default, there is very little recourse, and you will be stuck with an empty property until you can find a new tenant.

A *franchisee* tenant is typically a company that owns two or more franchises. For example, most McDonald's you drive by are not owned and operated by the McDonald's company. Instead, they are owned and operated by franchisees – individuals or groups of people who have invested in a McDonald's franchise. Some franchisees operate a couple of locations, but others may operate hundreds. I would hesitate to trust my retirement income to a franchisee who operates just a handful of locations, preferring my tenant to own and operate hundreds. That way, if they fail at the location I own, their other locations are likely to continue to do well and they can continue to pay rent even if they vacate my property.

A *corporate* guarantee is typically the strongest because the main corporation's full creditworthiness backs it. Instead of dealing with a small franchisee owner, your tenancy agreement is with the larger company – for example, McDonald's or 7-11.

Think about the industry. The world is rapidly changing. What was essential and popular just a few years ago may be a relic today (e.g., shopping malls, office buildings, movie theaters). This poses a challenge for NNN investors, given that the leases are often for 10, 20, or even more years. Who's to say your tenant who is financially strong and successful today will be in business a decade from now? In the past, when industries were more stable, it was easier to feel comfortable selecting long-term tenants. Now? You need to be careful. For example, a client was interested in exploring NNN investment properties, so we engaged a commercial agent specializing in these types of transactions. He would email us dozens of properties from across the country every morning – retail, fast-food, commercial, parking lots, and more. One industry, however, kept coming up over and over – automotive. Think nationally recognized companies focused on oil changes, auto parts, or gas stations. The terms of these deals were attractive, complete with high cap rates, long-term leases, strong financial guarantees, escalating rents, and good locations. The properties checked off all the boxes – except one. Will this business or industry exist in a decade? With the growth of electric vehicles, it's not just possible but probable that we will need a lot fewer oil changes, auto parts, and gas stations in the future. You don't want to commit to a tenant that may not exist for the full term of your lease.

Go national. Clients are often tempted to go for something nearby, but I always recommend broadening the search to the national level. There can be a much greater selection of deals nationally, as well as more diversified tenants. Since NNN investments require very little oversight, distance isn't a problem. Additionally, you may get tax benefits if you own property and earn income from a different state.

Tax breaks. Among the benefits of owning real estate are the many potential tax breaks from which you could benefit including depreciation and 1031 tax-deferred exchanges. You'll want to work with a competent tax advisor to help guide you, and I recommend doing the tax benefit analysis *before* you purchase. It's also better to know what your tax situation is going to be before you commit.

Environmental issues. Although NNN investments are generally hands-off, you (and not your tenant) may be liable if there are any environmental issues at your property. Years ago, a client inherited several gas stations, and I quickly learned the challenges of dealing with environmental issues. Even though he didn't operate the gas stations, he owned the property and was responsible for the environmental impact of a leaking underground tank. It cost several million dollars to fix, and he was liable for the full expense. So, when a different client expressed an interest in NNN gas stations and convenience stores, I discussed the liability and encouraged him to focus on convenience stores without gas stations.

No investment is perfect, and this is certainly true for NNN properties. It's important to explore the risks and compare them to other investments to determine if they make sense as part of your retirement income plan.

Reverse Mortgages

It's common for retirees to be "house rich but cash poor." A reverse mortgage allows those who are 62 or older to convert equity in their house into monthly income or a lump sum payment. What's the catch? The loan plus interest gets paid back when you pass away, move out of the house permanently, or sell it. This sounds like a great way to create a lifetime stream of income in retirement, and in the right circumstances, it is. Reverse mortgages are controversial, though. Fees can be high and the rules complex. Although reverse mortgages can provide a steady stream of income throughout retirement, they are not for everyone – especially in these three circumstances:

You may move. Reverse mortgage loans need to be repaid if you move. If you anticipate a move in the next five to ten years, it may not make sense to pay the fees and interest.

You have health issues. One of the requirements for a reverse mortgage is that you live in the house. If you have health issues and think you may require a different living situation (e.g., assisted living) at some point soon, a reverse mortgage is unlikely to be a good solution for you.

You can't afford basic payments. If, at any point, you become delinquent in paying property taxes, homeowner's insurance, HOA fees, or other costs associated with living in your home, you could be subject to defaulting on your reverse mortgage and be required to sell and pay back the loan balance.

As with Social Security, entire books have been written about reverse mortgages. This is not one of them. If you are interested in exploring reverse mortgages in more detail, you can find additional resources at BadassRetirement.com.

The goal for retirees who want to live a Badass Retirement is to create an amazing life free of financial worry. By generating a lifetime of income that is escalating, sustainable, and predictable, you can thrive throughout retirement. However, lifetime income isn't guaranteed. To truly be free of financial worry, you'll want to maximize your portfolio's longevity. That's what you'll learn to do in the next Challenge.

JOIN THE FAMILY

When one of the most influential and esteemed economists confesses that creating a lifetime of income in retirement is one of the "nastiest and hardest problems in finance," you know it's a challenge. That doesn't mean it's impossible, though. I've been helping clients do this for nearly three decades. Join the Badass Retirement Community for exclusive content and ongoing discussion on converting assets into a lifetime stream of income.

GO TO BADASSRETIREMENT.COM

11

CHALLENGE

Maximize
Portfolio Longevity

How to invest to reduce the risk of
running out of money in retirement.

CHALLENGE 11

When I first started as a financial advisor, I was introduced to a couple in their 30s who wanted to make the most of their high incomes. I went through all the fundamental steps of retirement planning with them, but something struck me that I hadn't realized during my financial training – because of their age and situation, they could take bigger risks and even make mistakes with their finances and still be just fine. At that point in my career, I already had a lot of financial education and training, but the only risk we talked about was investment risk, and client "mistakes" were certainly not part of the curriculum. So, what does a new financial advisor with few clients and a lot of free time do? He creates art!

As I thought more about their situation, I developed a better understanding of the dynamics of age and risk – and not just portfolio risk, but career, business, and life risk as well. If you are in your 20s or 30s, you can take an absurd number of risks and still have time to recover from any potential setbacks before retirement. Playing it safe, in their situation, might not have been the safe choice after all. But the experience also led me to an even more profound realization. As you get closer to retirement, the margin for error becomes very narrow. A bad financial decision or a missed opportunity at work can derail retirement and make it difficult or even impossible to fully recover.

To help explain this to my clients, I created a visual like the one below. I told them to imagine they were playing a game. Their goal was to navigate their character toward the finish line – retirement – while staying within the boundaries of the playing field. I also told them that because they were young, had already amassed an investment portfolio, were highly educated, and had thriving careers, they were starting at the base of the pyramid.

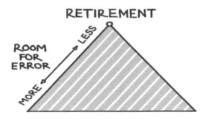

The younger you are, the more room you have for error. As you get closer to retirement, you have less room for mistakes.

I explained that the base of the pyramid is wide and green, representing their freedom to deviate widely and take detours without any long-term negative consequences. They could make mistakes and face setbacks, but they had plenty of room to get back on track and reach their retirement goal.

I cautioned that, as they grew older and closer to retirement, they would have less wiggle room to make mistakes or take risks and still recover – as they move up the pyramid, the guardrails would become tighter and tighter. If a risk was too high or a mistake too large, it would push them outside the pyramid, and they wouldn't successfully reach their goal. Thanks to the visual, they could easily grasp that the closer they came to retirement, the less room they'd have for excessive risk or mistakes.

They loved the explanation and graphic. In fact, they said they were going to frame the "art" and hang it on their wall (although I never did see it adorning their home!). As a new advisor trying to please his clients, that made me feel great! But years later I discovered I had made a mistake. I missed something crucial.

I fell victim to the false belief that "retirement" only refers to the destination. Remember, the goal with traditional retirement planning is simply to reach retirement – earn, save, and grow your investment portfolio so you can retire. But that's a rather short-sighted view of retirement. If we expect to live 30% or 40% of our lives in retirement (or maybe even more – see the *Upgrade Health* Challenge!), we can't just make it to the destination and be satisfied.

By viewing retirement solely as a destination, I was only seeing half the picture. I focused so much on getting *to* retirement that I neglected to consider what happens *during* retirement. It turns out, the same dynamic with my pyramid plays out in retirement . . . except inverted.

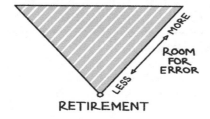

In the early days of retirement, you are subject to much greater risk than in the later years of retirement.

The primary financial goal in retirement (there are many non-financial goals) is to have sufficient income and financial resources to last through the rest of your lifetime. The keyword here is "lifetime." Once again, time becomes a critical element. The earlier you begin retirement, the longer your life expectancy and the greater the number of years your portfolio will need to provide you with income. As you get older, your life expectancy will decrease and the number of years you withdraw from your portfolio will reduce. It's the pyramid in reverse.

During retirement, there is initially much less room for risk and mistakes, but as you get older, your ability to withstand risk surprisingly increases. I know this seems counterintuitive because it goes against the typical narrative that we need to take fewer risks as we get older – but that's only partially true. We absolutely should be concerned about risk, but not in the same way we've been led to believe.

The greatest risk does not come at a very old age, but when you're nearing retirement. The Retirement X Zone extends over 10 years – a few years leading up to retirement and the first several years in retirement.

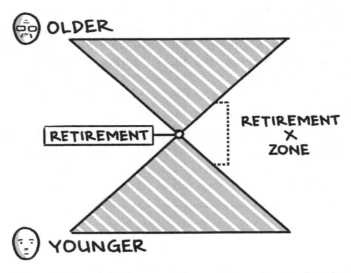

The Retirement X Zone is the few years before and after retirement where there is the greatest risk to our financial assets and income.

This novel approach to retirement risk may take some time to wrap your head around, and that's perfectly fine. At this point, just understand that retirement isn't the finish line. If you view retirement as the end of a journey, you are likely to be more cavalier about the risks you take at the very point in your life when you can least afford it. I made this very mistake at nearly 20,000 feet.

For six days, I had been hiking up Mt. Kilimanjaro in Tanzania with a group of friends and clients. We left camp around midnight to make our final push to the top. As the sun was coming up over the African Savannah, we made it to the final resting place before the summit. Perched at almost 19,000 feet, I gazed across the landscape, filled with gratitude and pride. We did it. All the training and preparation, sore muscles and blisters had been worth it. Sipping some water and chewing on an energy bar, I could almost see the famous sign at the summit. I packed up my things and with a little too much enthusiasm, trotted my way to the top. I took photos and reveled in standing at the highest point on the African continent – overjoyed that I had made it.

Except I hadn't made it. In fact, I'd only gone halfway. For every step I had taken to get to the top over the past week, I would have to take another step to get back down. It was right around this time I started to feel very sick. Apparently, in my excitement to reach the summit, I had walked a little too quickly. At nearly 20,000 feet, where there is very little oxygen, that is a big no-no. I struggled and stumbled my way back down the mountain – feeling a whole lot less triumphant and proud.

In doing this I committed THE cardinal sin of hiking . . . I mistook the summit for the end. Adventure guides are adamant that getting to the top is only half the journey. They'll tell you that most accidents occur on the way back down. That's when people get careless and lose focus.

Retirement is not the end. A stop along the way? Sure. A slight diversion? You bet. But a destination? Nope.

THE WEALTH RETIREMENT PARADOX

Standing on top of Mt. Kilimanjaro at nearly 20,000 feet, I was more confident than I had been at any other point. I had sacrificed and put in the work to get there. I felt strong and assured. It was (literally) downhill from there.

Retirees often feel something similar when they retire. They've spent decades saving and preparing for that very moment. Their portfolio balances are likely the largest they've ever been. They have the least amount of debt they've ever had. Financially, they are the strongest they've ever been in their lives . . . but they are also the most tenuous.

They are giving up the only stable source of income they've ever known, instead relying on the vagaries of a volatile investment portfolio and counting on Social Security to provide them with income for the rest of their lives. Their portfolios are under the maximum level of stress since, at this point, they need to survive the longest. Obtaining emergency credit or loans becomes much harder without employment. Unlike your working years, when stock market declines allowed you to dollar-cost average and buy investments "on sale," in retirement there is no new source of funds to buy the dip.

Entering retirement, you have the most, but you also have the most to lose.

This reality can lead to a fragile financial environment and financial worries.

It's hard to live a Badass Retirement if you are constantly worried about the stock market or running out of money. There are three principles to maximize portfolio longevity:

- Principle 1: The Sequence of Investment Returns Matters
- Principle 2: Build an Investment Asset Allocation
- Principle 3: Stay on Financial Track

PRINCIPLE 1: THE SEQUENCE OF INVESTMENT RETURNS MATTERS

Sequence matters. For example, imagine an airline pilot doing these three actions: checking the plane's fuel gauge, filling the fuel tank, and taking off. That sequence of events produces a safe and reasonable outcome. Now take these same three events but change the order: taking off, checking the fuel gauge, (trying to) fill the fuel tank. These are the same three events, but they would result in a very different outcome. The same is true of investing.

Imagine you have a nosy neighbor who is always in your business and loves to flaunt his new toys and how much money he spends. Unlike him, you are a much more diligent saver. You've worked hard and sacrificed for years to build your retirement portfolio. You are surprised when he tells you he is retiring early. You know a little about his financial situation because he loves to talk about it, so you know he has saved less than you. You wish him luck but say you want to work a few more years just to be safe. After a few years, you feel comfortable enough with your portfolio balance to go ahead and retire. You feel a sense of pride and accomplishment and are ready to enjoy retirement. And you do . . . until the stock market starts to drop. Then it drops even more. Your financial advisor says you must cut your expenses and reduce your monthly withdrawals from your portfolio or else you will run out of money. This is not how you had envisioned retirement. Your neighbor, however, seems to be doing better than you financially. How can that be? Does he have a less aggressive portfolio allocation? Does he have more of his income from fixed sources? Or did he simply retire at the right time?

When I started in the financial advice industry almost 25 years ago, it was common for retirement advisors to make projections using an average annual return in a spreadsheet. For example, an advisor might assume that, going forward, the annual average return of a client's portfolio was going to be 7.5%. In the spreadsheet, the portfolio would then be calculated to grow each year at 7.5%. Using this approach, the client could withdraw 7.5% of their portfolio each year and the balance of their account would never change. The "safe" amount to withdraw was calculated to be 7.5% in this example, but there is a significant problem with this approach.

Indeed, the average annual return of the portfolio may be 7.5% over 30 years, but it is more important to look at whether the portfolio will actually increase by this amount each year. If you've had any experience as an investor, you know the answer is a resounding *no!* The stock market is volatile. Some years the portfolio may grow more or less than 7.5% and in other years it may decline. If the average return is 7.5% it shouldn't matter, right? Wrong!

Poor investment performance in the early years of retirement has a much bigger negative impact on how much you can safely withdraw from your portfolio compared to experiencing poor returns later in retirement. You can have the same starting assets in retirement and the same portfolio withdrawal rate, but if you experience an adverse stock market in the time leading up to retirement or immediately following it, your financial success could be more compromised than someone else with the same assets and expenses but who happened to have better portfolio returns around their retirement date.

In two popular articles I wrote for *Forbes*, I shared the following scenarios. Both scenarios use these assumptions:

- Average annual portfolio return = 5.50%
- Time frame = 30-year period
- Starting portfolio value = $1 million
- Annual withdrawal = $40,000 (4% of the portfolio's starting value)

In the two examples we'll explore, we are starting with the same portfolio value, we are withdrawing the same amount per year, and the average annual return is the same, so you may be wondering what the point is in having both scenarios if everything is the same. Won't the results be identical? Well, this is where things get interesting. Everything is the same except that *the sequence of investment returns is different* for each of our three scenarios. In other words, the investment performance will vary each year. Will this make a difference? Let's find out.

In this first scenario, we have several years of strong investment performance, but after nearly 30 years, the markets and our investment return both turn negative...

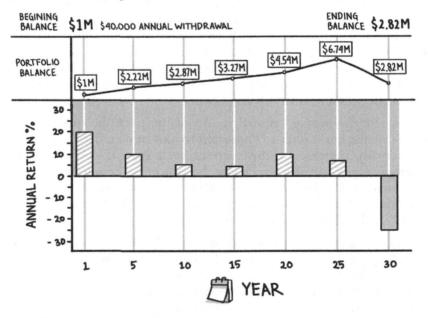

Strong returns early in retirement outweigh weaker returns later in retirement.

In this second scenario the *average* return is the same as the first scenario (5.50%), but the negative returns occur first rather than at the end. What do you notice with the portfolio balance? You run out of money in Year 15. How is that possible?

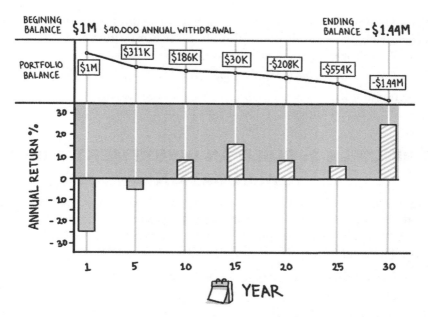

BEGINING BALANCE $1M $40,000 ANNUAL WITHDRAWAL ENDING BALANCE -$1.44M

PORTFOLIO BALANCE $1M $311K $186K $30K -$208K -$554K -$1.44M

ANNUAL RETURN %

Negative returns early in retirement can derail even the best financial plan.

When the portfolio experienced negative returns early on, it was never able to recover, even with the high returns later. Basically, your portfolio got stuck in a hole, and with the yearly $40,000 withdrawals, the improved investment returns were too little and too late. This is obviously not the outcome you want in retirement.

This is the dirty little secret in the investing and retirement planning world that few people like to talk about – sequence of returns risk. Why don't they want to bring it up? Three reasons. First, it doesn't feel like you have a great deal of control over this type of risk. Second, it doesn't feel fair, as your retirement success shouldn't depend so heavily on how lucky you are when you decide to retire. Third, many financial advisors specializing in retirement may not be aware of the outsized impact made by sequence of returns risk or they don't have the knowledge or tools to minimize the risk.

The Retirement X Zone – the few years leading up to retirement and the first several years during retirement – is when your retirement nest egg is most vulnerable to sequence of investment returns risk. Specifically, the year you retire is when you face the *greatest* portfolio risk.

Are there strategies to help mitigate this type of risk? Absolutely. The often-discussed 4% rule regarding retirement income was formulated while studying the problem of sequence of investment returns risk. It's a good rule of thumb but is not perfect and should be customized for your unique situation.

Another strategy to minimize the risk from experiencing an insurmountable portfolio drop at the onset of retirement is to implement a non-traditional allocation. We'll explore this strategy next.

PRINCIPLE 2: BUILD AN INVESTMENT ASSET ALLOCATION

The income from your portfolio is only as sustainable as the portfolio itself. In other words, if the value of your portfolio reaches zero, the 4%, 5%, or whatever percentage you take out each year will also reach zero. The math is simple: 4% of $0 is $0.

Unlike other sources of income – such as Social Security – in order to withdraw income from your investment portfolio, you need an actual investment portfolio. If you withdraw too much and/or if the value of your investments decline, you may face the dire situation that every retiree works to avoid – running out of money. In "chicken speak," we need to keep the chicken alive and healthy.

That's where asset allocation comes in. Asset allocation refers to how your investment portfolio is invested across different asset classes or types of investments – for example, how much is invested in stocks versus bonds versus real estate. It's also possible to divide your portfolio into very narrow asset classes, so instead of just focusing on stocks in general, you decide to focus more narrowly on small company stocks outside the United States.

In the research paper presenting the 4% rule, the author assumed that half of the portfolio would be allocated to large U.S. companies, with the other half going to intermediate-term U.S. bonds. The author could have chosen a breakdown of 65% U.S. stocks and 35% bonds, or even 70% large U.S. stocks, 10% small U.S. stocks, and 20% bonds – or really any other combination.

What's important is that your portfolio has an asset allocation – for instance, 100% cash or 100% Disney stock. Your investment portfolio's asset allocation determines your investment return in retirement. Since you'll likely be living off money from your portfolio for 30 or more years in retirement, you need your portfolio to do well over a long time.

Research suggests that a portfolio with a stock allocation less than 40% to 50% won't be able to grow enough over time.[97] Alternatively, a portfolio with a stock allocation over 75% is subject to a great deal of volatility and risk. Most retirement investment advisors will suggest a stock allocation of somewhere between 40% and 75%.

I have some clients who take in more than enough income from real estate and other sources, so they don't need to withdraw money from their investment portfolios. These clients prioritize long-term growth and feel comfortable taking greater risks with their investments, with the goal of building a larger estate they can leave for their children. Other clients can't afford to take that same level of risk with their portfolios because they are withdrawing money each month for living expenses.

Most investors take the view that, when you are young, you should have more stocks in your portfolio, then, as you get older, you should reduce the amount invested in stocks. This is the traditional approach for asset allocation in retirement – gradually trim your stocks over time as you age – and can be a successful strategy.[98] The popular "Rule of 100" says you should subtract your age from 100 to determine the percentage of stocks you should have. So, if you're 40 years old you should have 60% in stocks and if you are 60 years old you should have 40% in stocks, etc.

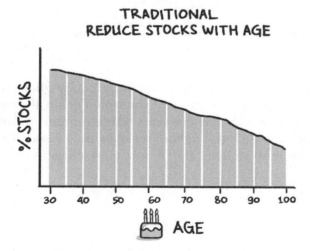

**TRADITIONAL
REDUCE STOCKS WITH AGE**

The common approach to investing in retirement is to reduce your allocation to stocks as you age.

One of the most significant risks to your portfolio's longevity is when your portfolio experiences a sharp and/or prolonged drop right before or after you retire – the sequence of returns risk discussed earlier. Your portfolio is especially vulnerable the year you retire and during the subsequent few years. Using a safe withdrawal rate (e.g., the 4% rule) is one approach to reducing this risk, but another is to use a non-traditional allocation strategy in which you decrease stocks as you approach retirement and then increase them as you age in retirement.

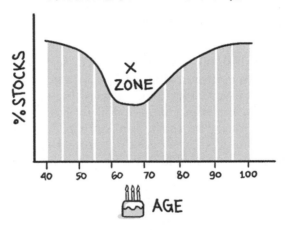

An alternative approach to help minimize sequence of returns risk: Reduce your level of stocks before retirement and then increase your allocation with age.

This approach is referred to as a "rising equity glide path."[99] If you followed this investment strategy, you would gradually lower your stock allocation approximately five years before retirement. You would then gradually increase it throughout retirement. For example, if your goal is to retire at 60 and you are 55 now, your allocation might look like this:

Age	% Stocks
55	70%
56	65%
57	60%
58	55%
59	50%
60	45%
61	45%
62	50%
63	55%
64+	60%

There are many variations to the glide path strategy – constant, rapidly decreasing, rapidly increasing, V-shaped, etc. There is no one-size-fits-all approach when it comes to retirement allocation, and what's best for you depends on dozens of individual factors. Be wary if you use any online tools or services that give you an asset allocation just based on your answers to a few questions. To really determine an appropriate allocation for your investments, I'd recommend working with someone who can analyze your cash flow needs, income sources, taxes, risk tolerance, risk capacity, and other factors to create an allocation that makes sense for your taxable accounts and tax-deferred accounts.

Whether you are building your own retirement asset allocation and managing your own investments or if you are working with an advisor, you don't want to find yourself in a situation like the one faced by an individual who contacted me several years ago...

I received a call from a woman who began by apologizing for calling, primarily because she wasn't sure why she called or what exactly she needed. She had been working with an investment advisor at one of the largest banks in the United States for several years. Her portfolio performance seemed to be good, yet she felt confused. She said that she didn't understand her statements or even what she was investing in. She then told me that she was 68 years old and that her only assets were her house and her investments with this advisor.

She made a point of telling me she was more concerned about losing money than making money, and that her advisor told her she had a "conservative allocation." I told her to send me her statements so I could have a look at how she was invested. Within 20 seconds of reviewing her statements, I knew she had a problem.

Her multimillion-dollar portfolio was 98.8% invested in stocks, which, for her age and risk tolerance, was wildly inappropriate. After digging deeper, I discovered that most of her holdings were in high-tech companies, including many ultra-high-risk Chinese internet companies! I was stunned.

I requested some of her historical statements to get a better idea of how and when her portfolio became so concentrated and risky. The strange thing was that the advisor hadn't always been so aggressive with her portfolio. After reviewing older statements, it was clear that the advisor grew more and more aggressive the longer he worked with her. What started out as an appropriate allocation eventually turned into a high-flying, risk-it-all allocation. Because she had a discretionary account – a common type of investment account where an advisor can buy and sell at will – her advisor was able to shift not only the investments but also the allocation from a sane approach to an insane approach. The advisor went rogue with her portfolio. But why? Why did the advisor take so much risk?

Sometimes this happens as advisors attempt to make up for earlier losses or bad investments – the familiar Las Vegas strategy of doubling down to try to recoup losses. But that's not always the reason. Sometimes advisors become too confident in their abilities, convincing themselves they cannot lose. Simply put, they forget their clients' goals and objectives, instead focusing on their own goals and objectives. Fortunately, we took immediate action and she didn't get hurt.

One way to prevent yourself or your advisor from deviating from the plan is to create investment guardrails. Most large pension funds and college endowments use guardrails – which they call an investment policy statement – to set certain restrictions on how their portfolio is to be invested. You should also consider setting parameters for how your portfolio should be managed, whether you are managing your own portfolio or working with a financial advisor. To see an example of an Investment Policy Statement with investment criteria, go to BadassRetirement.com.

INVESTMENT RISK PARADOX

There is another dilemma all investors must face: risk versus reward. I think of this as a battle with safety, security, and stability on one side and growth on the other. How we balance between these two opposing goals will have significant consequences on our portfolio allocation, volatility, potential growth, and ultimately, the success or failure of your finances in retirement. What makes this choice more challenging is the investment risk paradox.

This paradox says that what seems like, looks like, and feels like the least risky choice most often ends up being the riskiest choice. It also says that what seems like, looks like, and feels like the riskiest choice is often the least risky choice. This conundrum is the result of the risk illusion, where we tend to focus on short-term risks and disregard long-term risks. In the non-investment world, we gladly wear a seatbelt because the consequences of an accident are immediate, but we'll eat poorly because the impact on our health may not be realized for years or decades.

As investors, we are keenly aware of our portfolios' values right now, placing great emphasis on retaining that value. In volatile investment markets, some investors look at their portfolios several times a week or even several times a day. The value of time gets condensed so that the only thing that matters is this precise moment. Behavioral economics refers to this tendency as "temporal discounting" – we perceive a desired result in the future to be less valuable than one in the present. In investment speak, we don't care at all about the possibility of growth in our portfolio tomorrow when we are losing money today.

This tendency can lead to bad investment decisions and poor returns, especially when retirees think they are doing the "safe" thing by buying CDs, money market funds, and bonds while selling "risky" stocks. Over short periods of time, the safe assets really are safer, and stocks really are riskier. That's what makes the investment risk paradox so challenging – it's based in truth . . . at least in the short-term.

If you are saving to buy a house or make another large purchase in the short term, it makes sense to overemphasize safety, since you need the money relatively soon. However, over longer periods of time (e.g., retirement), the long-term benefit of owning stocks is much more important than any short-term volatility.

It might surprise you, but a higher allocation to stocks can create a larger safe withdrawal rate over time. Alternatively, low(er) stock allocations create a smaller safe withdrawal rate. For example, an all-bond portfolio (what many retirees would consider safe and conservative) has been shown to produce a maximum safe withdrawal rate of only 2.5%. In this case, the so-called "safe" portfolio of all bonds and no stocks produced the *lowest* safe withdrawal rate. What seemed the safest was actually the riskiest! How's that for safe?

As a rule of thumb, the safer your portfolio is today, the riskier it is in the future. Conversely, the riskier your portfolio is today, the safer it is in the future. This isn't always true, of course. You could bet your entire retirement nest egg on black on a Vegas roulette table, which would definitely be risky in the short term but isn't likely to be safe in the long term! But outside of such extreme examples, this rule of thumb tends to be true.

As you think about your investment portfolio allocation in retirement, be aware of your brain's strong tendency to focus on short-term risk. Your goal should be to create an asset allocation that supports your ability to feel comfortable with short-term volatility for the benefit of greater long-term growth. One way to navigate this balancing act is to have a good handle on your risk capacity and risk tolerance.

RISK CAPACITY & RISK TOLERANCE

When establishing your asset allocation in retirement, you need to determine your financial ability to withstand risk (risk capacity) and your emotional ability to withstand risk (risk tolerance).

Risk capacity attempts to answer the question *How much can I afford to lose without jeopardizing my financial success in retirement?* Risk tolerance, on the other hand, answers a very different question: *How much can I handle losing before I decide to change my allocation?*

Risk capacity addresses your financial ability to deal with losses, while risk tolerance deals with your emotional ability to deal with them. It's common for your capacity for risk to be different from your tolerance for risk.

Risk Matrix

	RISK CAPACITY − ... +	
RISK TOLERANCE +	DANGEROUS	MORE AGGRESIVE
−	VERY CONSERVATIVE	GET COMFORTABLE WITH RISK

It's important to know your risk capacity and risk tolerance. Which quadrant are you in?

High risk capacity/High risk tolerance (More Aggressive). You have the greatest opportunity for long-term growth if you have both high capacity for risk and high tolerance for risk. In this instance, you can afford to seek greater growth opportunities, but you'll need to watch your portfolio carefully to avoid taking more risk than you can deal with financially or emotionally.

Low risk capacity/High risk tolerance (Dangerous). This is the most dangerous combination because, while your appetite for risk is high, your ability to withstand a financial shock is low (that is, you can't afford to lose too much money without affecting your retirement's financial stability). As a result, you may be inclined to take more investment risks than you should. Paraphrasing the movie *Top Gun*, your ego may write checks your portfolio can't cash.

High risk capacity/Low risk tolerance (Get Comfortable with Risk). In this situation, you are likely able to take more investment risk than you feel comfortable taking. If you don't require a high amount of growth in your portfolio, you may be able to keep a low-risk portfolio. With time, however, you may get more comfortable taking on additional risk or separating your investment accounts into different accounts (this will be discussed more later).

Low risk capacity/Low risk tolerance (Very Conservative). Here, your ability and tolerance for investment risk are both low. It's important that you ensure your portfolio doesn't have too high an allocation in stocks and that you rebalance regularly.

Knowing your investment risk capacity and risk tolerance is critical in retirement. If you take too many risks, your portfolio may not be able to recover. If you take too few risks, it may not grow enough to sustain several decades of withdrawals. It's really no wonder that creating an income stream in retirement is one of the "hardest and nastiest" problems in finance, especially considering the countless inputs that can lead to limitless variations. Even a small, seemingly insignificant change in one input can create a significant impact in the future. This is like the proverbial butterfly effect, in which a butterfly flapping its wings in Asia can cause a chain of events leading to a storm in Chicago – except, in this situation, we are dealing with thousands of "butterflies."

Risk Capacity

How can you determine your risk capacity and risk tolerance? The simple truth is that it's hard to do. Your risk capacity is ultimately determined by how much money you can afford to lose and still be financially secure. But what do "afford to lose" and "financially secure" really mean? Every retiree has an amount of income they would like to have available throughout retirement to cover their basic living expenses and any travel, hobbies, or other "non-essential" expenses that make retirement more enjoyable. Your true risk capacity focuses on your basic living expenses, but many retirees want to be confident they can afford not just the basics, but also any extras that arise. To you, being financially secure may mean that you have enough to cover the basics, but to someone else, it may mean also having enough to travel, engage in hobbies, give gifts, etc. As you can see, risk capacity is personal. If you are trying to calculate this for yourself, start by determining what it would cost to cover just the essentials – your basic living expenses such as rent, food, utilities, insurance, etc. This becomes your income "floor" – the amount you need per month to survive. After you examine your income sources, such as Social Security, you can then calculate how much money you need to withdraw from your portfolio. Finally, to determine the minimum investment portfolio you would need, divide the annual dollar amount you calculated by 4%.

Here's how this might look:

- Your basic living expenses are $120,000 per year.
- Social Security will provide you with $32,000 per year.

- You need to withdraw $88,000 per year from your investment portfolio.

- Your portfolio would need to be at least $2,200,000 if you withdrew 4% per year.

- If your current portfolio was valued at $3,000,000, you would have a risk *capacity* to lose $800,000 – 26% of your portfolio.

This is intentionally a very simple example. There are many other factors that would and should be considered. A financial advisor who specializes in retirement planning would be able to help you calculate this. There are also many sophisticated software programs that are excellent for considering and analyzing myriad factors that can't be calculated manually.

Risk Tolerance

Risk tolerance is equally challenging to determine but for different reasons. Unlike risk capacity, which is more based in mathematics, risk tolerance involves our feelings, fears, and emotions. There are numerous risk tolerance assessments you can take online, and if you work with an advisor, they likely have their own questionnaires. Regardless of which method you use, the goal is to determine how much your portfolio can decline before you become uncomfortable to the point of losing sleep and/or deciding to sell your investments to avoid losing any more money.

The assessments are helpful – I've used many versions of them for years. They do, however, have a significant limitation. You are asked to imagine hypothetical losses and report how they would affect you. After doing thousands of these over the years, I've learned one thing – hypothetical and actual are two very different paradigms.

The same people who said they would celebrate a 20% decline as a buying opportunity are as fearful and unwilling to buy as everyone else when the market is down. As a result, risk tolerance is a moving target and is difficult to pin down. It reminds me of boxer Mike Tyson's famous quote, "Everybody has a plan until they get punched in the mouth." Everyone has a cerebral sense of their risk tolerance until the market drops. The best predictor of your risk tolerance is investment experience, which, after several decades of investing, you likely have. What you don't have, though, is investment experience *as a retiree*. Is there a difference? Absolutely! There's a huge difference.

Once you shake that last hand and walk away from your career, you are not the same person you were just moments earlier. You are now retired. Your greatest source of income is likely your investment portfolio. During your working years, you had the advantage of being able to spread your investment purchases over months, years, and even decades. If the market declined by 30%, you continued to save and invest – buying assets at lower prices. You never woke up in the middle of the night worried you were going to run out of money or not be able to pay your bills at the end of the month. Your work salary provided a stable income and a mental/emotional cushion, even in recessions and down markets. In retirement? That all goes away. There is no stable source of income from work. You aren't buying investments as they decline. There is no cushion.

As a result, risk tolerance can change dramatically upon retirement. It's possible your risk tolerance has changed, but unless you face a market drop, you may not even notice the change since nobody thinks or cares about risk tolerance when the market is on the rise. This is why I encourage you to re-assess your risk tolerance as you enter retirement and in retirement. Take advantage of the popular online assessment tools, as they can at least help you *imagine* different scenarios and get you thinking about your comfort level for market declines before you actually *experience* a big decline.

Once your retirement investment plan is in place, it needs consistent attention, tweaking, and nurturing. It's one thing to start your retirement journey in the right direction, but it's another to stay on track.

PRINCIPLE 3: STAY ON FINANCIAL TRACK

As nice as it would be to set everything up and then forget about it while you enjoy your retirement, the fact is that you can't. Managing your portfolio is critical for long-term investment and retirement success. Remember the chicken we referred to earlier? You must keep it alive and healthy, which means paying attention to it. Fortunately, this doesn't mean you have to be glued to your computer screen. You can do this work yourself or you can outsource it to a financial advisor. Either way, there are a few key issues to pay attention to throughout retirement:

Rebalancing

One of the advantages workers have is the ability to earn, save, and invest over time. This steady supply of new investment cash allows pre-retirees to make purchases over all types of market cycles – up markets, sideways markets, and down markets. If the market dropped 20% when you were working and saving, those new dollars you invested were buying investments at a 20% discount from where they were previously. The more the market dropped, the more shares you could buy with the same saved and invested dollars.

Compare this to retirees with no new source of cash with which to invest. If the market drops, they aren't earning, saving, and investing new money in the market. As a result, retirees don't experience the same "benefit" of a market decline.

This doesn't mean you are doomed in retirement, however. Although you likely won't have new cash to invest, you can still take advantage of market drops and market gains by rebalancing. The long-term investment advantage of rebalancing is similar to the dollar-cost averaging workers are able to do over the span of their careers – you get to buy assets at a "discount," even though you don't have new cash to invest. If you have already invested for decades, you are probably familiar with portfolio rebalancing. Even though investors know about rebalancing, there is usually a reluctance to follow through with it. This makes sense because rebalancing requires you to sell assets that are doing well and buy assets that are not doing as well. That's hard to do.

Here are two examples:

Imagine you calculate your ideal target asset allocation to be 65% stocks and 35% bonds based on your risk capacity, risk tolerance, and other personal factors. Let's also imagine that the stock market does very well and as a result, your allocation shifts to 75% stocks and 25% bonds. Rebalancing would have you sell your well-performing stocks and buy more of the not-as-well-performing bonds. Seems reasonable on paper, but this can be a challenge in practice. "But my stocks are doing so well. Why would I want to sell those and buy more bonds?" you may ask.

Or consider the opposite example. Again, your target allocation is 65% stocks and 35% bonds, but in this scenario, the stock market has lost value. Your allocation shifts to 55% stocks and 45% bonds. Rebalancing would have you sell some of your stable and well-performing bonds and buy more stocks, even though stocks have dropped in value. Again, it's easy to talk about the merits of rebalancing, but it's entirely different to sell what's working and buy something that is actively losing value.

Some of the best investors are those that keep emotion out of their investment decisions. They rebalance because their portfolios require it and disregard how they might feel. It can help to work with an advisor who will do this unemotional rebalancing on your behalf. If you manage your own portfolio, make rebalancing part of your regular investment schedule.

Knowing the Difference Between Possible and Probable

One of the greatest risks to your investment success has nothing to do with the stock market, the economy, or the Federal Reserve – instead, it has everything to do with you.

I included over 100 financial lessons in my book, *Get Money Smart*. The following is one of those lessons, and it may be one of the most important in the entire book for financial success in retirement.

Which of the following is *possible*?

1. North Korean cyberterrorists hack into our banking system and wipe out our wealth.

2. A magnitude 15 earthquake strikes California, causing the state to sink into the Pacific Ocean.

3. Artificially intelligent robots replace 99% of global jobs, leaving the population without work and income.

4. The U.S. government eliminates the Federal Reserve and returns to a gold standard.

5. A large-scale electromagnetic pulse is detonated over the United States, destroying our power grid, cell phone networks, TVs, radios, and the electronics in our vehicles.

If you answered yes to all of these, you are correct! All these doomsday threats are theoretically possible. It's hard to argue that any of the above threats (or any others you've heard) could never happen. They absolutely could. In fact, it's possible all five of them could happen on the same day!

Now, however, you must ask yourself which of them are *probable*?

As an investor, the difference between possible and probable is one of the most important lessons you can learn. Why? When I was starting out as an advisor, I'd have clients frantically call me because they read something or saw a video about some impending disaster. Their immediate reaction was to be afraid that they'd be financially ruined or that the stock market would crash and wipe out their wealth. As a novice, I'd even get a bit frantic myself. However, once I got past the scary headlines and did more research, I'd find that while the threat was indeed possible, the chance of it actually happening was infinitesimally small.

Could an asteroid strike Manhattan, killing millions and decimating the country's economy and financial system? Yes! But is it probable? Despite what you may read or watch online, not at all.

Forget what's possible and instead focus on what's probable.

Once you've asked yourself whether the threat is probable, you can then ask yourself if the threat is *actionable*. Is there anything you can do to protect yourself or your wealth? According to late night TV or the radio, the solution might be as simple as "Buy gold!" The common thinking is that gold will always have some value and that, if the country or the financial system collapsed, you could use gold. It's a bit of a longshot, but let's just say that's true. Okay, so you sell all your investments and buy gold. How long does that last you? Forever? Until the asteroid hits? This is where things start to make much less sense.

You are afraid that a one-in-a-billion event will occur and you'll lose your money, so you sell everything (incurring taxable gains) and buy gold, which is highly volatile and regularly drops in value by double digits? This is what they mean by jumping out of the frying pan and into the fire.

Before you give in to a fear-based headline or scary YouTube video prophesizing the collapse of something or the other, ask yourself what the consequences of your reaction might be. Every single time I've done this with a client, their planned reaction posed a much greater threat to their wealth than the scary event they were trying to avoid.

The consequences of acting on whatever could possibly happen can be as devastating as the event itself.

In the aftermath of the financial crisis, I visited a potential client at her house. She had several million dollars but was worried that another financial crisis would occur and wipe out the entire global financial system. She didn't want to invest or do any traditional financial planning. Instead, she was building a shelter and learning how to create a sustainable garden in her backyard. While the threat was possible, it was not probable. If her worst-case need-to-live-off-the-land doomsday scenario came true, her money in the bank would probably be worthless anyway. Sadly for her, she missed out on several million dollars of investment gains because she was so focused on what might happen that she didn't want to consider whether the event was probable or if her reaction would have dire consequences.

Before you make an emotional investment move in retirement, first ask yourself if the threat is possible (it almost always is), and then ask yourself if the threat is probable. Doing this will help you stay calm and maintain your wealth throughout retirement.

CLEAR MONEY MENTALITY

True or false? The financial media such as business channels, personal finance magazines, market focused newsletters, and investing websites are designed to help you make smart long-term financial decisions and reach your goals.

If you answered true, you've been duped. The financial media does not care about the growth of your Roth IRA or if you can afford to pay for your grandkid's college tuition.

In the publishing world, the adage is, "If it bleeds, it leads." Magazines, newspapers, TV producers, and radio hosts have one and only one goal. It's not to inform; it's to hold your attention. That means they must titillate, frighten, and shock you with one story after another.

All this financial babble, or as it is often called, "financial pornography," is just a bunch of marketers trying to get you to click on or tune in so they can sell more ads. They are not trying to educate you. They are not trying to help you become better investors. They are trying to scare the hell out of you so you keep coming back day after day to figure out what you should do next.

We are programmed to respond to threats and fear – to focus on what's happening right now, by being hyper vigilant to any sign of danger and making quick emotional decisions that prioritize near-term safety over analytical decisions with a longer timeframe in mind.

The media are experts at exploiting this natural trait in each of us. It's a vicious financial downward spiral:

Watch or read something that creates fear and urgency...

Concerned about financial loss, make a short-term and emotional decision...

Lose money because of a bad decision...

Filled with more anxiety and uncertainty from losing money, try to find answers and guidance by watching more business news and reading more financial articles...

The solution? If you follow the markets too closely, watch the business TV networks, read too many financial blogs, or listen to too many financial experts, you'll be inclined to want to "do something." That something is often to buy or sell, and it is usually the worst thing you can do.

Retirees who get sucked into this cycle live with heightened anxiety and worry. They'll be glued to their TV and constantly swiping from one article to the next, checking their portfolio throughout the day. Does that sound like a Badass Retirement to you? It sounds horrible. I've worked with enough people stuck in this cycle, and they will be the first to tell you just how agonizing it is.

There's so much financial pollution – everyone trying to get your attention through fear and uncertainty. Your perspective can quickly and easily get clouded. Instead, adopt a Clear Money Mentality where you dismiss the day-to-day blather, focus on your long-term goals, and stick to your plan. To paraphrase Timothy Leary, Turn off the noise; Tune out the chatter; Drop in to living your life without worry and fear. How?

Limit the amount of business news from TV, articles, podcasts, and YouTube videos you ingest. Reduce how often you are checking your portfolio to once a month. Restrict the number of trades you make in your investment accounts. If you are married, agree to make any investment or financial decisions together. Think about partnering with a financial advisor to take some of the day-to-day burden from your shoulders and have an impartial party help you make the best long-term financial decisions.

By choosing a Clear Money Mentality, you'll likely not only boost your investment performance, but as a welcome side benefit, you'll enjoy your days more and sleep better at night.

Track Your Spending Against Target Income

The danger I've witnessed time and time again for retirees and non-retirees alike is called *expense creep*. This is where a client will start off with expenses that match their income, but over time, their expenses increase, and they start spending more than they can afford. This is why a "set it and forget it" approach is dangerous.

You must continuously track your spending against your withdrawal rate, monitoring both at least every quarter if not every month. A month or two may not make a trend, but if you see several months of increasing outflows, you should adjust before too much damage is done.

Fortunately, most retirees don't need to budget or keep detailed notes of their spending, though you will still want to keep abreast of where your money is going or, at the very least, how much is going. When clients or their bookkeepers want to track their expenses, I recommend using software such as Quicken. Programs like these provide all the necessary details of your financial situation. Clients may not necessarily care, but it allows me to spot trends and make better projections. For example, it's a red flag when I see a client's fixed expenses increasing. If they remain high and fixed, it limits their flexibility if the ever need to reduce their expenses. By monitoring this, we can spot the trend early and take action to get them back on track.

At a minimum, review your monthly withdrawals yourself and/ or with your advisor to make sure you are staying within your plan. This is especially important in the early days of your retirement as you grow accustomed to your new lifestyle and income level. With time and experience, you may be able to review this every quarter or even every year.

Monthly Reports

You can also stay on track by reviewing a couple of key financial reports each month. The first is your net worth. You'll want to review your net worth at least once a month in the beginning and then, as you become more comfortable, at least once a year. If you are spending too much and having to withdraw funds from your investment accounts, or if you increased your liabilities, this will be reflected in your net worth.

While you shouldn't be concerned about fluctuations in your monthly net worth, you should look for trends and issues so you can make changes sooner rather than later. If you or your advisors don't track these closely, your net worth could continue to decline for months or even years and erode your security in retirement.

In addition to a net worth report, you should also review your investment accounts. These accounts will experience volatility, going up and down each month, but you should still be aware of what is happening. I've found that the clients who are most nervous about investing become much more comfortable just by reviewing what happens in their accounts over time.

Another way to stay on track is very simple: don't get off track in the first place. Some retirees adapt quickly to their new situation and stick closely to their spending plans, but others struggle. If you find that you are making impulse purchases and/or consistently spending too much, consider creating a spending review system with your advisor. For example, make a commitment that you and your advisor will review all purchases over a certain dollar amount before you buy, and/or allow for a "cooling off" period between the impulse and the purchase.

Stopping the Snowball Effect

Every retiree's greatest fear is running out of money. By staying on track, however, you can avert any problems early so they don't grow into bigger problems that can impact the financial success of your retirement. But what happens if your finances go awry, and you don't notice until your financial security is already off the rails?

One of the most dangerous financial situations in retirement – especially in the early years – happens when you withdraw an amount from your portfolio that exceeds the growth of your portfolio.

Let's say, as you enter retirement, you decide you need $40,000 a year from your portfolio to cover your lifestyle expenses. Your portfolio balance is $1 million, so the $40,000 you take out represents a 4%

withdrawal rate. During your first few years of retirement, however, the economy experiences a recession, with negative investment returns for several years. Your fixed living expenses are high, and you continue to withdraw $40,000 from your portfolio despite the negative returns.

As you can see, what started out as a 4% withdrawal rate quickly escalates to high single digits and even double digits. Even after the market recovers and your portfolio starts to earn a positive return, the damage has already been done.

Although the amount you withdraw from your portfolio stays the same at $40,000, since your portfolio has declined in value, that

$40,000 starts to represent a larger and larger percentage of your account's total value until, ultimately, you run out of money. This is the snowball effect – the withdrawal percentage increases faster and faster as you withdraw more.

WITHDRAWAL RATE SNOWBALL

If your portfolio withdrawal rate is too high, it can deplete your portfolio causing the level dollar amount to become a larger percentage of a smaller and smaller portfolio.

The goal here is to slow or even stop this snowball effect as early as possible. If you can respond quickly enough, there is a much greater chance you can salvage your portfolio.

The following are a few strategies you can consider if your withdrawal percentage starts to creep up.

Monitor your withdrawal percentage. If you aren't aware that your withdrawal percentage is rapidly increasing, you won't be able to act. That's why tracking your percentage is extremely important throughout retirement – but especially if your portfolio suffers. It's an easy calculation – just divide your annual dollar withdrawal amount (e.g., $40,000) by your portfolio balance ($1 million). As a rule of thumb, you can use these ranges to see if you need to take action:

Green Zone: 4% or less

With this withdrawal rate, you should feel fairly safe and confident. There is a lower chance you will outlive your money if your withdrawal percentage stays in this zone.

Yellow Zone: 4% to 6%

A month or two in the Yellow Zone shouldn't be cause for too much concern, but if you find yourself there for an extended period, it could turn into a larger problem. Think about reducing your withdrawal rate closer to 4% as quickly as you can.

Red Zone: 6%+

It's called the Red Zone for a reason – withdrawing 6% or more from your portfolio for an extended period will drastically increase the chance of experiencing the snowball effect and running out of money. Work with an advisor if necessary to lower your withdrawal rate.

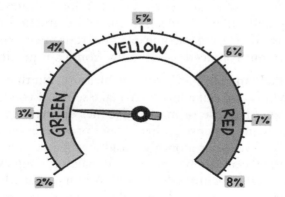

Make sure your portfolio withdrawal rate is in the Green Zone.

Be flexible with withdrawals. The more flexibility you have regarding the amount you need to take out of your portfolio, the better. If you absolutely must withdraw a certain amount per month to cover your living expenses, you won't have the ability to reduce that amount. It's best if you can keep your fixed expenses lower while having higher discretionary expenses. That way, if you need to reduce how much you are pulling from your portfolio for a few months, you can cut back on your discretionary expenses while still covering your fixed expenses. I understand that cutting back on your monthly income is not ideal – nobody wants to have to lower their income in retirement – however, you want to stop the snowball effect as early and quickly as possible. Reducing your monthly income for a few months could help you prevent much longer-term and more consequential negative outcomes.

Take Social Security earlier. You already read about Social Security strategies earlier in the book and that it's often wise to delay taking Social Security at least until you reach full retirement age (FRA) or even until you're 70. However, if you haven't started Social Security retirement benefits yet and if you find yourself in the Yellow or Red Zone for too long, you may want to consider starting Social Security earlier. You could then decrease the amount you are withdrawing from your portfolio by the amount you are receiving in Social Security benefits. This decrease in monthly withdrawals could shift you from the Yellow or Red Zone back to the Green Zone. Knowing when to start Social Security can be complicated, and there are many factors that should be evaluated before deciding, so be sure to seek out competent counsel before you decide to start your benefits early.

Consider an annuity. As you learned earlier, annuities can provide a steady source of income that is guaranteed and will not fluctuate regardless of what the stock market does. Although annuities are confusing and often not ideal, in the right situation they can be beneficial parts of a total income plan in retirement and can help reduce the amount you need to withdraw from your portfolio.

Take out a loan. This is an extreme measure, but there are certain situations when taking out a loan may make sense. If you find yourself in the Red Zone because of market declines and you cannot reduce your monthly living expenses, a loan could provide enough cash flow to allow you to lower your monthly withdrawal percentage. Of course, it's not ideal to take a loan in retirement to pay for living expenses, but it's also not ideal to stay in the Red Zone. A home equity line of credit or a reverse mortgage loan – discussed earlier – may provide enough income to get you out of the Red Zone for an extended period. Before you take out any loan, however, I strongly suggest working with your CPA or financial advisor to see if there are better alternatives.

When you stay on track with your financial plan, you will only have to make minor adjustments to ensure you don't run out of money in retirement.

Preventing Bad Investments

One of the most popular and effective set of investment guidelines I've created has been the Green, Yellow, and Red Investment Guide. I wrote about this in *The Sudden Wealth Solution* years ago, and I still get emails thanking me for it to this day. The guide is meant to provide you with guardrails while you think about investing your retirement assets, either by yourself or with an advisor.

According to this guide, you'll want to invest in green investments, be cautious of yellow investments, and generally avoid red investments. Download the free guide at BadassRetirement.com.

A lifetime of good decisions can be ruined by a single bad decision. Our goal is to avoid that, instead making a series of smart financial, legal, and tax decisions throughout your retirement.

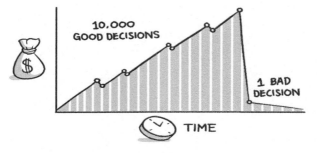

Years of hard work and smart decisions can evaporate with just one bad decision.

Total Financial Security can't exist if you are worried about your finances. In the next Challenge, you will learn 10 strategies for de-risking your finances. If you implement these strategies effectively, one bad decision won't destroy decades of work and sacrifice.

JOIN THE FAMILY

What's the right investment allocation for your portfolio? How much risk should you take? When should you rebalance? What should you do if there is a stock market drop? I hope you got a little closer to answering these questions by reading this Challenge, but the economy, market, and your portfolio are dynamic. Join the Badass Retirement Community to get regular updates, content, and ideas on investing in your retirement portfolio.

GO TO BADASSRETIREMENT.COM

12

CHALLENGE

De-Risk Finances

You only need to do a handful of things to create financial security throughout retirement.

CHALLENGE 12

Do you want to know the tell-tale sign of financial success in retirement? I'll tell you what it sounds like – silence. The clients who are truly living Badass Retirements and going on adventures, working hard to stretch their limits, making an impact, and pursuing their mission feel financial peace and contentment. They don't worry about their finances or the stock market. These clients don't call me any time they are concerned about a CNBC clip or a *Wall Street Journal* article. They don't call me just because they saw that the market was down that day or are anxious about what the Federal Reserve may do next. They don't call me because of rumors of a possible recession or geopolitical problems in Asia. Silence. The phone doesn't ring. They are too busy enjoying retirement to the fullest.

Of course, this doesn't mean they bury their head in the sand and just hope and pray everything works out. That's a strategy for uncertainty and anxiety. Instead, the retirees who want to live more and think less about their finances are the ones who de-risk their finances. But what does that mean?

The goal of de-risking your finances is to minimize financial injury. The 10 concepts you will learn in this Challenge are a combination of strategies that will protect and prevent financial disasters. Many retirees are too passive when it comes to protecting their finances. This can be a recipe for financial anxiety at the best and financial disaster at the worst. Neither are ingredients of a Badass Retirement.

The following 10 strategies are proactive actions you can take today that will put you in a stronger financial position. So even if you experience a financial setback, you will be less likely to experience deep or long-term financial injury as a result.

Here are the 10 financial strategies to de-risk your finances:

1. Part-time retirement
2. Retirement radar
3. Income taxes in retirement
4. Build your retirement team
5. Prevent financial fraud

6. Help children/family the right way

7. Minimize lawsuits

8. Estate planning

9. Protect assets in marriage/re-marriage

10. Long-term care planning

1. PART-TIME RETIREMENT

Are you nervous about transitioning into full-time, traditional retirement and/or do you need a stronger financial cushion? One of the best ways to de-risk your finances is through part-time retirement. Is this approach right for you? Maybe. As part of my routine when creating a retirement plan for a client, I will almost always model what part-time retirement might look like for them compared to traditional retirement.

As you've learned, traditional retirement is one of the most significant life and financial transitions we can experience. For 30 or 40+ years, you've had a daily routine that, for many people, includes waking up in the morning, getting ready, eating breakfast, driving to work, working eight to ten hours, and then driving home. This daily routine is often done five days a week for several decades. The job might change, and the commute might differ, but the general routine doesn't. Then, one day, it does. Radically. The day before, you had a reason to wake up, a place to be, things to do, people to engage with, and responsibilities to handle. But this daily routine changes overnight when you retire. Understandably, this transition can be difficult for some.

When we think of retirement, we assume it is all or nothing – we are either fully working or fully retired. But it turns out that, for retirement, gray can be good. Does that mean there is another option? The answer is an emphatic yes, and it's called part-time retirement. A part-time retirement is where you gradually transition from full employment to full retirement over some time.

Research suggests that anywhere between 10% and 20% of retirees work in retirement.[100] Many of these retirees do so for strictly financial reasons – they cannot afford to stop working completely. However, part-time retirement is not just for those who need the extra money and cannot afford to retire fully. The best part-time retirements have many significant financial and non-financial benefits I would suggest you at least explore, even if you are financially prepared for retirement and don't need the extra income. I've had many financially successful clients who approached retirement age and decided to adopt a part-time retired lifestyle, even though they could have easily afforded to retire completely. They saw the advantages of staying engaged and in the game, opting for this part-time approach. Granted, they received many financial benefits, and their finances became meaningfully stronger because of choosing a part-time retirement, but the motivations behind working part-time weren't exclusively financial.

The questions I always get from clients are likely the same ones you may be asking yourself: *What would a part-time retirement look like for me? Would I get a job as a Walmart greeter? What work would I be doing? Who would even hire me?*

There are countless variations of what work may look like in a part-time retirement, but it can be helpful to think in terms of two dimensions: novelty and autonomy.

Novelty. Novelty refers to having new experiences in your part-time work compared to the work you've been doing for years. It is interesting to note that I've had just as many retirees want to stick with what they know at the same companies — but on a part-time basis — as I've had clients who wanted to do something completely different.

Autonomy. Autonomy is all about freedom. Retirees who don't want or need autonomy tend to be employees. Those who value autonomy often choose to become independent contractors or start their own businesses.

By combining these two dimensions, you get a matrix with four primary types of work you can consider if you want a part-time retirement.

Part-Time Retirement Matrix

	−	NOVELTY	+
+ AUTONOMY −		**1099 SAME COMPANY**	**START OWN BUSINESS**
		EMPLOYEE SAME COMPANY	**EMPLOYEE NEW COMPANY**

Which quadrant of the Part-Time Retirement Matrix interests you the most?

1. **Working for the same company.** Although I'm still looking for more data on this, my experience is that this is the most common arrangement for part-time retirement. It's logical because it is the most seamless for both the retiree and the company. There are certainly many potential benefits to staying at the same company as an employee. You know the work and the people. You are used to the company's culture and systems. You may be able to continue to receive employee benefits such as health insurance and 401(k) participation. The disadvantage of this work-retirement arrangement is that it may not feel like much of a retirement since very little has changed – you are doing the same work for the same company and working with the same people. You are just doing it for fewer hours each week.

2. **Working as an independent contractor for the same company.** This has become a more popular option. Here, you retain many of the advantages – you get to do work you know and are good at with people you've likely become close to over the years. As an independent contractor, however, you probably won't qualify for health insurance benefits or 401(k) matching. There are advantages to being an independent contractor, though, including tax opportunities, larger contributions to retirement accounts, and more flexibility with your work schedule.

3. **Working at a new company and/or industry.** Some retirees want a change. They like the idea of continuing to earn money and contributing to retirement, but the thought of doing the same thing they've done for years isn't appealing. Instead of

continuing to work for the same company, they may do part-time work for a different company in the same industry or even venture out and try something totally different. Retirees who choose this work-retirement arrangement may feel more "retired" since they are doing something unique and perhaps adventurous.

4. **Starting your own company.** For retirees who want the greatest flexibility and novelty, starting a company is a viable option. I've seen spouses team up to start a new venture and even bring their kids into the business. It can be a rewarding experience, but it can also be a lot of work. Many who retire and start a business say they work harder and longer in "retirement" than they ever did before!

Regardless of which arrangement you choose, there are advantages to a part-time retirement. Though many retirees want nothing to do with work ever again, it can be a perfect arrangement for those looking to strengthen their finances and who feel they just aren't ready to stop working completely.

Advantages of Part-Time Retirement

- **Additional income.** This is an obvious benefit of continuing to work – even if it is just part-time. Many pre-retirees do not realize just how impactful this extra income is. If you are approaching retirement age, chances are you are saving money and adding to your nest egg. If you transition into a part-time retirement and continue to earn income, you may not be able to save like you did when working full-time, but that's okay. Your part-time income may be enough to cover some or all your living expenses. If so, this is a huge financial benefit. Every year that you cover your living expenses through employment is one less year your investment portfolio needs to support you and one more year it can grow without any withdrawals. This is an important advantage that is hard to appreciate without running the numbers and seeing your retirement plan's impact.

  I've modeled this comparison – working part-time versus retiring completely – hundreds of times for clients, and the financial impact is substantial. By delaying distributions from your retirement portfolio, you can dramatically increase the overall success of your financial plan in retirement. If your goal is to de-risk your finances and create more financial security in retirement, it's difficult to find a better solution.

- **Health insurance.** One of the biggest expenses in retirement is health insurance. By continuing to work part-time, you may still qualify for employer-paid health insurance. Not all companies offer this for part-time employees, but it is something you could negotiate with your employer.

- **Delay Social Security Retirement benefits.** As you learned in Challenge 10, the longer you can delay receiving Social Security the larger your monthly benefit becomes (up to age 70). If you are in good health and expect to live a long life, waiting until you're 70 to start receiving benefits can greatly increase your Social Security Retirement income. By engaging in a part-time retirement, you may be able to delay Social Security by a few months or even a few years. This is an often-overlooked advantage.

- **Continue to contribute to Social Security.** Your Social Security Retirement benefit is calculated using your averaged indexed monthly earnings during your highest-earning 35 years of employment. If you have lower-earning years or don't have 35 years of credited work, you may be able to increase your Social Security payout by continuing to work (even part-time).

- **401(k) match.** By working part-time, you may not be able to contribute the maximum amount to your employer's 401(k) plan, but you may be able to contribute enough to get the full company match. It's free money that you wouldn't get if you didn't continue to work.

- **Make large(r) retirement plan contributions.** Being an independent contractor or starting your own business both open the door to many retirement plan options you either didn't have access to as an employee or that had been limited in terms of how much you could contribute. As an employee, the maximum you could contribute to your employer's 401(k) was less than $30,000 per year. This is more than enough for many retirees, but others wish they could contribute more and get a larger tax break. Similarly, the most you could contribute to an IRA is less than $10,000 a year. If your employer doesn't offer a pension plan (and most don't), you couldn't open one yourself. I gave a speech once and told the crowd that, as an independent contractor or business owner, you could do things that would get regular employees arrested. Instead of being capped at contributing less than $30,000 to a 401(k), how would you like to contribute $60,000 or more? Instead of a maximum contribution into an IRA of less than $10,000, how about contributing close to $60,000? Or, instead of being blocked from contributing to a pension plan, how would you like to contribute $200,000 or more per year and get the tax deduction as well? The IRS has two sets of rules: a very limited one for employees and a much more generous one for independent contractors or business owners. Is it fair? Not at all. It makes absolutely no sense. But so long as these beneficial rules exist, you may be able to take advantage of them in a part-time retirement.

- **Contribute to Roth/traditional IRA.** As a part-time worker, you may qualify to contribute to a Roth or traditional IRA, though you will need to look at your own financial and tax situation to determine if this is an option. Still, I typically find that contributing the maximum to a Roth IRA (for you and for your spouse) is an excellent financial strategy. Since Roth and traditional IRAs require earned income, this is a big advantage that won't be available if you completely retire.

- **Health benefits.** Research has identified several non-financial benefits of part-time retirement, including better mental and physical health and fewer major diseases.[101]

- **Possible tax benefits.** The tax consequences of continuing to work as an employee or independent contractor can be complicated. I recommend you discuss your tax situation with a CPA who can model different scenarios to see which options make the most sense for you. One strategy I'm quite fond of for people living in a state with higher income tax is to shift to part-time retirement AND move to a new state with lower income tax. I've run this scenario for countless pre-retirees and the financial benefits are significant. For example, if you've been living and working in a high tax state such as California, it's possible you could save tens of thousands of dollars a year during your part-time retirement by moving to another state. The benefit is even greater for part-time retirees than full-time retirees since your income is likely to be higher when you are still working – even part-time. If you have any interest in experiencing a new part of the county, are a little adventurous, and can work part-time remotely, this is an incredible strategy you should consider. I've had several clients successfully combine a reduction in work with a move to a different state. For example, a client who lived in New York traded the East Coast and a 10+% income tax for the rolling hills of wine country – and 0% income tax – in Washington State. When I ran the financial projections of what they would save in state income tax, it exceeded the mortgage on their new and larger house in Washington. The client remarked, "So you're telling me that, if I move, I get a free house?!" In a part-time retirement, since you are still earning an income from work, the income tax savings of a move can be even greater than if you move after you fully retire.

- **Stay engaged with people.** The abrupt transition from work to retirement can be especially difficult if your social network is closely tied to your work. By continuing to work part-time, you get to stay socially engaged while growing your relationships outside of work in advance of full retirement.

- **Provide a sense of purpose and structure.** One of the hardest challenges for some retirees is struggling with feelings of emptiness. In their working years they felt like they were doing something important, and that people counted on them. They felt valued and needed. That's hard to give up, and some retirees struggle with this. If you sense this could be a problem for you, a part-time retirement can make the transition much smoother and give you just enough time to develop new hobbies and a sense of purpose outside of work.

- **Easier to go back to full-time work.** Nobody goes into part-time retirement hoping they can eventually go back to full-time work, but under certain circumstances, you may need to. If there is a serious financial shock and/or your expenses unexpectedly rise, you may need a full-time income. If you retire fully, it can be challenging to start working again a few years later. If you have been working part-time, however, the transition back to full-time will be much easier. This is especially true if you are a professional – such as a CPA, attorney, or medical professional – with designations or licenses that require continuous work activity.

- **Ability to time joint retirement with spouse.** In an earlier Challenge, you learned that both spouses retiring together is often ideal. This can be accomplished easier if one spouse wants to cut back while the other still wants or needs to continue working for a few more years.

- **Less time with spouse.** I know this sounds funny to some readers, but it's actually a common concern among married soon-to-be retirees. Remember, retirement can be less of a transition and more of a disruption. The thought of having their spouse at home full-time can be alarming and disconcerting for some. A part-time retirement can bridge the two phases and allow spouses to adjust more smoothly.

- **Retire earlier.** For those who want to retire as early as possible and scoff at working part-time in retirement, this advantage is for you. By engaging in a part-time retirement, you may be able to retire sooner. For example, I had a client who was anxious to retire and explore the world but financially needed to work full-time for another seven years. He wasn't thrilled about working for several more years but understood that it was necessary to ensure financial success in retirement. I told him there was another option – part-time retirement. I created a successful financial model that had him working full-time for four years and part-time for another four to five years. Although he would be working an extra year or two, he would cut back to part-time work much earlier. For him, this was perfect. Part-time work provided him with plenty of free time to go on adventures and travel the world – all while he was still relatively young and energetic. It was a trade-off he was more than happy to make – and he's not alone. This is a strategy that many clients are thrilled to make because it allows them more time to do the things they really want while still improving their financial situations. Many who have done this decide they want to work part-time even longer than necessary because they enjoy the benefits of this combination of work and retirement. If you are anxious to retire but are not comfortable making the financial leap to full-time retirement, a part-time retirement may help you partially retire earlier.

- **Easier to get a loan/refinance.** It is far easier to qualify for a new loan or to refinance a mortgage if you have earned income – even part-time income. Regardless of your investment portfolio's size, most lenders want to see stable earned income from employment. If interest rates drop and you want to take advantage of a lower monthly mortgage payment or if you want to get a loan on a vacation cottage, you will be able to qualify much easier if you are still working.

A part-time retirement is not perfect and doesn't work for everyone. It can lead to some retirees complaining that they don't feel retired and are just as stressed as when they were working full-time but with only half the pay. Even for those who think they would enjoy a part-time retirement, such an arrangement can be hard to negotiate with their employers. Some companies jump at the chance to retain experienced workers part-time, but others are just not set up for it.

If you think you would enjoy and benefit from a part-time retirement, it's worth exploring further. Determine whether the financial benefits and tax ramifications make it worthwhile in your situation. Work with your financial advisor and/or tax expert so you can see the economic consequences of this type of arrangement.

2. RETIREMENT RADAR

Risk is the result of uncertainty regarding an unknown future. Since we don't know what the future will bring, one of the best ways to de-risk our finances is to do our best to peek into the future.

When I gave the commencement speech for my Ph.D., I told the graduates and their families in attendance that I think financial advisors are superheroes with the power to see into the future. I explained that we routinely gather clients' financial information, talk to them about their goals, and then run financial projections to see what their financial lives might look like in the future. We then incorporate certain factors – expenses, rates of return, buying a second house, increasing the travel budget, etc. – to see how doing each or all these things will impact their financial lives.

But unlike Tarot Card readers we don't stop there. It's not enough to merely *predict* the future . . . we help *create* the future! Our job and our gift is the ability to see our clients' futures *and* help guide their decisions today to create the futures they desire. I can't think of a more impactful and rewarding profession, and that's exactly what I told the group that day.

So, how can we predict the future? Through something I refer to as the Retirement Radar. After collecting as much information as we can about the client, their finances, and their expectations about the future, we then use sophisticated software that considers taxes, inflation, investment returns, assets, liabilities, income streams, expenses, and a myriad of other factors to glimpse into what the future may look like throughout their retirement. Do they run out of money? Do they have lifetime income? Do they deplete their investment portfolio, or does it grow over time? We can help answer these questions and more. What if there is a stock market drop? Another financial crisis? A long-term care event? Can they pay for an annual cruise for their extended family? Can they afford to climb Mt. Everest?

Please understand this is not a sales pitch for working with a retirement financial advisor. It's simply our value proposition. I'm not sure how retirees make important financial decisions without thoroughly examining possible outcomes. If you aren't sure of the short- and long-term consequences of buying a vacation house – not just the immediate effect of the down payment, but the mortgage payments, property taxes, maintenance, tax considerations, and insurance expenses that can have impacts decades into the future – how can you make a confident decision?

Retirement Radar is the process of creating a comprehensive financial retirement plan and running different "what if" scenarios. What if you work for another year? What if you had a part-time retirement for three years? What if the market underperforms for the next five years? What if you get an inheritance? What if you need to move to an assisted living facility at 85 years old?

There are many different software programs available to you and/or your financial advisor. The best ones implement Monte Carlo simulations. Monte Carlo is a model that runs simulations to predict the probability of future outcomes. Monte Carlo is the "radar" in Retirement Radar. Through thousands of investment return simulations, it determines the probability of running out of money (or not) in retirement. Here, success is defined as not running out of money, while failure is running out of money before you pass away. Insert a transaction where you buy a second house, and you can see how that affects your success or failure rate. Increase expenses by $5,000 a month for the first five years in retirement, and you can see today how that might impact your financial success in not just five years but 10, 20, or 30 years into your retirement.

Additionally, it's helpful to look at worst-case scenarios. What happens if the market drops by 40% the day after I retire? What happens if I need to increase my expenses? What happens if the cost of healthcare doubles every five years? What happens if I buy a second house, increase my expenses by $5,000 a month, and then the market drops by 40%?

Monte Carlo analyses aren't perfect by any means. Very small and seemingly insignificant changes to inputs can produce very real and dramatic changes to the results. For example, assuming your portfolio has a 5% future growth rate and a 2% inflation rate will produce a much rosier outlook than a 4% future growth rate and a 3% inflation rate. The old computer adage is true here: garbage in, garbage out.

These programs are most beneficial when you have the experience and knowledge to know what information and assumptions to use. The investment you make into working with a retirement financial advisor – even temporarily – will be well worth it. You can enter or enjoy retirement with greater financial confidence in your decisions and your finances.

Retirement Radar is one of the best ways to de-risk your finances. Want to know another way? Strengthen your finances by paying less in taxes. Let's look at how to do just that.

3. INCOME TAXES IN RETIREMENT

The biggest expense for nearly all my clients is taxes. If you can legally and ethically reduce your taxes, you can keep more of your money. That means you can withdraw less from your portfolio or spend more on adventures or gifts to causes you support.

Tax planning is like playing a game of chess. You must abide by the game's rules, but the rules offer a lot of flexibility. The tax game's rules are contained in the tax code – a set of complicated rules, explanations, formulas, and opinions on all things related to federal income tax. These rules are so complicated that the tax code is approaching 100,000 pages! And don't forget about state income taxes. This is daunting for any retiree doing their own taxes, but it can be a blessing for others since there is so much latitude. If your tax situation is even a little complicated, one of the best investments you can make is working with an experienced and knowledgeable tax advisor. If your tax situation is even slightly complex, they may save you a lot more than you pay them. We'll talk about this more in the next section.

Here are a couple of specific tax ideas to consider:

Roth IRA Conversions

If you have money in a traditional IRA or a 401(k), you may benefit from converting some of those assets into a Roth IRA. The distribution will be taxable, but being retired means you are likely now in a lower tax bracket. It can make sense to spread the Roth conversions over several years to spread the income and take advantage of the lower tax brackets.

Moving to a Lower Tax State

Many of my clients live in California, and this is a frequent topic of discussion. California has a high income tax rate, but many other states have high rates as well, including Hawaii, New York, Connecticut, New Jersey, Washington D.C., Oregon, Minnesota, Iowa, Wisconsin, Vermont, Maine, South Carolina, and Montana. As states grapple with budget shortfalls, look for this list to expand. More clients are entertaining the idea of moving out of their high income tax states in favor of lower or no income tax states such as Washington, Nevada, Texas, Tennessee, Florida, Wyoming, Alaska, or South Dakota. This is especially attractive to retirees who expect to have moderate-to-high income levels in retirement.

Thinking about moving to a low or no income tax state?
Better do it the right way.

I've had several clients move out of California and New York and relocate to lower tax states. In doing so, they save tens of thousands of dollars (sometimes even more) in state income taxes every year. They often save so much that they can afford a new house mortgage or can use the tax savings to go on more adventures, make a bigger impact, or help their kids.

Even when the financial savings are not quite that dramatic, clients who want a change of scenery can often still benefit from a lower cost of living in another state. But making the move takes more than filling a few boxes and renting a U-Haul. High income tax states don't like losing residents and the taxes they pay. If you are only pretending to move out of state, you are likely to be audited and caught. It's important you are diligent and document your move to prove you truly are a resident of the new state. This gets complicated if you plan to keep your house in the high tax state and buy a new house in a lower tax state. Each state has its own residency rules, so it's important to get good tax counsel.

For additional information, you can read an article I wrote for *Forbes* that goes into more detail on this.[102] If leaving your high income tax state interests you at all, read that article and work with a CPA to ensure you are doing it correctly.

4. BUILD YOUR RETIREMENT TEAM

Here, I will make a case for building your team. I've specialized in financial planning and investment management for nearly three decades, but I still have my own advisory team. There is too much at stake not to have the best minds and latest strategies available to help create your best retirement. If your goal is to de-risk your finances and create more financial strength and confidence, you'll want to work with a few professionals to help guide you and make the best financial, tax, and legal decisions.

I've written about the importance of having a team for years. I've been beating the drum for a long time, and most of this section has been covered in other books, speeches, and articles I've written or in my TV interviews and podcasts. Although it's not a new idea, too few retirees have the right team (or any team at all). That's a mistake that can derail even the best retirement plans.

I'm not shy about promoting the value of working with smart, experienced, and ethical advisors because I've seen the benefits of good advice compared to no advice. I once watched a client write a $15 million check to the IRS for federal income tax. At first, that sounds like a disastrous amount, but if she hadn't hired a team of experts, that check would have been closer to $25 million. By working with the right specialists, she saved close to $10 million on state and federal income taxes. If her team had been made up of a typical accountant, a general business attorney, and a normal financial planner, she would have left millions of dollars on the table. That $10 million of "found" money could be worth well over $100 million in her lifetime if invested.

This section's goal is to become familiar with who should be on your team, what role each member plays, what their qualifications should be, and most challenging of all, how to find them.

Who Should Be on Your Team?

Each retiree has their own unique tax, legal, and financial challenges and opportunities. At a minimum, however, you should expect to have (at least) the following three types of advisors on your team: attorney, tax professional, and a retirement financial planner. These three advisors represent your team's foundation – what I call *the advisor triad*. Think of them as three legs of a stool. You need all three to form a stable base so you can be secure in knowing the tax, legal, and financial issues that come with retirement are being addressed.

Your advisor triad consists of a financial advisor, attorney, and accountant.

Attorney

A good attorney is worth her weight in gold, but the problem is knowing what type of attorney you need. There are hundreds of specialties within the legal profession – from criminal to copyright to bankruptcy to divorce to real estate and everything in between. Think of law like the medical field, where "doctor" is a general term for anyone who has gone to medical school. You wouldn't go to a dermatologist for an appendectomy, and you wouldn't want to hire a business attorney for tax matters.

Having an estate plan is critical in retirement (more on this later). Estate attorneys, also called trust attorneys, specialize in minimizing estate/gift taxes and drafting documents that address the distribution of your assets before and after death. If you don't already have an estate plan or a relationship with an estate planning attorney, now is the time.

There are a few things you should consider when hiring an attorney. We have already introduced the first. Make sure you hire a specialist in the area(s) you need rather than a one-size-fits-all legal generalist. Specialists will cost more, and you may have to hire more than one, but they will pay for themselves many times over.

Second, does it make more sense to hire an attorney from a big firm or a small firm? I think the same rule applies to music. You don't listen to songs because Universal Music Group is the record label. You play the *artists* you like. Law firms are a collection of attorneys. Don't hire the firm; hire the attorney. Some of the very best attorneys in the country are with law firms with fewer than 10 employees.

Lastly, each state regulates attorneys who are licensed to practice law in their state. An attorney only licensed in California cannot provide legal advice if you live in Missouri, so your attorney must be licensed to practice law in your home state.

CPA/Accountant

A CPA, or certified public accountant, is a broad designation provided to someone who has passed a comprehensive exam administered by the National Association of State Boards of Accountancy and who meets additional state education and experience requirements. CPAs perform a vast range of services, from auditing to forensic accounting to corporate finance. The CPA you hire should focus on taxes, specifically tax minimization and preparation. A CPA is not a hired gun you bring in for a limited time to help address a specific issue. Your CPA will be a long-term and critical member of your retirement advisory team. You'll work with them throughout the year to minimize state and federal income taxes, and they'll help calculate your estimated taxes and prepare your tax returns.

CPAs can be sole practitioners, work on a team at one of the big accounting firms, or fall somewhere in between. CPAs will also typically specialize in personal returns (tax matters for individuals) or business returns (tax matters for companies). If you plan on owning and/or operating a business in retirement, a firm with more than one accountant may provide a greater depth of services and research to support your needs.

Financial Advisor

The third leg of the stool – completing the advisory triad – is the financial advisor. A good financial advisor will work with you before and after you retire. They can run the Retirement Radar (Monte Carlo simulations) and manage your assets. They should provide ongoing reporting, monitoring, and adjustments to your plan and investments throughout retirement.

Many retirees complain about working with several professionals and say that none of them know what the others are doing – the CPA doesn't know what the estate attorney is doing and is not aware of the insurance agent's recommendations. This can lead to inefficiency, extra fees, sub-optimal planning, and gaping holes in your estate, asset protection, and financial retirement plan.

The financial advisor is usually best equipped to manage the other advisors, to coordinate and oversee the plan, and to serve as the person you call first when you have a question. When the financial advisor fills this role, they are called the "financial quarterback" because they oversee all the moving parts of the client's tax, legal, and financial life. They are the ones who can identify when to bring in other experts and make sure all your financial bases are covered.

But why is the financial advisor best equipped for this role? Many aren't, which is why it's important to work with a comprehensive financial planner, someone who can provide expertise in the areas of insurance, cash-flow management, retirement planning, taxes, estate planning, asset protection, and investments. This sounds like a tall order, and it is. Most financial advisors are simply not qualified (regardless of what their websites, TV ads, or brochures claim), but you can learn how to separate the pros from the amateurs by asking the right questions. Download the top 12 questions to ask your financial advisor by going to BadassRetirement.com.

So, where should you look? A good place to start your search is through association websites. For example, you can go on the Certified Financial Planner™ website to search for retirement advisors by zip code, or you can reach out to me through the Badass Retirement Community, and I'll try to point you in the right direction. To find an attorney, you can use the American Bar Association's website. The

American Institute of CPAs also offers a "Find a CPA" tool as a way to start your search. You can find all these links at BadassRetirement.com.

Another strategy is to find one member of your triad – either the attorney, CPA, or financial advisor – and then tap into their connections to find the remaining members of your team. The idea here is that, if you find, for example, a great estate planning attorney, they can refer you to other retirement professionals in their network.

5. PREVENT FINANCIAL FRAUD

On December 11, 2008, anyone with an investment or banking account collectively gasped as Bernie Madoff was arrested by the FBI on suspicion of running the largest Ponzi scheme in history. Ultimately, thousands of clients were bilked out of billions of dollars. Unfortunately, Madoff was not the only advisor stealing from clients. In the days and months that followed his arrest, hundreds of other Ponzi schemes were exposed.

There are numerous ways to lose your money – divorce, spending too much, making bad investments – but fraud is a different animal. It's theft – plain and simple. Although media reports give the impression that financial fraud runs rampant, its frequency and degree of damage are far smaller than divorce or some of the other threats to your assets. Nevertheless, theft does occur, and it can devastate your finances overnight.

There are hundreds of different types of financial fraud. Bernie Madoff operated a classic Ponzi scheme, but there are many others out there. Some types can wipe out a significant amount of money instantly (e.g., wire fraud), whereas others are more gradual (e.g., skimming).

A good investment advisor will know more about you and your finances than almost anyone else in your life. They'll know how much you make, how you spend your money, how much you give to charity, and will often know about your relationship issues before others do. They'll know your background and who you are as a person. This can make for a deep, intimate, and satisfying relationship – built on trust, often lasting for decades. Unfortunately, it can also lead to financial abuse.

Crooked investment advisors can use your trust, coupled with their access to your financial accounts, to take advantage of you. Unless systems are in place, they could wire funds out of your account, overcharge you in fees, and make investments in bogus companies, amongst other unsettling possibilities. A good rule of thumb is to trust *but verify*. Regardless of how long you have known them, and even if they come to your children's birthday parties or were referred by a family member or friend, never let your guard down.

Don't blindly trust! Instead, download the "10 Tips to Prevent Investment Fraud" from BadassRetirement.com.

6. HELP CHILDREN/FAMILY THE RIGHT WAY

As a parent, I'd do almost anything to protect my child, give her opportunities, and help her create a better life. In fact, I'm likely to do more for her than myself. After working with hundreds of retirees for decades, I know I'm not alone in that sentiment. Parents will do things for their kids that they wouldn't do for themselves, and they will sometimes do things even though they know it will hurt them financially. As a result, if you have children and suspect you'd jeopardize your own financial security to help or protect them, you should consider these measures to de-risk your finances.

It's common for kids to struggle financially. They may have to live with you, or, even if they live on their own, they may not be able to afford necessities like health insurance. If they get into an accident or suffer an illness without health insurance, you may be inclined to cover these costs from your retirement portfolio – even if doing so endangers your financial health. A better option may be to help them buy health insurance before something like that happens. I have several clients who pay for their children's health insurance (or automobile or umbrella liability insurance) premiums every month. Ideally, the kids will get to the point where they can pay this themselves, but until then, most clients would rather pay a little more each month to minimize the possibility of a much larger expense down the road.

Some of you may balk at the idea of paying for your child's automobile or liability insurance, but you should look at it as an investment instead. It's not an investment that will appreciate over time or generate income; it's an investment against your own financial damage. When I was just starting out as a financial advisor, I had a conversation with clients who wanted to reduce their living expenses but who were paying their adult son's auto insurance premiums. I suggested they reduce their expenses by letting their son pay the premiums himself, but they said he couldn't afford proper coverage.

Sure, they might save a few hundred dollars a month, but what would happen if he got in an accident or was sued and didn't have proper coverage? Would they sit back and watch their only son suffer? They knew themselves well. They knew they'd pull even more money out of their accounts to help him in a crisis. Paying for his insurance looked like a bad financial decision on the surface, but was actually brilliant. They could afford to pay the monthly premiums, but they couldn't afford a much bigger financial hit if their son didn't have insurance and needed help.

When I work with clients in similar situations now, I tell them to do it for themselves as much as they are doing it for their children.

Some children may need substantially more financial help than others. Some parents make it clear they are not going to help their adult kids – they are on their own – while others grapple with wanting them to be independent but not wanting them to suffer. There are many reasons why our kids may need financial help – everything from mental illness, lack of motivation, drug abuse, physical impairment, poor work habits, or countless other reasons. Nobody wants to see their child hungry or homeless. Our natural reaction is to help – usually, in part, with money. Sometimes, a little financial boost is all that is needed to help them get through a rough patch, but often it requires a lot more financial help over the years. This is where it can impact your retirement's financial success. Parents will help even though it hurts them and their future.

There are no easy solutions when it comes to helping kids in need. There is often a constant tension between wanting to help but not wanting to hurt – either hurting your child or your own financial security. Here are a few ideas that I've seen work well with retirees.

Teach a Child to Fish

One of the best ways to help a child in need is not just to give them a quick fix but provide them with the skills and tools to create a better life for themselves. Your child's greatest financial asset is themself – their skills, education, experience, and future potential.

You're probably familiar with the saying *Give a man a fish, and you feed him for a day. Teach a man to fish, and you've fed him for a lifetime.* It's common to try to fix the symptom but neglect the cause. For example, let's say your unemployed daughter asks you to help pay her mortgage. If you want to help the right way, you need to look beyond the surface instead of transferring her money. Maybe she is unemployed because she doesn't have the right skills or has difficulty getting along with others. Maybe she works in a low-skill industry with low pay and high turnover. Dig deeper and see how you can truly help – not just today, but for the rest of her life. A discerning reader will recognize that this approach not only helps the child but also the parent in the long term.

When you invest in others, you are making a deposit that will pay dividends for life. Instead of paying off your son's credit card debt, what if you paid for him to attend a personal finance seminar to learn how to manage his finances better? And after that class you could pay for him to finish his degree or get an advanced designation at a local community college. There is power when you invest in others. For example, a one-night class can earn a 100,000% return on tuition. How is that possible? If your son currently makes $20 an hour as an administrative assistant, how much more would someone pay him per hour if he could also maintain the company's website and make minor changes when necessary? What if he learned how to use QuickBooks? What if he learned how to set up and run the company's blog? Would he be worth $30 an hour? Maybe $50? A $100 class at the local community college could earn him an additional $60,000 a year for the rest of his career.

Focus less on the immediate need and start to think about what will best benefit them in the long term. What skills can they learn that will make them more valuable? When you invest in your children, it's good for them and good for you.

Buy an Annuity

If you want to help, consider buying an annuity for your child or family member – but only if you can afford it. Annuities have the advantage of providing income for life. Because the money doesn't come all at once, an annuity protects the funds from financial mismanagement. The steady stream of income your child will receive also protects you from having to write additional checks if they make bad financial decisions.

Annuities are also highly customizable. Work with your tax and financial advisors on gift tax consequences to determine if it makes more sense for your child to be the annuity's owner or for you to be the owner.

Make it Clear

Seek clarity when it comes to helping a family member. The temporary discomfort of discussing the details is much better than the potential long-term relationship damage that can result from not being clear. What should you make clear? If you are going to give them a one-time loan, investment, or gift, make it known what it is. If you're not willing to do more, let them know.

Clearly, you care about them and want to see them succeed. Help them best help themselves by letting them know what you will and won't do to help. What will be best for them? If they know they have only one shot, they may think harder about asking you for help, and it may force them to dig deep to figure out the best way you can help them.

One of my clients said it best, "It's like a roll of toilet paper. When there's a big roll, you don't think much about it, but when it's running low, you start to think a whole lot more about how best you're going to use each square." Give them a roll and tell them they better make the most of it.

Distinguish Between Charity and Investment

I always ask my clients who want to give money to family members whether it is an investment or charity. If you understand the difference, you can set expectations up front and avoid relationship issues down the road.

For example, a client wanted to give money to his brother-in-law to help his struggling business. In this case, the client could afford it and wanted to do it. But was it charity or an investment?

An investment is where you anticipate making a return. You invest

$100,000, thinking it will grow to $125,000. An investment can lose money, but you expect to see some growth. The criteria for investment are numerous, and an investment requires a calculated assessment of the risks and potential reward. It requires due diligence and contracts. The motivation for an investment is to make a profit. On the other hand, the motivation for charity is to make a difference. Charity has no such expectation for profit. Charity is simply a gift where you don't expect a return on your money, and you don't expect your money to be returned at all.

The brother-in-law needed help with his business, but despite his intentions, this was not an investment. If my client went into this transaction thinking it was an investment, he would have been disappointed. Once he realized it was a terrible investment but a wonderful way to make a difference in his sister's life, the decision became easy. Communicating his desire to make it a gift took all the pressure off his brother-in-law and sister. They didn't feel the need to perform, quickly pay the money back, or worry about awkward silences and tension when the families got together.

Don't trick yourself or your advisors into thinking you are investing when you are really making a gift. They often look the same on the surface but have very different outcomes. Call it what it is, and everyone will be much better off.

7. MINIMIZE LAWSUITS

The primary goal of de-risking your finances is to protect your assets. One of the quickest and most financially devastating events is a lawsuit.

Imagine you are sitting at home one quiet evening, and there's a knock at your door. You open the door, and a stranger is staring back at you. "Are you so-and-so?" they ask. After you answer in the affirmative, they respond, "You have just been served." You tremble as you take the package and open it. Inside is a letter from an attorney, and the first sentence grabs you: "So-and-so is suing you for an undetermined amount." The rest of the words fade away. An undetermined amount?! Flashes of living under a bridge and eating out of a can flood your mind.

Lawsuits are terrifying, but if you haven't protected yourself, they can also ruin your retirement, putting your house, investments, and other assets at risk.

The best way to avoid getting hurt in an accident is to not get in an accident. Similarly, the best way to protect your assets from a lawsuit is not to get sued. But there is little you can do to avoid lawsuits. You can get sued by anyone, for anything, at any time. This means that everything you've worked so hard to build can be wiped away with just one lawsuit.

Excess Liability Insurance

As I wrote in my first personal finance book, my most recent personal finance book, and nearly everywhere else, the first line of defense is to have a personal liability insurance policy.

A personal liability insurance policy is designed to protect you against judgments from property damage, bodily injury, and personal injury lawsuits. The personal liability policy is sometimes called an "umbrella" liability policy because it sits on top of your automobile and homeowner's insurance policies and covers claims that are either not covered by those policies or that are beyond their limits.

Umbrella liability insurance is relatively inexpensive. Coverage starts at $1 million of liability protection and in most cases, should cost less than $300 a year. A good rule of thumb is to get a policy that is either at least $5 million or twice as much as your net worth. For example, if your net worth is $5 million, you'll get $10 million of liability insurance. If your net worth is $3 million, you'll get $6 million of insurance.

Umbrella liability insurance is an inexpensive way to safeguard what you've worked so hard to achieve.

8. ESTATE PLANNING

I've written extensively about basic estate planning strategies such as wills and living trusts, as well as advanced strategies like family limited partnerships, irrevocable life insurance trusts, charitable trusts, and nearly everything in between. For our purposes, we will stick to the basics here. If you think you might benefit from more advanced estate planning techniques, work with your estate planning attorney.

At a minimum, your estate plan should include a will, power of attorney for financial and healthcare matters, advance healthcare directive or so-called "living will," and for most retirees, a living trust. Many retirees buy into the need for these documents, but I've found not everyone wants or understands a living trust. A living trust can be critical to a retirement plan and provide valuable benefits you can't get with just a simple will.

A living trust goes by many names – living trust, revocable living trust, family trust, and *inter vivos* (Latin for "lifetime") trust. Regardless of the different names, a living trust is created when you are alive and is revocable – meaning you can modify or terminate it at any time.

A living trust has two primary benefits. It allows you to avoid probate and have greater control of your assets.

Avoiding probate is a tremendous advantage, but you may not fully appreciate this benefit unless you are familiar with the probate court process. Probate court is the state court that handles the orderly transfer of your assets according to your wishes as expressed in your will or, if you don't have a will, by your state's intestate laws.

You may be thinking, "What's so wrong with probate?" Depending on your estate's size and your state's laws, the probate process can be time-consuming, difficult to navigate, expensive, and public.

The second advantage a living trust has over a will is that it allows you to retain more control over your assets, including how and when they are distributed to your heirs. With a will, once probate is complete, your heirs immediately receive your assets. There are many situations (e.g., unmotivated adult children, spendthrift spouse, special needs child, real estate owned out of state) in which it makes more sense to use a living trust to limit how and when your heirs receive assets.

There are two other estate planning tools that are optional, but some retirees find them incredibly valuable: a letter and an autobiography.

The "letter" is simply a letter you write to your loved ones about what they've meant to you, what you've learned from them, what you want them to learn from your experiences, or anything else you want them to know. This can be a great way to impart your values to your loved ones. What can be difficult to express out loud can be surprisingly easy on paper. You can have one letter for everyone, or you can write separate letters. How you format it is entirely up to you. Be sure to mention this letter or letters in your will so they can be given to the appropriate people.

Some people find great joy in writing an autobiography. Your autobiography can be a handful of pages or a 50-page document. It can be an incredible experience to learn about a loved one's trials, tribulations, successes, and fears. If the idea of writing your life story doesn't excite you or you want something a little different, you can hire a company to help you create a video biography. Many firms will take you step by step through the entire process, helping you decide on the video's purpose and conducting the interviews, as well as shooting and editing the video (I've been recommending this to clients for so many years that I used to talk about recording it on a VHS tape!). Most people who go through this process find it to be an incredible and rewarding experience.

9. PROTECT ASSETS IN MARRIAGE/RE-MARRIAGE

The statistics on divorce are sobering. The U.S. Census Bureau reports the highest divorce rates are among men and women aged 55 to 64.[103] Even more sobering, the "gray divorce" rate has doubled over the past few decades.[104] Think about that. Right at the cusp of retirement or shortly into it is when divorces are most common. Each year, millions of people who have diligently saved, invested, and planned for their retirement can see their assets and income cut in half overnight.

Anyone who has experienced a divorce will tell you it is a tumultuous experience in which no one wins. Emotions aside, few single events can do more damage to your finances as a separation or divorce. In addition to the legal expenses – it can easily exceed six figures to resolve a contested divorce – it's not only possible but probable that you will lose at least half of your assets to your ex-spouse, as well as being required to make ongoing payments for years to come.

The only thing more heated and emotional than talking about divorce is talking about how to protect your assets in a divorce. Let me come clean so you know where I'm coming from or, maybe more accurately, not coming from. I'm not going to show you how to take advantage of an unsuspecting spouse. My goal is to share with you a few strategies that have been used for decades to protect the assets that come in during a marriage.

Although many people assume these strategies are only used by rich guys and their new young wives, this is not the case. More and more women are implementing the ideas I'm going to share with you to protect themselves in retirement. If you have money and want to protect it in case you get divorced, this lesson is for you. Period.

The laws related to divorce are complex and vary by state, so it's important to work with an experienced family law attorney to help you navigate these issues. It's helpful to think in terms of pre-marriage and post-marriage when looking at how to protect your wealth. There are different tools and strategies available before you get married and others once you are already married.

If you are not yet married (or remarried) and want to protect your retirement assets, explore these ideas with your legal and financial team:

Cohabitation Agreement

A client once joked, "The best way to protect yourself from divorce is never get married!" His advice may protect you from many negative financial issues surrounding divorce, but even this extreme position won't protect you from all the problems. Why? Many states have cohabitation laws or recognize common law marriages. This means that, if you live with your partner, you may have some financial liability, even if you never get married and then separate. Even in states such as California, where common- law marriages are not recognized and there are no automatic rights for non-marital cohabitants, there could still be a claim if there was an expressed or implied agreement between the parties.

What does this mean in the real world? Your ex-partner may find an attorney who will argue you made an agreement to provide support, even if you didn't. In other words, married or not, you need to be aware of this threat. One way to protect yourself is to enter into a cohabitation agreement with your partner. A cohabitation agreement is a document that outlines how property, assets, and debt will be divided, as well as how financial support will be handled, among other issues.

Speak to a family law attorney about the financial risks you face if the relationship dissolves. Find out if a cohabitation agreement makes sense for you.

Prenuptial Agreement

A prenuptial agreement (often called a prenup or a premarital agreement) is an agreement you enter before marriage that spells out who owns what, how income earned during the marriage will be treated, and whether there will be spousal support, among other issues. Without a prenup, your ex-spouse can be entitled to a large portion of your assets. The laws are tricky and different in each state, but if you have a properly drafted prenup, it can save you hundreds of thousands or millions of dollars in legal fees, spousal support, and assets.

If you are getting married, work with a family law attorney who specializes in prenups – ideally, at least 90 days before you get married. Prenups are binding agreements with strong case law and precedent, but if yours is to be held up in court, it must be done correctly. This means your partner must have their own legal representation and adequate time to review the document. The court needs to see evidence that your partner was not cajoled into signing it the night before the wedding. Prenups are not inexpensive to draft, but they can save you millions of dollars in case of divorce.

If you are uncomfortable speaking to your partner about a prenup, talk to your attorney for ideas on broaching the subject or have your attorney facilitate the discussion in a joint meeting.

As I said, a divorce can wipe out 50% or more of your assets overnight. If you are in a relationship, talk to an attorney about your options to protect your retirement assets in the unfortunate case of a separation or divorce. Even if you are uncomfortable with the idea, talk to an attorney to discuss which strategies may make sense for you.

10. LONG-TERM CARE PLANNING

When I wrote my first personal finance book nearly 20 years ago, I dedicated an entire chapter to long-term care planning. I just re-read it recently, and times sure have changed. Although most of the statistics on who needs long-term care, average stays, and types of long-term care are still similar, long-term care *planning* has changed dramatically since I first wrote on the subject.

Twenty years ago, it was easy to de-risk your finances by buying a standalone long-term care insurance policy that provided increasing daily benefits for a low monthly premium that was guaranteed not to increase. Today? It's a whole new (and not as hospitable) world.

This is unfortunate because the need for long-term care in retirement has only increased. Do an internet search for *long-term care statistics in retirement,* and you will be flooded with innumerous statistics. The U.S. government reports that someone turning 65 today has a 69% chance of needing some type of long-term care support in their remaining years and that 37% of people require care in a facility for more than one year.[105] Those statistics are both staggering and sobering.

After the fear of running out of savings, the most common fear for retirees is about their health and the need for long-term care. But there is one statistic that caught my eye and perfectly summarized the challenge of long-term care planning – *while one-third of today's 65-year- olds may never need long-term care support, 20% will need it for more than five years.*[106] That single statistic illustrates the uncertainty and difficulty for retirees in planning for long-term care. Other research comes to the same conclusion – about a quarter won't need any care, another quarter will require long-term care, and the remaining 50% will require some but not extensive care.[107]

How do you plan with those probabilities?

Clients who were faced with this dilemma 20 years ago had an easy (and often affordable) solution – buy a long-term care insurance policy. Today, those policies are scarce, provide fewer options, and cost a lot more.

Fortunately, there are only two long-term care strategies:

1. Do nothing
2. Do something

Do Nothing

This is a legitimate long-term care strategy. Doing nothing, however, isn't the same as ignoring any planning. Doing nothing means you've evaluated the options and concluded that not doing anything was the best strategy for you. Doing nothing requires great effort and careful analysis. And for the right situation it's a perfectly viable strategy. So, what's the right situation? There are several factors to consider.

Good current health. Research shows that being healthy in your late 60s is a strong indicator of the level of assistance you will need. Do you have any underlying health conditions, or are you generally in good health? Although there are no guarantees, the healthier you are today, the less likely you are to need extended long-term care in the future.

Favorable family health history. Although not a perfect indicator, you can look to older siblings. Are they in good health or do they have any heritable health issues such as diabetes, cancer, or heart disease? What about your parents? Are they still living? Any health problems? If they passed away, at what age and from what? Your family medical history can provide a great deal of insight into your health future.

Healthy lifestyle. Your genes may influence your future, but they don't dictate it. Lifestyle factors such as exercise and diet play an important role in your current and future health. If you take care of yourself, research shows you are less likely to require long-term care.

Prevention focused. One of the best indicators of long-term health is your focus on early detection and prevention. This means regular checkups and screening. The earlier your health team detects a problem or anomaly, the sooner they can treat the condition and prevent it from becoming a larger problem. I've never met anyone who loved going to the doctor to get poked and prodded, which is why 8% to 10% of people 65 or older don't go to the doctor.[108] If you are focused on detecting and preventing disease, however, by regularly taking blood tests, getting screening procedures, and seeing doctors, you may be able to minimize or avoid serious long-term care stays.

Financial resources. Long-term care planning has long been thought to be a middle-class problem. The thinking is the affluent have enough money to pay for their own long-term care, and the poor can rely on Medicaid to cover their long-term expenses. If you are in either of these camps, there may be less need for you to do something. This is where running different scenarios with the Retirement Radar can be very helpful. Can you afford to pay for a three-year long-term care stay? How about an eight-year stay? What effect does this have on your finances? You may survive the long-term care event, but will your finances? If you model different long-term care scenarios and have a high financial success rate, you may not need additional long-term care planning.

Demographic factors. There are several other factors that research has found to correlate with requiring no or limited long-term care. These include being married, better educated, and/or white.[109] Again, these are correlations and are not causal relationships. If you fall into these categories, however, you may be less likely to need long-term care planning.

So, does it make sense for you to do nothing? The list above is not exhaustive and should only be your starting point. Even if you determine you are in a favorable position for each of the factors discussed, that is no guarantee you won't need long-term care.

Do Something

After reviewing the list of factors above, you may determine that your risk is high enough to warrant additional long-term care planning. What are your options? Again, there are only a handful of viable strategies.

Family. Over half of long-term care is carried out in the home.[110] Your plan could include moving in with your children, having them move in with you, or relying on a spouse to care for you. If your children are willing and able to care for you, this is certainly a viable option. The key word here is "able." While your children may be willing to care for you and are part of a two-income family, it may be difficult to provide the level of support you need. In addition, moving in with children involves a lot of practical questions. Will someone be home or available 24 hours a day? Is there an extra bedroom? Is the bedroom on the first floor? Are there pet allergies? How close is the nearest hospital? Are there sidewalks for exercise?

As long as the children can provide the right kind of support and the parents and children work out the arrangement's details, a multi-generational household can be a wonderful experience for everyone. My wife's grandparents lived with her family for several years. She frequently tells stories of running home from grade school and spending her afternoons playing with them and watching TV in their bed.

I've had a few clients who have built a casita – a separate housing structure – on their property, renting them out for income but also anticipating either moving in themselves or moving their children in if they need long-term care. Others have moved closer to family members – siblings or children – as part of their long-term care plans.

Personal finances. If you have the financial resources, you can pay for the cost of care out of your own assets. Most clients decide they will self-fund any care they may need after looking at the cost of long-term care insurance and running different projections using their own assets. This requires careful analysis, as the cost of extended care can be expensive – a price that is rapidly accelerating. Any future projections need to account for liberal costs and high rates of growth for those costs.

Government assistance. Don't count on Medicare to pay for your long-term care. The Medicare website plainly states that "Medicare doesn't cover long-term care."[111] Even when it does, it offers a narrow range of services. It is difficult to qualify for service, and if you do, the services are provided for only a limited time.

The good news is that Medicaid offers long-term care coverage. Medicaid is a very different program from Medicare, though. Most seniors, rich and poor, rely on Medicare for health insurance. As long as you have contributed to the Social Security system for the required number of quarters, you are eligible for Medicare, regardless of your income or net worth.

Think of Medicaid as the equivalent of college financial aid. If you have the resources to pay for a college education, you will not qualify for financial aid. Similarly, Medicaid is for those people who don't have the resources to pay for care themselves.

Qualifying for Medicaid is both easy and difficult. It is easy because it is the provider of last resort. If you are in a nursing home and have completely run out of money, you will not be sent home to care for yourself. Medicaid will intervene and pay your bill, though you will likely have to move to a Medicaid-approved nursing home.

The caveat is that, to qualify for Medicaid, you must have very little monthly income and few assets. If you have assets that can be used to pay for your long-term care, you will not qualify for Medicaid. Medicaid is sponsored by the federal government and by each state. As a result, the program varies depending on where you live. If you think Medicaid might be a viable long-term care solution for you, I recommend working with an elder law attorney or other professionals in advance.

Insurance. As I mentioned earlier, the long-term care planning landscape has changed dramatically in a short period. While it used to be relatively easy and inexpensive to get a long-term care insurance policy, it has become difficult at best and impossible at worst. Why? Because the insurance companies made a big mistake.

In the early years of long-term care, all the insurance companies (big and small) wanted a piece of this business. They aggressively priced their products to attract customers but also underestimated the number of claims they would have to pay in addition to the number of policyholders that would retain their policies. In short, they made several big actuarial and policy miscalculations that made this line of insurance much more expensive than they anticipated. The result? Most companies stopped offering new long-term care insurance policies. In just 15 years, the number of stand-alone long-term care insurance plans dropped by 90%.[112] Additionally, they dramatically increased the insurance's cost for the clients who already had policies. Some policyholders saw 30% increases in their premiums for several years in a row. The insurance companies wanted out of long-term care insurance.

As a result, long-term care insurance planning has become challenging. There are still some companies that offer standalone long-term care insurance policies, but there has been a transition to life insurance policies with a long-term care benefit. The majority (84%) of new long-term care insurance policies purchased now are through this newer hybrid insurance model.[113] Here's how they work...

Under a "linked benefit" structure, the long-term care benefit – the number of dollars you have available to pay for your long-term care – is approximately five times the premium you pay for the policy. For example, if you pay $100,000 for the life policy, you might have up to $500,000 of long-term care available. Adding a long-term care rider on a life insurance policy is another option, but it generally doesn't provide as many long-term care dollars. Married couples can use a pooled policy that provides long-term care benefits for both spouses – albeit typically at a reduced amount.

The hybrid policy's main advantage is that, if you don't use the long-term care benefit – because it is a life insurance policy – a death benefit gets paid to your spouse or heirs. One of the complaints with traditional standalone long-term care insurance is that you could pay for the policy for decades and pass away having never needed it. With the hybrid policy, your beneficiaries typically get back at least the premiums you put in.

The other advantage is that your premiums will not increase. The reason they won't increase, however, is also one of the main disadvantages: they usually require a lump-sum premium payment. So, instead of making smaller monthly premium payments, you'd need to write one large check.

These hybrid policies are a reasonable solution under the right circumstances. The only way to know if they make sense for you is to get quotes from several companies. Once you have the quotes, you can run a Retirement Radar analysis that considers the large lump-sum premium payment compared to forgoing the coverage but facing a long-term care event.

It's not possible to de-risk your finances in retirement completely, but if you implement the strategies in this Challenge, you will go a long way to reducing the financial risk you face.

You just read three Challenges focused on retirees' greatest concern – money – but there is another issue that dwarfs even concerns about running out of money, and it explains why an 80-year-old billionaire would do anything to switch places with a broke 20-year-old: Health.

A full 96% of retirees say health is more important than money in living well in retirement – and that figure rises to 99% for retirees 75 or older.[114] The lesson? Money is the most important thing we all think about, stress over, and plan around in retirement until we are faced with a health problem. Money is still incredibly important – even more so if we are sick – but it becomes secondary when we are in pain, debilitated, or faced with a life-threatening condition. Suddenly, all the financial projections become less significant, and plans for the future become increasingly uncertain.

How well you feel physically and mentally and the amount of energy you have are key levers of living a Badass Retirement. It's hard to live to your potential, make an impact, and tackle big challenges when you are in chronic discomfort or lack the energy to get out of bed, let alone embark on an adventure.

The next and final section is Momentum – specifically, how to create and sustain it throughout retirement. First up? Your health. Nothing will bring your Badass Retirement to a screeching halt faster than a health issue for you or a loved one. Learn how to upgrade your health in the next Challenge.

JOIN THE FAMILY

De-risking your finances isn't something to check off a to-do list; it's something you continuously do. Join the Badass Retirement Community and take part in our regular discussions, workshops, and courses so you can ensure you stay on top of your finances.

GO TO BADASSRETIREMENT.COM

SECTIONS

MAGNIFY

MINDSET

MEANING

MONEY

MOMENTUM

13

CHALLENGE

Upgrade
Health

Invest in your most valuable asset to
feel better, live longer, and to have
more energy throughout retirement.

CHALLENGE 13

I want you to become an athlete in retirement.

If you want to live an Average Retirement, take your Geritol and feel good about walking around the block every once and a while. If you think it's crazy or impossible to upgrade your health in retirement, that means you've bought into the Retirement Myth. If the thought of becoming an athlete in retirement seems absurd, you've bought into the Retirement Myth.

Why do I use the word "athlete"?

If you strip away the jerseys and the glitz, athletes are just individuals who invest their time and energy into improving their performance. Athletes want their bodies to perform at their best – nimbly, free from pain. They want to be durable, avoiding tension and injuries that can keep them sidelined, unable to train or perform. They want to be able to recover quickly and thoroughly so they are ready to face any obstacle the day might bring. They want ample energy and the stamina to perform at the highest level for years or even decades. Guess what! Everyone wants these things in their life – *especially* aging retirees!

Ronald Reagan may have been president and Madonna may have been playing on your boombox the last time you wore a uniform. That's okay. You may have never even competed in sports in your life. That's okay, too. Your past athletic endeavors and your current health are irrelevant. We all enter retirement in different conditions and at different levels of health. You may be an Ironman competitor with the bloodwork of a 20-year-old, or maybe you are pre-diabetic and have a hard time completing a hike. Doesn't matter. You may not look or feel like an athlete today. That doesn't matter, either. The goal is the same for everyone – upgrade your health in retirement by thinking and acting like an athlete and utilizing the 9 Health Levers discussed in this Challenge.

Your health is central to your experience and enjoyment of retirement. If you've ever had health issues, you know exactly what I mean. You can be in the middle of an exotic adventure with friends and having the time of your life, but the moment you get a throbbing toothache, none of it matters (this happened to me in Africa and I needed a root canal). Getting your health right is the most important thing you can do in retirement. This is why Upgraded Health is one of the **Badass 5** drivers. I want you to think and act like an athlete and invest in yourself so you can feel amazing, live longer, have more energy, and be pain free throughout retirement.

Here's the good news. It doesn't matter where you begin the journey to upgrade your health; you just need to take that first step. You might start by taking a multivitamin and walking 15 minutes a day, or you may do high intensity interval training and get weekly NAD+ IV infusions. Upgrading your health only requires you get started. However, if you want more, you're going to have to do more. You will need to think and act differently than the average person your age thinks and acts. You need to shed your gloomy perception of health and aging, and reevaluate what you think is possible.

You have more time and resources in retirement than you've ever had in your entire life. Retirees living an Average Retirement don't think it's possible to upgrade their health, so they fail to invest these ample amounts of time and resources into bettering their own bodies. Retirees will spend hours every week watching athletes, but few invest the same time into becoming athletes themselves.

Average Retirement means average health, and trust me, you do not want average health.

The statistics are sobering. According to the National Council on Aging, 80% of adults 65 and older have at least one chronic condition, and 68% have two or more – everything from hypertension to diabetes to coronary heart disease.[115]

This is what average health looks like over a lifespan:

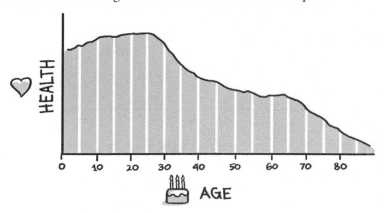

For most people their health declines over time with age.

You see a marked decline in health, fitness, and functioning in midlife. This is likely due to a focus on work and family at the expense of health. We sacrifice sleep to have more time for work. We opt for fast and processed foods because they save time. Exercise is something we might get to if we have time, but only after we've done everything else. As a result of these tradeoffs, the health of the average person drops between the ages of 40 and 60. Their stress, cholesterol, blood pressure, blood glucose, and weight all increase, while their energy, mobility, and muscle conditioning drop over the same period.

You may have bucked the typical midlife trend by making health a priority or you may have experienced the same drop in health that affects many in their working years. It doesn't matter. You may be scaling mountains in your free time, or you may even be able to get on a scale. It doesn't matter. You may regularly surf the waves, or you may only surf the internet. It doesn't matter.

Regardless of your past and where you are today, you can always upgrade your health. Remember, you have more money, resources, and time to devote to improving your health than ever before. The goal is to work hard and make good decisions so that you can experience a boost in health that benefits you for years in retirement.

The purpose of upgrading your health is not to live as *long* as possible, but to live as *well* as possible for as long as possible.

This is how I visualize what upgrading health looks like:

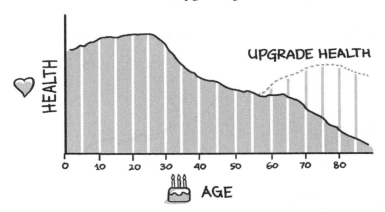

Can you actually improve your health with age in retirement?

In upgrading your health, you not only increase the number of years you'll live, but also the quality of those years. It's not about lifespan; it's about *healthspan.*

HEALTHSPAN > LIFESPAN

If you could extend your life by 20, 30, or even 100 years, would you? If you're like most people, your answer is most likely "no." In polls asking U.S. adults if they would use life extension technology to increase their lifespans, 65% of respondents have said they would not – or, at least, would have reservations about doing it.[116] A Pew Research Center survey showed that only 8% of respondents thought it was ideal to reach an age over 100 years, with nearly twice as many people (14%) saying they thought living to age 78 or less was ideal.[117] Another surprising finding is that, regardless of the age of the respondent, the answers were quite consistent – the younger and older alike shared similar views on the ideal life expectancy. So, what's going on here?

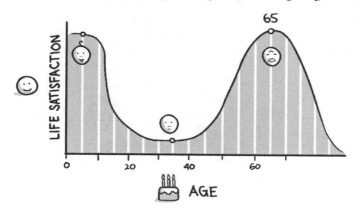

Life satisfaction can improve in retirement.

Research shows life satisfaction starts to decrease rapidly as we age.[118] The oldest experience the lowest levels of life satisfaction. Why? Our satisfaction and overall well-being are directly related to our health. It's not about the number of years we live, but how we live the years we are alive. The old model looked at health as a function of your lifespan – how long you live. That's a flawed model. Nobody wants to live longer if it involves being in pain or suffering from disease. This explains why few people want to live past 100. We all have a picture in our heads of what that looks like, and we don't want any part of it.

If lifespan is the old model, what is the new model? Healthspan. Lifespan only focuses on how long you live, while healthspan expands on this notion to include how long you live feeling well and healthy. My philosophy of health in retirement is simple. Feel good so you can make an impact, live your purpose, be bold, and take on adventures.

The aim of thinking and acting like an athlete is to live as long as possible while remaining healthy, mobile, and mentally sharp, with the energy to do all the things you want.

Under those conditions, aging doesn't have to be a death sentence.

In fact, it's more helpful to think of it as a life sentence.

LONGEVITY ESCAPE VELOCITY: THE RACE AGAINST TIME

Growing up, I couldn't wait for Saturday mornings cartoons – Bugs Bunny, Foghorn Leghorn, Wile E. Coyote, and the Road Runner. In every episode, Wile E. Coyote would chase the Road Runner, but just as he was about to catch up, the Road Runner would let out a "beep-beep" and speed out of reach. The Coyote could never catch his prey.

If we reach longevity escape velocity, death may never catch up with us.

Scientists think we are getting close to creating the same Coyote-Road Runner dynamic with life extension. Advancements in research and new technologies may get us to the point where science can extend our lives by more than a year for every year we are alive – the so-called "longevity escape velocity." If you make it until next year, the advancing technologies that are discovered and created in that year will help you live for more than another year, not giving death the chance to catch up.

Let that sink in.

Experts suggest that, because of overlapping advances in fields such as DNA sequencing, gene editing, supercomputing, precision medicine, and artificial intelligence – among many others – the date we reach longevity escape velocity could be closer than most of us think.

If you are part of the 92% who doesn't want to live past 100, would you change your mind if you knew you'd be healthy, active, and mobile? The goal for longevity is not just to be alive, but *to live*.

It's possible we could see dramatic advances in longevity in the coming years. When my clients express that they want to live longer and better, I tell them we are in a race against time. We need to live long enough for the science to improve to the point that we reach longevity escape velocity.

Until then, our job as athletes is to flourish physically and mentally. We need to both prevent disease and upgrade our health. Invest your resources – time and money – into improving your health. This is not the area to try to save a buck. If working with a private trainer is what you need to get exercise, hire them! If you need to invest money into a piece of exercise equipment, buy it! If you have to spend more money on healthier foods or nutritional supplements, order them! If you can afford it, do not hesitate to invest your money into your health. It's the best money you can spend in retirement.

Download the guide, "Staying in the Game: Preventing the 6 Most Common Diseases in Retirement" from BadassRetirement.com (if you're a man you must read #1 – it could save your life). You'll learn about the two mental conditions and the four physical afflictions that can significantly and negatively impact your life in retirement – even ending it prematurely.

The best time to dig a well is before you need the water. Don't put off upgrading your health until you're not feeling well. Do it now. The rest of this Challenge will walk you through the 9 Health Levers you can control to optimize your health.

THE 9 HEALTH LEVERS

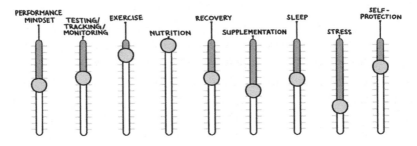

Want to upgrade your health in retirement? These are the 9 Health Levers you can control.

As an athlete in retirement, these 9 Health Levers are your greatest tools for controlling and upgrading your health and performance at any age:

1. Performance Mindset
2. Testing/Tracking/Monitoring
3. Exercise
4. Nutrition
5. Recovery
6. Performance-Enhancing Supplements
7. Sleep
8. Mental Health/Stress
9. Personal Self-Protection

A word of caution before you continue: Although I've been focused on exercise, nutrition, and health for decades, I'm not a health expert. I'm a "doctor," but not the kind that counts here. Even though I feel like I have a good sense of what works and what doesn't, please do not take anything I write here as medical advice. Your physical and mental health are too important to confine to a chapter in a book. Remember the Challenge *Take Control?* You need to take control of your health. Use these Health Levers as a starting point but continue to research and seek professional medical advice before making any changes to your diet or exercise routine.

Health Lever #1: Performance Mindset

Many years ago, I participated in my first triathlon. Even though it was a sprint – the shortest distance triathlon – I was a nervous wreck. I was a terrible runner, a bad cyclist, and an even worse swimmer. But I had trained and was ready to take the plunge – both literally and figuratively. Unsurprisingly, I struggled with the swim, the bike, and the run. My goal was simply to finish.

As I was nearing the end of the run, I heard race personnel calling out to the runners to guide us down the right path: "Athletes to the right. Athletes, make your way to the right." I nearly turned left before the thought occurred to me, *Is she talking to me? Am I an athlete? Whoa.* That hit me. I hardly remember anything about the event, but I can still hear her voice saying, "Athletes to the right." She *was* talking to me. I'd never thought of myself as an athlete in my life, but there I was – an athlete. She said it, and I was starting to believe it. That was a profound moment because I started to think differently about myself and what was possible.

I want you to experience the same mental shift, which begins with you asking yourself a few questions. What would your retirement look like if you were an athlete? How much better would you feel? How much more energy would you have? What could you do that you can't do now?

Lurched over at the end of the race, my legs aching, out of breath, I became an athlete.

You may be thinking that I wasn't *really* an athlete. Sure, I had just completed a very short swim, a casual bike ride, and a jog. It was no grand athletic achievement. I didn't win anything. I was just happy to have finished. Trust me – nobody would have mistaken me for an athlete. I didn't look like one. I didn't act like one. I didn't feel like one. But in that moment, I became one.

The greatest mistake you can make is to think change takes time. It doesn't. Change can happen in an instant with just a glance. A conversation. A lab result. A promise. A word. An act. A thought.

The consequences of change – losing weight, getting your degree, starting a company – can take months or years, but the outcome is secondary to the thought. Your identity can shape your actions just as much as your actions can shape your identity. There have been several critical times in my life where, in just an instant, I shifted my thinking and immediately set off on a new path. In many cases, the results took months and even years to realize, but the shift started with just one crucial moment.

The reason change can happen with just a thought is because it can change how you think about yourself – your identity. Your identity colors how you think and the decisions you make. Much of therapy is helping clients construct new and healthier identities. Psychologists know that people will fight to defend their identities – sometimes with words and sometimes with violence. Dale Miller, Stanford professor and author of the book, *The Power of Identity Claims*, writes, "Embracing an identity, more than just endorsing a self- description, involves making and defending claims about oneself. The satisfaction and dissatisfaction that we derive from identity-relevant actions are based less on what those actions do for us than on what those actions say about us."[119] When we change how we think about ourselves it changes who we are, what we perceive, our values, and our actions – it changes our identity.

You may be out of shape, struggling with addiction, or suffering from a chronic condition. Your current beliefs – e.g., that you're lazy and will never feel good, you can't quit, or your health will continue to slide – will continue to influence your every thought, decision, and action.

When you think about upgrading your health – exercising more, eating better, and becoming stronger, do you find yourself thinking, *Oh, I couldn't do that*, or *That's not me*? You're right. Your current identity wouldn't do it. Improving your health is not "you" because you do not identify as someone who exercises or eats well.

Being an athlete is as much mental as physical. The Performance Mindset shifts how you think about yourself and what is possible.

And what's incredible is that this shift can occur in an instant. You can immediately choose to think about yourself differently. Your identity can instantly shift and with it, your thoughts and actions.

How can you engage the Performance Mindset?

Expand what you think is possible. What is possible for your health? Would you lose 100 pounds? Would you complete a marathon? Would you lower your blood glucose to under 100 mg/dl? The more you can expand what you believe to be possible, the more you can expand your health identity.

Keep asking WWAD. In the early days, when we are still shaping our new health identities, it can be challenging to know what to do. We can undermine our own success by making less-than-ideal decisions. If you are faced with a decision regarding your health such as if you are going to work out, what you should eat, or if you should sign up for that 5K, don't look inward for an answer. We know what you would do, and it's likely less than ideal. Instead, ask, "What would an athlete do?" Then answer the question. As a reminder to yourself to always ask yourself what an athlete would do, download the printable "WWAD" sign and hang it on your bathroom mirror, office, or gym. You can find the poster at BadassRetirement.com.

Stop thinking; start doing. It's 6 am, dark, and drizzling outside. You're asking yourself, *Should I go for my morning jog or stay in my warm bed?* You've already lost the battle. As soon as you start thinking, you start asking questions and that leads to rationalizations. The best question is no question. Create a plan and then stop thinking. The less you think, the better.

Take actions consistent with the identity you want. It can be a challenge to change how you think about yourself. If you can make the mental shift – like I experienced when I was told I was an athlete – use that to propel you. However, it's not always that easy. Our identities are entrenched and can be hard to shift. So don't set out with the goal to transform yours. Instead, get out of your head and start acting in ways that are consistent with the identity you want. If you continue to do things compatible with your desired identity, you'll start thinking of yourself differently. If it looks like a duck and quacks like a duck, it's probably a duck. If you find yourself exercising like an athlete and eating like an athlete, you just might start to identify as an athlete.

Be an imposter. If you feel like an imposter, you're likely doing something right. Like a well-traveled path, your identity becomes more deeply rooted and intractable. Chances are you have years or decades of thinking of yourself in a certain way. If you start to think or act in way that clashes with this ingrained identity, you will feel like a fake. *Why am I doing this? Who am I kidding?* If you start to doubt yourself and feel like a phony, you're on the right path – or, more accurately, on a new path. Stick with it. It might take time to forge a new track, but with consistency, it will happen.

Find the right team. Several years ago, I saw a doctor about knee pain I was having. After careful examination, he told me that, because I was getting older, I needed to avoid strenuous exercises such as hiking, jogging, and cycling. I thanked him for his time, and then I proceeded to rebuild and strengthen my knee. Since that appointment, I've hiked mountains, completed marathons, and ridden thousands of miles on my bike – all with no knee pain. The doctor was well-intentioned, but completely misinformed.

Doctors and nearly everyone else under the spell of the Retirement Myth continue to view retirees as frail and fragile, in need of being coddled and protected. This is the hospice mentality of making someone's remaining time as easy and comfortable as possible. If you are preparing for death, this is a compassionate approach. If you are preparing for life, however, this is cruel.

If your healthcare providers share the view that retirees are weak and feeble, find new ones that see you for what you are – a strong and resilient athlete who wants to upgrade your health and functioning. For years, my primary care physician was someone with lots of credentials from top medical schools, but she focused on treatment rather than prevention. Now, I go to a sports and wellness medical doctor who prioritizes prevention and optimizing my health through an integrated approach. I pay a flat monthly membership fee for his service. I can text him at any time and schedule appointments for no additional charge. Although insurance doesn't cover the monthly fee, I view it as an investment in my health.

Health Lever #2: Testing/Tracking/Monitoring

As an athlete in retirement, you will benefit from testing and tracking your health data. Fortunately, there are simple and accessible tools to help you collect quality data beyond just steps.

Data is not your friend. *Usable* data is. It's important that the data you obtain is useful and actionable. Otherwise, it's just numbers on a screen. The goal is for you to have information you can use to upgrade your health, spot and address issues early, and prevent health problems.

We are living in an incredible time. Just a few years ago, you wouldn't have been able to get the type of health data you can get today. If the current trend continues, which I think it will (see the longevity escape velocity discussion earlier), we are sure to see accelerating advancements in the type and quality of health data to which we have access.

What health data should you track and how can you get it?

The following are several key metrics you should measure consistently throughout retirement. By tracking this data, you can optimize your health and catch health issues early. Because the science and tools are advancing so quickly, for specific product recommendations, join our community at BadassRetirement.com for the latest.

Blood pressure. Your blood pressure is one of the most important health metrics you can track. Per the CDC, nearly 50% of adults in the U.S. have high blood pressure, and for older adults, the statistics are even worse: 64% of men and 69% of women between 65 and 74 years old have high blood pressure.[120] Prolonged high blood pressure can wreak havoc on your arteries and heart, as well as increase your risk for stroke, vision loss, kidney disease, heart disease, and heart attacks. There are simple steps you can take to lower your blood pressure, such as limiting salt intake, exercising more frequently, limiting smoking and/or alcohol, and taking prescription medications, but you must be aware you are at risk.

High blood pressure is called the "silent killer" because it typically has no obvious symptoms. The American Heart Association says many people with high blood pressure don't even know they have it. Fortunately, it's easy and painless to track your blood pressure.

Typical over-the-counter home blood pressure monitors cost less than $50 and provide highly accurate readings. The Mayo Clinic recommends measuring your blood pressure twice a day – in the morning before you eat, drink coffee, or take medications and then again in the evening.[121] They recommend getting two or three readings each time to make sure the results are accurate. There are dozens of mobile apps that let you manually record your blood pressure over time. Track your blood pressure with our daily tracker form you can download for free at BadassRetirement.com. Alternatively, you can get a monitor that automatically syncs your readings to an app on your phone, saving you the step of having to manually enter the readings.

A reading of 120/80 mm Hg or less is considered normal. If you consistently get readings above this level, speak to your doctor about steps you can take to lower it.

Cholesterol. Harvard Health reports that one in every six American adults has high cholesterol, which makes them twice as likely to develop heart disease compared to those with lower cholesterol levels.[122] Similar to high blood pressure, you may not even know you have high cholesterol, which is why you need to stay on top of your cholesterol metrics.

We've learned a lot about cholesterol over the past few decades – specifically, we now know it's not just a single number. There is so-called "good" cholesterol and "bad" cholesterol, but it's more nuanced than you may think. Unfortunately, your Apple Watch can't measure blood lipid levels. To test your cholesterol, you will need to get a blood analysis. Doctors recommend yearly routine blood tests, but I get full blood panels at least twice a year. Remember, you're an athlete. Your body and your health are your livelihood – literally. I'd rather have more data earlier than less data later. The sooner you and your doctor notice an issue, the sooner you can address the problem.

Blood glucose. Diabetes is one of the most common diseases and top killers in the United States. The CDC recognizes regular blood glucose monitoring as the most important part of *managing* diabetes.[123] As is so often the case in our healthcare system, the focus is on treating disease. But wouldn't you rather *prevent* diabetes? If you and your doctor notice that your blood glucose is steadily rising, you may be able to take steps to slow or even reverse this increase without needing daily insulin shots.

There are two simple ways you can test your blood glucose level. The first is by using a blood glucose monitor. Reliable and accurate monitors cost less than $30. You prick your finger and use a test strip to instantly check your levels.

Another option is a continuous blood glucose monitor. Unlike the manual test strip method, a continuous monitor is attached to your upper arm and tests your glucose levels throughout the day. Diabetics are often prescribed the continuous monitor, but it may make sense for you even if you don't have diabetes.

For those focused on upgrading their health, tracking how their bodies respond to certain foods provides them with important data they can use to alter their diets. For example, my blood glucose may spike and subsequently crash after eating a plate of pasta, but yours may not. My levels may not budge after a bowl of oatmeal, but yours may spike. There is no such thing as a rule of thumb or common wisdom when it comes to how our blood glucose levels respond to different foods. If you are looking to hone your diet with foods that work best for you, you must test your blood glucose response across a variety of foods. You can do this with a manual test strip or with the continuous version.

There are even apps that integrate with the continuous monitors that can graph your blood glucose levels before, during, and after a meal.

Additionally, doctors recommend getting the A1C blood test twice a year. A1C test results show your average blood sugar over the previous three months. This test can be included in your semi-annual blood panel.

Resting heart rate. Resting heart rate is another crucial measure of cardiovascular health. Research has found that the higher an individual's resting heart rate, the greater their risk of premature death.[124] In the same study, the data showed that a resting heart rate between 81 and 90 doubled the chance of death and a resting heart rate greater than 90 tripled the chance of death compared to a resting heart rate of 50 or less.

So, what is a normal resting heart rate? The American Heart Association identifies a normal resting heart rate for adults as being between 60 and 100 beats per minute.[125] Age and gender, however, are contributing factors. The U.S. Department of Health and Human Services reports that an average resting heart rate for a man aged 40-79 is 67 to 76 beats per minute and 70 to 78 beats per minute for a woman.[126]

Testing and tracking your resting heart rate is even easier than testing your blood pressure. The old-school method is counting the beats of your pulse for 10 seconds and then multiplying that figure by six to get the number of beats per minute. But it's not 1983 anymore. I recommend using a wearable device such as an Apple Watch, Fitbit, or Garmin tracker. These devices automatically test and record your heart rate throughout the day and night, identifying its trends over weeks or months. If you see a sustained increase in your resting heart rate, you should share this data with your doctor and have a conversation about your next steps. More likely, as you upgrade your health, you may see a steady decline in your resting heart rate.

Heart rate variability. Relatively unknown to most people until just recently, heart rate variability (HRV) measures your nervous system – specifically, the variation in time between each heartbeat. Harvard Health calls HRV "a new way to track well-being."[127] Harvard's report found that higher variations indicate greater cardiovascular fitness and more resilience to stress, while a lower HRV is related to cardiovascular disease and even increased risk of death.

Your HRV level is considered one of the best metrics for measuring physical fitness. As you upgrade your health, you may notice a rise in your HRV over time. Additionally, one of the primary advantages of tracking your HRV is that it can tell you if your body has fully recovered to the point that it is ready to perform. There are several wearable devices that can track your HRV during the day and/or while you sleep. Some of these devices combine sleeping heart rate metrics with HRV to provide a readiness score.

Fitness activity. We've come a long way from the 10,000 steps goalpost. Modern wearable devices can track not just steps, but hundreds of different activities from running to swimming to biking to rock climbing. These devices and the data they measure can help you track caloric expenditure, but more importantly, they can serve as motivators. Reaching 10,000 steps, closing the Activity Ring, or reaching your Activity Goal can help motivate you to go just a little farther or for longer. As you upgrade your health through increased exercise, you'll not only feel better, but you can also point to the data to track your progress. Many of these devices and apps allow you to compete against friends and family. This can provide an extra motivational boost that some users appreciate.

Body weight/fat. Weight may be the oldest and most common health metric we track. Bathroom scales are ubiquitous, but it's time to ditch your old scale and upgrade to a smart scale. In just a few seconds, smart scales can measure, record, and track body weight, body fat, body mass index (BMI), muscle and bone mass, and other metrics. Even better, this data can be automatically imported to mobile apps such as Apple Health or others so you can monitor these metrics over months and years. For a list of specific devices, join our community at BadassRetirement.com.

Sleep. How well did you sleep last night? In the past, it was hard to define, but now there are several sleep-tracking devices that can provide you with not just how many hours you've slept, but your sleep efficiency, the number of hours of deep and REM sleep, restfulness, and your overall sleep score. These devices can provide suggestions on when to go to sleep and can help you wake up at the optimal time.

You spend a third of your life sleeping, so you should have some idea of how well you are doing. Instead of guessing or basing your opinion on how you feel in the morning, you can look to real data to determine if you need to make changes. For example, I've found that if I eat within a few hours of bed or have any alcohol, it negatively affects my sleep.

With your sleep data, you can test what works and what doesn't for getting an optimal night's sleep. For a list of wearable sleep trackers and even sleep-tracking mattresses, go to BadassRetirement.com.

Genetic testing. The Human Genome Project, launched in 1990, set out to sequence the first human genome.[128] It took 13 years and is estimated to have cost $2.7 billion. That figure dropped to $100 million two decades ago, and today, sequencing costs less than $600.[129] Experts predict the cost could further decline to $100 or less. As a result of increasing technologies and decreasing costs, several companies offer genetic health screening, though be sure not to confuse this testing with the popular DNA genetic tests from companies such as 23andMe or Ancestry, which aim to provide you with information on your family's geographic origins and connect you with long-lost ancestors. The genetic health tests analyze inheritable genes associated with common health conditions such as heart disease, Alzheimer's, and cancer. For example, the genetic test offered by one firm selects 30 genes strongly associated with the eight most common hereditary cancers.[130] Other services combine DNA testing with bloodwork and your lifestyle habits to alert you to abnormalities and offer personalized recommendations. The costs of these services range from $200 to $600 depending on the provider and the level of detail you desire.

That being said, genetic testing has its drawbacks. Testing does not conclusively identify whether you will develop a disease or not. Yes, most diseases are influenced by genetic variants, but these tests are limited to detecting only a few major genetic variants. For example, there are thousands of variants that are known to cause breast cancer, but most genetic tests analyze just three. Additionally, even if you have a concerning variant, most mutations are not actionable. These tests can also cause a great deal of anxiety. Not everyone is comfortable knowing they have a genetic mutation that increases their risk for cancer or heart disease, and on top of that, many are uncomfortable sharing their DNA data at all.

For those who are comfortable with the limitations, these genetic tests can alert you to potential areas requiring more of your attention and resources.

Gut microbiome testing. Your digestive track is home to trillions of microbes that play an important role in not only digestion, but your overall health. These tiny organisms can influence how well you age, as well as whether you develop heart disease and diabetes – among many other known (and likely unknown) factors. For less than $100, you can purchase a home microbiome test and get your results in a matter of weeks.

This is a relatively new and exciting line of science that is likely to advance our understanding of our health and promote personalized healthcare – identifying which foods, supplements, and medications are best for each of us. Personalized healthcare could revolutionize our relationships with our bodies, helping us optimize what we put into them. The science isn't there today, but I'm confident that with the acceleration of technology, it's not far off. If you want to get a head start, there are several companies that provide this service. Go to BadassRetirement.com for a list.

Traditional screening. There are common tests all of us should have done throughout retirement such as screenings for colorectal cancer, prostate cancer, and abdominal aortic aneurysms, as well as routine mammograms, pelvic exams, bone density tests, allergy tests, comprehensive metabolic panels, dental exams (you'd be surprised how much your dental health can affect your overall physical health), and others. Follow the advice of your doctor, who can track your results over time to determine if any treatment is necessary.

I get it. Nobody likes to be poked and prodded. I've never met anyone who looked forward to seeing their doctor. However, our new job in retirement is to stay healthy. Getting our health data is an essential part of this process. If you start to have second thoughts, just remember to ask yourself: *What would an athlete do?*

Health Lever #3: Exercise

If you're reading this book, there is a good chance you are already active. But are you doing enough? Have you pulled back on your activity leading up to or in retirement? Have you been distracted by other things? Are you in a rut? Just as you learned about the Retirement Gap – the chasm between where you are and where you would like to be – ask yourself if there is a gap between your current health and what you think it could be. This section is focused on helping you close the exercise gap.

I'll skip the lecture on how important exercise is for physical health, offering cardiovascular benefits and increased life expectancy. I also won't include any research that shows how physical activity is associated with improvements in mental health, well-being, cognitive function, and emotional and psychological functioning. Not a word from me on how exercise can contribute to quality of life either. You already know that.

Furthermore, I won't cite statistics showing that a large percentage of older adults are either not getting any physical activity or below the weekly recommended amount.[131] The last thing you need to hear is scary figures like the fact that 3.2 million people around the world die each year from . . . inactivity.[132]

Exercise is one of the most important tools you have for upgrading your health – but don't just take my word for it. Look at the research. In a study of nearly 9,000 participants, researchers found that high levels of physical activity translated into a nine-year biological advantage.[133] If a nine-year biological advantage isn't big enough for you, the Human Performance Lab at Ball State University published research in the *Journal of Applied Physiology* indicating that 70-year-old participants who exercised had the heart, lung, and muscle fitness of healthy people 30 years younger.[134] The director of the lab and co-author of the study, Scott Trappe, explains, "We assume that, as you get older, you become frail and weak. But just looking at the muscle of older exercisers compared to younger ones, we couldn't tell who was young and who was old."

If you want to upgrade your health in and throughout retirement, you need to make exercise a part of your life. Fortunately, improvements to your energy and health don't require six pack abs or 10% body fat. It's all about functional health – what can you do and how do you feel? You can use your upgraded health to live longer, contribute more, and experience greater adventures – across the world or in the backyard with your grandkids.

Again, you already know that.

The problem isn't that we are unaware of the benefits of exercise, or the many problems caused by inactivity. No. The problem is that we don't exercise (or don't exercise enough), even though we know the benefits of exercise and the drawbacks of inactivity.

Our challenge is not rooted in knowledge or awareness; it's based on action. And it may not even be our fault.

Harvard evolutionary scientist Daniel Lieberman believes we are wired for inactivity: "When people don't exercise, we label them as lazy, but they are actually doing what we evolved to do – which is to avoid unnecessary physical activity."[135] This avoidance may be evolutionarily wise, but we know better.

I've always been fascinated with the question of why we don't do what we know we should do. This question is relevant for exercise and eating well, but it's just as relevant in every other domain of life finances, relationships, work, etc. Think about that for a moment. We know what we should do to improve our lives, yet we don't. We know that walking two miles a day will improve our moods, reduce our chances for disease, give us energy, and help us live longer. We don't just know this; we firmly believe it is true. But most of the time we still choose not to do anything about it. Logically, this doesn't make any sense. Why would we intentionally choose to undermine our own success, happiness, and even life?

It's not because we are irrational.

We don't do what we know we should because we think we have a good reason not to. We may be wrong. We may be hurting ourselves. We may be short-sighted. But we are not irrational. If you struggle with starting or sustaining an exercise routine, you may have good reasons. Our goal is to help you think differently so that working out can be a part of your daily life in retirement.

Use the following ideas to help you incorporate activity into your retirement and close your exercise gap.

Do what you enjoy. If you forget everything else in this section, don't forget this. For you to stick with an exercise program, it must be enjoyable – especially if you are just getting started. If you hate to run, stop running! This sounds like obvious and unnecessary advice, but too often people think they need to do certain exercises or activities, even if they can't stand them. So, they power through a few times until they become demoralized and give up.

Choose a physical activity you enjoy. Make a list of all the activities you like to do and focus on those in the beginning. For instance, I'm happy to lift weights or jump on a bike, but please don't make me swim. Do what you enjoy, and it won't feel so much like working out.

Find a partner. Get your spouse or a friend to be your exercise partner. Having companionship can make exercise more fun and enjoyable. Just as important, you'll be accountable to someone else. A friend of mine needs an exercise partner to hold her accountable. She says she never feels like working out but shows up anyway because she knows her partner is counting on her. Nothing wrong with using guilt to motivate you!

Do it with friends. Get a group of friends and/or family members together for regular activities. For example, every Monday morning you get together to do yoga in the park, or every Friday afternoon you kayak on the local lake. For years, a group of guys and I met on Saturday mornings to go hiking. There are countless activities you can schedule.

Get connected. Connected fitness has grown rapidly over the past few years and for good reason. Even if you don't have friends or a partner with whom you can work out, you can still feel a sense of connection and camaraderie. It can be 10° outside, and you can still work out in your basement with friends from around the world. There are several cool products – such as the Peloton bike and treadmill, Hydrow Rower, Tonal, and Mirror – that can help you work up a sweat and connect with others.

Incorporate low-impact exercise. A common worry about starting a new exercise program is the fear of injury. Our tendons, ligaments, and muscles don't have the same resilience they had when we were younger. You may have had previous injuries or surgeries that you are wary of exacerbating. Not to worry. There are many low-impact activities you can do with little chance of injury, including yoga, Pilates, tai chi, swimming, or biking. Talk to your doctor about the best exercises for you.

Perpetual event. One of the best ways to stay both motivated and active is to always be training for a scheduled event. This could be an organized event, such as a 5K or triathlon, or it could be something you put together, like a longer hike or bike ride with friends. Lifting dumbbells, jogging on a treadmill, or sitting on a stationary bike can sometimes feel a bit meaningless. To give your workouts a little more meaning, do what athletes do: train for an event.

When you have an event scheduled a few weeks or months in the future, you not only have something to look forward to but also something that requires you to train. The more you can link your training to a purpose, the more likely it is you'll feel compelled to do the work. Part of this being a *perpetual* event is that, before the day of the event, you have to schedule a new one further out. This ensures that, even if you finish the race, hike the mountain, or complete the big ride, you've got another goal on the horizon.

Use fear. I use this trick often. If I'm feeling stuck or need a boost of motivation, I'll schedule something that pushes my limits and scares the hell out of me. This strategy doesn't work for everyone, but it gets me moving because fear is a strong motivator for me. I don't want to fail. I've been doing this long enough to know just how far to push myself – too little and the fear of failure won't be strong enough, but too much and I'll back out. What event can you and a few friends commit to that will test your abilities and require you to be in better shape than you are now? Make it big and make it bold, but just make sure the thought of it lights a fire under you.

Go on adventures. For the adventurous among us (and we all should be adventurous in retirement!), you can get a group of friends to do "adventure trips," as I like to call them. This is travel with a physical component – hiking to Machu Picchu or climbing Mt. Kilimanjaro, for example. This type of trip works well when you allow for time after the adventure component for sightseeing and a more relaxing itinerary. It's a great way to recover and see the world.

It's common for workers to schedule personal time around a business trip, such as setting aside a few days to explore the city after a conference. Now that you are retired, you can replace the cocktail receptions, bad finger food, and boring presentations with exciting adventures.

Link micro habits. Pair an existing behavior or routine with a desired behavior. For example, when you get out of bed, do 10 push-ups. It's like behavioral dominos – you do the habit you already have (e.g., brushing your teeth) and pair it with a new behavior you want to become a habit. Make a list of all the behaviors during your day that you don't even think about, and then think of a small new behavior you can do right before or after a few of them.

A few common routine behaviors include turning off the alarm clock, getting out of bed, brushing your teeth, having a cup of coffee, checking email, eating breakfast, etc. You don't have to think about doing any of these – you just do them automatically. They don't take any effort or motivation. You can try pairing your alarm clock with jumping jacks. When the alarm goes off, you can't turn it off until you finish five jumping jacks. A friend lays out her jogging clothes and shoes at her bedside and won't turn off her alarm until she puts them on. Maybe you could do a 30-second plank before you can check your email. The benefit to this approach is you can integrate micro workouts throughout the day without even thinking about it. Have fun with this!

Compete. Our desire to win – or at least to not finish in last place – can be a strong motivator. There are large national (and local) competitive organizations such as the Senior Olympics that you can join to compete against others.

You can also use technology to compete with others near and far. Apps such as <u>Strava</u> offer a running and cycling social network where you can connect and compete with others. Some products, such as Peloton, allow you to compete with others in your class. I'll tell you from firsthand experience – it can be a huge motivator when someone 20 years older than you is kicking your butt!

Get a dog. Need a little inspiration and some companionship? Get a dog. Research shows taking care of a furry four-legged friend is associated with many physical and mental benefits.[136] You are guaranteed to get more exercise even if you don't want it! It's cold and raining at 7am? Too bad. It's walk time.

It was only just a few years ago I got my first dog, and I can tell you she has improved my life in so many ways. My family jokes she is my BFF, and I can't argue that. If you are new to being a dog parent like I was, it can be challenging if you travel a lot or you don't think you will have the time/energy to provide them with the exercise and attention they need. If you are unsure, consider being a foster dog owner for a few weeks. It's a great way to test the waters.

Dialing in Your Exercise Routine

If you already have a solid exercise routine you enjoy, stick with it. If you are new to exercise and are unsure where to start, here are a few things to consider.

Start slow. If you are just getting started on your path to upgrading your health and haven't been active until now, let me be the first to congratulate you. It's not easy to change direction and start something new and may be foreign to you. It takes courage. Before you start, make sure you get the green light from your doctor.

The biggest mistake I've seen people make when they start exercising is that they go too hard, too quickly. And I completely understand that. You want to jump in and start feeling the benefits of exercise. Unfortunately, if you do too much, the only thing you'll feel is sore and maybe injured. Take your time if you're new to exercise. There's no rush. Start slowly and go easier than you think. You need to build your foundation for exercise, and this can take time. That's okay. You have time. Exercise needs to be a consistent part of your life throughout retirement – not for weeks or months but for years and decades.

To reap the benefits of exercise, you need to make it a meaningful part of your life – ideally a part of your daily life.[137] In our younger years, we could miss a workout (or several) and not feel any different. We could take weeks or months off before jumping back in without missing a beat. Now that we are older, however, we don't have that luxury. We cannot afford to miss workouts or take time off. We need to prioritize fitness and make it a part of our daily routine.

Beyond walking. For the elderly or those with mobility issues, a walk around the block is a workout and an accomplishment. Don't delude yourself into thinking a casual stroll is sufficient, though. If you really want to improve your health, you'll need to do more – if you can. Remember, you're an athlete. Most retirees do too little to enjoy the benefits.

Exercise scientist and aging researcher Larry Tucker conducted a large-scale study that examined the effects of frequency, intensity, and duration of 62 different physical activities on 5,823 adults.[138] His conclusion? "If you want to see a real difference in slowing your biological aging, it appears that a little exercise won't cut it. You have to work out regularly at high levels."[139]

How often, how intense, and for how long do you need to exercise? The CDC recommends getting at least 150 minutes of moderate-intensity aerobic activity a week.[140] This equates to 30 minutes of physical activity per day, five days a week, though I recommend you aim higher. This figure is the bare minimum, which even the CDC acknowledges. If you want even more health benefits, you should double the minutes of moderate-intensity activity to 300 per week or aim for 150 minutes of vigorous-intensity activity (or some combination of the two).

Include weight training. At least a few days a week, you can toss your aerobic leotard aside and pump some iron. It is essential for retirees to incorporate weight training into their weekly exercise routines. The benefits of weight training as we age are well documented and include an increased ability to perform functional tasks, a reduction in chronic disease, lower mortality rates, and increased bone density, in addition to staving off osteoporosis.[141] Experts recommend resistance training two or three days a week for optimum results.

Go hard. If you have your doctor's approval, consider polarized training or high-intensity interval training (HIIT), which includes intervals of short but intense bouts of exertion followed by a brief recovery break. For example, a common interval would be a 20-second sprint followed by a 40-second rest. Common HIIT exercises are sprinting, biking, rowing, squats, push-ups, and burpees. The trick is to go all out during the exertion phase – 100% intensity. The good news about HIIT training is that the total workout can be completed in just minutes. The bad news is that it's brutal.

HIIT training has earned mixed reviews – some people love it and others (understandably) hate it. What's not debated, however, are the benefits. There is a large and ever-growing body of research on the many health benefits of HIIT training including decreases in several markers related to aging.[142] And HIIT isn't just for 20-year-olds. The research shows that HIIT is beneficial for older adults and can increase aerobic capacity, balance, and cardiovascular function, as well as improving lipid metabolism.[143] HIIT has even been shown to be safe for individuals with diabetes or heart disease.[144]

If you are still not convinced in the merits of HIIT, consider a study that compared two groups of stationary bike riders over a two-week period – one group biked moderately between 90 and 120 minutes, three times a week, while the other group biked four to six HIIT sessions of 30 seconds each. If you're doing the math, one group biked about 12 hours over the course of two weeks while the other group biked about 12 minutes. The results? The HIIT group experienced the same, *if not better*, levels of fitness and positive cellular changes.[145] If you can suffer through HIIT – even if just occasionally – you are likely to experience rapid improvements in muscle tone, cardio fitness, and VO_2 maximum oxygen levels.

Get outside. The beneficial effects of exercise on your mental and physical health are real and numerous. For an extra boost, you can couple exercise with nature. Outdoor exercises offer great flexibility and there are nearly limitless ways to get a workout. One common complaint about exercising indoors is the boredom stemming from the limited options and from doing the same thing over and over – think treadmills, stationary bikes, basketball, swimming, racquetball, etc. When you bring your workout outdoors, the whole world becomes your gym. Take a walk in your local park, do a trail run, hike (or bike) a nearby mountain, or do Pilates on a beach. As you get more comfortable being active outdoors, you can take on organized events such as 5K runs and triathlons.

The research concludes that exercising outdoors can increase self- efficacy (remember how important self-efficacy is?), in addition to improving your well-being, mindfulness, and blood pressure.[146] In a meta-analysis of several studies, researchers attempted to determine if there were any different outcomes between exercising indoors and outdoors.[147] The results were conclusive: "Compared with exercising indoors, exercising in natural environments was associated with greater feelings of revitalization and positive engagement, decreases in tension, confusion, anger, and depression, and increased energy." In the investment world, the term "alpha" is the excess return an investment earns above its benchmark. Every investor wants alpha – it's a free lunch. This is how I think about spending time outside – especially exercising outside.

Seek adventure. For the more adventurous, you can bundle exercise with the wilder parts of our world. There are several groups like Ageless Adventures, Evergreen Club, ElderTreks, and Walking the World that organize physical adventures around the world. Even better, you can bring your spouse or a few friends for a truly unforgettable exercise adventure!

Not sure how to incorporate adventure in your life? Join others who make adventure a part of their retirement.

Health Lever #4: Nutrition

I've been focused on nutrition as long as I can remember. I had the benefit of being raised by a mom who was ahead of her time. Long before health food stores and supplement companies were mainstream, my mom was in the thick of it. She was an avid *Prevention* reader, and when I was very young, she increased her knowledge by working at a health food store. Even better, she liked to bring her work home with her. While the other kids took a single Flintstones Vitamin in the morning, I had a handful of vitamins, minerals, and other supplements. I was also the only ten-year-old taking performance-enhancing supplements. No, she didn't give me testosterone or growth hormones, but before each baseball game, I'd choke down a spoonful of bee pollen and brewer's yeast so I'd have more energy and focus. If only there was a natural powder to help me throw a fastball a little faster!

I've discovered that nutrition is as important – if not *more* important – than exercise when it comes to upgrading your health. Unfortunately, the science is not crystal clear. There isn't a single nutritional diet that is ideal for everyone.

That's not to say there isn't ample evidence of things you can eat to increase longevity and vitality. You might not like the findings of this research, and if you are adamant that your view of nutrition is the best, you can likely find studies that support your pre-existing beliefs. Do yourself and your health a favor, though, and keep an open mind.

Nutrition isn't math; it's probabilities. This means that you will never find the one right answer. There are too many variables and factors to identify definitively what is ideal for each unique body. That's okay, though. We don't need perfect. We can still get close by using probabilities. You just have to discover the foods and the approach to nutrition that is most likely going to produce the best answer to the question: *What will help me feel better and live longer?*

My philosophy on food is that it's nothing more than fuel. I know the foodies will scoff at that, but I truly view nutrition as something that can be optimized to help me perform and feel my best. I'll eat or do pretty much anything to upgrade my health. If that means eating crickets, pour me a bowl. If it's eating spinach, make me a salad. If it's choking down a nasty green shake, bottoms up.

Our challenge in finding the foods that are best for us is not the lack of information; it's the lack of *actionable* information. Do a Google search for "nutrition" and you'll get over a billion results. Thousands of new research papers, books, and articles on nutrition flood the market every year. A lot of their information is conflicting. Milk does a body good. Except it doesn't. There are volumes of independent, peer-reviewed studies that find milk doesn't do the body any good. You probably remember growing up being told that fat was bad and would kill you – turns out that may not be true. Or what about carbohydrates? We were told to eat lots of whole grain carbs because they fuel your body. But now we hear a low-carb diet is healthier for us. What about the adage that you need meat for the protein? Do you, though? Is fish good or does it have too many toxins? Is Paleo or plant-based better? What about the keto approach? What about a carnivore diet?

It's no wonder we don't know what's good for us! You can find a study that supports or discredits nearly any food or diet. A handful of poorly designed or potentially biased studies do not make for good science, but because they usually provide surprising findings, these are the papers that get the attention of the media and social networks. Just as commonly, a single individual will make a video or write a book about how a particular food or diet has cured them or changed their life. Others with that same condition or goal flock to them, and a nutritional movement is born based on no scientific evidence and a single study. These authors probably mean well – maybe the diet cured them or made them feel better, so they want to tell others. But what if the results are short-lived? What are the long-term consequences? What other health issues are being created because of the new diet? Not all evidence is created equally. This is your health – and by extension, your life – we are talking about.

The goal for this section isn't to settle the great food debate. There aren't enough pages in this book, and I'm not even remotely qualified. However, I've done considerable research over the last several decades and I lean on those who are qualified to help guide my approach to nutrition. My strategy for trying to make sense out of all of this (often conflicting) information is to focus on where there is <u>overwhelming scientific evidence</u>.

OVERWHELMING SCIENTIFIC EVIDENCE

Focus on what most of the scientific research finds to be true when making decisions about your health.

The good news is there is a specific diet that is optimal for your genetics and specific biochemistry that will provide you with the best physical and mental health. The bad news is you likely don't know what it is. That's okay. I'm still experimenting with my diet, and I've been tinkering for a few decades! Instead, the goal is to adjust and test – to gradually get closer to optimal.

Could you find a study that shows a diet of Skittles and hot dogs is good for you? Probably. But we need to raise the bar for what we find convincing. Overwhelming scientific evidence means there are hundreds if not thousands of peer-reviewed studies that support a finding. If you want to upgrade your health, following such evidence is key.

However, there is one gigantic caveat. If you follow the evidence but don't feel well, be open to experimenting. Remember, nutrition is not black and white. We all react to foods and process nutrients differently. You may feel amazing on a low-carb and high fat diet, but your spouse may feel perpetually lethargic. Your job is to adjust and experiment; to figure out what gets you moving and what leaves you feeling flat.

Start your journey by focusing on the evidence, but don't be afraid to mix things up if it's not working for you. Try vegan. Try keto. Try low-carb. Try carnivore. Test; don't trust.

So, what does the overwhelming scientific evidence tell us about nutrition? It's clean <u>and</u> functional. At least that's how I think about it…

Plant-focused. A plant-focused diet may provide the best health outcomes for most people. Plant-focused doesn't mean you have to become a vegetarian or vegan, but it does mean your diet should consist mainly of foods derived from plants.

In a recently published study in the *Journal of the American Heart Association*, the diets and health of nearly 5,000 adults were followed for 32 years.[148] The conclusion? The participants who ate a plant-focused diet were 52% less likely to have a heart attack or other cardiovascular-related incident. Furthermore, the participants who added even more of a plant focus to their plant-focused diets as they got older had even better results – they were 61% less likely to develop cardiovascular disease. Other research corroborates the physical and cognitive health benefits of a plant-focused diet in older age, such as decreased obesity, type 2 diabetes, cardiovascular disease, mortality, and incidence of Alzheimer's disease.[149]

How many servings of fruits and vegetables do you need a day? In another recently published large-scale study in the *Journal of the American Heart Association*, the diets and health of over 100,000 adults were followed over the years.[150] All participants entered the study free from cancer, diabetes, and cardiovascular disease. An analysis was conducted of the 33,898 who had died and those who were still living. The researchers found an intake of five servings of fruit and vegetables a day was associated with the lowest mortality.

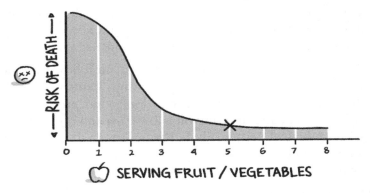

Try to get five servings of fruit/vegetables a day to minimize your risk of premature death.

Yes, there are many studies that find positive health benefits from eating meat – some showing stunning benefits from *only* eating meat. If you focus on probabilities, the evidence suggests that minimizing meat and increasing vegetables may be optimal for most people, but you are unique. This is why it is essential to test different diets to see what works best for you.

Minimize dairy. The weight of evidence suggests dairy may do more harm than good. A large percentage of the population suffers from the negative effects of lactose intolerance and may not even be aware of it. A staggering 95% of Asian Americans, 70% of African Americans, 53% of Mexican Americans, and 15% of Caucasians are lactose intolerant. Even if you are not lactose intolerant, there is ample research identifying the negative health effects of dairy consumption. But remember, nutrition is not math; it's probabilities. There are plenty of studies that show the health benefits o f d airy c onsumption. In a *Nutrition & Metabolism* study that combined and analyzed the data from 41 other studies, the researchers found that dairy provided several health benefits as well as negative effects.[151] They summarized their findings by stating, "Milk consumption does more good than harm for human health in this umbrella review."

That's an interesting summary – "does more good than harm." Is that the scale for how you evaluate the food you put into your body? More good than harm? Seat belts do more good than harm, and we dutifully put one on every time we get in a car because there isn't a better alternative. Dairy does provide protein and calcium, and if drinking a glass of milk was the only way to get protein and calcium, you'd have no choice. But you do have a choice. There are innumerable sources of protein and calcium that do *no* harm.

When it comes to food, the alternatives are nearly endless. Instead of settling for "more good than harm," how about we raise the bar and demand our food provides the *most* good and *no* harm?

What foods will help me feel the best and live the longest? It's likely not large amounts of dairy.

Consume healthy fats. When I was growing up in the 1970s and 1980s, I was indoctrinated to believe fat was the devil. The low-fat ideology was promoted by the federal government, physicians, the food industry, and the media, even though there wasn't clear evidence.[152] Food manufacturers quickly shifted to "low-fat" everything – even low-fat butter! Fast forward to today, when science and research are luckily putting a dent in this false doctrine.

But not all fats are created equally. Bad fats – or trans fats – were banned by the FDA but can still be found in pastries, shortening, fried foods, and processed foods such as cookies, frozen pizzas, and fast food. Trans fats should be avoided completely and are a good example of a food that does no good and all harm.[153] Saturated fats, although they are not believed to be as damaging as trans fats, are typically found in dairy and meat and should also be limited.[154]

Good fats are monounsaturated and polyunsaturated. They can be found primarily in vegetables, nuts, seeds, and certain vegetable oils such as olive and avocado. Research suggests these fats are best for long-term health.[155]

Is fat bad or good for you? Yes! You just need to know which types of fat you are consuming, emphasizing the good fats while limiting or avoiding the bad fats. Consider using only olive or avocado oils, adding more nuts and seeds to your diet, and limiting your intake of meat and dairy.

Cut out sugar. Added sugar is another example of a food that does no good and all harm. Sugar intake is associated with a swath of negative health outcomes that you do not want to experience, including high blood pressure, inflammation, weight gain, diabetes, liver disease, cancer, and death.[156] Retirement life is sweet; your diet doesn't need to be.

Focus on whole, unprocessed foods. Sometimes, knowing what to eat or not eat can be confusing. Other times, however, it just takes common sense. What do you think is better for you, a baked sweet potato or potato chips? How about a TV dinner or homemade vegetable soup? The closer you can get to a diet of whole and unprocessed foods, the better off you are going to be. The evidence is clear. Processed foods are unhealthy and should not be a big part of your diet if your goal is to upgrade your health.[157]

Stay hydrated. One of the most important – and also simplest– things you can do to improve your health, sleep quality, cognition, mood, and overall functioning is to drink a sufficient amount of water each day. While it may seem "easy," some people have a hard time drinking enough consistently. If you fall into that camp, I suggest buying a stainless steel water bottle. Having a dedicated and portable bottle you bring with you can be the reminder you need. Also, if you need a little flavor, consider adding electrolyte powders, Himalayan salt, or natural and unsweetened boosters.

Go Mediterranean. If you are still confused about what to eat and want an approach to follow, consider the Mediterranean diet. There is a great deal of research that shows a Mediterranean diet to have numerous health benefits and few drawbacks.[158]

The Mediterranean diet is straightforward:

Green light foods – Vegetables, fruits, nuts, seeds, whole grains, extra virgin olive oil, legumes, and moderate amounts of seafood.

Yellow light foods – Poultry, red meat, eggs, and dairy.

Red light foods – Added sugars, processed meat, refined oils, and highly processed foods.

What I like about the Mediterranean diet is that you'll likely be able to stick to it. Unlike other diets that require extreme amounts of willpower and self-discipline, the Mediterranean diet should be relatively easy to stick with throughout retirement.

But if you are unconvinced, you can look at the people around the world living longer than most others to see what they have in common. Areas across the globe that have been identified as pockets of longevity are known as Blue Zones. Turns out that the people who defy age tend to approach nutrition similarly – they stick to a plant-focused diet by eating plenty of vegetables, fruits, whole grains, nuts, beans, seeds, and olive oil. They eat meat from free-range animals a couple of times per week and avoid sugar and processed foods. If this sounds familiar, it should. Diets in Blue Zones share many of the same characteristics of the Mediterranean diet.

You could do a lot worse than the Mediterranean diet. It's simple, easy to follow, and is backed by overwhelming scientific evidence. It seems to be the approach to nutrition that does the most good and the least harm. But science marches on, and the field of nutrition is evolving, so we may find a better approach. For example, strategies such as intermittent fasting (something I've done for several years), the ketogenic diet (something else I've done on and off for years), and other non-traditional methods may be beneficial. Join the Badass Retirement Community if you want to follow these developments as we continue to try to answer the question: *What foods will help me feel better and live longer?*

Health Lever #5: Recovery

One of the most important aspects of upgrading your health is consistent exercise, but just like any athlete, your training needs to be followed by recovery. That's not to say that embracing recovery but neglecting training will lead to health improvements. To get the greatest health benefits, you need an optimum balance between training and recovery.[159]

The most common form of recovery is simply not exercising, but there may be more effective strategies that promote faster and deeper recovery so that you can continue to train at a high level. The following are several techniques you can consider adding to your intentional recovery program.

Active recovery. Active recovery involves performing lower-intensity exercise after engaging in higher-intensity exercise. For example, if you combine 20 minutes of HIIT with 20 minutes of weight training, active recovery might include a short swim, brief walk, or a few minutes on a stationary bike. Active recovery can also be incorporated into your training off days. For example, if you go on a long and strenuous hike and are feeling muscle fatigue and soreness the next day, it's better to get up off the couch and go on a walk. Research shows active recovery is superior to passive recovery.[160]

Stretching. Forget what you learned in gym class. What we used to think about stretching has changed, but that doesn't mean it's not important. In fact, as we age, we should aim to become even more limber. Increased flexibility can reduce your risk of injury, increase muscle blood flow, improve mobility, and help your joints. Do it after you've warmed up and look for a slow and deep (but not painful) stretch. Consider yoga, tai chi, or Pilates. One of my retired clients, who has had a long history of back pain, has been able to manage his pain and stay active by going to yoga classes three days a week. Stretching and flexibility exercises can help you recover and keep you in the game.

Massage. Massages feel good and do good. In a study that reviewed several recovery strategies, massage was the most effective at reducing muscle soreness and perceived fatigue.[161] If you can afford it, consider scheduling a weekly massage as part of your recovery program. It's likely to offer the biggest bang for your dollars.

Cryotherapy and cold immersion. If the thought of stripping down to your underwear and standing in a nitrogen-cooled tube for several minutes at sub- zero temperatures sounds like a good time, welcome to cryotherapy. The promise is faster recovery, pain management, and reduced inflammation. While the research does support moderate recovery benefits, it's not inexpensive.[162] If you don't mind spending $30 to $50 for each session, it may accelerate your recovery.

If you want to save a few bucks, you can skip the cryotherapy session and jump in a cold shower or ice bath at home. The research shows it may help reduce symptoms of depression, boost immunity, reduce inflammation, protect against cardiovascular and neurodegenerative disease, preserve muscle mass, and reduce morbidity.[163] There also appears to be some benefits from alternating between cold (ice bath) and hot (sauna). If you're feeling up for it, take a normal shower but turn the water as cold as it gets for the last minute. I'm not going to lie. It's not easy and it takes practice, but you'll feel vibrant and alive after!

Assess readiness. Wearable devices such as the Oura Ring or the Whoop Band – which combine heart rate, HRV, temperature, sleep, and other measures – can help you determine how well you've recovered. I wear the Oura Ring. Every morning I look at my "readiness" score, which is a proxy for how well I've recovered and how aggressive I can be about my day's training.

Health Lever #6: Performance-Enhancing Supplements

Athletes work hard but also look for opportunities to get an edge. They demand functional fitness – what is needed to perform better at their sport. The athlete's job is to function at their highest level throughout their career.

As an athlete in retirement, your job is to function at your highest over the course of your lifespan. Having the right mindset, exercising, dialing in your nutrition, and valuing sleep and recovery are essential building blocks for helping you upgrade your health. Just like a professional athlete, however, there may be supplements that can help you get an edge. Interventions can include testosterone replacement therapy, electromagnetic field therapy, cryotherapy, hormone replacement therapy, photobiomodulation treatment, stem cell therapy, IV infusion therapy, and exercise with oxygen therapy among many others. Supplements include vitamins, minerals, collagen, amino acids, spices, roots, CBD, oils, terpenes, coenzymes, ketones, and other compounds that *may* provide health benefits. There is evidence that supplementing in the areas where you are deficient can provide health benefits – for example, increasing your testosterone to a normal level or taking vitamin D3 to alleviate a deficiency. This is why it is important to get routine bloodwork done. You and your doctor will be in a better position to address deficiencies before they become problems.

Again, the science is rapidly evolving. Check out our membership community if upgrading your health through supplementation interests you and you want access to product discounts.

Health Lever #7: Sleep

I'll sleep when I die. That's a common refrain amongst the working folks. I get it and respect it. Sometimes, you need to work a little harder and a little longer, and when you are pulled in so many different directions, something has to give. And that something is usually sleep.

However, you are no longer among the working class. You are retired! Ideally, the only demands for your time are the demands you choose and enjoy. Still, many older adults do not get enough sleep. I think of sleep as not so much a tool to *upgrade* health but as a tool to not *undermine* your health.

You can exercise all you want, recover effectively, and eat the best foods, but if you don't dial in your sleep, you simply cannot reach your peak health. Poor sleep in older adults is linked to a long list of conditions and chronic diseases you would not wish upon your enemies, including cognitive decline, depression, cardiovascular disease, and death.[164] In one sleep study, UCLA researchers deprived some participants of sleep and compared their bloodwork against a control group whose sleep was not interrupted.[165] They found a "causal link" between sleep deprivation and biological aging. Participants who were only allowed a few hours of sleep for just one night showed increased gene activation associated with aging. After just one night of "bad" sleep, our bodies react. If your goal is to delay the negative health effects of aging, the lesson is to get sufficient sleep.

In another study, this one with 50,000 participants, researchers found that poor sleep was associated with increased blood markers of inflammation.[166] If you know anything about inflammation, you know it's often a precursor to disease in the body.

How much sleep do you need?

The National Sleep Foundation recommends between 7-8 hours of sleep for adults 65 and older. Other research finds a U-shaped relationship between hours of sleep and mortality – less than five hours or more than nine hours are both linked to increased mortality.[167]

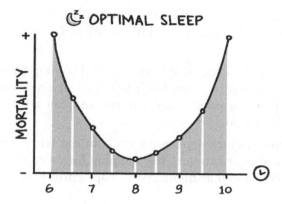

The research finds we need no less than seven hours and no more than nine hours of sleep a night.

While other studies have confirmed the negative health effects on older adults who get less sleep, some have not been able to confirm that *more* sleep has any negative health consequences.[168] If you sleep for more than nine hours a night, talk to your doctor to see if this is normal for you or if there are any other issues that may be at play.

You signed up for something bigger and better than Average Retirement. You have a mission and a compelling vision for your future. You do your best to be bold, make an impact, and go on adventures. Badass Retirement requires energy and for you to be at peak health. Sleep is a foundation of good health and energy. If you struggle with getting enough sleep or from common sleep complaints, invest in whatever you can to improve your sleep.

If you have sleep issues, you likely know the common sleep tricks – make your room as dark as you can, limit computer or cell phone usage a few hours before bed, set the room temperature to 65 degrees, minimize caffeine intake, etc. Here are a few less common tips that have been shown to help improve sleep:

Stick to a sleep schedule. Our bodies have a natural internal clock. According to research, if you can stick to a sleep schedule where you go to bed at the same time each night and wake up at the same time each morning, you will likely improve your sleep quality.[169]

Don't eat or drink before bed. Not drinking before bed makes sense. You don't want to have to go to the bathroom in the middle of the night. But no food? I've tested this on myself and can report that eating food within three hours of bed negatively affects my sleeping heart rate, HRV, body temperature, and other factors. Experiment with not eating or drinking several hours before bed to see what works for you.

Avoid alcohol. Some people use alcohol to help them fall asleep faster, but in exchange, they are likely to get a much worse night's sleep. Alcohol can increase poor sleep patterns and can alter your natural melatonin production.[170]

Limit naps. A quick nap after a workout can feel great and can be a healthy part of your recovery, but napping for more than 20 minutes could affect your sleep at night. Avoid naps entirely or limit them to 20 minutes.

Make it bright. No, not your bedroom. Research shows that exposure to natural sunlight during the day can improve your sleep duration and quality.[171] So, get outside and get some sunlight. This may be easier said than done in certain parts of the country – especially during the winter. No problem. You can use bright light therapy – also called phototherapy – to get the same benefits.[172]

Use natural supplements. There is plenty of research showing that taking as little as 2 mg of melatonin before bed can help you fall asleep faster and improve your overall sleep quality.[173] Other supplements, such as magnesium, lavender, and gingko biloba, may also aid in sleep.[174] Ask your doctor if taking melatonin or other natural supplements is a good idea for you.

Exercise. In one study of older adults, participants who were randomly assigned to training consisting of 16 moderate-intensity exercises showed significant improvements in sleep quality. The exercise group fell asleep nearly two times as fast and enjoyed an additional 41 minutes of sleep on average each night.[175] Keep in mind, the positive sleep benefits of exercise are eliminated if you exercise too closely to bedtime.

Gamify sleep. One of the first things I do in the morning is look at my sleep score. I wear an Apple Watch and an Oura Ring while I sleep, which track several different metrics related to sleep, including average heart rate, HRV, temperature, and many others, as well as your time spent in deep sleep and REM sleep. The Apple Watch has built-in sleep tracking, but I also use other third-party apps that provide even more data. The Oura Ring also provides a sleep score that I find useful. It's because of these apps and the Oura Ring data that I've been able to determine how food and alcohol affect my sleep. If you have any sleep issues or just want to have insight (and a little fun) tracking your sleep, there are several wearables from which you can choose.

Get a smart bed. Seems like everything is "smart" nowadays, including mattresses. What makes them smart? They monitor and report your respiratory rate, resting heart rate, and HRV, as well as smartly waking you at the optimum stage of sleep in the morning. Fortunately, you can get all these things with a device such as an Apple Watch, but what you can't get with a wearable is temperature control. Some brands of beds automatically adjust the mattress temperature based on room temperature, humidity, and your body. This can be a big benefit if you find yourself waking up hot throughout the night. Popular smart bed brands include <u>Sleep Number</u> and <u>EightSleep</u>.

Health Lever #8: Mental Health/Stress

I was hunched over on the side of the freeway. Cars were speeding by me as I threw up on the shoulder. It just got worse from there. I had experienced intermittent stomach and intestinal pain for the preceding couple of weeks. The pain became so severe I went to an urgent care, where they gave me a shot of morphine.

Over the course of several weeks, I had a battery of tests completed (e.g., MRI, CT scan, etc.) to rule out cancer or other diseases. The results were normal, so I was assigned the diagnosis of irritable bowel syndrome (IBS) – a disorder that affects the large intestine and causes intense abdominal pain, cramping, and bloating.

The treatment? A drug called Zelnorm, which I dutifully took each morning for several months until I got the disturbing news they were taking it off the market because it was linked to heart attacks and strokes. I distinctly remember reading the news and thinking that something had to change. I hadn't turned 40 yet and was diagnosed with a disorder that was painful, lifelong, and severely impacting my quality of life. Even worse, the "treatment" could give me a heart attack or stroke. Remember the earlier discussion about how change can happen in an instant? That was one of those moments for me.

I started to investigate how my diet and lifestyle were affecting my IBS. I changed what I was eating – eventually eliminating all meat, dairy, and soda. I started juicing and then moved on to making green smoothies with various mixed greens and powders. I haven't experienced IBS since the morning I read about Zelnorm.

Was it the diet? I'm certain that was a big part of my recovery and how I've been able to avoid any IBS symptoms for the last couple of decades. But my poor diet was not the only factor. There was another contributor that may have been more – much more – to blame. Stress.

In the months leading up to my IBS symptoms, I lost a child in utero, became a new dad by adopting a baby, quit a job, started a new company, wrote a book, moved to a new city, and my mother-in-law and terminally ill father-in-law moved in with me. It's a wonder I didn't have to take morphine every day. But at the time, it just felt like life. Stressful? Sure, but I could handle it. Except I couldn't. The stress nearly destroyed me. It was a very difficult time, and only upon reflecting can I really appreciate how mental stress can undermine physical health.

If your goal is to live at peak health in and throughout retirement, one of the levers of improvement is managing stress. I'll admit that I'm not a pillar of stress management. I don't feel like I experience a great deal of stress, but just like it did in my 30s, it can sneak up unexpectedly. You think everything is fine and then you find yourself face down on an exam table getting a shot of morphine in your butt.

I have more to learn about managing stress, but the following practices are a great place to start after you've taken care of the low-hanging fruit of sleep and getting plenty of exercise (ideally outside).

Go green. If you want to decrease stress and live an even greater Badass Retirement, there is a simple approach we can all take – go green.

In a relatively new scientific field called ecotherapy, there is ample research that shows getting outside provides a host of mental and physical benefits. Just getting outside can help restore the mind from mental fatigue, and even help to restore the "brain drain" that occurs in urban settings. So called "green time" can help alleviate a host of mental health conditions, including attention deficit disorder, Alzheimer's and dementia, stress, depression, and anxiety, as well as providing cognitive benefits.[176]

The gift of green keeps giving. Spending time in nature is associated with numerous positive outcomes, including well-being, positive affect, happiness, positive social interactions and engagement, senses of purpose and meaning in life, and memory.[177] Being outdoors may even be a remedy for nature deficit disorder, the term Richard Louv coined to describe the range of negative outcomes associated with spending so little time outdoors.[178]

One of the best medicines is simply spending time outdoors.

Our disconnection from nature may also be one of the causes of depression, as Johann Hari argues in his book, *Lost Connections*. In his popular TedX talk, he says, "Most of the factors that have been proven to cause depression and anxiety are not in our biology. They're factors in how we live."[179]

A recent study of nearly 20,000 people found that those who spent just two hours a week in nature were significantly more likely to report good health and higher well-being.[180] The researchers found the results to be consistent even for those with long-term health issues and older adults. This is good news for retirees – especially for men. Jason Strauss, director of geriatric psychiatry at Harvard-affiliated Cambridge Health Alliance, explains, "Many men are at higher risk for mood disorders as they age, from dealing with sudden life changes like health issues, the loss of loved ones, and even the new world of retirement. They may not want to turn to medication or therapy for help, and for many, interacting with nature is one of the best self-improvement tools they can use."

The benefits are not just for men. Countless studies with older men and women show that greater physical, mental, and social benefits are achieved through nature.[181] In one study of 117 adults living in a retirement community, researchers found retirees who spent more time outside reported fewer depressive symptoms, increased bone health, and increased physical functioning.[182]

There are different theories on why nature is so beneficial to our mental and physical health. Some suggest an evolutionary trigger – our ancestors evolved in nature, so we have an innate drive to connect with nature. Others suggest the benefits we achieve are due to a physiological response that decreases our stress levels. A third hypothesis suggests nature calms our prefrontal cortex and restores our cognitive functioning, allowing us to concentrate and pay better attention. Most think it is a mix of these factors (and likely many others) that contribute to our positive green response.

Frankly, it doesn't really matter *why* we reap so many benefits from being outside, just that we do. In fact, the research shows we don't even need to be outside to experience some of the benefits. Listening to nature sounds or viewing images of nature were both associated with positive outcomes.[183] For those unable to go outside, virtual reality looks like a promising alternative. Although a study found that participants experienced greater benefits from being in nature, researchers concluded that virtual reality could be used as an alternative when it was not possible to experience the real thing.

What's interesting are the numerous positive benefits of just *being* in nature. No effort required. You don't need to do outdoor yoga, embark on a strenuous hike up the side of a mountain, or canoe in a lake to reap the rewards of nature. There is something magical that happens when we are outside experiencing nature. Peter H. Kahn, a professor of psychology at the University of Washington, acknowledges the benefits of gazing at nature, but recommends we do more than just look if we want to experience the greatest benefits: "We need to deepen the forms of interaction with nature and make it more immersive."[184]

Breathing. Imagine what it would feel like if you suddenly received millions of dollars and did not feel prepared or in control. Sudden wealth recipients can experience intense and sustained stress, which can cloud their judgment and affect their decision-making abilities. It's imperative for sudden wealth recipients to rapidly reduce their stress levels.

When I was writing my book, *The Sudden Wealth Solution*, I reached out to retired Navy SEAL and author Mark Devine to get his advice on how to reduce stress quickly and easily. His number one suggestion? Learn to breathe better. "Seriously, deep diaphragmatic breathing will negate stress in your life and turn you into the calm, cool character you need to be," he said. Mark shared with me a breathing technique called "box breathing."

Here's how to do it in Mark's words: "Inhale to a count of four, hold your breath for a count of four, exhale for a count of four, and hold the exhale for a count of four. Do this when you wake up in the morning for 10 minutes and whenever you feel stressed during the day."

The research backs up breathing exercises as a beneficial tool for improving health and reducing stress. In fact, research shows that it may be more effective than other common techniques like mindfulness training or cognitive therapy on reducing stress.[185] If you are looking for a no-cost, highly effective, and quick strategy for reducing stress that you can do anywhere, incorporate breathing techniques into your daily routine.

But box breathing is just one type. There are many other breathing techniques including resonant, Sitali breathing, deep, rhythmic, decompression, Wim Hof Method (my favorite), and many more. You can learn how to do any of these and others by watching videos on YouTube.

I recommend you try a few to find the one(s) you like best and then integrate them into your daily life.

Meditation. I struggle with meditation. I force myself to do it a couple of times a week, and I often skip it altogether. I know that there are incredible mental and physical health benefits, which is why I (occasionally) do it. But this is a good lesson for all of us trying to upgrade our health – it's not always easy or enjoyable. It takes willpower to do another set, bike another mile, choose the salad over the burger, or to stop after a couple of drinks.

As much as you try to make exercise enjoyable by doing activities you like and finding workout friends, there will be times when you just don't feel like it – maybe the new season of your favorite series was just released or the game is on. The same is true for nutrition. It's not always easy to choose between what *is* the best and what *tastes* the best. Sometimes you need to suck it up (literally) and do what's hard.

Who said being an athlete is easy?!

Even though I'll choose burpees over meditation, I still need to suck it up and meditate more often, though my most common form of "meditation" is my daily walk in a wooded area next to a stream.

I used to schedule phone calls or listen to podcasts during my hike, but I found that I wasn't present when I did this. I was so focused on the conversation or the podcast that I completely overlooked the tranquility of the experience.

If you have any experience with meditation, you probably already realize what took me months to figure out . . . my body was present but my mind wasn't.

One style of meditation is mindfulness. Mindfulness is the mental state of being fully present in the moment – not focused on the past or the future – and having an unjudgmental awareness of your ever-changing thoughts, bodily sensations, and feelings. Mindfulness therapy has been shown to be an effective treatment for stress, anxiety, and depression.[186] There are many styles and approaches to mindfulness training. Some include guided work with a therapist and others can be done by yourself – like a walk in the woods.

There are many other kinds of meditation, including focused, guided, transcendental, visualization, and others. In case you couldn't tell, I am but a novice when it comes to meditation, so the best I can do is point you in the right direction. There are dozens of meditation apps, such as Calm and Headspace, that are great places to start.

Gratitude. Although regular meditation isn't something I've incorporated (yet) into my weekly health training, I have been a proponent of gratitude awareness for years. Research has found a link between gratitude and improved physical outcomes (like less inflammation and better blood vessel function) as well as improved emotional outcomes, including greater well-being, lower reported depression and anxiety, better sleep, and increased happiness.[187]

If you've ever written in a gratitude journal or just thought about the things in your life for which you are appreciative, you don't need research to tell you it feels good and does good. I've practiced various forms of gratitude awareness on and off for years. In the moment, when I'm thinking about the things that are meaningful to me and for which I'm grateful, I feel a sense of calm and centeredness. But what is even more interesting are the lingering effects of the gratitude work. I feel what only can be described as a protective and peaceful layer enveloping me. I know it sounds strange, but there seems to be a form of emotional inoculation that occurs.

There is another benefit that you may experience. I call it the Instagram effect. The more you post to social media platforms like

Instagram, Facebook, or Twitter, the more you notice things in the real world to post. Several years ago, I went through a phase where I was posting on Twitter several times a week. At first, it was a challenge to figure out what to post, but after a few days, I started noticing more and more opportunities.

The same effect happens when I practice gratitude awareness regularly – I start to notice things throughout my day I'm grateful for and that I can include in my gratitude ritual. Gratitude exercises shift your perception to those things that are meaningful to you – just like a radio tuning to the right frequency. Gratitude work trains your awareness of what's important and where to focus.

There are several forms of gratitude awareness – from journaling to lying in bed counting your blessings. Here are a few you can try:

- **Gratitude journal.** Simple and effective. Every morning, write down a few things for which you are grateful, or if you prefer, the "journal" can just be a mental account of those things. I find I get a lot more out of writing in a journal, and as a bonus, it's a thrill to read the entries from years ago.

- **Three good things.** Similar to using a gratitude journal, this involves the added step of writing down not only three things you appreciate in your life, but the causes of those things. You can do this exercise every day, or, if you're pressed for time, you can limit this to just once a week.

- **Mental subtraction.** I don't have a lot of experience with this exercise, but it might be a fun occasional change of pace. The technique requires you to imagine what your life would be like if a positive event had never occurred – for example, the birth of a child, a job promotion, or a negative health test.

- **Think about the bad to feel good.** If you're having trouble coming up with things you are grateful for, just think back to a time in your life when you experienced a setback, were in pain, or suffered a tragedy. Use the tough times in your life to be thankful for the good days. It's easy to take feeling good for granted when things are going smoothly. It's important to appreciate the mundane because it can change quickly.

There are many more interventions to help reduce stress throughout retirement, from natural supplements such as CBD to wearable technology that engages your parasympathetic nervous system. Check out our website for more resources.

Health Lever #9: Personal Self-Protection

Your goal is to stay healthy, energized . . . and alive! The most significant threat we face as we age is getting sick from illness and disease. We are all just one bad diagnosis away from having our lives change instantly. The previous Health Levers will help you stay strong, feeling good, and healthy.

However, there is another health threat we all face that can just as quickly change our lives. This threat can't be minimized by eating well, getting sufficient sleep, or proper exercise. This threat is physical harm.

I am a strong advocate for gaining the tools and training to protect yourself and your loved ones. I think this is an important factor that often gets overlooked in retirement – maybe because our culture views retirees as weak and frail. Regardless of where you live or your circumstances, we all face some level of risk. Your job in retirement is not to dwell on the potential for danger, but simply to prepare and prevent.

How can you protect yourself?

This is going to look different for everyone, but at a minimum I'd recommend protecting your home with security cameras, high-grade locks, secure door frames, reinforced sliding doors, an alarm system, and sufficient lighting.

For the more adventurous (that's you!), I think it's smart to invest time and money learning how to protect yourself. That means getting trained in self-defense. It might be a two-hour seminar, a weekend training, or a lifelong commitment to a martial art. Whatever it is, you want to have hand-to-hand skills to defend yourself and your loved ones if needed. Not only will you have a better chance of surviving a violent encounter, you'll also feel more confident. (What's more badass than being able to kick ass?!)

You should also consider additional training such as active shooter preparation, severe trauma and first-aid, and the use of advanced personal self-defense tools (e.g., pepper spray, TASER, stun-gun, firearms).

A Badass Retirement is not one where you live in fear, but one where you live in confidence. Personal security preparation and training can help you do just that by helping you prepare – and even *prevent* – the worst from happening.

Invest in your health. Without question, it is the best investment you can make. Buy the bike, hire the chef, work with a trainer, get the fancy juicer, engage a therapist, sign up for healthy food delivery, order the supplements, upgrade your mattress, purchase the treadmill, or invest in *anything* that will upgrade your health. The only question you need to ask yourself is, "Will this upgrade my health?" If the answer is yes, do not hesitate. Just do it.

Through this Challenge's discussion of the 9 Health Levers, you've now learned how to become stronger physically and mentally. In the next Challenge, you'll learn how to become emotionally stronger in the face of setbacks and tragedies.

JOIN THE FAMILY

The most important asset you have is your health, but knowing what to do when it comes to nutrition, supplements, and fitness feels like a moving target for a good reason. If there is one area that changes more than any other, it's health. There are continuous advancements in nutrition and fitness that are hard to stay on top of, but if you want not just to live long but live well, upgrading your health must be one of your top priorities in retirement. Join the online Badass Retirement Community to get discounts on products and stay on top of developments that can improve your energy, health, and life.

GO TO BADASSRETIREMENT.COM

14

CHALLENGE

Build
Resilience

You can't escape from setbacks and challenges in retirement, but you can develop strength and strategies to help you recover.

CHALLENGE 14

"This is the doctor's office calling. We'd like you to come in to discuss your lab results…"

I've been there, and I'm sure you have also. Anyone who's been around for 50 or 60 years has experienced setbacks and challenges – even traumas and tragedies. We've faced minor disappointments like losing a job as well as major tragedies like the loss of a loved one.

Nothing can stop you in your tracks faster than a phone call with unexpected bad news: a lump that could end your spouse's life, a DUI that destroys your child's career, a drug addiction terrorizing your grandchild, a divorce that breaks your heart, or a devastating tragedy that breaks your will.

Let's face it – growing older can be depressing. Despite your best efforts, your health will eventually decline. Your friends or family may fall ill or pass away. You may be able to escape Average Retirement, but you're not going to be able to escape everything that accompanies retirement. I wish it weren't the case, but bad things will happen to the best of us. I'm sorry about that. Sometimes even Badass Retirement is, well, just bad.

You may experience things so profound that you'll feel like life will never be the same, and unfortunately, it may not be. Your life may be forever altered in an instant, but that doesn't mean you can't find a way to continue.

Despite adversity, resilience provides momentum – a way to move forward. Resilience can help get you through another day when all you want to do is curl up and disappear.

Since you are putting in the work to escape Average Retirement and create a Badass Retirement, I have no doubt your life in retirement will be filled with joy and happiness, meaning and purpose, and adventure and gratitude. Nevertheless, it will also include failures and adversity. There will be times in retirement where you feel stuck – like you've lost your mojo – and there will be times when you feel you can't move.

We will all face misfortune at some point in retirement. Sometimes, we'll face setbacks that pull us out of the game temporarily. We might be sidelined with a sprained ankle, require knee surgery, or have to help a child get back on his feet. In such times, the best response may be to shake it off and get back in the game, using the setback as a source of strength to emerge stronger on the other side.

Other times, we'll encounter events that shift the trajectories of our lives, changing us permanently – no bouncing back or recovering. We just don't move on from some events. At best we can only move forward. Life may never be the same. There is a sense of innocence that gets lost when we experience certain hardships.

These traumas are the "before and after" events in our lives that leave indelible marks – demarcations of moments that forever distinguish life before and after them.

Resilience is our ability to adapt and find a way to move forward. Resilience has many faces. Resilience can be brushing off a failure and coming back stronger and more determined, or it can be summoning the strength to get out of bed and brush your teeth.

After spending my professional career working with older adults, I can say with confidence that we are bound to experience more misfortunes and challenges later in life, and thank goodness for that. Older does not mean weaker. Older does not mean fragile. We've seen more and experienced more. This doesn't mean, however, that it will be easy. Some things we never fully recover from. That's when it just becomes about moving forward.

Resilience is like a seatbelt; it's not going to stop the accident, but it may help you walk away. Research shows that despite the adversities you face when you age, high resilience can help you improve your quality of life, your mental health, and your view of aging.[188] You may even live longer. Studies have linked high resilience with a lower risk of mortality – even among the very old.[189]

This was a hard Challenge to write because it's more fun to talk about the impact you will have on the world, the adventures you will take, and the fulfillment you will feel living your purpose. Living a Badass Retirement isn't about deluding yourself into believing that everything will be perfect, though. We know there will be pain and grief. Instead of pretending these factors won't impact your life, let's face them head-on.

Being bold isn't just about taking risks, it's also about confronting the things that scare you. You will experience events that rock you to your core and bring you to your knees. The upshot is that while you are guaranteed to face adversity as you age, and while there are some things from which you will never fully recover, building resilience can help you move forward.

THE RESILIENCE ALREADY WITHIN YOU

The good news is that you are likely more resilient than you think. If you imagine what life was like tens of thousands of years ago, it must have been nothing but trauma – death, famine, disease, and close encounters with hungry animals. Resilience is hard-wired. We have a stress-response system that has evolved over millions of years. Our species wouldn't have survived long if we just gave up and couldn't press on in the face of hardship and trauma.

One of the academics spearheading research on resilience is George Bonanno, a professor of clinical psychology at Columbia University. He coined the term "potentially traumatic event" to underscore that negative events don't necessarily have to lead to trauma. He rebukes the popular belief that trauma invariably leads to suffering or post-traumatic stress disorder (PTSD) and has the research to back it up. In one study on the aftermath of the terrorist attacks of September 11, 2001, he found that 65% of participants exhibited just one or even no symptoms of PTSD six months after the attack. Even those closer to the event – those involved in the rescue effort – had surprisingly few PTSD symptoms.[190]

In a larger study, Bonanno examined 54 previous studies that focused on individual well-being following traumatic events such as combat, bereavement, natural disasters, and injury. He found that 65% of the participants in these studies exhibited few or no negative symptoms after the event, concluding: "People follow common trajectories of response following major life stressors and potential trauma, and that resilience is the most common response. The majority adapt successfully to such adversity."[191] If you connect with this philosophy of resiliency, you'll want to read Bonanno's popular book, *The Other Side of Sadness*.

Even if you haven't been as steadfast when confronted by setbacks in the past, the good news is that you can learn to become more resilient. Resilience is not something that weakens with age. In fact, research shows that older adults can improve their resilience later in life.[192]

BUILDING RESILIENCE

When I think of adversity in retirement, I imagine a sailboat cutting through calm waters, occasionally facing storms along the way. These storms may just include cloudy skies and a little rain, but some are made up of strong winds and waves so violent they knock you into the cold, dark water. The longer you sail, the more opportunity you have to run into an unexpected storm. Your only hope is to make sure you have the resources to make your way back to safety.

The resilience-building process involves protective measures that will help you become more durable when confronted with adversity, giving you the tools that will support you when you are face to face with it. Fortunately, you've already learned many of these strategies throughout this book.

You can't prevent the unexpected events that tomorrow may bring, but that doesn't mean you are helpless. You can do things today that will help you adapt to these challenges and find a way to move forward.

Research finds the following mental, social, and physical strategies highly effective in building resilience.[193]

Mental Factors That Build Resilience

Meaning. When you get proverbially knocked down or feel like your life will never be the same, having a mission and a strong sense of purpose can help you move forward. The best example of this is recounted in the book *Man's Search for Meaning* by Viktor Frankl. I read this book as a teenager and have re-read it several times since. The book is about Viktor's life as a prisoner in a Nazi concentration camp during World War II. Reading his account of the trauma he endured and witnessed is difficult, but his message is one of hope. Viktor identifies meaning as the key – not only to surviving the Holocaust, but to life itself. His "why" was to see his wife again, to write about his experiences, and to develop his ideas on a new form of therapy he called logotherapy. It was his search for and discovery of what was meaningful that helped him survive the daily trauma of life in a concentration camp.

Review your mission and your purpose from Challenge 7. This provides your why – your meaning in life. While this will provide you with energy, passion, and direction, it will also give you solace and protection when you are faced with your own adversity.

Viewing the world differently. How can you and I both experience the same event but have completely different reactions? Psychologists would say it's because we look at the world differently – that we have different explanatory styles.

OPTIMISTIC	PESSIMISTIC
EXTERNAL "This isn't all my fault"	INTERNAL "This is all my fault"
TEMPORARY "Things will get better"	PERMANENT "This will last forever"
SPECIFIC "It's just this one thing"	GLOBAL "This is going to ruin everything"
CONTROLABLE "I can make this better"	UNCONTROLABLE "There is nothing I can do"

How you view the world can radically alter your quality of life and health.

There are infinite ways to view the world and the events that occur in our lives, but researchers have identified four important paradigms that give us either optimistic or pessimistic explanations of the events that happen to us.

- **External or Internal:** Are you to blame, or do you allow the possibility that it's not all your fault?

- **Temporary or Permanent:** Do you believe that you will make it through the adversity, or do you think it will persist forever?

- **Specific or Global:** Is this negative event limited to a single area in your life, or will it affect everything?

- **Controllable or Uncontrollable:** Do you have the ability to make things better, or is it outside of your control?

An optimistic explanatory style is associated with a significantly higher quality of life, greater physical well-being, and lower levels of depression compared to those who have more pessimistic perspectives.[194] An optimistic approach can provide a cushion of resilience when you face adversity. Even if you are not naturally optimistic, you can learn to see the world differently. A great resource is Martin Seligman's classic book *Learned Optimism*.

Gratitude. Gratitude has been shown to offer protection from adversity as well as resulting in positive outcomes following trauma.[195]

In his book *The Upward Spiral,* Dr. Alex Korb writes: "Gratitude is a state of mind. Strengthening that circuit brings the power to elevate your physical and mental health, boost happiness, improve sleep, and help you feel more connected to other people." These are all factors that support overcoming adversity and building resilience. Like an athlete preparing for an important match, you can incorporate the gratitude practices discussed in the Upgrade Health Challenge to prepare yourself for life's unexpected events.

Connect with a therapist. Therapy's success often has less to do with the experience, education, or style of the therapist and more to do with their relationship with the client.[196] If you've ever faced a challenge in life and tried to connect with a therapist, you may have been discouraged by the process. It can take time to find a therapist covered by your insurance and even more time building a connection where you feel comfortable exploring difficult topics. This is why I recommend you start that process now – before you need it. When adversity arrives, it does so quickly and often forcefully. It's best to already have a relationship with someone you can talk to – someone you know and trust. It helps to know that, if something bad happens in your life, there is someone who already knows you who is just a phone call away. Find someone local who you can see in person or use a virtual therapist you can talk to over the phone or in a video session.

Social Factors That Build Resilience

Create strong social networks. You don't need research to tell you that having close friends or a supportive family can help you get through the darkest days. Humans are social creatures, wired to both give and receive support from others from the moment they are born. For example, the single most important factor in early life is the bond with your primary caretakers.[197] If you expect to survive and move forward after life's hardest and most challenging adversities, you cannot expect to do it alone. One of the key takeaways from resilience research is that strong social networks help promote resilience.[198]

If you don't already have at least one confidant or trusted family member who is equipped to be a shepherd for you, you need to start to develop those relationships now. Unfortunately, it's not enough to simply have good friends or family members. While they may be well-intentioned, they may not have the appropriate bedside manner or be able to provide the advice you need. If you've ever experienced real pain and suffering, you know that clichés don't help:

Look on the bright side.

This will make you stronger.

You just need to bounce back.

Things could be worse.

You still have a lot to be thankful for.

Just try to move on.

In fact, they make you feel worse. I've heard all of these and more from some of my closest social relationships. You need someone who can offer more specific insight into your own situation and life. Try to identify or cultivate at least one person that can sit with you and help you get through the pain or the fear.

Lean on a higher power. If you are religious or spiritual, you have an incredible source of resilience to tap into. First, you may discover peace of mind knowing there is a larger plan at work in your life. No matter how bad things get, you have something working in the background on your behalf. This can provide immense relief and contentment even in the face of tragedy. Second, you may have a network of other like-minded people you can turn to for support. The belief that there is a reason for what you are going through and the social encouragement you receive can be a powerful one-two punch to help you overcome even the most difficult situations. Unfortunately, it's common to withdraw when things get tough. We retreat to our thoughts, fears, and anxieties and resist getting help from others. This is a mistake. As much as you may not feel social, force yourself to spend time around others.

Join a group. There is good reason for the existence of support groups. They offer a place where everyone knows exactly what it feels like to go through what you are experiencing, whether that is a health diagnosis or the loss of a loved one. Your friends and family may be supportive and caring, but they may not fully understand your experience. There are support groups – either in person or online – for nearly every hardship you may face in retirement. Sometimes these groups are exactly what you'd envision – a circle of people sitting in a room talking about their challenges – but others may incorporate a hike or making art as part of their process.

After my wife and I lost our son eight months into the pregnancy, we were devastated. We couldn't leave the house, and it felt like nobody really understood our pain. Our first substantive conversations were with a therapist who specialized in grief. She introduced us to a couple who had experienced a similar loss decades earlier. The couple couldn't have been more different than us. They were much older, a different religion, and from a different country. But despite these differences, our common loss connected us. We were then connected to another woman who had also experienced the loss of a child in utero. We had never met her before, but we instantly felt a bond – one that is still strong nearly 20 years later. When we decided to attend a support group, we were nervous to share our story, but when we looked around the room at the 15 other couples with stories of their own, we knew they would all understand our pain.

A support group can provide a venue where you don't feel like you are going through something alone. No matter what you are experiencing, there are others – a whole room full of others – that get it.

Help others. Sometimes, the best way to help yourself is by helping others. Volunteering can be a wonderful way to connect with others and set aside your challenges for a few hours. Studies show that volunteering after a loss can protect against depression and help create feelings of purpose in life.[199] After my father-in-law passed away from pulmonary fibrosis just a couple of years into his retirement, my wife and mother-in-law were grief-stricken, struggling to find meaning in life. They summoned their strength and courage and decided to find purpose in their pain by organizing a walk in his name to raise money for the Coalition for Pulmonary Fibrosis.

After our son died, my wife and I also wanted to help others who had experienced similar tragedies. My wife volunteered at a burgeoning non-profit called Forever Footprints, serving on its board for years. Look for opportunities to help others experiencing what is challenging you. You may find you get as much as you give.

Physical Factors That Build Resilience

Get physical. If it sounds like I'm saying exercise is a panacea for nearly everything, it's because it just might be. The research shows that resilience is another benefit of being physically active.[200] The beneficial effects that exercise has on one's mood are well documented. If you are struggling, the last thing you feel like doing is exercise. Our natural tendency is to want to curl up on the couch, but you need to fight this. Make yourself go for a walk. Get a friend to exercise with you, combining its social benefits with its physical benefits. Hire a personal trainer. Knowing that you are paying them may give you the extra nudge you need to get moving.

Shinrin-yoku. You learned about the numerous physical, mental, and emotional benefits of nature earlier in the book. If you are struggling with adversity, get out of the house and into nature – go for a hike, watch a stream flowing by, or sit in a forest. In Japan, the latter is referred to as *shinrin-yoku* ("forest bathing"). The health and psychological benefits of simply sitting in a forest are astounding. There have been numerous studies on the healing effects of *shinrin-yoku*, which include improved cardiovascular and immune functions, decreased self-reported anxiety and cortisol levels, improved relaxation, and increases in cancer-fighting white blood cells.[201] John Muir, the so-called "Father of National Parks," may have recognized the healing properties of nature long before scientists did. He is quoted as saying, "Climb the mountains and get their good tidings. Nature's peace will flow into you as sunshine flows into trees. The winds will blow their own freshness into you and the storms their energy, while cares will drop off like autumn leaves." If that doesn't sound like a prescription for quelling adversity, I don't know what is.

Forest bathing has been found to have many positive physical and mental health benefits.

Eat well. If you've ever faced hardship, you may have reached for a pint of ice cream or some homemade mac and cheese. Why is it so common to crave comfort foods high in fat and sugar when we are going through difficult times? The science tells us that these foods really do provide some comfort.[202] If you are dealing with a painful experience, do what you need to get through the first few days. At some point, do what you can to incorporate better nutrition into your diet. Although the comfort foods may provide some relief, it is temporary. Moving forward with a clear head and able body requires energy. Although it may not feel like it (and you may not even want it), your body needs all the nutrition you can give it. Studies also find that eating well can promote greater resilience for older adults.[203]

If there is one thing my experience and research on resilience has taught me, it is that while we cannot avoid hardship, we don't have to just suffer through it. Sometimes, trauma can lead to negative consequences, but other times, we can grow from trauma. What's the difference? We don't fully know the answer, but science tells us that it's possible to experience post-traumatic growth.

POST-TRAUMATIC GROWTH

Nietzsche wrote, "That which does not kill us makes us stronger," but you and I both know that's not always true. I'm sure you've seen people who have experienced traumatic events and never fully recovered, instead becoming weaker in response. PTSD is a prime example of this. Soldiers and victims may have survived the trauma of war or violent crimes, but they would hardly consider themselves stronger from it. So, are we destined to suffer? Or is it possible to experience growth in the aftermath of trauma? It seems we can.

Post-traumatic growth (PTG) is a theory developed by psychologists Richard Tedeschi and Lawrence Calhoun that explains the experience of positive transformation and growth in the aftermath of trauma.[204] They acknowledge that highly stressful and traumatic events are disturbing and often lead to distressing emotions, sadness, depression, guilt, anger, anxiety, and even numbness. They argue that this response does not preclude the possibility for positive transformation. In fact, the response often acts as a precursor to growth. PTG psychology makes it clear, however, that it's not the trauma that can lead to growth. It is the individual's struggle in the aftermath of adversity that provides the possibility for positive transformation.

Their research has identified five factors for post-traumatic growth:

1. **Increased appreciation for life.** You often don't appreciate what you have until it is jeopardized. When you are faced with your own mortality or lose a loved one, it is common to experience a greater appreciation for life. Even the smallest tasks – taking the garbage out or gazing up at the night sky – can provide joy. Everything you took for granted before the adversity takes on a new meaning. Another shift that can occur post-trauma is an altered sense of priorities. A common PTG outcome is a re-evaluation of your life and how you spend your time. This greater appreciation for life and for the small things is a powerful and positive outcome made possible by adversity.

2. **More meaningful relationships.** It's also possible to experience closer and more intimate relationships with friends and family after encountering trauma. After my son died, the outpouring of support from friends, family, and even strangers was incredible. We connected with them on a deeper level – something we wouldn't have experienced without the trauma. Adversity can create new relationships by leading you to meet others who have experienced similar challenges as well as fostering re-connections between those who have drifted apart.

3. **Greater sense of personal strength.** Surviving adversity can create the belief that you can survive anything. What you used to think were big problems may now seem to be no big deal. This "shield of armor" can help you view future hardships as less challenging. Paradoxically, the research also finds that a sense of vulnerability often accompanies this newfound personal strength. Even though you are battle-tested, there is an awareness and appreciation that bad things can happen.

4. **Recognition of new possibilities.** Most retirees create a stable and predictable structure for their lives, ensuring that they are on a certain trajectory. Following adversity, it isn't uncommon for individuals to look at their lives from a new perspective – to see new possibilities – and want to create a new path. Maybe it's starting a non-profit, going on more adventures, or moving closer to grandkids. This new path never would have presented itself if it had not been for the adversity. This is exactly what my wife and I experienced just a few months after our son died. We received a call from someone we had recently met who knew about our loss. She told us about a woman pregnant with a baby girl who wanted to find a good home for her. I had never thought about or considered adoption in my life, but suddenly, the option presented itself. This new path was only

created because of our loss. That little baby girl has been our daughter from the moment she was born. Out of loss, there can be gain. New possibilities can be created, putting your life on a new trajectory you never could have imagined.

5. **Spiritual growth.** When you are down, it's common to look up. PTG can create a spiritual awakening. You may start asking all the big questions about life and meaning. Why am I here? What is my purpose? Some find solace and meaning in religion and spirituality – connecting with a higher power and with other believers.

Adversity doesn't guarantee growth, but it certainly doesn't have to lead to lifelong despair either. Healing and transformation occur because the journey through adversity causes you to look at the world and your place in it differently.

Lance Armstrong was diagnosed with stage three testicular cancer. By the time they discovered it, the cancer had spread to his lymph nodes, lungs, brain, and abdomen. After several surgeries and rounds of chemotherapy, Lance beat the odds and overcame cancer, much to the shock of his doctors. His outlook on that experience may surprise you: "Looking back, I wouldn't change anything. Had I not been sick, I wouldn't have met my wife. I don't feel unlucky to have had to go through this. I learned a lot and grew tremendously the last two years."[205] From tragedy to transformation. Growth isn't inevitable, but it's possible.

Sometimes the adversity we experience has been with us for years, often in the form of regret. Other times, however, we mourn things that have yet to occur, including our own death. Psychologists call this anticipatory grief, and it can derail even the best retirement if you let it.

EMBRACING YOUR OWN MORTALITY

I took the offramp toward Harbor Boulevard in Anaheim just like I had hundreds of times before. When my daughter was younger, we had annual passes for Disneyland. There were years when we went several times a month, and even now that she is older, we try to go at least once or twice a year. At the stoplight just past the offramp, the muscle memory in my hands wanted to turn right toward "The Happiest Place on Earth." I thought about all the good times and the memories of our many visits – the soft pretzels, popcorn, rides, princess shows, and parades. It felt like just yesterday that I walked my daughter into this magical place for the first time. On this day, however, I had to turn left.

All those nights driving home after the fireworks with my daughter fast asleep in the backseat, I'd pass a small city of buildings near Disneyland: the UCI Medical Center. I'd gaze up at the towers from the freeway and wonder what was happening in the patients' rooms with lights on. Why were they there? What were their stories?

My trip to the hospital.

On this night, though, I knew the answer for one of those rooms since it would soon be my story. I had to have surgery to remove skin cancer. If you or your loved ones have had other types of cancers or illnesses that required more intense treatments, removing skin cancer may seem prosaic, but the diagnosis shook me to the core. For as long as I can remember, I have told people I was going to live to be at least 120. Clients would send me birthday cards and joke about my prediction. I've exercised my whole life and have always been dedicated to upgrading my health. Cancer? I may have lost one square centimeter of skin, but I gained a ton of doubt. The surgeons removed more than cancer that evening; they removed part of my identity.

I know there are a lot of people who have come to terms with death, comfortable with the fact that they will pass away one day. I am not one of those people. I know there is a peace that comes with accepting death and anxiety that comes with denying it. After that experience, I had to confront my own mortality. It's been a process, but in working with many older clients over the years, I've found that facing death can help you live more fully. Research supports this as well.

Studies have found that there are positive benefits that come from thinking about your own death, including improved physical health, the reprioritization of goals and values, and help in creating a life of greater significance and meaning.[206] Irvin Yalom, a professor of psychiatry at Stanford University and author of the book *Staring at the*

Sun: Overcoming the Terror of Death, suggests we can use an "awakening experience," such as the death of a loved one or a negative health diagnosis, as an opportunity to confront our mortality.

If you are struggling with your own mortality, you are not alone. Research has found that most people have low-to-moderate levels of death anxiety – and that the fear of death is just as likely for younger people as it is those of us who are older.[207] Surprisingly, there was no association between religious affiliation and reduced death anxiety. How can you transition from death avoidance to death acceptance? It helps to first identify the cause of the fear.

Psychologists say thanatophobia – the fear of dying – takes three forms:

(1) You may fear the experience of dying. This may stem from the fear of pain or feeling ill or from the loss of control and dignity that comes with dying.

(2) Your fear may be about being dead. This could be a fear of the unknown or of abandoning family. Some people have a fear of eternal punishment in an afterlife. Others may experience a combination of fear and sadness about what they will miss after they are gone (e.g., weddings, Christmas mornings).

(3) A combination of being afraid of the process of dying and of being dead.

If you are struggling with your mortality, here are a few ideas to consider:

Use fear to take better care of your health. If you are afraid of dying, live longer. Research finds that, if you have a greater appreciation for the gravity of death, you are more likely to take better care of yourself. Use your anxiety to upgrade your health by exercising, eating well, and getting regular checkups.

Do not put off important things for tomorrow. In his work *On the Shortness of Life*, Roman philosopher Seneca writes, "You will hear many men saying: 'After my fiftieth year I shall retire into leisure, my sixtieth year shall release me from public duties.' And what guarantee, pray, have you that your life will last longer? How late it is to begin to live just when we must cease to live!"

I wrote earlier about my mom missing her opportunity to visit Paris. What do you want to do and experience? Do not wait for the "right" time. Do the things that you desire – all of them. The list may include big adventures or even just conversations you know you need to have. Whatever they are, now is the time to do them.

Appreciate each day. In William Shakespeare's *Julius Caesar*, the titular character remarks, "A coward dies a thousand times before his death, but the valiant taste of death but once." Those who are preoccupied with dying can never truly live. Post-traumatic growth theory tells us we can use our fear for transformation, but have you ever tried to *not* think of something? Invariably, you think of the thing you are trying not to think of! Anxiety and fear are created and perpetuated by thoughts. Instead of avoiding them, which doesn't work, acknowledge the fear and reframe it. Tell yourself that you're going to make the most of your life – whether you have five more days or five more decades. Tell yourself that you will be ready whenever that day comes. At least, that is what the research on the terminally ill tells us to do. Those who are at the ends of their lives often accept it and make peace with it. I've seen this with relatives and clients alike. Have faith that, when your time comes, you will be able to look back and smile with contentment.

Focus on your mission and purpose. When I was being wheeled in for surgery, I knew I wasn't going to die, but I thought about death. I was grateful that it was "just" skin cancer and that I still had a full life expectancy. Nevertheless, I started to think about my life. I was nervous and hated that I was there, but I can tell you that I felt a kernel of comfort because I knew I lived for something. Whenever my time comes, I know that I've made the most of my life and that I've made an impact. Do the work laid out in Challenge 7 so you are clear on your mission, your purpose, and the impact you want to make.

Learn from others. There are wonderful books that explore facing death and mortality, including *On the Shortness of Life* by Seneca, *Staring at the Sun: Overcoming the Terror of Death* by Irvin Yalom, *Being Mortal* by Atul Gawande, *How We Die: Reflections of Life's Final Chapter* by Sherwin B. Nuland, *No Death, No Fear: Comforting Wisdom for Life* by Thich Nhat Hanh, and *The Other Side of Sadness* by George Bonanno. There are also countless presentations and TED Talks on the subject.

Practice Visualization. This may sound morbid, but some therapists suggest that, rather than running from the fear, you should dive into it instead. Visualize what your last days, hours, or minutes might feel like. Will you have regrets? Will you imagine the things you didn't do or conversations you didn't have? Get comfortable sitting with your fear. If this is too difficult, work with a therapist who can guide you.

Use therapy. If you have more than just casual thoughts about death or suffer from more intense fear, consider working with a therapist. Cognitive-behavioral therapy (CBT) is an effective style of therapy for treating anxiety and phobias. It focuses on overcoming cognitive distortions and behaviors and developing coping strategies. Another form of therapy to consider is existential therapy. As the name suggests, existential therapists are trained on issues related to human existence – including the meaning of life and matters of death.

Of course, if you're like me, you can always hope for the day we reach longevity escape velocity so we can cheat death! I know, that's not embracing my mortality. Like I said, it's been a process.

DIP > DROP

Sometimes, building resilience isn't about life or death but something more mundane like spraining an ankle on a hike or getting into an argument with your spouse. It's the small things – not the existential threats – that throw us off our game more frequently. To create momentum in retirement, we must be vigilant in order not to let the small setbacks derail us.

There have been several times when I've felt I was not just in the game, but winning. I felt a connection to my purpose, which inspired me to get out of bed every day. I was physically in the best shape of my life and was boldly doing everything I could to achieve and experience more. Then, a setback – maybe something big like a surgery or even something insignificant such as a vacation – would take me out of the game. I know you've also been there.

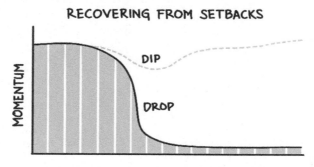

Don't confuse a dip with a drop. Dips are short- lived and you can get back on track while drops are permanent.

You work so hard to build momentum only for it to grind to a halt in an instant. We must fight to keep that from happening, but it's difficult. Everything is interrelated – we pull a hamstring so we can't exercise, but then we also aren't eating as well because we aren't working out, which leads to poor sleep, which leads to less mental focus and energy, and so on. The challenge is to stop the snowball from growing, spreading, and undermining your momentum.

After years of being derailed following minor setbacks, I've learned a few things that have helped me bounce back faster and continue creating momentum.

When things are going well, we think they will continue to do so forever, and when they don't, we get surprised. "How could this have happened?" we ask ourselves. That's the wrong approach. We shouldn't be shocked when challenges conspire to derail us. We should expect them. Setbacks are not strangers. We encounter them enough that they are more like acquaintances. When they show up at your door, don't be surprised. Don't let their presence startle you and divert you from what's important.

When you drop-out, you quit. You stop and move on to something else. A drop is permanent. A dip, however, is something quite different. A dip is momentary. You will face setbacks and you'll stop doing the things that help you live a Badass Retirement. This I guarantee. You might experience a rough fall off your snowboard when trying a double black diamond or you may accidentally fall off a curb on your way out of Baskin-Robbins. Stuff happens. Your job is not to fight the setbacks – they are inevitable – but to reframe the drops as just temporary dips. A dip from exercising. A dip from doing your daily gratitude work. A dip from pursuing your mission. A dip from making an impact.

A drop is the end of the game; a dip is just a brief pause. The only difference between a fleeting dip and a lasting drop is your perception. Language matters. Label your setback a drop and you can kiss your progress goodbye. Reframe it as a brief dip and you'll be back in action shortly.

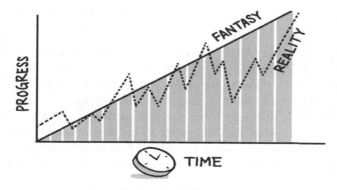

We think progress is a steady climb but it's often much less of a straight line than we expect.

One trick that has helped me and others re-engage after a dip is the one day, one week, one month strategy. After a setback, even a minor one, it can feel daunting to commit to action. Sometimes the last thing you feel like doing is anything – even when you know it's the right thing to do. Instead of getting overwhelmed, just promise you'll do whatever you know you need to do (e.g., exercise, stop smoking, skipping dessert, waking up early) for just one day. Don't commit to anything longer. After you do it for a day, then only commit to doing for a week. If you backslide after a few days, just start over and commit to a day again. If you successfully complete a week, commit to a month. Again, if you experience another dip go back to a day. The reason I think this is so effective is that it takes all the pressure off. The next time you experience a setback – and you will – remember to frame it as a temporary dip and commit to getting back into action.

RULE OF THIRDS

I recently learned about the "rule of thirds" – a simple but powerful lesson on facing adversity. It describes something I've intuitively felt without being able to articulate it as clearly as the rule does. Although the rule of thirds was developed by Ian Dobson, a former Olympic runner and current long-distance track coach, I heard about it from his track student, Alexi Pappas.

Alexi is also a long-distance runner and Olympian. In a *Wall Street Journal* article, she recounts the story of a bad training session leading up to the Rio Olympics.[208] She couldn't reach her pace on the track and became frustrated, starting to cry. That's when Ian shared the rule of thirds with her.

Ian told her that, when you're training, chasing a big goal in life, or doing anything hard, you're supposed to feel good a third of the time, okay a third of the time, and crappy a third of the time. He said if you're feeling bad or struggling, just chalk it up to a crappy day. If the ratio is wildly different from the rule of thirds, you should make a change. For example, if you feel great all the time, it means you are not pushing yourself hard enough. If you feel bad all the time, you need to adjust. Alexi has internalized the rule and has made it her own.

THE RULE OF THIRDS

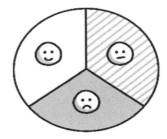

Working hard toward something? About 1/3 of the time you will feel good, 1/3 of the time you will feel okay, and 1/3 of the time you'll feel crappy. And that's okay.

In a Rich Roll podcast interview, Alexi explains, "In those days where creativity doesn't come or you don't feel great, you still show up because maybe that's your crappy day. It doesn't mean you quit the goal. It doesn't mean you freak out. It means you show up and live through that crappy day or the dip because you're chasing a dream and doing something hard."[209]

You don't need to be training for the Olympics to apply this rule to your life. You can use it when you are making an impact or fulfilling your mission. Alexi used this approach when she was writing her book, *Bravery: Chasing Dreams, Befriending Pain, and Other Big Ideas.* On the days she struggled to find the words, she persevered anyway. She says, "On the good days, you grow your confidence. On the crappy days, you grow your patience, courage, and resilience."[210]

I just love this. You show up, even – especially – when you don't feel like it. Momentum is about movement, not about motivation. Motivation is elusive. If you wait for it to grace you with its presence, you may find yourself waiting for a long time. Instead of waiting to feel inspired, just start doing the work. That means you take your walk, even though it's raining. You drink your nutritional shake, even though you don't feel like it. You sit down at the computer and start typing, even though each word is a battle. You fulfill your commitment to volunteer, even though you'd rather watch the game.

The phrase "going through the motions" has negative connotations – like you are phoning it in and doing as little as possible. Sometimes, however, doing as little as possible is enough. It's okay to go through the motions. The key is that you are moving – however slowly that occurs. The minute you stop, it becomes exponentially harder to start again. I could get into a big discussion about kinetic friction versus static friction, but if you've ever pushed a stalled car, you'll know exactly how this feels. It's incredibly hard to get the car moving, but once it starts to roll – even just a little – it becomes so easy a child could push it. Don't let the momentum stop.

Badass Retirement isn't free from pain or hardship. You can do everything right, but sometimes, things still go wrong. There will be moments when you feel like curling up, but you must do whatever you can to keep moving forward.

Next, we will focus on the one thing you can do to create and sustain momentum throughout retirement . . . Seek Impossible! Read on, but brace yourself, it's not for the weak or the faint of heart.

JOIN THE FAMILY

It's hard to face tough times and challenges alone. Foster relationships with family and friends so you have people you can lean on when you experience setbacks. Also, a group of people are ready to support you in the Badass Retirement Community. We'd love to have you join us.

GO TO BADASSRETIREMENT.COM

15

CHALLENGE

Seek
Impossible

There are no do-overs. Retirement is
your last opportunity to do everything
you thought impossible.

CHALLENGE 15

There is something fascinating brewing just below the surface of our culture. In this age of widespread streaming and binge-watching, we are witnessing another type of surge.[211] This other surge doesn't require an internet connection, TV, or couch. You just need a pair of running shoes, a whole lot of determination, and some would say, a little insanity.

Ultrarunning – basically, taking part in any race longer than a marathon – has soared in popularity. Research shows that participation has increased 345% globally in just the last decade.[212] Estimates suggest there are 10,000 or more of these races each year, which often span upwards of 200 miles over multiple days. It's not just the distance that makes these events grueling, however, as the geography often plays a villainous role.

Some examples include the Marathon des Sables – a six-day, 156-mile race across the Sahara Desert. Dubbed the "Toughest Footrace on Earth," it promises temperatures over 120 degrees and bloody feet. What's more surprising is that these warnings are not buried in the fine print of their legal disclaimers. These are selling points displayed front and center on the homepage. And the Marathon des Sables is just one of thousands of events that advertise pain, punishment, and ultimately, the opportunity to test your mind and body to see if you can rise to the challenge. There is the HURT 100 in Hawaii (the name says it all), the Arctic Ultra 380-mile race across upper Canada (for the less ambitious, they offer a shorter 120-mile option), the Everest Marathon (yes, *that* Everest), the 200km Revenant with 16,000 meters of ascent on the South Island of New Zealand (with the tagline, "A true challenge is when failure is the most likely outcome."), the Spartan Death Race (with the appropriate website address, www.youmaydie.com) and the Badwater 135, which is a 135-mile race across Death Valley . . . in the heat of July.

The harder, more grueling, and more brutal the event the happier it makes some participants.

If you want to test your limits but running is not your thing, there are plenty of other grueling endurance events you can tackle. Such ultra-events have expanded beyond running to include almost anything you can imagine. For example, the Iditarod Trail Invitational includes battling temperatures as low as negative 50 degrees while you bike, hike, and ski across 1,000 miles of frozen tundra over 30 days. Or there's the Atlantic Challenge, which requires you to row 3,000 miles across the Atlantic Ocean.

The rapid rise in ultra-endurance events is certainly interesting, but what's even more intriguing is the simultaneous decline of traditional 5K races. Furthermore, what was once considered *the* racing challenge – the marathon – has all but plateaued during the same timeframe.

We've transitioned from plain vanilla events (like the 5K) that maximize the number of participants who can complete them to events that are much harder and instead use the dismal finishing rate as a marketing lure!

In fact, go to any of the events' websites and you'll encounter basically the same marketing copy. *Pay us money so you can participate in a grueling event where you will experience more pain and anguish than any other event you've experienced. There is a high probability of minor injury and a meaningful chance of serious injury or death. You will be subjected to extreme environmental conditions, get little to no sleep, and compete over several days with a very small chance of successfully finishing.*

I wouldn't dismiss the participants as just young and crazy. It's not just brash young men full of testosterone signing up for these events. Men and women of all ages are flocking to these challenges.

Have we gone mad?

No, I think we've gone easy.

THE MAGIC OF CHALLENGE

Dean Karnazes is an author and ultrarunner (think 100+ miles). He has tackled countless amazing physical and mental feats over the years. He has a unique view on how true happiness is achieved in life: "We think that, if we had every comfort available to us, we'd be happy. We equate comfort with happiness. And now we're so comfortable we're miserable. There's no struggle in our lives. No sense of adventure. We get in a car, we get in an elevator, it all comes easy. What I've found is that I'm never more alive than when I'm pushing and I'm in pain, and I'm struggling for high achievement, and in that struggle, I think there's a magic."[213]

Obviously, Dean is operating on a different level than most of us mere mortals who feel accomplished after finishing a 5K. I think there's wisdom in that approach, though – not just in retirement but in life. I also think you can achieve this kind of magic without ever lacing up your running shoes!

I think we are searching for challenge – for something that pushes us and tests our limits. I think many of us feel we can do and achieve more. There is a gnawing feeling that we haven't tapped into our full potential. A friend of mine describes it as having "another gear." The participants who enter these extreme events are not crazy. In fact, they're perfectly rational. They're more pleasure seekers than they are masochists. But how could someone who rows across the Atlantic be a rational pleasure seeker?

The incremental steps that bring someone to that point are invisible. Nobody goes from the couch to being able to run across the Sahara Desert.

APPRECIATE THE GAP

Try this experiment. Ask 10 of your friends or family – retired or not – if they think they are living up to their full potential or if they think they could do, achieve, or become more. I guarantee that all 10 will admit they could be doing more. This might suggest a rather bleak picture of humanity – that we are habitual underachievers – but I think this realization is a gift.

This gap we feel can either depress and demotivate us, or it can give us inspiration and drive. Not everyone, however, feels this potential gap. It's possible some of these people really are living up to their full potential, but it is more likely they just don't realize what they can do. This might explain the paradox that those who are doing the most and pushing their limits the furthest are often the ones that feel the biggest gap between potential and reality, while those who do the least feel the smallest gap. The more you do, the more you realize you can do. The less you do, the less you think you can do.

The Retirement Myth – that less is more – perpetuates the belief that you are capable of less because you are doing less. This is one of the pernicious outcomes of living an Average Retirement. It's like a snowball rolling down a hill but getting smaller and smaller. Our belief of what we can do, achieve, experience, and become decreases over time. It's a vicious cycle that accelerates in retirement.

How can we stop the cycle and live closer to our full potential in retirement? That's really what living a Badass Retirement is all about – elevating your view of what's possible in retirement, and in turn, what you are capable of achieving in retirement.

IT FEELS GOOD TO BE CHALLENGED

Think about a sport or hobby you really enjoy and that gives you immense satisfaction. Maybe it's playing the piano or golfing. Imagine you woke up tomorrow morning and you could play every song flawlessly or you could hit a hole-in-one on every swing. That would be amazing, right? You'd show off your new talent as often as you could. And then what would happen? Think about it. Really imagine yourself in this situation. After the novelty wore off, you'd get bored, wouldn't you? There would be no challenge. Even worse, the hobby that used to give you so much gratification would become unenjoyable at best and a curse at worst. How could being perfect at the thing you love to do cause you so much anguish?

The enjoyment you derive from your hobby doesn't come in *spite of* your frustration on the golf course or learning a tough chord progression. Nope. It's *because* of these challenges that you keep coming back. You love your hobby because there is a challenge – there is room for improvement and room to grow. You can try new things to get better. There is a gap between where you are and perfection, and it is that gap that provides interest, exploration, and motivation.

This is a big reason why golf is not only hugely popular but also quite addictive. The intermittent reinforcement – 100 bad-to-mediocre hits for every two great ones – is the same phenomenon that keeps gamblers at the slot machines. Golf is also impossible to master, which means you are always striving to learn and get better. It also provides immediate feedback. Because of its intermittent rewards, high difficulty of mastery, and instant feedback, golf is a potent cocktail that can be all-consuming. If you golf or know people who do, you'll know exactly what I mean – it's a recipe for obsession.

Of course (pun intended!) we don't need golf to experience this high level of engagement. Most of our hobbies provide varying levels of these sticky elements that keep us hooked and coming back for more.

Life is better when you have the impossible in your crosshairs, but seeking the impossible can ring hollow if it isn't tied to your purpose. Without a deeper meaning, the impossible becomes a façade – just something to check off a list as you move on to the next thing.

An impossible feat that is grounded in purpose, however, is the stuff of legend. Impossible provides challenge, excitement, and the ability to learn and grow as you chase it down. Impossible is the antidote to boredom and restlessness. Impossible that is connected to your purpose is a shot in the arm, providing focus, direction, and meaning. It gets you out of bed in the morning and keeps you up at night.

WHAT DOES IT MEAN TO SEEK IMPOSSIBLE?

Seek Impossible sounds like a recipe for disaster. We've been told we should set realistic and achievable goals. We shouldn't aim too high because we'll just get frustrated and give up. We're told to set small goals we can check off to keep the momentum moving forward.

Impossible is, well, impossible. Why would you want to dedicate your retirement to something unattainable?

Small doesn't inspire. Trivial doesn't move. Easy doesn't motivate. Something being within reach doesn't excite us. Spare yourself the drudgery of the realistic and the practical. These minor "goals" are affronts to our real potential.

Impossible is out there, far out on the horizon. You can barely see it, and you have no idea how you are going to accomplish it, but it's pulling you. It's beckoning you despite the perceived absurdity of the challenge. Your mind is trying to talk you out of it, but your heart has already accepted the challenge. That's the power of impossible.

Small can't compete. Small feels like a to-do list. If you think you can achieve something, it's not impossible enough. If you only focus on what you think you can achieve, you will habitually underperform because we habitually underestimate ourselves.

What's that thing you always thought about doing but never thought you could achieve? Finish a marathon? Write a novel? Get your black belt? Start a bakery? Win the StorySLAM championship? Give speeches to high school students? Finish your degree? Ride your bicycle across the country? Teach English in a foreign country? Launch a non-profit? Start a podcast? Live in 10 countries in the first 10 years of retirement? Participate in the NCHA World Finals? Grow a YouTube channel to 100,000 subscribers? Lose 200 pounds? Write a Billboard top 100 song? Run a five-minute mile? Walk a mile? Visit every continent? Hike the Appalachian Trail? Write a *New York Times* bestselling book? Perform standup at the Comedy Store in Hollywood? End animal suffering? Become a Congressperson? Start an animal shelter? Complete the Seven Summits? Go into space? Start a non-profit that provides equine therapy to teens? Raise and donate $1 million to a cause? Sell your artwork? Win the Palm Springs International ShortFest? Become a Master Scuba Diver? Visit every home of your ancestors as far back as you can trace? Run a thriving online community of badass retirees? :)

Remember, if it's easy or not much of a stretch, it's not impossible. You need to find that thing that you've put off. That thing that causes your heart to skip a beat when you think about it. That thing that you've pushed aside thinking you couldn't do it. That, my friend, is your impossible. And that's what you are going to go after in retirement. But, but, but. I know. You're afraid. You feel anxious even thinking about it. That's okay. You don't want to fail. That's okay, too.

In our working years, we did well by accomplishing the possible, but we're playing a different game in retirement. Back then, we had other forces working with us that made the possible respectable and worthwhile. That's over. When we retire, let's also retire that line of thinking. What is possible doesn't serve us in the same way that it did when we were working. Why? There were consequences if we failed.

Our livelihoods were built on our ability to reach outcomes, so it made sense to aim for and achieve the possible. In retirement, there are no consequences for failure.

Let that sink in.

There are no consequences for failure in retirement, but that doesn't mean it won't scare you or others...

IMPOSSIBLE CAN BE INTIMIDATING

When you set big goals and chase after your most important dreams, many of your friends and family will rise to the occasion and be supportive of your efforts and vision. They will cheer you on as you slay your dragons and try to conquer what had once seemed impossible.

When you Seek Impossible, it's infectious. Those around you may join in your effort, or you may inspire them to find their own impossible. You may have already experienced this in your life.

Have you ever started an exercise routine or a new diet and others joined you? We love being part of something, and sometimes, all it takes is seeing someone else act to give us the motivation to jump in ourselves. Seek Impossible is attractive. Those on a mission have a purpose – a reason for being. They have a focus and intention that draws people in like a gravitational pull. It can also repel.

Mere mention of the word "impossible" scares people. Although you might be up for the challenge, others may not. When you Seek Impossible, it can be intimidating for those around you. If you are attempting to achieve hard things, don't expect a parade honoring your effort. You may get pushback from friends and family. They may scoff at your dreams. They may discourage your efforts. They may think you are crazy to focus your time and energy on striving for the impossible. It's important that you are aware that not everyone will be as excited about your passion as you are.

If you experience a negative reaction, your response should reflect the value of your relationship. If it is an acquaintance or casual friend, you may want to limit your interaction with them or drop them completely. Does it make sense to be around those that discourage you from achieving fulfillment? Obviously, you can't cut a close friend or spouse out of your life just for giving you a negative response, but a heartfelt conversation about why you are going after the impossible and what it means to you will often alleviate any negativity. Asking for their support or help can also be a great tool to get them on board.

If you continue to experience conflict, however, working with a therapist can be an effective way to explore the issues and (hopefully) come to a resolution – or at least a better understanding. Seek Impossible is challenging by itself, and although it can give you purpose and energy to go after your big goals, it is still hard work and can be frustrating at times. You don't need cheerleaders pumping you up at every turn, but you certainly don't need the people around you discouraging you and making your journey to the impossible even more arduous. It will be a better experience if you can inspire those around you to seek their own impossible or to help you on your mission.

WHAT YOU COULD DO > WHAT YOU HAVE DONE

"I am consistently overestimating what I can achieve . . ." said no one ever.

Our problem (mine, yours, and everyone else's) is that we are bad at predicting what we can do. We habitually underestimate ourselves, keeping our sights set too low. We are short-sighted in what we think we can do, so instead of having big and bold visions, we tend to accept small and meek goals. Why do we habitually underestimate our potential? I think there are a few reasons:

- **We look to the past.** If I asked you "What can you do?" you would immediately start to think about what you have already done. This is human nature, and we all do this. I think this is one of the reasons that those who accomplish great things tend to continue accomplishing great things. The historical bar of past achievements is higher for them than for most of us. When they look back, they are reminded of past challenges they successfully overcame. It becomes an approach to life for them. They may not have any idea *how* they are going to do it, but they are confident that they will be able to figure it out. Those of us without this "can do" approach constantly gaze into the rearview mirror to determine what we think we can do. If we've done X before, we may try to do X+1, but we'd never attempt X+100 or even X+10.

- **We don't have good role models.** Have you ever been around someone that had an energy or spark about them that was contagious? Didn't you feel like you could do so much more? Maybe it was finding a workout routine, eating better, writing a book, or starting a business. Being around others who dream big and tackle tough challenges is infectious. Some of their energy and zeal rubs off on us, making us want to do more. Unfortunately, most of us don't have enthusiastic role models around us. The adage that we are the average of our five closest friends has merit. Often these five closest friends also struggle with setting the bar too low. I'm sure you've experienced feeling lethargic or pessimistic after being around someone negative or with a small-scale vision for their future. It would be ideal if we could generate motivation ourselves – independent of others – but most of us are influenced by those around us.

- **Our "why" is not big enough.** Friedrich Nietzsche wrote, "If we have our own 'why' of life, we shall get along with almost any 'how.'" Without a sufficiently meaningful "why," it's easy to understand why we set our sights too low and do not live up to our potential. In retirement, it's easy to fall into the "doing less is better" trap, especially if our "why" is simply to relax and enjoy life. If your "why" is to take it easy, you're not setting grandiose goals that could improve your life or the lives of those around you.

- **We are lazy.** It's true. Even in our working years, most of us had at least an area or two where we struggled to act. Maybe we didn't always make the time to develop strong relationships, help others, improve our health, or learn new things. Our rationale was that, with work occupying our daily life, there just wasn't enough time to do everything. Unfortunately, we often bring this mindset with us after we stop working, and such lackadaisical tendencies only increase in retirement.

- **It's scary.** The impossible is frightening because it is overwhelming. We don't have all the answers, we feel incapable of tackling the project, and we feel smaller and weaker as our challenges get bigger and harder.

- **Fear of ridicule.** Even though we've all read countless books and we "thumbs up" posts that encourage us to "chart our own destiny" and "be ourselves," we care what other people think.

We don't want to look like a dope in the eyes of our family and friends. What's a great way to immediately look like a dope? Saying you're going to rise to a challenge and then failing miserably. Shame and embarrassment are powerful drivers. It's a lot less threatening to underestimate your ability and succeed than it is to overestimate and fail.

- **Better to stay with the pack.** There are benefits to being pack animals, including mutual collaboration, the division of duties, and protection from threats. There are unspoken agreements within each of our social networks that can influence our behavior, our goals, and what we attempt. Some networks thrive on pushing limits. They consider members to be abnormal or out of place if they have mundane visions and are not clawing to grasp the impossible. Think about the networks that form around adventure athletes who push the boundaries of physics and sport or the tech titans who are continuously inventing and reimagining what's possible. It's no wonder these super achiever networks form clusters – often geographically and temporally. Their social dynamics encourage and motivate progress. Even though most of us aren't lucky enough to have an environment like this, we still exist in networks with unwritten rules for us and our fellow members. Those unwritten (but very real) rules temper what is normal. This dynamic comes up a lot in my work with sudden wealth recipients – average people who come into windfalls that change their entire financial lives overnight. As soon as they start to use their money in ways that differ from others in their social group, such as joining a country club or buying a luxury vehicle, they feel the friction and it can create a divide. Social dynamics have a hidden but powerful influence over our beliefs, decisions, and actions.

As a result of all these hurdles and many others, we err on the side of the known and manageable. Our natural approach is to underestimate what we can do. The deck seems stacked against us, and it is.

If you want an Average Retirement, continue to set tepid goals for your retired life. You may avoid feeling fear, embarrassment, or self-doubt, but I promise you that your possible goals will not inspire you to jump out of bed in the morning. Your predictable vision won't inspire those around you, and your lackluster mission won't create a remarkable retirement. So, what's the solution?

HOW TO SEEK IMPOSSIBLE

- **Make your impossible meaningful.** The promised land in retirement isn't a life exclusively defined by ease and comfort. Based on what you already know or what you've read so far, you may appreciate that impossible isn't easy. Our natural inclination may be to pull away from what feels like work or effort. "I retired so I wouldn't have to do hard stuff anymore" is a common refrain. But it's different when you get to choose the hard stuff you do. The difference is akin to babysitting someone else's young kids versus caring for your own grandkids. Hard is only unpleasant when it's not a choice and it's not meaningful. However, hard can be deeply gratifying when it's your choice and it is connected to your purpose.

- **What impossible thing(s) do you want to do in retirement?** This is a good place to start, although I've found that most initial answers are mundane and not very "impossible." That's okay, though. Just jot down all the impossible things you'd like to do. If your list starts with "golf three days a week," just keep writing. Again, we are not good at predicting what we can achieve. Start with the easy and then move onto the more challenging. Over time, you may start to dance with the impossible.

- **What work would you do even if you weren't getting paid?** This is a common question for young adults to help them determine their career paths. I don't want to spoil the surprise, but guess what? You just described retirement. What would you dedicate your life in retirement to doing . . . for free?

  When you take money out of the equation, you can focus on all the non-economic benefits. If you weren't getting paid and the work wasn't providing you with meaning, fulfillment, or joy, why would you do it? In our working years, we may have had to sacrifice because earning an income was the priority. Now that you aren't just concerned with getting money, what other form of compensation would this work have to provide you?

- **What do you want to be the best in the world at?** This is a fun game to play with kids and is a great exercise to help you elevate your view of what's possible. If you could be the best in the world at something, what would it be? Singing? Empathy? Lawn darts? Listening? Krav Maga? Poetry? Psychological profiling? Really think about it. Your first response may not be what you really want. Dig deeper. You are not looking for a knee-jerk answer. This exercise may take 20 minutes, or you may find that you are still thinking about this a week from now. Good. I hope this question provokes you. I hope it burrows itself into your psyche and irritates you until you resolve it. I want it to provide just enough agitation that discovering the answer gives you a sense of relief. That's how you know you've found something meaningful.

- **Succumb to (the right kind of) peer pressure.** Who says peer pressure must be negative? We might as well adapt our natural tendency to stick with the pack to our benefit. This means you need to have at least one person in your life who is pushing their limits and who sees the potential for greatness in you – even if you may not. Better still, find more than just one person – maybe even find yourself a whole tribe of go-getters that can act as models for you. Rather than eliminating old friends or family members who might not elevate you, a more compassionate approach is to add new friends. One of the quickest ways to accelerate your view of what's possible is to join a group made up of people who are doing the thing you want to do. If you've been living far below your potential for some time, seeing what other people can do – people just like you – can be an awakening. If you are struggling to light your own fire, use the inferno an ambitious group can provide.

- **Create an "unsafe" space.** The world can be a tough place. Friends and family can be insensitive. Sometimes we just need to be told that we are okay and we are good enough. For a friend to tell us everything will work out, and we are perfect just the way we are. I get it. We all need comfort and security . . . but we shouldn't live in it.

Sometimes what we really need is a kick in the ass.

Create an uncomfortable space. No, not a place where you'll be beaten down or criticized, but a place you are surrounded by so much greatness that you feel vulnerable but also inspired. A place where you witness others going after their dreams, taking risks, and trying to become the best versions of themselves that you feel challenged to aim a little higher yourself.

Who you are is who you know.

Create an environment that challenges you physically but also one that can stretch you intellectually – where people are going after big goals and making an impact. Find older people doing things that inspire you and make you question what you think is possible as you age. Create community with younger people to remind yourself of the vitality and sense of wonder that's within you.

Be the "slacker" in at least one of your friend groups or social circles – not because you aren't trying to crush it – but because everyone else is pushing even harder.

Don't run from reality; embrace it. It's too easy to let things such as your health, relationships, passions, hobbies, and goals slip in retirement. Be vigilant and brutally honest with yourself. What's working? Where are you falling behind? On what areas do you need to focus more time and energy?

You want to get comfortable feeling uncomfortable.

Every time I get on my Peloton I enter an uncomfortable space, but not for the reasons you may think. The instructors couldn't be more encouraging with their praise. The other riders are supportive with their virtual "high fives." What makes this a vulnerable space for me is that I'm challenged. I can't hide. The numbers don't lie. I'm either pushing myself and getting better or I'm not.

Other examples of unsafe spaces could include CrossFit gyms where you come face-to-face with trying to push and better yourself, a group where the members are stretching their comfort zones physically or mentally, or something as simple as having an accountability partner that keeps you on track.

Whatever the source, it might not feel comfortable, but that's the point.

- **Become, achieve, do, contribute.** If you are new to thinking in terms of impossible (aren't most of us?) and need guardrails to help you focus, think of what impossible could mean across these domains: *Become, Achieve, Do*, and *Contribute*. Who do you want to become in retirement? A child trauma counselor? What would becoming impossible look like? What impossible do you want to *achieve*? Earn a Ph.D.? Write a bestselling novel? What impossible do you want to *do*? Start a drug rehab shelter for homeless youth? Ride a bicycle from Los Angeles to Buenos

Aires? What impossible *contribution* could you make? Ending animal suffering? Freeing the innocent from death row?

- **Explore all areas of your life.** Impossible isn't limited to one domain. Review the major aspects of your life – financial, social, relational, health, growth, etc. – to see if one area pulls at you a little more than the others. One client described this as "scratching an itch." He said that, when he explored one area of his life, it jumped out at him like an itch that needed to be scratched. He knew that was the area that needed his focus. But don't think you have to limit yourself to just one impossible. You can Seek Impossible in more than one area of your life.

- **Don't try to impress.** My impossible isn't necessarily going to invigorate you. In fact, you may scoff at what I think is impossible. You may think my impossible isn't hard enough or maybe it's too selfish. Guess what? The joy of retirement is that we get to say goodbye to bosses and customers who we need to appease. Retirement is the time in our lives when we get to invest our time and energy in anything we want without retribution from anyone else (though this is different if you are in a relationship as discussed in Challenge 9). If I choose to spend my retirement exploring the Himalayas, so be it. If you choose to spend your retirement helping the homeless, so be it.

- **Imagine you've obtained the impossible.** Imagine not just trying to reach the impossible but also achieving it. No, really imagine it. Close your eyes and put yourself in the future when you have already conquered the impossible. What does that feel like? Try to avoid making the mistake of intellectualizing how you *should* feel. Instead, try to experience what you *would* feel. If your response is a tepid "that's cool" or "neat," that's an indication you haven't found the right target or that the stakes aren't high enough. The impossible requires perseverance, grit, and determination in the face of ridiculous odds. If "meh" is your reward, keep searching.

- **What if you don't achieve the impossible?** Imagine you are near the end of your life, and you haven't achieved your impossible. How does that make you feel? Apathetic? If all you can muster is "Oh well, whatever, nevermind," find a new impossible goal. You should be angry that you don't have more time. Furious that your impossible is still looming out there, unfinished. Those strong feelings are the qualities that will drive you in retirement. It must mean something if it stirs so much emotion in you. On the line between interested and obsessed, you need to be closer to obsessed. The right impossible goal is not a nice-to-have but rather a need-to-have. Judge your impossible with the feelings that arise when you imagine not reaching it. That will help you determine if your impossible is significant enough for you.

- **Dial up the crazy.** Impossibility requires a certain level of craziness. Humdrum and reasonable approaches just aren't going to cut it. The best response you can hear is, "You want to do what?!" Small, tepid, and achievable are not words associated with the impossible. Dial up the crazy to the point that it scares you. The purpose of impossible isn't for you to feel comfortable. It's for you to feel unsure, agitated, and energized. When you Seek Impossible, it immediately creates a gap between where you are and what is impossible. This gap creates agitation because you want it filled. The agitation creates energy and purpose. That's why your impossible must be challenging. Nothing garners energy like the impossible. Grand is what gets us out of bed. It's hard to be moved when the stakes are inconsequential. If your impossible only warrants a "Who cares?" you haven't found the right target or you need to rachet up the stakes.

- **Make a friend.** I have a friend that yells and curses at me when I'm struggling and want to give up. He always seems to know the right time to show up and work his profane magic on me. Sometimes, I try not to let him in – to just ignore him. That never seems to work well. He just yells louder, and the ~~encouragement~~ insults just get crueler and more personal. He's annoying, and he only comes around when I'm in a dogfight with my goals. I hate to admit it, but he's almost always right. I can do more. I can hang in there a little longer. I can push just a little harder. As irritating as he is, I love him. This friend is retired Navy Seal and ultra-endurance athlete David Goggins.[214] He's become a personal mentor of mine. I guess you could call him a mental coach. Oh, and he has no idea who I am. We've never met (I talked to him once on Christmas Eve, but that's another story). David is a real person, but our relationship is in my head. Who can you invite into your head when you invariably struggle on the path to impossible?

Think about a couple of people who inspire you because they are blazing trails. What would they say to you when you are feeling sorry for yourself or insecure?

My "friend" David Goggins providing me with encouragement.

It's not a race to see how quickly you can find your impossible. Your retirement could easily last 40+ years. Take your time. If you are like others, this process can take weeks or even months. The quickest answer isn't always the best, but you must do the work. It's not going to be delivered to you with a bow. Keep thinking, exploring, and iterating. If you find something that takes your breath away and all you can think is, "I have no idea where I would even start," you're on the right track. Keep chiseling at the idea until you have your muse that carries you along.

You've come a long way, but you are not quite done. The last 300+ pages have prepared you for this. I hope you learned a few things and are maybe starting to see retirement and what you can achieve differently, but what would really make me happy is if you took what you learned and used it each day to improve your life. That's next...

JOIN THE FAMILY

The impossible doesn't happen overnight or easily. Get your daily dose of inspiration in the Badass Retirement Community while you go out into the world and Seek Impossible!

GO TO BADASSRETIREMENT.COM

THE BADASS RETIREMENT SYSTEM

You've reached the end of the book, but I hope this milestone is only the beginning of your journey. Creating a Badass Retirement starts with desire, but the process never ends.

What's next? Where should you go from here?

What I've found after working with retirees for so many years is that it's easy to enter retirement with big hopes and goals, but it's even easier to get complacent. Relax a little too much. Exercise less often. Neglect the things that provided us with meaning. Lose touch with friends. Stop doing the things that created excitement and thrill.

How can you ward off Average Retirement and continue to live your very best life? Consistently pursue the Badass 5. Think of making an investment across these five areas each day – what I imagine as making "daily deposits." It is the only way I know how to give yourself the best opportunity to live an amazing life . . . not just for a few months or years but for the rest of your life.

Committing to the **Badass 5** is an investment. It requires your attention, focus, and energy. But putting effort into each of these drivers is the single best investment you can make and will pay dividends throughout retirement.

Here's your Badass Retirement blueprint...

THE BADASS RETIREMENT SYSTEM

Badass Driver #1: Greater Meaning

Goal: Passion & Fulfillment

Outcome: Feel that your days and life have purpose, you are needed, and you are growing and becoming.

Focus Areas:

- **Impact.** Make a difference, be a part of something bigger than yourself, pursue your mission, go after your big cause, volunteer, and help others.

- **Grow, Learn, Improve.** Never-ending march to grow as an individual, learn new things, and improve who you are, your skills, and abilities.

- **Create.** Build, invent, and create. Focus on projects where you bring to life something new – a business, art, book, organization, event, etc.

- **Impossible.** Set gargantuan-sized goals that take your breath away, make consistent progress to reach them.

- **Be a Hero.** Create opportunities to have responsibility, to be valued, and for others to count on you.

- **Gratitude.** Incorporate daily gratitude practices.

Badass Driver #2: Total Financial Security

Goal: Peace & Confidence

Outcome: Feel financially secure, less worry about money or the stock market.

Focus Areas:

- **Lifetime Income.** Calculate a safe withdrawal rate, seek multiple sources of income, determine optimized Social Security strategy, track withdrawal rate, modify as needed.

- **Portfolio Longevity.** Determine your risk tolerance and capacity, create an appropriate asset allocation, rebalance, shift assets between investment buckets, and monitor portfolio.

- **De-risk Finances.** Focus on all ten financial de-risking strategies such as review finances, insurance, estate plan, withdrawal rate, expenses, and net worth reports, as well as prevent financial fraud, minimize lawsuits, build your retirement team, rebalance your portfolio, etc.

- **Clear Money Mentality.** Limit financial news, avoid excessive trading, don't obsess over the stock market or fixate on the daily moves in your portfolio, etc.

Badass Driver #3: Upgraded Health

Goal:　　　Energy & Ability

Outcome:　　Feel good, live longer, have energy, be pain free and mobile.

Focus Areas:

- **Performance Mindset.** Expand what you think is possible, think and act like an athlete, build the right health team.

- **Test/Track/Monitor.** Track vital health metrics such as blood pressure, cholesterol, blood glucose, resting heart rate, body weight/fat, among others.

- **Exercise**. Aim for daily exercise such as weight training, walking, and cardio.

- **Nutrition.** Focus on a clean and simple plant-focused diet with little meat, dairy, bad fats, and sugar.

- **Recovery.** Engage in active recovery such as massage, walking, yoga, tai chi, and stretching.

- **Performance-Enhancing Supplements.** Dial in the right amount and combination of supplements such as vitamins, minerals, electrolytes, and explore whether you'd benefit from alternative supplements such as hormones, testosterone, CBD, and others.

- **Sleep.** Target seven to nine hours of sleep a night by sticking to a sleep schedule, limiting naps, avoiding alcohol before bed, getting sufficient exercise during the day, using natural supplements, etc.

- **Mental Health/Stress.** Reduce negative stress and increase your mental well-being by spending time in nature, meditating, doing breathing techniques, exercise, and daily gratitude work.

- **Personal Self-Protection:** Learn how to protect yourself. Get training in self-defense, first aid, and the use of advanced personal self-defense tools (e.g., pepper spray, TASER, stun-gun, firearms). Personal security preparation and training can help you prepare – and even prevent – the worst from happening.

Badass Driver #4: Deeper Relationships

Goal: Connection & Belonging

Outcome: Feel wanted and connected with others, experience love and belonging.

Focus Areas:

- **New Relationships.** Invest time and energy into building new relationships.

- **Existing Relationships.** Daily actions that bring you closer to your partner, family, and friends.

- **Your Tribe.** Find connection and belonging with others who share similar interests and passions.

Badass Driver #5: Real Adventure

Goal: Enthusiasm & Joy

Outcome: Feel alive, have fun, and experience a rush and excitement.

Focus Areas:

- **Boldness.** Do things that create fear and excitement, push past your comfort zone.

- **Hobbies.** Engage in activities and hobbies that provide you with joy, thrill, challenge, and community.

- **Adventure.** Schedule and participate in adventures that push your mental and physical limits.

- **Novelty.** Focus on doing things differently, experimenting with new activities and recreations, changing your routines.

- **Nature.** Spend time outside and in nature.

- **Short Game.** Reprogram how you think about time and prioritize today over tomorrow.

The framework above is just a rough outline and a starting point. It provides the structure and the essential elements for creating your best life in retirement, but it is ever evolving. You can download the latest printer-friendly version at BadassRetirement.com. Some readers will digest what they read over the last 15 Challenges, download the system, and run with it.

But if you're like me and many others, you might benefit from more specific step-by-step actions. Remember, it's easy to start off strong and determined, but it's even easier to get off track if you're not careful.

Over the years, I've developed and honed daily, weekly, monthly, quarterly, and yearly actions you can take to ensure you have the best shot at living and sustaining a Badass Retirement. Daily actions include:

Is someone better off because of something I did?

Did I text or call a friend?

Did I write in my gratitude journal?

Did I avoid checking my investment portfolio?

Did I sweat?

Did I learn something new?

Did I do something that pushed me outside of my comfort zone?

And so many others…

In addition to daily action items, there are also weekly, monthly, quarterly, and yearly actions, check-ins, and prompts you can incorporate that focus on the **Badass 5**:

- **Greater Meaning** (e.g., Do you feel connected to your mission, and did you make progress toward it? What specifically have you done to get closer to your Impossible goal?).

- **Total Financial Security** (e.g., Calculate your current monthly withdrawal rate, Check your property and casualty insurance coverage).

- **Upgraded Health** (e.g., Get your blood panel taken, Schedule a skin check).

- **Deeper Relationships** (e.g., Did you see at least one friend in person? Do you feel connected to a tribe?).

- **Real Adventure** (e.g., Do you have an adventure activity scheduled? How much time have you spent in nature?).

I've always loved the saying, "Success isn't owned. It's leased, and rent is due every day." Think of these actions as not so much a to-do list, but a *get-to-do* list. You get to incorporate any combination of these actions and check-ins that resonate with and make sense to you. I've learned a lot working with retirees over my professional career, but

I certainly don't have all the answers. What's cool is that I've added items to the framework throughout the years based on suggestions from clients, friends, and other retirees. This is an evolving and dynamic blueprint that grows and develops over time. To view the full system (and maybe even make a suggestion or two of your own!), go to BadassRetirement.com.

Lastly, if I've learned anything over the last nearly three decades working with retirees, it's that we need others. Creating and sustaining a Badass Retirement is actually quite simple – you just need to incorporate the **Badass 5** into your daily life – but it's not easy. It takes effort and dedication. It's also infinitely easier and more rewarding when you are part of a group who are committed to the same goal.

Remember, your environment is everything. You get to choose who you want in your life. Who you surround yourself with plays a huge role in who you become and what you achieve in retirement. The people in your life will influence your level of happiness and health, joy and adventure, and meaning and fulfillment.

I am looking for retirees who want to escape Average Retirement . . . together. A tribe of motivated retirees who crave something more – something bolder, more meaningful, more rewarding – who want to be in a powerful community with others who work each day to create their best possible lives in retirement.

If the message of this book resonated with you, and you want to experience more and be around others living retirement at the highest level, apply to be a part of the Badass Retirement Community. We have workshops, courses, book clubs, videos, forums, and other resources that will help you live your best life in retirement. Even better, you'll be among friends – like-minded retirees who are achieving, experiencing, and becoming more each day.

We don't accept every application for membership because we want to ensure only those who are a good fit become part of the community. If you've made it this far in the book, though, there's a good chance you have the characteristics we look for in our members. You have one shot at retirement. Let's make the most of it with each other.

Remember, Average Retirement is a death sentence – you go there to die. A Badass Retirement is a life sentence – you go there to live.

This is your retirement. This is your life. Now go live it...

ABOUT THE AUTHOR

Hello. My name is Robert Pagliarini. For over 25 years I have helped hundreds of clients escape average retirement and create more meaning and purpose, joy and adventure, energy and confidence, and growth and impact than they ever thought possible.

My investment and wealth management firm, Pacifica Wealth Advisors, specializes in helping clients manage, grow, and preserve their wealth and create extraordinary lives in retirement.

I have a Ph.D. in financial and retirement planning. Additionally, I am a Certified Financial Planner™, an Enrolled Agent with the IRS, and have a master's degree in psychology.

This is my fifth personal finance book. The four others were #1 bestselling *The Six-Day Financial Makeover: Transform Your Financial Life in Less Than a Week* (St. Martin's Press, 2006), *The Other 8 Hours: Maximize Your Free Time to Create New Wealth & Purpose* (St. Martin's Press, 2010), *The Sudden Wealth Solution: 12 Principles to Transform Sudden Wealth Into Lasting Wealth* (Harbinger Press, 2015), and *Get Money Smart: Simple Lessons to Kickstart Your Financial Confidence & Growth Your Wealth* (Harbinger Press, 2018).

Over the years, I've also had the privilege of appearing on several TV shows including Dr. Phil, 20/20, Good Morning America, Fox Business, Katie Couric, and many others.

I also practice what I preach. I co-founded a non-profit organization that supports orphanages and helps kids across SE Asia. I've dedicated my professional life to teaching and helping others create richer lives. Despite setbacks and challenges over the years (and a wife and daughter who love to make fun of the chunky nutritional shakes I drink, new exercise routines, or health gadgets I try), I make it a daily practice to upgrade my health.

I've also tried to create and live an adventurous and bold life. A couple times a year, I travel to exotic places around the world. I've climbed Mt. Kilimanjaro, hiked the Inca Trail to Machu Picchu, hang-glided in Brazil, ice-climbed in Colorado, camped at the bottom of the Grand Canyon, mountain biked in Burma, trekked to the Great Wall of China, sky-dived in Fiji, explored the jungles of Thailand, journeyed over trails in New Zealand, white water rafted in Costa Rica, explored islands in the Philippines, biked through the streets of New Delhi, rode camels in Morocco, "surfed" in Nicaragua, hiked in Patagonia, hot air ballooned in the deserts of United Arab Emirates, jumped off waterfalls in Malaysia, and completed an Ironman with clients (yes, they beat me, but I was just happy to finish!).

I've come a long way from eating government cheese and simply *watching* adventures on TV, but there is still so much left to do.

I'm on this journey with you...

ENDNOTES

1   https://www.yahoo.com/now/americans-retiring-increasing-pace-145837368.html

2   Atchley, R. C. (1976). *The sociology of retirement*. Wiley.

3   Sohier, L., Van Ootegem, L., & Verhofstadt, E. (2021). Well-being during the transition from work to retirement. Journal of Happiness Studies, 22, 263–286. https://doi.org/10.1007/s10902-020-00228-6

4   Wang, M. (2007). Profiling retirees in the retirement transition and adjustment process: Examining the longitudinal change patterns of retirees' psychological well-being. *The Journal of Applied Psychology*, 92, 455–474. doi:10.1037/0021-9010.92.2.455

5   Retirement Triggers Research Report (2015). *Ameriprise Financial*. http://ameriprise.com/retirementtriggers

6   Health and Retirement Study Survey Research Center. (2000). *Health and retirement study*. Retrieved from http://hrsonline.isr.umich.edu

7   Jordan, B. (2005). Science-based assessment of animal welfare: Wild and captive animals. *Revue Scientifique et Technique*, 24(2), 515–528. https://pubmed.ncbi.nlm.nih.gov/16358505/.

8   Csikszentmihalyi, M., & LeFevre, J. (1989). Optimal experience in work and leisure. *Journal of Personality and Social Psychology*, 56(5), 815–822.

9   https://www.pacificawealth.com/robert-pagliarini-earns-phd-in-financial-retirement-planning/

10 Cialdini RB. (2008) Influence: Science and Practice (5th edn). Boston, MA: Allyn & Bacon.

11 https://twitter.com/elonmusk/status/1433713164546293767

12 Wrosch, C., Bauer, I., & Scheier, M. F. (2005). Regret and quality of life across the adult life span: The influence of disengagement and available future goals. *Psychology and Aging*, 20(4), 657–670. http://citeseerx.ist.psu.edu/viewdoc/download?doi=10.1.1.704.1374&rep=rep1&type=pdf

13 Wrosch, C., Bauer, I., & Scheier, M. F. (2005). Regret and quality of life across the adult life span: The influence of disengagement and available future goals. *Psychology and Aging*, 20(4), 657–670. http://citeseerx.ist.psu.edu/viewdoc/download?doi=10.1.1.704.1374&rep=rep1&type=pdf

14 Gilovich, T., & Medvec, V. H. (1994). The temporal pattern to the experience of regret. *Journal of Personality and Social Psychology*, 67(3), 357–365.

15 Davidai, S., & Gilovich, T. (2018). The ideal road not taken: The self-discrepancies involved in people's most enduring regrets. *Emotion*, 18(3), 439–452. https://doi.org/10.1037/emo0000326

16 https://journals.sagepub.com/doi/full/10.1177/1461444819888720

    https://scholarship.claremont.edu/cgi/viewcontent.cgi?article=1749&context=cmc_theses

    Tesser, A., & Collins, J. (1988). Emotion in social reflection and comparison situations: Intuitive, systematic, and exploratory approaches. *Journal of Personality and Social Psychology*, 55(5), 695–709.

    Festinger, L. (1954). A theory of social comparison processes. *Human Relations*, 7(2), 117–140.

    Fiske, S. (2011). Envy up, scorn down: How comparison divides us. *The American Psychologist*, 65(8), 698–706.

    Marsh, H. W., Trautwein, U., Lüdtke, O. & Köller, O. (2008). Social comparison and big-fish-little-pond effects on self-concept and other self-belief constructs: Role of generalized and specific others. *Journal of Educational Psychology*, 100, 510–524.

    Marsh, H. W. (1987). The big-fish-little-pond effect on academic self-concept. *Journal of Educational Psychology*, 79, 280–295

    Collins, R. L. (1995). For better or worse: The impact of upward social comparison on self-evaluations. *Psychological Bulletin*, 119(1): 51–69. doi:10.1037/0033-2909.119.1.51

    Taylor, S. E., & Lobel, M. (1989). Social comparison activity under threat: Downward evaluation and upward contacts. *Psychological Review*, 96(4), 569–575. doi:10.1037/0033-295X.96.4.569

    Aspinwall, L. G., & Taylor, S. E. (1993). Effects of social comparison direction, threat, and self-esteem on affect, self-evaluation, and expected success. *Journal of Personality and Social Psychology*, 64(5), 708–722. doi:10.1037/0022-3514.64.5.708

17 https://psycnet.apa.org/record/1996-01401-005?doi=1

    https://www.tandfonline.com/doi/abs/10.1080/15213269.2013.878663

    Guyer, J., & Vaughan-Johnston, T. (2018). "Upward and downward social comparisons: A brief historical overview." In V. Zeigler-Hill & T. K. Shackelford (Eds.), *Encyclopedia of personality and individual differences*. Springer. 10.1007/978-3-319-28099-8_1912-1.

18 Martin, P., & Priest, S. (1986). Understanding the adventure experience. *Adventure Education*, 3(1), 18–21.

19 https://ajph.aphapublications.org/doi/full/10.2105/AJPH.2010.192245

20 Cater, C. (2006). Playing with risk? Participant perceptions of risk and management implications in adventure tourism. *Tourism Management*, 27, 317–325.

    McGillivray, D., & Frew, M. (2007). Capturing adventure: Trading experiences in the symbolic economy. *Annals of Leisure Research*, 10(1), 54–78.

    Hattie, J., Marsh, H. W., Neill, J. T., & Richards, G. E. (1997). Adventure education and outward bound: Out-of-class experiences that make a lasting difference. *Review of Educational Research*, 67, 43–87.

21 https://www.ncbi.nlm.nih.gov/pmc/articles/PMC6723984/

22 https://link.springer.com/article/10.1007/s11482-009-9091-9

    https://journals.sagepub.com/doi/abs/10.1177/0956797614546556

    https://journals.sagepub.com/doi/10.1177/135676670200800406

https://www.ustravel.org/sites/default/files/media_root/document/PlanningTravel_MichelleGielan.pdf

https://pubmed.ncbi.nlm.nih.gov/17500652/

23   https://www.ncbi.nlm.nih.gov/pmc/articles/PMC3860931/

https://pubmed.ncbi.nlm.nih.gov/31096566/

https://www.brightquest.com/blog/benefits-adventure-therapy-treatment-severe-mental-health-disorders/

Mutz, M., & Müller, J. (2016). Mental health benefits of outdoor adventures: Results from two pilot studies. *Journal of Adolescence*, 49, 105–114.

O'Brien, K., & Lomas, T. (2017). Developing a Growth Mindset through outdoor personal development: Can an intervention underpinned by psychology increase the impact of an outdoor learning course for young people? *Journal of Adventure Education & Outdoor Learning*, 17, 133–147.

Filep, S., Klint, L. M., Dominey-Howes, D., & DeLacy, T. (2013). Discovering what matters in a perfect day: A study of well-being of adventure tourists. In S. Taylor, P. Varley, & T. Johnston (Eds.), *Adventure Tourism: Meanings, Experience and Learning* (pp. 33–46). Oxon.

https://www.ncbi.nlm.nih.gov/pmc/articles/PMC2535823/

Brymer, E., & Schweitzer, R. (2013). Extreme sports are good for your health: A phenomenological understanding of fear and anxiety in extreme sport. *Journal of Health Psychology*, 18(4), 477–487.

Ewert, A., & Yoshino, A. (2011). The influence of short-term adventure-based experiences on levels of resilience. *Journal of Adventure Education & Outdoor Learning*, 11, 35–50.

Hattie, J., Marsh, H. W., Neill, J. T., & Richards, G. E. (1997). Adventure education and outward bound: Out-of-class experiences that make a lasting difference. *Review of Educational Research*, 67, 43–87.

Scarf, D., Kafka, S., Hayhurst, J., Jang, K., Boyes, M., Thomson, R., & Hunter, J. A. (2018). Satisfying psychological needs on the high seas: Explaining increases self-esteem following an adventure education programme. *Journal of Adventure Education & Outdoor Learning*, 18, 165–175.

Sheard, M., & Golby, J. (2006). The efficacy of an outdoor adventure education curriculum on selected aspects of positive psychological development. *Journal of Experiential Education*, 29(2), 187–209.

Sibthorp, J., Paisley, K., Gookin, J., & Furman, N. (2008). The pedagogic value of student autonomy in adventure education. *Journal of Experiential Education*, 31, 136–151.

24   https://gufaculty360.georgetown.edu/s/contact/00336000014RYGZAA4/abigail-marsh

25   https://selfdeterminationtheory.org/wp-content/uploads/2021/04/2020_MackenzieHodge_Adventure_Manuscript.pdf

26   Csikszentmihalyi, M. (1990). *Flow: The psychology of optimal experience*. Harper & Row.

27   *The Sudden Wealth Solution: 12 Principles to Transform Sudden Wealth Into Lasting Wealth*

Plan Z: How to Survive the 2009 Financial Crisis (and even live a little better) Covid-19 Financial Survival Guide

28   Csikszentmihalyi, M. (1992). *Flow: The psychology of happiness*. Ridler.

Dustin, D., McAvoy, L., & Beck, L. (1986). Promoting recreationist self-sufficiency. *Journal of Park and Recreation Administration*, 4(4), 43–52.

Smith, D. H., & Theberge, N. (1987). *Why people recreate: An overview of research*. Life Enhancement Publications.

29   https://www.researchgate.net/publication/50232804_Exploring_the_Motivations_of_BASE_Jumpers_Extreme_Sport_Enthusiasts

Lyng, S. G. (Ed.). (2005). *Edgework: The sociology of risk taking*. Routledge.

30   https://selfdeterminationtheory.org/wp-content/uploads/2021/04/2020_MackenzieHodge_Adventure_Manuscript.pdf

31   Ewert, A., & Hollenhorst, S. (1989). Testing the adventure model: Empirical support for a model of risk recreation participation. *Journal of Leisure Research*, 21, 124–139.

Houge Mackenzie, S., & Brymer, E. (2020). Conceptualizing adventurous nature sport: A positive psychology perspective. Annals of Leisure Research. 23. 79-91. 10.1080/11745398.2018.1483733.

Houge Mackenzie, S.; Hodge, K. Adventure Recreation and Subjective Well-Being: A Conceptual Framework. Leis. Stud.2020,39, 26–40.

Kerr, J. H., & Mackenzie, S. H. (2012). Multiple motives for participating in adventure sports. *Psychology of Sport and Exercise*, 13(5), 649–657.

Swarbrooke, J., Beard, C., Leckie, S., & Pomfret, G. (2003). Adventure tourism: *The new frontier*. Butterworth-Heinemann. Ewert, A., & Hollenhorst, S. (1989). Testing the adventure model: Empirical support for a model of risk recreation participation. *Journal of Leisure Research*, 21, 124–139.

Beedie, P., & Bourne, G. (2005). Media constructions of risk: A case study of the Stainforth Beck incident. *Journal of Risk Research*, 8(4), 331–339.

Pomfret, G. (2006). Mountaineering adventure tourists: A conceptual framework for research. *Tourism Management*, 27(1), 113–123.

Clough, P., Houge Mackenzie, S., Mallabon, L., & Brymer, E. (2016). Adventurous physical activity environments: A mainstream intervention for mental health. *Sports Medicine*, 46, 963–968.

Brymer, E., & Schweitzer, R. (2013). Extreme sports are good for your health: A phenomenological understanding of fear and anxiety in extreme sport. *Journal of Health Psychology*, 18(4), 477–487.

Lee, K., & Ewert, A. (2018). Understanding the motivations of serious leisure participation: A self-determination approach. *Annals of Leisure Research*, 22(1), 76–96. doi:10.1080/11745398.2018.1469420

32   Panicucci, J. (2007). Cornerstones of adventure education. In D. Prouty, J. Panicucci, & R. Collinson (Eds.), *Adventure education, theory and applications* (pp. 33–48). Human Kinetics.

33   Panicucci, J. (2007). Cornerstones of adventure education. In D. Prouty, J. Panicucci, & R. Collinson (Eds.), *Adventure education, theory and applications* (pp. 33–48). Human Kinetics.

34   Priest, S., & Bunting, C. (1993). Changes in perceived risk and competence during whitewater canoeing. *Journal of Applied Recreation Research*, 18(4), 265–280.

35   https://www.econstor.eu/bitstream/10419/162583/1/890596670.pdf
      https://pubmed.ncbi.nlm.nih.gov/32283536/
      https://www.researchgate.net/publication/325738704_The_Empty_Nest_Syndrome_Critical_Clinical_Considerations
      https://journals.plos.org/plosone/article?id=10.1371/journal.pone.0218704#sec007

36   Retirement Triggers Research Report (2015). Ameriprise Financial. http://ameriprise.com/retirementtriggers

37   Gilbert, D. T., Pinel, E. C., Wilson, T. D., Blumberg, S. J., & Wheatley, T. (1998). Immune neglect: A source of durability bias in affective forecasting. *Journal of Personality and Social Psychology*, 75, 617–638.

      Gilbert, D. T., Lieberman, M. D., Morewedge, C. K., & Wilson, T. D. (2004). The peculiar longevity of things not so bad. *Psychological Science*, 15, 14–19.

      Gilbert, D. T., & Ebert, J. E. J. (2002). Decisions and revisions: The affective forecasting of changeable outcomes. *Journal of Personality and Social Psychology*, 82, 503–514.

      Gilbert, D. T., Gill, M. J., & Wilson, T. D. (2002). The future is now: Temporal correction in affective forecasting. *Organizational Behavior and Human Decision Processes*, 88(1), 430–444.

      Lench, H. C., Levine, L. J., Perez, K., Carpenter, Z. K., Carlson, S. J., Bench, S. W., & Wan, Y. (2019). When and why people misestimate future feelings: Identifying strengths and weaknesses in affective forecasting. *Journal of Personality and Social Psychology*, 116(5), 724–742.

      Flynn, E., Hovasapian, A. & Levine, L. J. (2020). Affective forecasting. In K. Sweeny, M. L. Robbins, & L.M. Cohen (Eds.), *The Wiley Encyclopedia of Health Psychology* (pp. 21–29). John Wiley & Sons. https://doi.org/10.1002/9781119057840.ch46

38   Geirland, J.(1999, September 1). Go with the flow. *Wired*.

39   Cohen, R., Bavishi, C., & Rozanski, A. (2016). Purpose in life and its relationship to all-cause mortality and cardiovascular events: A meta-analysis. *Psychosomatic Medicine*, 78(2), 122–133. doi:10.1097/PSY.0000000000000274

      Wood, A. M., & Joseph, S. (2010). The absence of positive psychological (eudemonic) well-being as a risk factor for depression: A ten year cohort study. *Journal of Affective Disorders*, 122(3), 213–217. doi:10.1016/j.jad.2009.06.032

      Kim, E. S., Strecher, V. J., & Ryff, C. D. (2014). Purpose in life and use of preventive health care services. *Proceedings of the National Academy of Sciences of the United States of America*, 111(46), 16331–16336. doi:10.1073/pnas.1414826111

      Rasmussen, N. H., Smith, S. A., Maxson, J. A., Bernard, M. E., Cha, S. S., Agerter, D. C., & Shah, N. D. (2013). Association of HbA1c with emotion regulation, intolerance of uncertainty, and purpose in life in type 2 diabetes mellitus. *Primary Care Diabetes*, 7(3), 213–221.

40   Cohen, R., Bavishi, C., & Rozanski, A. (2016). Purpose in life and its relationship to all-cause mortality and cardiovascular events: A meta-analysis. Psychosomatic Medicine, 78(2), 122–133. doi:10.1097/PSY.0000000000000274

      Hill, P. L., & Turiano, N. A. (2014). Purpose in life as a predictor of mortality across adulthood. *Psychological Science*, 25(7), 1482–1486. doi:10.1177/0956797614531799

      Boyle, P. A., Barnes, L. L., Buchman, A. S., & Bennett, D. A. (2009). Purpose in life is associated with mortality among community-dwelling older persons. *Psychosomatic Med*, 71(5), 574–579. doi:10.1097/PSY.0b013e3181a5a7c0

41   Alimujiang, A., Wiensch, A., Boss, J., Fleischer, N. L., Mondul, A. M., McLean, K., Mukherjee, B., & Pearce, C.L. (2019). Association between life purpose and mortality among US adults older than 50 years. *JAMA Network Open*, 2(5). doi:10.1001/jamanetworkopen.2019.4270

42   Sone, T., Nakaya, N., Ohmori, K., Shimazu, T., Higashiguchi, M., Kakizaki, M., Kikuchi, N., Kuriyama, S., & Tsuji, I. (2008). Sense of life worth living (ikigai) and mortality in Japan: Ohsaki Study. *Psychosomatic Medicine*, 70(6), 709–715. doi:10.1097/PSY.0b013e31817e7e64

      Tanno, K., Sakata, K., Ohsawa, M., Onoda, T., Itai, K., Yaegashi, Y., & Tamakoshi, A. (2009). Associations of ikigai as a positive psychological factor with all-cause mortality and cause-specific mortality among middle-aged and elderly Japanese people: Findings from the Japan Collaborative Cohort Study. *Journal of Psychosomatic Research*, 67(1), 67–75. doi:10.1016/j.jpsychores.2008.10.018

43   Steptoe, A., & Fancourt, D. (2019). Leading a meaningful life at older ages and its relationship with social engagement, prosperity, health, biology, and time use. *Proceedings of the National Academy of Sciences*, 116(4), 1207–1212. doi:10.1073/pnas.1814723116

44   https://www.adultdevelopmentstudy.org/

45   https://www.theatlantic.com/magazine/archive/2009/06/what-makes-us-happy/307439/

46   Collinson, C., Rowey, P., & Cho, H. (2021). Living in the COVID-19 Pandemic: The Health, Finances, and Retirement Prospects of Four Generations (2021). Transamerica Center For Retirement Studies. Retrieved from https://transamericacenter.org/docs/default-source/retirement-survey-of-workers/tcrs2021_sr_four-generations-living-in-a-pandemic.pdf

47   https://www.edwardjones.com/sites/default/files/acquiadam/2021-01/Edward-Jones-4-Pillars-US-report.pdf

48   https://www.greatcall.com/docs/default-source/newsroom-files/fighting-social-isolation-among-older-adults.pdf

      Anderson, G. O., & Thayer, C. (2018). Loneliness and Social Connections: A National Survey of Adults 45 and Older. AARP Research. Retrieved from https://www.aarp.org/research/topics/life/info-2018/loneliness-social-connections.html?CMP=RDRCT-PRI-HOMFAM-073118

      Perissinotto, C. M., Stijacic Cenzer, I., & Covinsky, K. E. (2012). Loneliness in older persons: A predictor of functional decline and death. *Archives of Internal Medicine*, 172, 1078–1084.

Cudjoe, T., Roth, D. L., Szanton, S. L., Wolff, J. L., Boyd, C. M., & Thorpe, R. J. (2020). The epidemiology of social isolation: National health and aging trends study. *The Journals of Gerontology: Series B, Psychological Sciences and Social Sciences*, 75(1), 107–113. https://doi.org/10.1093/geronb/gby037

49 https://www.wsj.com/articles/baby-boomers-get-more-selective-about-friends-1531918772

50 https://www.barna.com/research/friends-loneliness/

51 https://www.edwardjones.com/sites/default/files/acquiadam/2021-01/Edward-Jones-4-Pillars-US-report.pdf

52 Panadero, S., Guillén, A. I., & Vázquez, J. J. (2015). Happiness on the street: Overall happiness among homeless people in Madrid (Spain). *American Journal of Orthopsychiatry*, 85(4), 324–330. https://wjsspapers.com/wp-content/uploads/2020/04/Happiness-and-Homelessness-A-Case-Study-of-Happiness-Awareness-among-Homeless-People.pdf

53 Mehta, K. M., Yaffe, K., & Covinsky, K. E. (2002). Cognitive impairment, depressive symptoms, and functional decline in older people. *Journal of the American Geriatrics Society*, 50(6), 1045–1050.

54 Umberson, D., & Montez, J. K. (2010). Social relationships and health: A flashpoint for health policy. *Journal of Health and Social Behavior*, 51, S54–S66. https://doi.org/10.1177/0022146510383501

55 Aquino, J. A., Russell, D. W., Cutrona, C. E., & Altmaier, E. M. (1996). Employment status, social support, and life satisfaction among the elderly. *Journal of Counseling Psychology*, 43(4), 480–489.

Steptoe, A., Shankar, A., & Rafnsson, S. The Links Between Social Connections and Wellbeing in Later Life. Department of Epidemiology and Public Health at University College London. Retrieved from https://ilcuk.org.uk/wp-content/uploads/2018/10/The-links-between-social-connections-and-wellbeing-in-later-life.pdf

Amati, V., Meggiolaro, S., Rivellini, G., & Zaccarin, S. (2018). Social relations and life satisfaction: The role of friends. *Genus*, 74(7). https://doi.org/10.1186/s41118-018-0032-z

Zhang, Z., & Zhang, J. (2015). Social participation and subjective well-being among retirees in China. *Social Indicators Research*, 123(1), 143–160. http://www.jstor.org/stable/24721595

56 Chopik, W. J. (2017). Associations among relational values, support, health, and well-being across the adult lifespan. *Personal Relationships*, 24(2), 408–422. doi:10.1111/pere.12187

57 Everson-Rose, S. A., & Lewis, T. T. (2005). Psychosocial factors and cardiovascular diseases. *Annual Review of Public Health*, 26, 469–500.

Ertel Karen, A., Glymour, M., & Berkman, L. F. (2009). Social networks and health: A life course perspective integrating observational and experimental evidence. *Journal of Social and Personal Relationships*, 26, 73–92.

Sutin, A. R., Yannick, S., Luchetti, M., & Terracciano, A. (2020). Loneliness and risk of dementia. *The Journals of Gerontology: Series B*, 75(7), 1414–1422. https://doi.org/10.1093/geronb/gby112

Valtorta, N. K., Kanaan, M., Gilbody, S., Ronzi, S., & Hanratty, B. (2016). Loneliness and social isolation as risk factors for coronary heart disease and stroke: Systematic review and meta-analysis of longitudinal observational studies. *Heart*, 102(13), 1009–1016.

58 Berkman, L. F., & Syme, S. L. (1979). Social networks, host resistance, and mortality: A nine-year follow-up study of Alameda County residents. *American Journal of Epidemiology*, 109(2), 186–204.

House, J. S., Landis, K. R., & Umberson, D. (1988). Social relationships and health. *Science*, 241(4865), 540–545.

Perissinotto, C. M., Stijacic Cenzer, I., & Covinsky, K. E. (2012). Loneliness in older persons: A predictor of functional decline and death. *Archives of Internal Medicine*, 172, 1078–1084.

Brummett, B. H., Barefoot, J. C., Siegler, I. C., Clapp-Channing, N. E., Lytle, B. L., Bosworth, H. B., Williams, R. B. Jr., & Mark, D. B. Characteristics of socially isolated patients with coronary artery disease who are at elevated risk for mortality. *Psychosomatic Medicine*, 63(2), 267–272.

59 Holt-Lunstad, J., Smith, T. B., & Layton, J. B. (2010) Social relationships and mortality risk: A meta-analytic review. *PLoS Medicine* 7(7), e1000316. https://doi.org/10.1371/journal.pmed.1000316

Holt-Lunstad, J., Smith, T. B., Baker, M., Harris, T., & Stephenson, D. (2015). Loneliness and social isolation as risk factors for mortality: A meta-analytic review. *Perspectives on Psychological Science*, 10(2), 227–237. https://doi.org/10.1177/1745691614568352

60 https://www.apa.org/monitor/2019/05/ce-corner-isolation

61 Cole, S. W., Capitanio, J. P., Chun, K., Arevalo, J. M., Ma, J., & Cacioppo, J. T. (2015). Myeloid differentiation architecture of leukocyte transcriptome dynamics in perceived social isolation. *Proceedings of the National Academy of Sciences of the United States of America*, 112(49), 15142–15147. https://doi.org/10.1073/pnas.1514249112

62 Castiello, U., Becchio, C., Zoia, S., Nelini, C., Sartori, L., Blason, L., D'Ottavio, G., Bulgheroni, M., & Gallese, V. (2010) Wired to be social: The ontogeny of human interaction. *PLoS ONE*, 5(10), e13199. https://doi.org/10.1371/journal.pone.0013199

https://dana.org/article/in-sync-how-humans-are-hard-wired-for-social-relationships/

63 https://newsroom.ucla.edu/releases/we-are-hard-wired-to-be-social-248746

64 https://www.cambridge.org/core/journals/children-australia/article/abs/making-the-world-safe-for-our-children-downregulating-defence-and-upregulating-social-engagement-to-optimise-the-human-experience/502AEEB10946FBD6C529F344C502A22C

65 Perissinotto, C. M., Stijacic Cenzer, I., & Covinsky, K. E. (2012). Loneliness in older persons: A predictor of functional decline and death. *Archives of Internal Medicine*, 172, 1078–1084.

66 Nguyen, T., & Szymanski, B. (2012). Using location-based social networks to validate human mobility and relationships models. *Proceedings of the 2012 IEEE/ACM International Conference on Advances in Social Networks Analysis and Mining*, 1215–1221.

Preciado, P., Snijders, T. A., Burk, W. J., Stattin, H., & Kerr, M. (2012). Does proximity matter? Distance dependence of adolescent friendships. Social Networks, 34(1), 18–31. https://doi.org/10.1016/j.socnet.2011.01.002

Latané, B., Liu, J. H., Nowak, A., Bonevento, M., & Zheng, L. (1995). Distance matters: Physical space and social impact. *Personality and Social Psychology Bulletin*, 21, 795–805.

67   Rohrer, J. M., Keller, T., & Elwert, F. (2021). Proximity can induce diverse friendships: A large randomized classroom experiment. *PLoS ONE* 16(8): e0255097. https://doi.org/10.1371/journal.pone.0255097

68   Wann, D. L., Hackathorn, J., & Sherman, M. R. (2017). Testing the team identification–social psychological health model: Mediational relationships among team identification, sport fandom, sense of belonging, and meaning in life. *Group Dynamics: Theory, Research, and Practice*, 21(2), 94–107. https://doi.org/10.1037/gdn0000066

69   https://www.huffpost.com/entry/sports-fan-mental-health-benefits_n_6565314

70   Cacioppo, J. T., Fowler, J. H., & Christakis, N. A. (2009). Alone in the crowd: The structure and spread of loneliness in a large social network. *Journal of Personality and Social Psychology*, 97(6), 977–991. https://dash.harvard.edu/bitstream/handle/1/4276347/christakis_alonecrowd.pdf?sequence=2

Fowler, J., & Christakis, N. (2008). Dynamic spread of happiness in a large social network: Longitudinal analysis over 20 years in the Framingham Heart Study. *BMJ (Clinical research ed.)*, 337, a2338. doi:10.1136/bmj.a2338

Christakis, N. A., & Fowler, J. H. (2007). The spread of obesity in a large social network over 32 years. *New England Journal of Medicine*, 357(4), 370–379.

Fowler, J. H., & Christakis, N. A. (2008). Estimating peer effects on health in social networks: A response to Cohen-Cole and Fletcher; and Trogdon, Nonnemaker, and Pais. *Journal of Health Economics*, 27(5), 1400–1405.

Christakis, N. A., & Fowler, J. H. (2008). The collective dynamics of smoking in a large social network. *New England Journal of Medicine*, 358(21), 2249–2258.

Rosenquist, J. N., Murabito, J., Fowler, J. H., & Christakis, N. A. (2010). The spread of alcohol consumption behavior in a large social network. *Annals of Internal Medicine*, 152(7), 426–433, W141.

Fowler, J., & Christakis, N. (2008). Dynamic spread of happiness in a large social network: Longitudinal analysis over 20 years in the Framingham Heart Study. *BMJ (Clinical research ed.)*, 337, a2338. doi:10.1136/bmj.a2338

Rosenquist, J. N., Fowler, J. H., & Christakis, N. A. (2011). Social network determinants of depression. *Molecular Psychiatry*, 16(3), 273–281.

Mednick, S. C., Christakis, N. A., & Fowler, J. H. (2010). The spread of sleep loss influences drug use in adolescent social networks. *PLoS One*, 5(3), e9775.

McDermott, R., Fowler, J., & Christakis, N. (2013). Breaking up is hard to do, unless everyone else is doing it too: Social network effects on divorce in a longitudinal sample. *Social Forces*, 92(2), 491–519.

Rowe, D. C., Chassin, L., Presson, C. C., Edwards, D., & Sherman, S. J. (1992). An epidemic model of adolescent cigarette-smoking. *Journal of Applied Social Psychology*, 22, 261–285.

Connolly, T., & Aberg, L. (1993). Some contagion models of speeding. *Accident Analysis and Prevention*, 25, 57–66.

Ennett, S. T., Flewelling, R. L., Lindrooth, R. C., & Norton, E. C. (1997). School and neighborhood characteristics associated with school rates of alcohol, cigarette, and marijuana use. *Journal of Health and Social Behavior*, 38, 55–71.

Jones, M. B., & Jones, D. R. (1995). Preferred pathways of behavioural contagion. *Journal of Psychiatric Research*, 29, 193–209.

71   Hall, J. (2018). How many hours does it take to make a friend? *Journal of Social and Personal Relationships*, 36(4), 1278–1296. doi:10.1177/0265407518761225.

72   Brody, J. (2016). The challenges of male friendships. The Sydney Morning Herald. Retrieved from https://www.smh.com.au/lifestyle/life-and-relationships/the-challenges-of-male-friendships-20160628-gptcep.html

73   https://www.americansurveycenter.org/why-mens-social-circles-are-shrinking/

74   https://www.americansurveycenter.org/research/the-state-of-american-friendship-change-challenges-and-loss/

75   Helliwell, J. F., & Huang, H. (2013). *Comparing the happiness effects of real and on-line friends* [Working paper No. 18690]. National Bureau of Economic Research. http://www.nber.org/papers/w18690.pdf

Stack, S. (1998). Marriage, family and loneliness: A cross-national study. *Sociological Perspectives*, 41, 415–432. http://dx.doi.org/10.2307/1389484

Russell, D. (2009). Living arrangements, social integration, and loneliness in later life: The case of physical disability. *Journal of Health and Social Behavior*, 50, 460–475. http://dx.doi.org/10.1177/002214650905000406

Petersen, J., Kaye, J., Jacobs, P. G., Quinones, A., Dodge, H., Arnold, A., & Thielke, S. (2016). Longitudinal relationship between loneliness and social isolation in older adults: Results from the Cardiovascular Health Study. *Journal of Aging and Health*, 28, 775–795. http://dx.doi.org/10.1177/0898264315611664

76   Helliwell, J. F., & Huang, H. (2013). *Comparing the happiness effects of real and on-line friends* [Working paper No. 18690]. National Bureau of Economic Research. http://www.nber.org/papers/w18690.pdf

77   https://zety.com/blog/afraid-of-retirement

https://cdn.ameriprisecontent.com/cds/alwp/advisor/joseph.c.amodei/cuserssbisch1desktopfinal-retirement-triggers-research-report-02011563574539104896871 0.pdf

78   Chopik, W. J. (2017). Associations among relational values, support, health, and well-being across the adult lifespan. *Personal Relationships*, 24(2), 408–422. doi:10.1111/pere.12187

79   https://msutoday.msu.edu/news/2017/are-friends-better-for-us-than-family

80   Umberson, D., & Montez, J. K. (2010). Social relationships and health: a flashpoint for health policy. *Journal of Health and Social Behavior*, 51, S54–S66. https://doi.org/10.1177/0022146510383501

Helliwell, J. F., & Huang, H. (2013). *Comparing the happiness effects of real and on-line friends* [Working paper No. 18690]. National Bureau of Economic Research. http://www.nber.org/papers/w18690.pdf

Anderson, G. O., & Thayer, C. (2018). Loneliness and Social Connections: A National Survey of Adults 45 and Older. AARP Research. Retrieved from https://www.aarp.org/research/topics/life/info-2018/loneliness-social-connections.html?CMP=RDRCT-PRI-HOMFAM-073118

81   Tomini, F., Tomini, S. M., & Groot, W. (2016). Understanding the value of social networks in life satisfaction of elderly people: A comparative study of 16 European countries using SHARE data. *BMC Geriatrics*, 16, 203. https://doi.org/10.1186/s12877-016-0362-7

82   https://adaa.org/understanding-anxiety/social-anxiety-disorder

83   https://www.nytimes.com/2019/10/28/smarter-living/the-benefits-of-being-alone.html

84   https://journals.sagepub.com/doi/pdf/10.1177/0146167297234003

85   Moen, P., Kim, J. E., & Hofmeister, H. (2001). Couples' work/retirement transitions, gender, and marital quality. *Social Psychology Quarterly*, 64(1), 55–71. https://doi.org/10.2307/3090150

86   https://news.cornell.edu/stories/2001/04/marital-road-retirement-bumpy

87   Szinovacz, M. E., & Davey, A. (2004). Honeymoons and joint lunches: Effects of retirement and spouse's employment on depressive symptoms. *The Journals of Gerontology: Series B*, 59(5), 233–245. https://doi.org/10.1093/geronb/59.5.P233

88   Walen, H. R., & Lachman, M. E. (2000). Social support and strain from partner, family, and friends: Costs and benefits for men and women in adulthood. *Journal of Social and Personal Relationships*, 17, 5–30.

      Kiecolt-Glaser, J. K., & Newton, T. L. (2001). Marriage and health: His and hers. *Psychological Bulletin*, 127(4), 472–503.

      Umberson, D., Williams, K., Powers, D. A., Liu, H., & Needham, B. (2006). You make me sick: Marital quality and health over the life course. *Journal of Health and Social Behavior*, 47(1), 1–16.

89   Funk, J. L. & Rogge, R. D. (2007). Testing the ruler with item response theory: Increasing precision of measurement for relationship satisfaction with the Couples Satisfaction Index. Journal of Family Psychology, 21, 572-583. Retrieved from https://backend.fetzer.org/sites/default/files/images/stories/pdf/selfmeasures/ Self_Measures_for_Marital_Satisfaction_COUPLES_SATISFACTION_INDEX.pdf

      Locke, H. J., & Wallace, K. M. (1959). Short Marital-Adjustment and Prediction Tests: Their Reliability and Validity. *Marriage and Family Living*, 21(3), 251–255. Test retrieved from https://fetzer.org/sites/default/files/ images/stories/pdf/selfmeasures/Self_Measures_for_Marital_Satisfaction_MARITAL_ADJUSTMENT_ TEST.pdf

      Hendrick, S. S. (1988). A generic measure of relationship satisfaction. Journal of Marriage and the Family, 50, 93–98. Retrieved from https://backend.fetzer.org/sites/default/files/images/stories/pdf/selfmeasures/ Self_ Measures_for_General_Relationship_Satisfaction_RELATIONSHIP.pdf

90   Thompson, D. (2010, April 15). Friends, not grandkids, key to happy retirement. HealthDay.

      Szinovacz, M. E., & Davey, A. (2004). Honeymoons and joint lunches: Effects of retirement and spouse's employment on depressive symptoms. *The Journals of Gerontology: Series B*, 59(5), 233–245. https://doi.org/10.1093/geronb/59.5.P233

      Moen, P., Kim, J. E., & Hofmeister, H. (2001). Couples' work/retirement transitions, gender, and marital quality. *Social Psychology Quarterly*, 64, 55–71.

      Myers, S. M., & Booth, A. (1996). Men's retirement and marital quality. *Journal of Family Issues*, 17, 336–358.

      Szinovacz, M. (1996). Couple's employment/retirement patterns and marital quality. *Research on Aging*, 18, 243–268.

      Thompson, D. (2010, April 15). Friends, not grandkids, key to happy retirement. *HealthDay*. https://consumer.healthday.com/senior-citizen-information-31/misc-aging-news-10/friends-not-grandkids-key-to-happy-retirement-638050.html

91   Szinovacz, M. E., & Davey, A. (2004). Honeymoons and joint lunches: Effects of retirement and spouse's employment on depressive symptoms. *The Journals of Gerontology: Series B*, 59(5), 233–245. https://doi.org/10.1093/geronb/59.5.P233

92   https://zety.com/blog/afraid-of-retirement

93   https://www.allianzlife.com/-/media/files/allianz/documents/ent_991_n. pdf?la=en&hash=1DB3AED9D8744BF645AAE77C04BC5A0864E52F7E

94   Pagliarini, R. (2019, November 13). *17 surprising facts you probably don't know about the retirement income 4% rule.* Forbes. Retrieved from https://www.forbes.com/sites/robertpagliarini/2019/11/13/17-surprising-facts-you-probably-dont-know-about-the-retirement-income-4-percent-rule

95   https://www.morningstar.com/lp/the-state-of-retirement-income

      https://www.financialplanningassociation.org/article/4-percent-rule-not-safe-low-yield-world

      Finke, M., Pfau, W. D., & Williams, D. (March 2012). Spending flexibility and safe withdrawal rates. *Journal of Financial Planning*. Retrieved from https://www.financialplanningassociation.org/article/journal/MAR12-spending-flexibility-and-safe-withdrawal-rates

      [Counter Argument] https://www.kitces.com/blog/4-percent-rule-bengen-morningstar-report-the-state-of-retirement-income-safe-withdrawal-rates

96   https://www.wsj.com/articles/cut-your-retirement-spending-now-says-creator-of-the-4-rule-11650327097

97   https://www.retailinvestor.org/pdf/Bengen1.pdf

98   https://www.financialplanningassociation.org/article/journal/FEB15-revisiting-optimal-distribution-glide-path

99   Pfau, W. D. & Kitces, M. E. (January 2014). Reducing retirement risk and a rising equity glide path. *Journal of Financial Planning*. Retrieved from https://www.financialplanningassociation.org/article/journal/JAN14-reducing-retirement-risk-rising-equity-glide-path

100   Collinson, C., Rowey, P., & Cho, H. (2018). A precarious existence: How today's retirees are financially faring in retirement. Transamerica Center for Retirement Studies. Retrieved from https://www.transamericacenter.org/docs/default-source/retirees-survey/tcrs2018_sr_retirees_survey_financially_faring.pdf

      Hannon, K. (2019, September 6). How working in retirement became a reality. *Forbes*. Retrieved from https://www.forbes.com/sites/nextavenue/2019/09/06/how-working-in-retirement-became-a-reality

101   Zhan, Y., Wang, M., Liu, S., & Shultz, K. S. (2009). Bridge employment and retirees' health: A longitudinal investigation. *Journal of Occupational Health Psychology*, 14, 374–389.

Griffin, B., & Hesketh, B. (2008). Post-retirement work: The individual determinants of paid and volunteer work. *Journal of Occupational and Organizational Psychology, 81*, 101–121.

Kim, S., & Feldman, D. C. (2000). Working in retirement: The antecedents of bridge employment and its consequences for quality of life in retirement. *Academy of Management Journal, 43*, 1195–1210.

Wang, M. (2007). Profiling retirees in the retirement transition and adjustment process: Examining the longitudinal change patterns of retirees' psychological wellbeing. Journal of Applied Psychology, 92, 455-474.

102   Pagliarini, R. (2020, February 12). Moving out of a high income tax state to save money? You need to know this first. *Forbes.* Retrieved from https://www.forbes.com/sites/robertpagliarini/2020/02/12/moving-out-of-a-high-income-tax-state-to-save-money-you-need-to-know-this-first

103   https://www.census.gov/newsroom/press-releases/2021/marriages-and-divorces.html

104   Brown, S. L., Lin, I. F., Hammersmith, A. M., & Wright, M. R. (2019). Repartnering following gray divorce: The roles of resources and constraints for women and men. *Demography, 56*(2), 503–523. https://doi.org/10.1007/s13524-018-0752-x

Brown, S. L., & Lin, I-F. J. (2012). The gray divorce revolution: rising divorce among middle-aged and older adults, 1990-2010. *The Journals of Gerontology: Series B, 67*(6), 731–741.

Kennedy, S., & Ruggles, S. (2014). Breaking up is hard to count: The rise of divorce in the United States, 1980-2010. *Demography, 51*(2), 587–598.

105   https://acl.gov/ltc/basic-needs/how-much-care-will-you-need

106   https://acl.gov/ltc/basic-needs/how-much-care-will-you-need

107   https://crr.bc.edu/briefs/what-level-of-long-term-services-and-supports-do-retirees-need/

108   https://www.census.gov/newsroom/releases/archives/health_care_insurance/cb12-185.html

https://www.nia.nih.gov/sites/default/files/2017-06/health_and_retirement_study_0.pdf

109   https://crr.bc.edu/briefs/what-level-of-long-term-services-and-supports-do-retirees-need/

110   Centers for Disease Control and Prevention. (2013). Long-term care services in the United States: 2013 overview. *Vital and Health Statistics, 3*(37). https://www.cdc.gov/nchs/data/nsltcp/long_term_care_services_2013.pdf

111   https://www.medicare.gov/coverage/long-term-care

112   https://www.naic.org/documents/cipr_current_study_160519_ltc_insurance.pdf

113   https://www.aaltci.org/news/long-term-care-insurance-association-news/long-term-care-insurance-purchased-by-350000-americans-in-2018

114   https://www.edwardjones.com/sites/default/files/acquiadam/2021-01/Edward-Jones-4-Pillars-US-report.pdf

115   https://www.edwardjones.com/sites/default/files/acquiadam/2021-01/Edward-Jones-4-Pillars-US-report.pdf

116   https://www.sciencedirect.com/science/article/abs/pii/S0890406521000219

https://www.sciencedirect.com/science/article/abs/pii/S0890406510000757?via%3Dihub

117   https://www.pewforum.org/2013/08/06/living-to-120-and-beyond-americans-views-on-aging-medical-advances-and-radical-life-extension/

118   Gwozdz, W., & Sousa-Poza, A. (2009). Ageing, health and life satisfaction of the oldest old: An analysis for Germany. *Institute for the Study of Labor Discussion Paper Series*, 4053. https://d-nb.info/993455255/34

119   Miller, D. T. (2020). *The power of identity claims: How we value and defend the self* (1st ed.). Routledge. https://doi.org/10.4324/9781003011590

120   https://www.cdc.gov/bloodpressure/facts.htm

121   "Get the Most out of Home Blood Pressure Monitoring." *Mayo Clinic.* 18 Sept. 2020, https://www.mayoclinic.org/diseases-conditions/high-blood-pressure/in-depth/high-blood-pressure/art-20047889

122   https://www.health.harvard.edu/heart-health/managing-your-cholesterol

123   https://www.cdc.gov/diabetes/managing/managing-blood-sugar/bloodglucosemonitoring.html

124   Jensen, M. T., Suadicani, P., Hein, H. O., & Gyntelberg, F. (2013). Elevated resting heart rate, physical fitness and all-cause mortality: A 16-year follow-up in the Copenhagen Male Study. *Heart, 99*, 882–887.

125   All About Heart Rate (Pulse). American Heart Association, https://www.heart.org/en/health-topics/high-blood-pressure/the-facts-about-high-blood-pressure/all-about-heart-rate-pulse. Accessed October 20, 2021.

126   https://www.cdc.gov/nchs/data/nhsr/nhsr041.pdf

127   https://www.health.harvard.edu/blog/heart-rate-variability-new-way-track-well-2017112212789

128   https://www.genome.gov/human-genome-project/Completion-FAQ

129   https://www.genome.gov/about-genomics/fact-sheets/DNA-Sequencing-Costs-Data

130   https://www.color.com/product/science

131   Dumith, S. C., Hallal, P. C., Reis, R. S., & Kohl, H. W. (2011). Worldwide prevalence of physical inactivity and its association with human development index in 76 countries. *Preventive Medicine, 53*(1-2), 24–28.

132   World Health Organization. (2013). *Diet and physical activity factsheet, 2013.* http://www.who.int/dietphysicalactivity/factsheet_inactivity/en/index.html

133   Tucker, L. A. (2017). Physical activity and telomere length in U.S. men and women: An NHANES investigation. *Preventive Medicine, 100*, 145–151. https://doi.org/10.1016/j.ypmed.2017.04.027.

134   Gries, K. J., Raue, U., Perkins, R. K., Lavin, K. M., Overstreet, B. S., D'Acquisto, L. J., Graham, B., Finch, W. H., Kaminsky, L. A., Trappe, T. A., & Trappe, S.. (2018). Cardiovascular and skeletal muscle health with lifelong exercise. *Journal of Applied Physiology, 125*(5), 1636–1645.

135   King, A. "Evolved to Run – but Not to Exercise." Irish Times, 3 Dec 2020. Retrieved from https://www.irishtimes.com/news/science/evolved-to-run-but-not-to-exercise-1.4412604

136   Cherniack, E. P., & Cherniack, A. R. (2015). Assessing the benefits and risks of owning a pet. Canadian Medical Association Journal, 187(10), 715–716. https://doi.org/10.1503/cmaj.150274

Hawkins, R. D., Hawkins, E. L., & Tip, L. (2021). I can't give up when I have them to care for: People's experiences of pets and their mental health. Anthrozoös, 34(4), p. 543-562. DOI: 10.1080/08927936.2021.1914434

Kramer, C.K., Mehmood, S., & Suen, R. S. (2019). Dog ownership and survival: A systematic review and meta-analysis. Circulation: Cariovascular Quality and Outcomes, 12(10), https://doi.org/10.1161/CIRCOUTCOMES.119.005554

Powell, L., Edwards, K.M., McGreevy, P. et al. (2019). Companion dog acquisition and mental well-being: A community-based three-arm controlled study. BMC Public Health, 19, 1428. https://doi.org/10.1186/s12889-019-7770-5

Wu Y., Luben R., Jones A. (2017). Dog ownership supports the maintenance of physical activity during poor weather in older English adults: Cross-sectional results from the EPIC Norfolk cohort. Journal Epidemiology Community Health. 71, p. 905-911.

137 https://www.nhs.uk/live-well/exercise/physical-activity-guidelines-older-adults/

138 Tucker, L. A. (2017). Physical activity and telomere length in U.S. men and women: An NHANES investigation. Preventive Medicine, 100, 145–151. https://doi.org/10.1016/j.ypmed.2017.04.027.

139 https://news.byu.edu/news/high-levels-exercise-linked-nine-years-less-aging-cellular-level

140 https://www.cdc.gov/physicalactivity/basics/older_adults/index.htm

141 Engelke, K., Kemmler, W., Lauber, D., Beeskow, C., Pintag, R., & Kalender, W. A. (2006). Exercise maintains bone density at spine and hip EFOPS: A 3-year longitudinal study in early postmenopausal women. Osteoporosis International, 17(1), 133–142.

Gale, C. R., Martyn, C. N., Cooper, C., & Sayer, A. A. (2007). Grip strength, body composition, and mortality. International Journal of Epidemiology, 36(1), 228–35.

Bohannon, R.W. (2008). Hand-grip dynamometry predicts future outcomes in aging adults. Journal of Geriatric Physical Therapy, 31(1), 3–10.

Ling, C. H., Taekema, D., de Craen, A. J. M., Gussekloo, J., Westendorp, R. G. J., & Maier, A. B. (2010). Handgrip strength and mortality in the oldest old population: The Leiden 85-plus study. Canadian Medical Association Journal, 182(5), 429–435.

Ruiz, J. R., Sui, X., Lobelo, F., Morrow Jr., J. R., Jackson, A. W., Sjöström, M., & Blair, S. N. (2008). Association between muscular strength and mortality in men: prospective cohort study. BMJ, 337, a439.

Bolam, K. A., van Uffelen, J. G., & Taaffe, D. R. (2013). The effect of physical exercise on bone density in middle-aged and older men: A systematic review. Osteoporosis International, 24(11), 2749–2762.

142 https://www.cell.com/cell-metabolism/pdfExtended/S1550-4131(17)30099-2

143 Lee, C. L., Kuo, Y. H., & Cheng, C. F. (2018). Acute high-intensity interval cycling improves postprandial lipid metabolism. Medicine & Science in Sports & Exercise, 50(8), 1687–1696. https://doi.org/10.1249/MSS.0000000000001613

https://www.ncbi.nlm.nih.gov/pmc/articles/PMC6658199/

https://www.bmj.com/content/371/bmj.m3485

O'Brien, M. W., Johns, J. A., Robinson, S. A., Bungay, A., Mekary, S. A. I. D., & Kimmerly, D. S. (2020). Impact of high-intensity interval training, moderate-intensity continuous training, and resistance training on endothelial function in older adults. Medicine and Science in Sports and Exercise, 52(5), 1057–1067. https://doi.org/10.1249/MSS.0000000000002226

Jiménez-García, J. D., Hita-Contreras, F., de la Torre-Cruz, M., Fábrega-Cuadros, R., Aibar-Almazán, A., Cruz- Díaz, D., & Martínez-Amat, A. (2019). Risk of falls in healthy older adults: Benefits of high-intensity interval training using lower body suspension exercises. Journal of Aging & Physical Activity, 27(3), 325–333. https://doi. org/10.1123/japa.2018-0190

144 Villelabeitia-Jaureguizar, K., Vicente-Campos, D., Senen, A. B., Hernández Jiménez, V., Garrido-Lestache, M.E. B., & Chicharro, J. L. (2017). Effects of high-intensity interval versus continuous exercise training on post- exercise heart rate recovery in coronary heart-disease patients. International Journal of Cardiology, 244, 17–23.

145 Gibala, M. J., Little, J. P., van Essen, M., Wilkin, G. P., Burgomaster, K. A., Safdar, A., Raha, S., & Tarnopolsky, M. A. (2006). Short-term sprint interval versus traditional endurance training: similar initial adaptations in human skeletal muscle and exercise performance. The Journal of Physiology, 575(3), 901–911. https://doi. org/10.1113/jphysiol.2006.112094

146 https://www.sciencedirect.com/science/article/pii/S014019711600049X

https://pubmed.ncbi.nlm.nih.gov/16416750/

https://www.dora.lib4ri.ch/wsl/islandora/object/wsl%3A5348

https://pubmed.ncbi.nlm.nih.gov/26895993/

Improving Mental Health: The Power of Outdoor & Adventure. Adventure Explorations. https://www. adventureexplorations.com/wp-content/uploads/2021/02/AE-Outdoor-and-Adventure-Whitepaper- Feb-2021-1.pdf. Accessed October 28, 2021.

https://www.sciencedirect.com/science/article/abs/pii/S2213078015000511?via%3Dihub

147 https://pubmed.ncbi.nlm.nih.gov/21291246/

148 Choi, Y., Larson, N., Steffen, L. M., Schreiner, P. J., Gallaher, D. D., Duprez, D. A., Shikany, J. M., Rana, J. S., & Jacobs Jr., D. R. (2021). Plant-centered diet and risk of incident cardiovascular disease during young to middle adulthood. Journal of the American Heart Association, 10, e020718. https://doi.org/10.1161/JAHA.120.020718

149 Kahleova, H., Levin, S., & Barnard, N. D. (2021). Plant-based diets for healthy Aging. Journal of the American College of Nutrition, 40(5), 478–479. doi:10.1080/07315724.2020.1790442

Morris, M. C., Tangney, C. C., Wang, Y., Sacks, F. M., Bennett, D. A., & Aggarwal, N. T. (2015). MIND diet associated with reduced incidence of Alzheimer's disease. Alzheimer's & Dementia, 11, 1007–1014. https://doi. org/10.1016/j.jalz.2014.11.009

Medawar, E., Huhn, S., Villringer, A., & Witte, A. V. (2019). The effects of plant-based diets on the body and the brain: a systematic review. *Translational Psychiatry*, 9(226). https://doi.org/10.1038/s41398-019-0552-0

Wang, X., Ouyang, Y., Liu, J., Zhu, M., Zhao, G., Bao, W., & Hu, F. B. (2014). Fruit and vegetable consumption and mortality from all causes, cardiovascular disease, and cancer: systematic review and dose-response meta-analysis of prospective cohort studies. *BMJ (Clinical research ed.)*, 349, g4490. https://doi.org/10.1136/bmj.g4490

World Health Organization. (2003). Diet, nutrition and the prevention of chronic diseases. *World Health Organization Technical Report Series*, 916.

National Academy of Sciences CoDaH, National Research Council. (1989). *Diet and health: Implications for reducing chronic disease risk*. National Academy Press.

150   Wang, D. D., Li, Y., Bhupathiraju, S. N., Rosner, B. A., Sun, Q., Giovannucci, E. L., Rimm, E. B., Manson, J. E., Willett, W. C., Stampfer, M. J., & Hu, F. B. (2021). Fruit and vegetable intake and mortality results from 2 prospective cohort studies of us men and women and a meta-analysis of 26 cohort studies. *Circulation*, 143, 1642–1654. https://doi.org/10.1161/CIRCULATIONAHA.120.048996

151   Zhang, X., Chen, X., Xu, Y., Yang, J., Du, L., Li, K., & Zhou, Y. (2021). Milk consumption and multiple health outcomes: Umbrella review of systematic reviews and meta-analyses in humans. *Nutrition & Metabolism*, 18(7). https://doi.org/10.1186/s12986-020-00527-y

152   La Berge, A. F. (2008). How the ideology of low fat conquered America. *Journal of the History of Medicine and Allied Sciences* 63(2), 139–177. https://doi.org/10.1093/jhmas/jrn001

153   Hu, F. B., & Willett, W. C. (2002). Optimal diets for prevention of coronary heart disease. *Journal of the American Medical Assocsiation*, 288(20), 2569–2578.

    Dhaka, V., Gulia, N., Ahlawat, K. S., & Khatkar, B. S. (2011). Trans fats - Sources, health risks and alternative approach - A review. *Journal of Food Science and Technology*, 48(5), 534–541. https://doi.org/10.1007/s13197-010-0225-8

    Iqbal, M. P. (2014). Trans fatty acids: A risk factor for cardiovascular disease. *Pakistan Journal of Medical Sciences*, 30(1), 194–197. https://doi.org/10.12669/pjms.301.4525

    de Souza, R. J., Mente, A., Maroleanu, A., Cozma, A. I., Ha, V., Kishibe, T., Uleryk, E., Budylowski, P., Schünemann, H., Beyene, J., & Anand, S. S. (2015). Intake of saturated and trans unsaturated fatty acids and risk of all cause mortality, cardiovascular disease, and type 2 diabetes: Systematic review and meta-analysis of observational studies. *BMJ*, 351, h3978. doi:10.1136/bmj.h3978

    Remig, V., Franklin, B., Margolis, S., Kostas, G., Nece, T., & Street, J. C. (2010). Trans fats in America: A review of their use, consumption, health implications, and regulation. *Research Review*, 110(4), 585–592. doi:https://doi.org/10.1016/j.jada.2009.12.024

154   Food and Agriculture Organization of the United Nations (FAO). (2010). Fats and fatty acids in human nutrition. Report of an expert consultation. *FAO Food Nutrition Paper*, 91.

    Food and Nutrition Board, Institute of Medicine. (2002). *Dietary reference intakes for energy, carbohydrate, fiber, fat, fatty acids, cholesterol, protein, and amino acids*. The National Academies Press.

    U.S. Department of Health and Human Services & U.S. Department of Agriculture. (2015). *Scientific report of the 2015 dietary guidelines advisory committee*. U.S. Department of Agriculture.

    Eckel, R. H., Jakicic, J. M., Ard, J. D., de Jesus, J. M., Miller, N. H., Hubbard, V. S., Lee, I-M., Lichtenstein, A. H., Loria, C. M., Millen, B. E., Nonas, C. A., Sacks, F. M., Smith Jr., S. C., Svetkey, L. P., Wadden, T. A., & Yanovski, S. Z. (2014). AHA/ACC guideline on lifestyle management to reduce cardiovascular risk: A report of the American College of Cardiology/American Heart Association task force on practice guidelines. *Journal of the American College of Cardiology*, 63(25 Pt B), 2960–2984.

    Kris-Etherton, P. M., & Krauss, R. M. (2020). Public health guidelines should recommend reducing saturated fat consumption as much as possible: YES. *The American Journal of Clinical Nutrition*, 112(1), 13–18. https://doi.org/10.1093/ajcn/nqaa110

155   Liu, A. G., Ford, N. A., Hu, F. B., Zelman, K. M., Mozaffarian, D., & Kris-Etherton, P. M. (2017). A healthy approach to dietary fats: Understanding the science and taking action to reduce consumer confusion. *Nutrition Journal*, 16(1), 53. https://doi.org/10.1186/s12937-017-0271-4

156   Yang, Q., Zhang, Z., Gregg, E. W., Flanders, W. D., Merritt, R., & Hu, F. B. (2014). Added sugar intake and cardiovascular diseases mortality among US adults. *JAMA Internal Medicine*, 174(4), 516–524. doi:10.1001/jamainternmed.2013.13563

    https://sugarscience.ucsf.edu/latest-sugarscience-research.html

157   https://www.hsph.harvard.edu/nutritionsource/processed-foods/

    Srour, B., Fezeu, L. K., Kesse-Guyot, E., Allès, B., Méjean, C., Andrianasolo, R. M., Deschasaux, M., Hercberg, S., Galan, P., Monteiro, C. A., Julia, C., & Touvier, M. (2019). Ultra-processed food intake and risk of cardiovascular disease: Prospective cohort study (NutriNet-Santé). *BMJ*, 365, l1451. doi:10.1136/bmj.l1451

    Rico-Campà, A., Martínez-González, M. A., Alvarez-Alvarez, I., Mendonça, R. D., de la Fuente-Arrillaga, C., Gómez-Donoso, C., & Bes-Rastrollo, M. (2019). Association between consumption of ultra-processed foods and all cause mortality: SUN prospective cohort study. *BMJ*, 365, l1949. doi:10.1136/bmj.l1949

    Hall, K. D., Ayuketah, A., Brychta, R., Walter, P. J., Yang, S., & Zhou, M. Ultra-processed diets cause excess calorie intake and weight gain: An inpatient randomized controlled trial of ad libitum food intake. *Clinical and Translational Report*, 30(1), 67–77. https://doi.org/10.1016/j.cmet.2019.05.008

158   Di Daniele, N., Noce, A., Vidiri, M. F., Moriconi, E., Marrone, G., Annicchiarico-Petruzzelli, M., D'Urso, G., Tesauro, M., Rovella, V., & De Lorenzo, A. (2017). Impact of Mediterranean diet on metabolic syndrome, cancer and longevity. *Oncotarget*, 8(5), 8947–8979. https://doi.org/10.18632/oncotarget.13553

    Grosso, G., Buscemi, S., Galvano, F., Mistretta, A., Marventano, S., La Vela, V., Drago, F., Gangi, S., Basile, F., & Biondi, A. (2013). Mediterranean diet and cancer: Epidemiological evidence and mechanism of selected aspects. *BMC Surgery*, 13(Suppl 2). S14.

    Sureda, A., Bibiloni, M., Julibert, A., Bouzas, C., Argelich, E., Llompart, I., Pons, A., & Tur, J. A. (2018). Adherence to the Mediterranean diet and inflammatory markers. *Nutrients*, 10(1), 62. https://doi.org/10.3390/nu10010062

Dominguez, L. J., Di Bella, G., Veronese, N., & Barbagallo, M. (2021). Impact of Mediterranean diet on chronic non-communicable diseases and longevity. *Nutrients*, 13(6), 2028. https://doi.org/10.3390/nu13062028

Martini, D. (2019). Health benefits of Mediterranean diet. *Nutrients*, 11(8), 1802. https://doi.org/10.3390/nu11081802

Mentella, M. C., Scaldaferri, F., Ricci, C., Gasbarrini, A., & Miggiano, G. (2019). Cancer and Mediterranean diet: A review. *Nutrients*, 11(9), 2059. https://doi.org/10.3390/nu11092059

159   Meeusen, R., Duclos, M., Foster, C., Fry, A., Gleeson, M., Nieman, D., Raglin, J., Rietjens, G., Steinacker, J., Urhausen, A., European College of Sport Science, & American College of Sports Medicine. (2013). Prevention, diagnosis, and treatment of the overtraining syndrome: Joint consensus statement of the European College of Sport Science and the American College of Sports Medicine. *Medicine & Science in Sport & Exercise*, 45(1), 186–205.

Soligard, T., Schwellnus, M., Alonso, J. M., Bahr, R., Clarsen, B., Dijkstra, H. P., Gabbett, T., Gleeson, M., Hägglund, M., Hutchinson, M. R., Janse van Rensburg, C., Khan, K. M., Meeusen, R., Orchard, J. W., Pluim, B. M., Raftery, M., Budgett, R., & Engebretsen, L. (2016). How much is too much? Part 1: International Olympic Committee consensus statement on load in sport and risk of injury. *British Journal of Sports Medicine*, 50(17), 1030–1041.

160   Menzies, P., Menzies, C., McIntyre, L., Paterson, P., Wilson, J., & Kemi, O. J. (2010). Blood lactate clearance during active recovery after an intense running bout depends on the intensity of the active recovery. *Journal of Sports Sciences*, 28(9), 975–982. doi:10.1080/02640414.2010.481721

Ortiz Jr., R. O., Sinclair Elder, A. J., Elder, C. L., & Dawes, J. J. (2019). A systematic review on the effectiveness of active recovery interventions on athletic performance of professional-, collegiate-, and competitive-level adult athletes. *Journal of Strength and Conditioning Research*, 33(8), 2275–2287. doi:10.1519/JSC.0000000000002589

Yamagishi, T., & Babraj, J. (2019). Active recovery induces greater endurance adaptations when performing sprint interval training. *Journal of Strength and Conditioning Research*, 33(4), 922–930. doi:10.1519/JSC.0000000000002787

Dupuy, O., Douzi, W., Theurot, D., Bosquet, L., & Dugué, B. (2018). An evidence-based approach for choosing post-exercise recovery techniques to reduce markers of muscle damage, soreness, fatigue, and inflammation: A systematic review with meta-analysis. *Frontiers in Physiology*, 9, 403. https://doi.org/10.3389/fphys.2018.00403

161   Dupuy, O., Douzi, W., Theurot, D., Bosquet, L., & Dugué, B. (2018). An evidence-based approach for choosing post-exercise recovery techniques to reduce markers of muscle damage, soreness, fatigue, and inflammation: A systematic review with meta-analysis. *Frontiers in Physiology*, 9, 403. https://doi.org/10.3389/fphys.2018.00403

162   Lombardi, G., Ziemann, E., & Banfi, G. (2017). Whole-body cryotherapy in athletes: From therapy to stimulation: An updated review of the literature. *Frontiers in Physiology*, 8, 258. https://doi.org/10.3389/fphys.2017.00258

Dupuy, O., Douzi, W., Theurot, D., Bosquet, L., & Dugué, B. (2018). An evidence-based approach for choosing post-exercise recovery techniques to reduce markers of muscle damage, soreness, fatigue, and inflammation: A systematic review with meta-analysis. *Frontiers in Physiology*, 9, 403. https://doi.org/10.3389/fphys.2018.00403

163   Huttunen, P., Kokko, L., & Ylijukuri, V. (2004). Winter swimming improves general well-being, *International Journal of Circumpolar Health*. 63(2), p. 140-144. DOI: 10.3402/ijch.v63i2.17700

Kunutsor, S. K., Laukkanen, T., & Laukkanen, J. A. (2018). Longitudinal associations of sauna bathing with inflammation and oxidative stress: The KIHD prospective cohort study. *Annals of Medicine*. 50(5), p. 437-442. DOI: 10.1080/07853890.2018.1489143

Patrick, R. P., & Johnson, T. L. (2021). Sauna use as a lifestyle practice to extend healthspan. Experimental Gerontology. 154(15). https://doi.org/10.1016/j.exger.2021.111509

Shevchuk N. A. (2008). Adapted cold shower as a potential treatment for depression. Medical hypotheses, 70(5), 995–1001. https://doi.org/10.1016/j.mehy.2007.04.052

Siems, W.G., Brenke, R., Sommerburg, O., Grune, T. (1999). Improved antioxidative protection in winter swimmers. *QJM: An International Journal of Medicine*, 92(4), p. 193–198. https://doi.org/10.1093/qjmed/92.4.193

164   Vaz Fragoso, C. A., & Gill, T. M. (2007). Sleep complaints in community-living older persons: A multifactorial geriatric syndrome. *Journal of the Ammerican Geriatric Society*, 55(11), 1853–1866.

165   Carroll, J. E., Cole, S. W., Seeman, T. E., Breen, E. C., Witarama, T., Arevalo, J. M. G., Ma, J., & Irwin, M. R. (2016). Partial sleep deprivation activates the DNA damage response (DDR) and the senescence-associated secretory phenotype (SASP) in aged adult humans. *Brain, Behavior, and Immunity* 51(1), 223–229.

166   Irwin, M. R., Olmstead, R., Breen, E. C., Witarama, T., Carrillo, C., Sadeghi, N., Arevalo, J. M. G., Ma, J., Nicassio, P., Bootzin, R., & Cole, S. (2015). Cognitive behavioral therapy and tai chi reverse cellular and genomic markers of inflammation in late-life insomnia: A randomized controlled trial. *Biological Psychiatry*, 78(1), 721–729.

Irwin, M. R>, Olmstead, R., Carrillo, C., Sadeghi, N., Breen, E. C., Witarama, T., Yokomizo, M., Lavretsky, H., Carroll, J. E., Motivala, S. J., Bootzin, R., & Nicassio, P. (2014). Cognitive behavioral therapy vs. tai chi for late-life insomnia and inflammatory risk: A randomized controlled comparative efficacy trial. *Sleep*, 37(1), 1543–1552.

167   Cappuccio, F. P., D'Elia, L., Strazzullo, P., & Miller, M. A. (2010). Sleep duration and all-cause mortality: A systematic review and meta-analysis of prospective studies. *Sleep*, 33(5), 585–592.

168   Lauderdale, D. S., Chen, J-H., Kurina, L. M., Waite, L. J., & Thisted, R. A. (2016). Sleep duration and health among older adults: Associations vary by how sleep is measured. *Journal of Epidemiology and Community Health*, 70(4), 361–366.

169   Kang, J. H., & Chen, S. C. (2009). Effects of an irregular bedtime schedule on sleep quality, daytime sleepiness, and fatigue among university students in Taiwan. *BMC Public Health*, 9, 248. https://doi.org/10.1186/1471-2458-9-248

Van Dongen, H. P., & Dinges, D. F. (2003). Investigating the interaction between the homeostatic and circadian processes of sleep-wake regulation for the prediction of waking neurobehavioural performance. *Journal of Sleep Research*, 12(3), 181–187. https://doi.org/10.1046/j.1365-2869.2003.00357.x

170   Taasan, V. C., Block, A. J., Boysen, P. G., & Wynne, J. W. (1981). Alcohol increases sleep apnea and oxygen desaturation in asymptomatic men. *The American Journal of Medicine*, 71(2), 240–245. https://doi. org/10.1016/0002-9343(81)90124-8

Ekman, A. C., Leppäluoto, J., Huttunen, P., Aranko, K., & Vakkuri, O. (1993). Ethanol inhibits melatonin secretion in healthy volunteers in a dose-dependent randomized double blind cross-over study. *The Journal of Clinical Endocrinology and Metabolism*, 77(3), 780–783. https://doi.org/10.1210/jcem.77.3.8370699

171   Sanassi, L. A. (2014). Seasonal affective disorder: Is there light at the end of the tunnel? *JAAPA*, 27(2), 18–23. https://doi.org/10.1097/01.JAA.0000442698.03223.f3

Sloane, P. D., Figueiro, M., & Cohen, L. (2008). Light as therapy for sleep disorders and depression in older adults. *Clinical Geriatrics*, 16(3), 25–31.

Tuunainen, A., Kripke, D. F., & Endo, T. (2004). Light therapy for non-seasonal depression. *The Cochrane Database of Systematic Reviews*, 2004(2), CD004050. https://doi.org/10.1002/14651858.CD004050.pub2

Campbell, S. S., Dawson, D., & Anderson, M. W. (1993). Alleviation of sleep maintenance insomnia with timed exposure to bright light. *Journal of the American Geriatrics Society*, 41(8), 829–836. https://doi. org/10.1111/j.1532-5415.1993.tb06179.x

172   "Bright Light Therapy." Stanford Health Care, https://stanfordhealthcare.org/medical-conditions/sleep/ advanced-sleep-phase-syndrome/treatments/bright-light-therapy.html. Accessed November 1, 2021.

173   van Geijlswijk, I. M., Mol, R. H., Egberts, T. C., & Smits, M. G. (2011). Evaluation of sleep, puberty and mental health in children with long-term melatonin treatment for chronic idiopathic childhood sleep onset insomnia. *Psychopharmacology*, 216(1), 111–120. https://doi.org/10.1007/s00213-011-2202-y

Lemoine, P., Nir, T., Laudon, M., & Zisapel, N. (2007). Prolonged-release melatonin improves sleep quality and morning alertness in insomnia patients aged 55 years and older and has no withdrawal effects. *Journal of Sleep Research*, 16(4), 372–380. https://doi.org/10.1111/j.1365-2869.2007.00613.x

174   de Baaij, J. H., Hoenderop, J. G., & Bindels, R. J. (2015). Magnesium in man: Implications for health and disease. *Physiological Reviews*, 95(1), 1–46. https://doi.org/10.1152/physrev.00012.2014

Lewith, G. T., Godfrey, A. D., & Prescott, P. (2005). A single-blinded, randomized pilot study evaluating the aroma of Lavandula augustifolia as a treatment for mild insomnia. *Journal of Alternative and Complementary Medicine*, 11(4), 631–637. https://doi.org/10.1089/acm.2005.11.631

Hemmeter, U., Annen, B., Bischof, R., Brüderlin, U., Hatzinger, M., Rose, U., & Holsboer-Trachsler, E. (2001). Polysomnographic effects of adjuvant ginkgo biloba therapy in patients with major depression medicated with trimipramine. *Pharmacopsychiatry*, 34(2), 50–59. https://doi.org/10.1055/s-2001-15182

175   King, A. C., Oman, R. F., Brassington, G. S., Bliwise, D. L., & Haskell, W. L. (1997). Moderate-intensity exercise and self-rated quality of sleep in older adults: A randomized controlled trial. *JAMA*, 277(1), 32–37.

176   Taylor, A. F., Kuo, F. E., & Sullivan, W. C. (2001). Coping with ADD: The surprising connection to green play settings. *Environment and Behavior*, 33(1), 54–77.

Martyn, P., & Brymer, E. (2016). The relationship between nature relatedness and anxiety. *Journal of Health Psychology*, 21(7), 1436–1445.

Taylor, A. F., & Kuo, F. E. (2009). Children with attention deficits concentrate better after walk in the park. *Journal of Attention Disorders*, 12(5), 402–09.

Kuo, F. E., & Taylor, A. F. (2004). A potential natural treatment for attention-deficit/hyperactivity disorder: Evidence from a national study. *American Journal of Public Health*, 94(9), 1580.

Mooney, P., & Nicell, P. L. (1992). The importance of exterior environment for Alzheimer residents: Effective care and risk management. *Healthcare Management Forum*, 5(2), 23–29.

Rappe, E. (2005). *The influence of a green environment and horticultural activities on the subjective well-being of the elderly living in long-term care*. University of Helsinki, Department of Applied Biology.

Ulrich, R. S. (2002). *Health benefits of gardens in hospitals* [Paper presentation]. Plants for People, International Exhibition Floriade, Haarlemmermeer, Netherlands.

Chalfont, G. E., & Rodiek, S. (2005). Building edge: An ecological approach to research and design of environments for people with dementia. *Alzheimer's Care Today*, 6(4), 341.

Hull, R. B., & Michael, S. E. (1995). Nature-based recreation, mood change, and stress restoration. *Leisure Sciences*, 17(1), 1–14.

Davis, J. (2004). *Psychological benefits of nature experiences: An outline of research and theory*. Naropa University. MIND. (2007). Ecotherapy: The green agenda for mental health. Mind.

Blumenthal, J. A., Babyak, M. A., Moore, K. A., Craighead, W. E., Herman, S., Khatri, P., Waugh, R., Napolitano, M. A., Forman, L. M., Appelbaum, M., Uurali, D. P., & Krishnan, K. R. (1999). Effects of exercise training on older patients with major depression. *Archives of Internal Medicine*, 159(19), 2349–2356.

Berman, M. G., Kross, E., Krpan, K. M., Askren, M. K., Burson, A., Deldin, P. J., Kaplan, S., Sherdell, L., Gotlib, I. H., & Jonides, J. (2012). Interacting with nature improves cognition and affect for individuals with depression. *Journal of Affective Disorders*, 140, 300–305.

de Vries, S., ten Have, M., van Dorsselaer, S., van Wezep, M., Hermans, T., & de Graaf, R. (2016). Local availability of green and blue space and prevalence of common mental disorders in the Netherlands. *BJPsych Open*, 23(2), 366–372.

https://journals.sagepub.com/doi/10.1177/0963721419854100

177   Bowler, D. E., Buyung-Ali, L. M., Knight, T. M., & Pullin, A. S. (2010). A systematic review of evidence for the added benefits to health of exposure to natural environments. *BMC Public Health*, 10, 456.

Berman, M. G., Kross, E., Krpan, K. M., Askren, M. K., Burson, A., Deldin, P. J., Kaplan, S., Sherdell, L., Gotlib, I. H., & Jonides, J. (2012). Interacting with nature improves cognition and affect for individuals with depression. *Journal of Affective Disorders*, 140, 300–305.

Wilson, E. O. (1984). *Biophilia*. Harvard University Press.

https://www.researchgate.net/publication/282749159_The_Nature_of_Happiness_Nature_Affiliation_and_ Mental_Well-Being

White, M. P., Alcock, I., Wheeler, B. W., & Depledge, M. H. (2013). Would you be happier living in a greener urban area? A fixed-effects analysis of panel data. *Psychological Science*, 24, 920–928.

Orban, E., Sutcliffe, R., Dragano, N., Jöckel, K.-H., & Moebus, S. (2017). Residential surrounding greenness, self-rated health and interrelations with aspects of neighborhood environment and social relations. *Journal of Urban Health*, 94, 158–169.

Jennings, V., & Bamkole, O. (2019). The relationship between social cohesion and urban green space: An avenue for health promotion. *International Journal of Environmental Research and Public Health*, 16, 452.

Hartig, T., Evans, G. W., Jamner, L., Davis, D., & Gärling, T. (2003). Tracking restoration in natural and urban field settings. *Journal of Environmental Psychology*, 23, 109–123.

O'Brien, L., Burls, A., Townsend, M., & Ebden, M. (2011). Volunteering in nature as a way of enabling people to reintegrate into society. *Perspectives in Public Health*, 131, 71–81.

Berman, M. G., Kross, E., Krpan, K. M., Askren, M. K., Burson, A., Deldin, P. J., Kaplan, S., Sherdell, L., Gotlib, I. H., & Jonides, J. (2012). Interacting with nature improves cognition and affect for individuals with depression. *Journal of Affective Disorders*, 140, 300–305.

Stevenson, M. P., Schilhab, T., & Bentsen, P. (2018). Attention Restoration Theory II: A systematic review to clarify attention processes affected by exposure to natural environments. *Journal of Toxicology and Environmental Health*, Part B, 21, 227–268.

Ten Brink, P., Mutafoglu, K., Schweitzer, J.-P., Kettunen, M., Twigger-Ross, C., Baker, J., Kuipers, Y., Emonts, M., Tyrväinen, L., Hujala, T., & Ojala, A. (2016). *The health and social benefits of nature and biodiversity protection. A report for the European Commission*. Institute for European Environmental Policy.

Frumkin, H. (2001). Beyond toxicity: Human health and the natural environment. *American Journal of Preventive Medicine*, 20(3), 234–240.

Thompson, C. J., Boddy, K., Stein, K., Whear, R., Barton, J., & Depledge, M. H. (2011). Does participating in physical activity in outdoor natural environments have a greater effect on physical and mental wellbeing than physical activity indoors? A systematic review. *Environmental Science & Technology*, 45(5), 1761–1772.

Williams, F. (2017). *The nature fix: Why nature makes us happier, healthier, and more creative*. W. W. Norton & Company.

Durr, L. I. (2009). Optimal challenge: The impact of adventure experiences on subjective well-being. *The Journal of Experimental Education*, 31, 451–455.

Smith, M. K., & Diekmann, A. (2017). Tourism and wellbeing. *Annals of Tourism Research*, 66, 1–13. https://www.outwardbound.org/lib/file/manager/Final%20PMM%202016%20-%20OB%20manuscript.pdf

Humberstone, B. (2015). Embodiment, nature and wellbeing: More than the senses? In M. Robertson, R. Lawrence, & G. Heath (Eds.), *Experiencing the outdoors* (pp. 61–72). Sense Publishers.

Little, J. (2012). Transformational tourism, nature and wellbeing: New perspectives on fitness and the body. *Journal of Rural Studies*, 52, 257–271.

Brymer, E., Cuddihy, T. F., & Sharma-Brymer, V. (2010). The role of nature-based experiences in the development and maintenance of wellness. *Asia-Pacific Journal of Health, Sport and Physical Education*, 1, 21–27.

Bell, S., Tyrväinen, L., Sievänen, T., Pröbstl, U., & Simpson, M. (2007). Outdoor recreation and nature tourism: A European perspective. *Living Reviews in Landscape Research*, 1, 1–46.

Aspinall, P., Mavros, P., Coyne, R., & Roe, J. (2013). The urban brain: Analysing outdoor physical activity with mobile EEG. *British Journal of Sports Medicine*, 49, 272–276.

Frumkin, H., Bratman, G. N., Breslow, S. J., Cochran, B., Kahn, P. H., Jr., Lawler, J. J., Levin, P. S., Tandon, P. S., Varanasi, U., Wolf, K. L., & Wood, S. A. (2017). Nature contact and human health: A research agenda. *Environmental Health Perspectives*, 125(7). doi:10.1289/EHP1663

Mutz, M., & Müller, J. (2016). Mental health benefits of outdoor adventures: Results from two pilot studies. *Journal of Adolescence*, 49, 105–114.

Pretty, J., Peacock, J., Sellens, M., & Griffin, M. (2005). The mental and physical outcomes of green exercise. *International Journal of Environmental Health Research*, 15, 319–337.

Ryan, R. M., Weinstein, N., Bernstein, J., Brown, K. W., Mistretta, L., & Gagné, M. (2010). Vitalizing effects of being outdoors and in nature. *Journal of Environmental Psychology*, 30, 159–169.

178   http://richardlouv.com/books/last-child

179   https://www.ted.com/talks/johann_hari_this_could_be_why_you_re_depressed_or_anxious?language=en

180   https://www.nature.com/articles/s41598-019-44097-3

181   https://www.sciencedirect.com/science/article/pii/S1353829215000672#bib45

182   https://www.ncbi.nlm.nih.gov/pmc/articles/PMC3546779/

183   https://journals.sagepub.com/doi/10.1177/0013916508319745
       https://link.springer.com/article/10.3758%2Fs13423-018-1539-1

Ulrich, R., Simon, R., Losito, B., Fiorito, E., Miles, M., & Zelson, M. (1991). Stress recovery during exposure to natural and urban environments. *Journal of Environmental Psychology*, 11, 201–230.

184   https://e360.yale.edu/features/ecopsychology-how-immersion-in-nature-benefits-your-health

185   Ma, X., Yue, Z. Q., Gong, Z. Q., Zhang, H., Duan, N. Y., Shi, Y. T., Wei, G. X., & Li, Y. F. (2017). The effect of diaphragmatic breathing on attention, negative affect and stress in healthy adults. *Frontiers in Psychology*, 8, 874. https://doi.org/10.3389/fpsyg.2017.00874

Yadav, A., Kaushik, R. M., & Kaushik, R. (2021). Effects of diaphragmatic breathing and systematic relaxation on depression, anxiety, stress, and glycemic control in type 2 diabetes mellitus. *International Journal of Yoga Therapy*. Advance online publication. https://doi.org/10.17761/2021-D-19-00061

Seppälä, E. M., Bradley, C., Moeller, J., Harouni, L., Nandamudi, D., & Brackett, M. A. (2020). Promoting mental health and psychological thriving in university students: A randomized controlled trial of three well-being interventions. *Frontiers in Psychiatry*, 11. https://www.frontiersin.org/article/10.3389/fpsyt.2020.00590

Goldstein, M. R., Lewin, R. K., & Allen, J. J. B. (2020). Improvements in well-being and cardiac metrics of stress following a yogic breathing workshop: Randomized controlled trial with active comparison. *Journal of American College Health*. Advance online publication. doi:10.1080/07448481.2020.1781867

186 Maxwell, L., & Duff, E. (2016). Mindfulness: An effective prescription for depression and anxiety. *The Journal for Nurse Practitioners*, 12(6), 403–409.

Khourya, B., Lecomtea, T., Fortina, G., Massea, M., Theriena, P., Bouchardb, V., Chapleaua, M.-A., Paquina, K., & Hofmannc, S. G. (2013). Mindfulness-based therapy: A comprehensive meta-analysis. *Clinical Psychology Review*, 33(6), 763–771.

187 Emmons, R. A., & McCullough, M. E. (2003). Counting blessings versus burdens: An experimental investigation of gratitude and subjective well-being in daily life. *Journal of Personality and Social Psychology*, 84(2), 377–389.

https://scottbarrykaufman.com/wp-content/uploads/2021/05/davis2016.pdf

Dickerhoof, R. M. (2007). Expressing optimism and gratitude: A longitudinal investigation of cognitive strategies to increase well-being. *Dissertation Abstracts International*, 68, 4174B.

Celano, C. M., Beale, E. E., Beach, S. R., Belcher, A. M., Suarez, L., Motiwala, S. R., Gahdni, P. U., Hanna, G., Januzzi Jr., J. L., Healy, B. C., & Huffman, J. C. (2016). Associations between psychological constructs and cardiac biomarkers after acute coronary syndrome. *Psychosomatic Medicine*, 79(3), 318–326. https://doi.org/10.1097/PSY.0000000000000404

McCraty, R., Atkinson, M., & Tiller, W. (1995). The effects of emotions on short-term power spectrum analysis of heart rate variability. *The American Journal of Cardiology*, 76(14), 1089–1093.

Ng, M.-Y., & Wong, W.-S. (2013). The differential effects of gratitude and sleep on psychological distress in patients with chronic pain. Journal of Health Psychology, 18(2), 263–271. http://dx.doi.org/10.1177/1359105312439733

Peterson, C., Ruch, W., Beermann, U., Park, N., & Seligman, M. E. P. (2007). Strengths of character, orientations to happiness, and life satisfaction. *The Journal of Positive Psychology*, 2(3), 149–156. https://doi.org/10.1080/17439760701228938

Hill, P. L., & Allemand, M. (2011). Gratitude, forgivingness, and well-being in adulthood: Tests of moderation and incremental prediction. *The Journal of Positive Psychology*, 6(5), 397–407. https://doi.org/10.1080/17439760.2011.602099

188 Smith, J. L., & Hollinger-Smith, L. (2015). Savoring, resilience, and psychological well-being in older adults. *Aging & Mental Health*, 19(3), 192–200.

Jeste, D. V., Savla, G. N., Thompson, W. K., Vahia, I. V., Glorioso, D. K., Martin, A. S., Palmer, B. W., Rock, D., Golshan, S., Kraemer, H. C., & Depp, C. A. (2013). Association between older age and more successful aging: Critical role of resilience and depression. *American Jouranl of Psychiatry*, 170(2), 188–196.

Netuveli, G., & Blane, D. (2008). Quality of life in older ages. *British Medical Bulletin*, 85, 113–126.

189 Shen, K., & Zeng, Y. (2010). The association between resilience and survival among Chinese elderly. *Demographic Research*, 23(5), 105–116.

Zeng, Y., & Shen, K. (2010). Resilience significantly contributes to exceptional longevity. *Current Gerontology and Geriatrics Research*. doi:10.1155/2010/525693

190 Bonanno, G. A., Galea, S., Bucciarelli, A., & Vlahov, D. (2006). Psychological resilience after disaster: New York City in the aftermath of the September 11th terrorist attack. *Psychological Science*, 17(3), 181–186. https://doi.org/10.1111/j.1467-9280.2006.01682.x

191 Galatzer-Levy, I. R., Huang, S. H., & Bonanno, G. A. (2018). Clinical Psychology Review, 63. Retrieved from https://www.tc.columbia.edu/media/centers/ltc-lab/peered-review-journals/2018_Galtzaer_Levy-Huang--Bonanno_REVIEW.pdf

192 Resnick, B. A., & Inguito, P. L. (2011). The resilience scale: Psychometric properties and clinical applicability in older adults. *Archives Psychiatric Nursing*, 25(1), 11–20.

193 MacLeod, S., Musich, S., Hawkins, K., Alsgaard, K., & Wicker, E. R. (2016). The impact of resilience among older adults. *Geriatric Nursing*, 37(4), 266–272. https://doi.org/10.1016/j.gerinurse.2016.02.014

194 Jowsey, S. G., Cutshall, S. M., Colligan, R. C., Stevens, S. R., Kremers, W. K., Vasquez, A. R., Edwards, B. S., Daly, R. C., & McGregor, C. G. (2012). Seligman's theory of attributional style: optimism, pessimism, and quality of life after heart transplant. *Progress in Transplantation*, 22(1), 49–55. https://doi.org/10.7182/pit2012451

Buchanan, G. M., & Seligman, M. E. P. (Eds.). (1995). *Explanatory style*. Lawrence Erlbaum Associates, Inc.

195 Vieselmeyer, J., Holguin, J., & Mezulis, A. (2017). The role of resilience and gratitude in posttraumatic stress and growth following a campus shooting. *Psychological Trauma: Theory, Research, Practice, and Policy*, 9(1), 62–69. https://doi.org/10.1037/tra0000149

196 Ardito, R. B., & Rabellino, D. (2011). Therapeutic alliance and outcome of psychotherapy: Historical excursus, measurements, and prospects for research. *Frontiers in Psychology*, 2, 270. https://doi.org/10.3389/fpsyg.2011.00270

197 Levine, S. (2003). Psychological and social aspects of resilience: A synthesis of risks and resources. *Dialogues in Clinical Neuroscience*, 5(3), 273–280. https://doi.org/10.31887/DCNS.2003.5.3/slevine

198 Netuveli, G., Wiggins, R. D., Montgomery, S. M., Hildon, Z., & Blane, D. (2008). Mental health and resilience at older ages: Bouncing back after adversity in the British Household Panel Survey. *Journal of Epidemiology and Community Health*, 62, 987–991.

Lamond, A. J., Depp, C., Allison, M., Langer, R., Reichstadt, J., Moore, D. J., Golshan, S., Ganiats, T. G., & Jeste, D. V. (2008). Measurement and predictors of resilience among community-dwelling older women. *Journal of Psychiatric Research*, 43(2), 148–154.

199 Li, Y. (2007). Recovering from spousal bereavement in later life: Does volunteer participation play a role? *The Journals of Gerontology: Series B*, 62(4), S257–S266. https://doi.org/10.1093/geronb/62.4.S257

Greenfield, E. A., & Marks, N. F. (2004). Formal volunteering as a protective factor for older adults' psychological well-being. *The Journals of Gerontology: Series B*, 59(5), S258–S264. https://doi.org/10.1093/geronb/59.5.S258

Felix, H. C., Adams, B., Cornell, C. E., Fausett, J. K., Krukowski, R. A., Love, S. J., Prewitt, T. E., & West, D. S. (2014). Barriers and facilitators to senior centers participating in translational research. *Research on Aging*, 36(1), 22–39.

200   Childs, E., & de Wit, H. (2014). Regular exercise is associated with emotional resilience to acute stress in healthy adults. *Frontiers in Psychology*, 5(161). doi:10.3389/fphys.2014.00161

Resnick, B. A., & Inguito, P. L. (2011). The resilience scale: Psychometric properties and clinical applicability in older adults. *Archives of Psychiatric Nursing*, 25(1), 11–20.

Gill, T. M., Robison, J. T., & Tinetti, M. E. (1997). Predictors of recovery in activities of daily living among disabled older persons living in the community. *Journal of General Internal Medicine*, 12, 757–762.

201   Lee, J., Tsunetsugu, Y., Takayama, N., Park, B. J., Li, Q., Song, C., Komatsu, M., Ikei, H., Tyrväinen, L., Kagawa, T., & Miyazaki, Y. (2014). Influence of forest therapy on cardiovascular relaxation in young adults. *eCAM*, 2014(834360). https://doi.org/10.1155/2014/834360

Li, Q. (2010). Effect of forest bathing trips on human immune function. *Environmental Health and Preventive Medicine*, 15(1), 9–17. https://doi.org/10.1007/s12199-008-0068-3

Ochiai, H.; Ikei, H.; Song, C.; Kobayashi, M.; Miura, T.; Kagawa, T.; Li, Q.; Kumeda, S.; Imai, M.; Miyazaki, Y. Physiological and Psychological Effects of a Forest Therapy Program on Middle-Aged Females. Int. J. Environ. Res. Public Health 2015, 12, 15222-15232. https://doi.org/10.3390/ijerph121214984

Park, B.-J., Tsunetsugu, Y., Kasetani, T., Hirano, H., Kagawa, T., Sato, M., & Miyazaki, Y. (2007). Physiological effects of shinrin-yoku (taking in the atmosphere of the forest) using salivary cortisol and cerebral activity as indicators. *Journal of Physiological Anthropology*, 26(2), 123–128. https://doi.org/10.2114/jpa2.26.123

Li, Q., Kobayashi, M., Wakayama, Y., Inagaki, H., Katsumata, M., Hirata, Y., Hirata, K., Shimizu, T., Kawada, T., Park, B. J., Ohira, T., Kagawa, T., & Miyazaki, Y. (2009). Effect of phytoncide from trees on human natural killer cell function. *International Journal of Immunopathology and Pharmacology*, 22(4), 951–959. https://doi.org/10.1177/039463200902200410

Li, Q., Kobayashi, M., Wakayama, Y., Inagaki, H., Katsumata, M., Hirata, Y., Hirata, K., Shimizu, T., Kawada, T., Park, B. J., Ohira, T., Kagawa, T., & Miyazaki, Y. (2009). Effect of phytoncide from trees on human natural killer cell function. *International Journal of Immunopathology and Pharmacology*, 22(4), 951–959. https://doi.org/10.1177/039463200902200410

Park, B. J., Tsunetsugu, Y., Kasetani, T., Kagawa, T., & Miyazaki, Y. (2010). The physiological effects of Shinrin-yoku (taking in the forest atmosphere or forest bathing): Evidence from field experiments in 24 forests across Japan. *Environmental Health and Preventive Medicine*, 15(1), 18–26. https://doi.org/10.1007/s12199-009-0086-9

202   Troisi, J. D., Gabriel, S., Derrick, J. L., & Geisler, A. (2015). Threatened belonging and preference for comfort food among the securely attached. *Appetite*, 90, 58–64. https://doi.org/10.1016/j.appet.2015.02.029
https://www.sciencedirect.com/science/article/pii/S0195666315000768

203   Gill, T. M., Robison, J. T., & Tinetti, M. E. (1997). Predictors of recovery in activities of daily living among disabled older persons living in the community. *Journal of General Internal Medicine*, 12, 757–762.

204   https://www.researchgate.net/profile/Richard-Tedeschi/publication/247504165_Tedeschi_RG_Calhoun_LG-Posttraumatic_growth_conceptual_foundations_and_empirical_evidence_Psychol_Inq_151_1-18/links/548aee-9a0cf225bf669f7e6c/Tedeschi-RG-Calhoun-LGPosttraumatic-growth-conceptual-foundations-and-empiri-cal-evidence-Psychol-Inq-151-1-18.pdf
https://books.google.com/books?hl=en&lr=&id=BHEABAAAQBAJ&oi=fnd&pg=PP1&dq=post+trau-matic+growth&ots=o5yLEgdzFo&sig=I1T0LuIxvND3O6yvI8ZdB6Vl5qY#v=onepage&q=post%20trauma-tic%20growth&f=false

205   https://www.realclearscience.com/articles/2012/08/07/can_trauma_make_you_a_better_person_106342.html

206   Vail, K. E., Juhl, J., Arndt, J., Vess, M., Routledge, C., & Rutjens, B. T. (2012). When death is good for life: Considering the positive trajectories of terror management. *Personality and Social Psychology Review*, 16(4), 303–329. doi:10.1177/1088868312440046

Society for Personality and Social Psychology. (2012, April 19). How thinking about death can lead to a good life. *ScienceDaily*. www.sciencedaily.com/releases/2012/04/120419102516.htm

Neimeyer, R. A. (2005). From death anxiety to meaning making at the end of life: Recommendations for psychological assessment. *Clinical Psychology: Science and Practice*, 12(3), 354–357.

Tomer, A. (Ed.) (2000). Death attitudes and the older adult: *Theories, concepts, and applications*. Brunner-Routledge Tomer, A., Eliason, G. T., & Wong, P. T. P. (2008). *Existential and spiritual issues in death attitudes*. Erlbaum.

207   Furer, P., & Walker, J. R. (2008). Death anxiety: A cognitive-behavioral approach. *Journal of Cognitive Psychotherapy*, 22(2), 167–182. https://doi.org/10.1891/0889-8391.22.2.167

Tsai, J. S., Wu, C. H., Chiu, T. Y., Hu, W. Y., & Chen, C. Y. (2005). Fear of death and good death among the young and elderly with terminal cancers in Taiwan. *Journal of Pain and Symptom Management*, 29(4), 344–351. doi:10.1016/j.jpainsymman.2004.07.013

208   https://www.wsj.com/articles/can-the-pandemic-make-us-stronger-endurance-athletes-tell-us-how-11620154800

209   https://www.richroll.com/podcast/alexi-pappas-579/

210   https://www.wsj.com/articles/can-the-pandemic-make-us-stronger-endurance-athletes-tell-us-how-11620154800

211   https://www.usatoday.com/story/tech/2021/08/10/streaming-tv-still-growing-despite-lifting-covid-19-restric-tions/5540265001/

212   https://runrepeat.com/state-of-ultra-running

213   The 5-Step Self-Improvement Overhaul. (2007, January 4). *Outside Magazine*. Note: No page numbers were provided for this article.

214   https://www.instagram.com/davidgoggins/

DISCLAIMER

I want you to live the very best life possible in retirement, and I hope this book helps you realize this even in some small way. You're going to read a lot about incorporating adventure in your life, investment ideas, thoughts on how to improve your health, and everything in between. I've distilled what I've learned over the past nearly 30 years and put it into this book. But keep in mind that the information in the book is not advice. Everyone's situation is different, so please make sure you work with professionals when necessary. And now the formal disclaimer...

This book is intended to provide general guidelines that are for informational purposes only and is sold with the understanding that the publisher and author are not engaged in rendering professional services or in providing specific investment advice. The application of general guidelines involving regulatory, accounting, and legal practices, which may differ from locality to locality, and which are constantly changing, is highly dependent on an evaluation of individual facts and specific circumstances. With regard to any decisions that can potentially have significant financial, legal, tax, or other consequences, no book can take the place of individualized professional advice. Readers should not regard this book as a substitute for consulting with a competent lawyer, accountant, or other financial professional, as appropriate to the nature of their particular situation. Different types of investments involve varying degrees of risk, and there can be no assurance that the future performance of any specific investment, investment strategy, or product discussed in this book will be profitable or suitable for any one reader's portfolio. If readers have any questions regarding the applicability of any investment strategy or product discussed in this book to their particular financial situation, they should consult with a professional advisor. The publisher and the author make no guarantees concerning the level of success you may experience by following the advice and strategies contained in this book, and you accept the risk that results will differ for each individual. The publisher and the author are providing this book and its contents on an "as is" basis and make no representations or warranties of any kind with respect to this book or its contents. Although the publisher and the author have made every effort to ensure that the information in this book was correct at press time and while this publication is designed to provide accurate information in regard to the subject matter covered, the publisher and the author assume no responsibility for errors, inaccuracies, omissions, or any other inconsistencies herein and hereby disclaim any liability to any party for any loss, damage, or disruption caused by errors or omissions, whether such errors or omissions result from negligence, accident, or any other cause. The content of this book is for informational purposes only and is not intended to diagnose, treat, cure, or prevent any condition or disease. This book is not intended as a substitute for consultation with a licensed practitioner. Please consult with your own physician or healthcare specialist regarding the suggestions and recommendations made in this book. The author is not a licensed healthcare provider and represents that they have no expertise in diagnosing, examining, or treating medical conditions of any kind or in determining the effect of any specific exercise on a medical condition. You should understand that there is the possibility of physical injury when participating in any exercise or exercise program. If you engage in any exercise program, you agree that you do so at your own risk, are voluntarily participating in these activities, assume all risk of injury to yourself, and agree to release and discharge the publisher and the author from any and all claims or causes of action, known or unknown, arising out of the contents of this book. The use of this book implies your acceptance of this disclaimer. Under no circumstances, including but not limited to negligence, will the publisher or author be liable for any special or consequential damages. You agree not to attempt to hold the publisher or author liable for any decisions, actions or results that you make or experience in business or in life due to the content in this book at any time, under any circumstance.

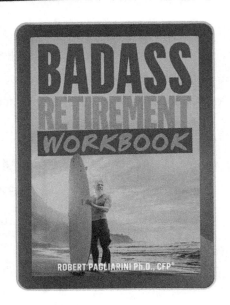

Made in the USA
Coppell, TX
20 October 2024

38969194R00207